KT-158-039

INTERNATIONAL AND COMPARATIVE EMPLOYMENT RELATIONS

GLOBALISATION AND CHANGE

Fifth Edition

Edited by

Greg J. Bamber, Russell D. Lansbury
and Nick Wailes

SAGE

Los Angeles | London | New Delhi
Singapore | Washington DC

The book G.J. Bamber, R.D. Lansbury and N. Wailes and in
individual chapters with their authors, 2011

First published in Australian in 2011 by Allen & Unwin
Reprinted 2014

Apart from any fair dealing for the purposes of research or
private study, or criticism or review, as permitted under the
Copyright, Designs and Patents Act, 1988, this publication
may be reproduced, stored or transmitted in any form, or
by any means, only with the prior permission in writing of
the publishers, or in the case of reprographic reproduction,
in accordance with the terms of licences issued by the
Copyright Licensing Agency. Enquiries concerning
reproduction outside those terms should be sent to the
publishers.

SAGE Publications Ltd
1 Oliver's Yard
55 City Road
London EC1Y 1SP

SAGE Publications Inc.
2455 Teller Road
Thousand Oaks, California 91320

SAGE Publications India Pvt Ltd
B 1/I 1 Mohan Cooperative Industrial Area
Mathura Road
New Delhi 110 044

SAGE Publications Asia-Pacific Pte Ltd
3 Church Street
#10-04 Samsung Hub
Singapore 049483

Library of Congress Control Number: 2010934958

British Library Cataloguing in Publication data

A catalogue record for this book is available from the British
Library

ISBN 978-1-84920-723-2 (paperback)

ISBN 978-1-84920-722-5 (hardback)

Typeset in 10.5/13pt Garamond by Midland Typesetters,
Australia
Printed and bound by CPI Group (UK) Ltd, Croydon, CRO 4YY
Printed on paper from sustainable resources

MIX
Paper from
responsible sources
FSC
www.fsc.org   FSC® C013604

To our immediate families: Dale, Alex, Kate, Gwen, Owen, Nina, Sharon and Stella
In loving memory of Freda, Betty and Doug

This book is also in loving memory of Professor C.S. Venkata Ratnam, the late Director of the International Management Institute, New Delhi, India. Unfortunately he died in 2010, after co-authoring the last chapter in this book.

(Royalties from this book will contribute to research into cancer.)

Foreword

This fifth edition of *International and Comparative Employment Relations* is another welcome contribution to and timely update of the literature in this growing field of study and teaching. The book embodies the best principles of international scholarship. By assembling a premier group of experts from different countries to address a similar set of issues, Greg Bamber, Russell Lansbury and Nick Wailes have produced a book that provides rich and detailed country specific knowledge and information from which readers can make informed comparisons.

This new edition rightly focuses more intensively on the impact of globalisation on employment relations in key developing and developed market economies. The new chapters on China, India and Denmark reflect, on the one hand, the growing impacts of two developing giants and, on the other, a country that has been proactive in responding to the challenges of globalisation in ways that keep it competitive and support high living standards. I am pleased to see this, given the heightened sensitivities (and tensions) globalisation has generated in recent years and the growing role that it is playing in employment relations in all countries.

Indeed it is not too much to say that some of the biggest intellectual puzzles and practical challenges facing our field today and in the future lie in managing globalisation in ways that benefit the world economy and enhance the standards of living and employment rights and opportunities for people in developing and developed countries alike. This will not happen by the workings of some invisible hand of market forces; it requires public policies and private practices and institutions that are informed by experiences and evidence on the ground. The data and evidence included in this edition provide a good starting point for addressing these challenges.

The field of international and comparative employment relations is well on its way to renewal, having come alive in recent years following a long period when most researchers focused on developments within their national systems. Stronger analytical frameworks that build on studies of the varieties of capitalism, global supply chains, transformed work systems, and contemporary tripartite bodies and processes are available to support macro and micro (industry, enterprise, and workplace) comparisons across and within national systems. This is producing new empirical evidence, new cross-national research networks, and a new generation of researchers. Continuing to support this cross-national and cross-cultural learning process is critical to the successful performance of world markets and regional trading blocs, as well as to the development of effective labour market and employment institutions in new or fragile democracies in Europe, Asia, and Latin America. Moreover, experiences in these countries will need to be brought to bear if we are ever to build sustainable democracies and peaceful and prosperous societies in the Middle East and Africa. Meeting this challenge will feature prominently on the world agenda for many years to come.

Understanding these developments increases the range of options from which managers, union leaders, and government policy-makers can choose in shaping their own employment practices. Our challenge as teachers, researchers, students and practitioners is to determine which employment-relations institutions and practices can be effectively transferred across international borders and can be adapted satisfactorily to different local settings. Yet, as the material in this book attests, there are significant limitations to this transfer process, given the desire by most parties to maintain well-established traditions and the fear of changing existing power relationships. Understanding and appreciating the importance of the country and culture-specific features of work and employment practices is therefore equally important for managers, union leaders and policy makers.

Greg Bamber, Russell Lansbury, Nick Wailes and their chapter authors put the emerging frameworks and empirical evidence to good use throughout this book. This edition should serve as a valuable point of reference for advancing the cross-national learning needed to support the policy debates underway within and among these countries.

I am delighted that the authors and editors continue to use to good avail the meetings and members of the International Labour and Employment Relations Association and draw on the results of the cross-national research teams and projects promoted by our Association in producing this book. My hope is that the Association will continue to serve as host to similar international and comparative projects in the future.

Thomas A. Kochan
Sloan School of Management, Massachusetts Institute of Technology;
Former President, International Industrial Relations Association
and Industrial Relations Research Association

Contents

Contributors

Søren Kaj Andersen is Associate Professor and Director of FAOS, Employment Relations Research Centre, Department of Sociology, University of Copenhagen, Denmark. He is also Visiting Associate Professor at the International Centre for Business and Politics, Copenhagen Business School.

Lucio Baccaro is Professor of Sociology at the University of Geneva, Switzerland. Previously he taught at Case Western Reserve University and MIT in the United States. He also held senior research positions at the International Labour Organization.

Greg J. Bamber is Professor and Director of Research, Department of Management, Monash University, Melbourne, Australia. His publications include *Up in The Air: How Airlines Can Improve Performance by Engaging their Employees* (Cornell UP, 2009) with J. Gittell, T. Kochan and A.von Nordenflytch; and 'Regulating Employment Relations, Work and Labour Laws: International Comparisions between Key Countries', *Bulletin of Comparative Labour Relations*, No. 74 (Kluwer, 2010) with P. Pochet and others.

Alexander J.S. Colvin is Associate Professor of Collective Bargaining and Conflict Resolution at the ILR School, Cornell University in the United States. His research and teaching focus on employment dispute resolution, with a particular emphasis on procedures in non-union workplaces and the impact of the legal environment on organisations.

Fang Lee Cooke is Professor of Human Resource Management and Chinese Studies and Deputy Head of School (Research and Innovation), School of Management, RMIT University, Melbourne, Australia. She is the author of *HRM, Work and Employment in China* (Routledge, 2005) and *Competition, Strategy and Management in China* (Palgrave Macmillan, 2008).

Jesper Due is Professor at FAOS, Employment Relations Research Centre, Department of Sociology, University of Copenhagen, Denmark.

Janine Goetschy is a political scientist and sociologist. She is a Senior Research Fellow at the National Center for Scientific Research (CNRS) and presently a member of IDHE-University of Nanterre. She is also part-time Professor at the Institute for European Studies of the University of Bruxelles. She is currently involved in various EU level research projects and networks financed by the European Commission. She has been publishing extensively in the field of social Europe and EU labour relations.

Annette Jobert is Director of Research at the Centre National de la Recherche Scientifique (CNRS) and is teaching industrial relations at the Ecole Normale Supérieure de Cachan. She is involved in the European project 'Capright' (Resources, rights and capabilities: in search of social foundations for Europe) and a member of the CRIMT Centre de Recherche Inter-universitaire sur la Mondialisation et le Travail—Canada). She is the author and editor of several books on European Industrial relations, including *Sociologie du Travail: les Relations Professionnelles* (with Antoine Bevort, Armand Colin, 2008) and *Les Nouveaux cadres du Dialogue Social, Europe et Territoires* (Peter Lang, 2008).

Harry C. Katz is the Kenneth F. Kahn Dean and Jack Sheinkman Professor of Collective Bargaining at the School of Industrial and Labor Relations, Cornell University. His major publications include *An Introduction to Collective Bargaining and Industrial Relations* (4th ed., with Thomas Kochan and Alexander Colvin, McGraw Hill/Irwin, 2007), *Converging Divergences: Worldwide Changes in Employment Systems* (with Owen Darbishire, Cornell University Press, 2000) and *The Transformation of American Industrial Relations* (with Thomas Kochan and Robert McKersie (2nd ed., Cornell University Press, 1994).

Berndt K. Keller is Emeritus Professor of Employment Relations at the University of Konstanz, Germany. He is the author and editor of several books and volumes on German and European employment relations, including *Einführung in die Arbeitspolitik. Arbeitsbeziehungen und Arbeitsmarkt in sozialwissenschaftlicher Perspektive* (7th ed., Oldenbourg Wissensch.Vlg, 2008) and *Industrial Relations and European Integration: Trans- and Supranational Developments and Prospects* (with Hans Platzer, Ashgate, 2003). He is co-editor of *Industrielle Beziehungen: The German Journal of Industrial Relations* and was a member of the Executive Committee of the International Industrial Relations Association (2003–09).

Anja Kirsch is a Lecturer in Work and Organisational Studies at the University of Sydney, Australia. Her current research interests include union mergers as a revitalisation strategy, gender equity in unions and the impact of globalisation on employment relations and human resource management in the retail banking and automobile assembly industries.

Katsuyuki Kubo is Professor in the School of Commerce at Waseda University, Japan. His recent papers include 'The Relationship Between Financial Incentives for Company Presidents and Firm Performance in Japan', *Japanese Economic Review*, 59(4): 401–18.

Russell D. Lansbury is Emeritus Professor of Work and Organisational Studies in the Faculty of Economics and Business at the University of Sydney, Australia. He is a Fellow of the Academy of Social Sciences Australia and former President of the International Industrial Relations Association. His recent research has focused on the impact of management strategies in multinational enterprises on employment relations and labour practices.

Byoung-Hoon Lee is a Professor in the Department of Sociology, Chung-Ang University, Seoul, South Korea. He is a Vice-president of the Korea Industrial Relations Association and the Chair of Social Labor Committee, People's Solidarity. His recent research has focused on labour market segmentation and non-standard employment, revitalisation of labour union movements and labour regime of service societies.

Jørgen Steen Madsen is professor at FAOS, Employment Relations Research Centre, Department of Sociology, University of Copenhagen, Denmark.

Mick Marchington is Professor of Human Resource Management at Manchester Business School, the University of Manchester, United Kingdom. He is co-organiser of the HRM study group of the IIRA and is co-editor of the *Human Resource Management Journal*.

Valeria Pulignano is Professor of Sociology of Labour and Industrial Relations at the University of Leuven, Belgium. She taught at the University of Warwick in the United Kingdom, where she is currently Associate Fellow. She is also co-researcher at the Interuniversity Research Center on Globalisation and Work (CRIMT) at the University of Montréal, Canada.

C.S. Venkata Ratnam was Director, International Management Institute, New Delhi, India. Sadly, he died in 2010 after co-authoring the last chapter in this book. Therefore, the editors see this book as a tribute to him. He was a lovely man and one of the leading authorities on industrial relations in India. He also had an outstanding inter-national reputation.

Hiromasa Suzuki is a Professor in the School of Commerce at Waseda University, Japan. He worked for the ILO in Geneva from 1970 to 1986. His recent publications include a chapter in *Korekarano Koyou Senryaku* (Towards a future employment strategy) (Japan Institute for Labour Policy and Training, 2007).

Daphne G. Taras is Associate Dean (Research) and Director of the PhD Program in the Haskayne School of Business at the University of Calgary, Canada. Within industrial relations, her principal research interest is formal non-union forms of employee representation. Recent publications include *Perspectives on Disability and Accommodation* (with Kelly Williams-Whitt, National Institute for Disability Management and Research, 2009) and *Canadian Labour Relations: Understanding Union–Management Challenges and Choices* (with Morley Gunderson, Pearson, 2008).

Mark Thompson is Professor Emeritus in the Organizational Behaviour and Human Resources Division at the Sauder School of Business, University of British Columbia, Canada.

Andrew R. Timming is an Assistant Professor in International and Comparative Human Resource Management at Manchester Business School, the University of Manchester, United Kingdom. His main research interests centre around the development of HR/IR metrics.

Anil Verma is Director, Centre for Industrial Relations & Human Resources and Professor, Rotman School of Management, University of Toronto, Canada.

Jeremy Waddington is Professor of Industrial Relations at the University of Manchester, United Kingdom, and Project Coordinator for the European Trade Union Institute, Brussels. He has written extensively on topics associated with trade union membership, structure and organisation, and European works councils.

Nick Wailes is Associate Professor in Work and Organisational Studies at the University of Sydney. He teaches strategic management and comparative employment relations. His current research interests include the diffusion and spillover of employment relations practices in multinational corporations and the strategic impact of human resource information systems.

Figures and tables

Acronyms and abbreviations

AC	Akademikernes Centralorganisation (Danish Confederation of Professional Associations)
ACAS	Advisory, Conciliation and Arbitration Service (UK)
ACCI	Australian Chamber of Commerce and Industry
ACFTU	All-China Federation of Trade Unions
ACM	Australian Chamber of Manufacturers
ACSPA	Australian Council of Salaried and Professional Associations
ACTU	Australian Council of Trade Unions
ADVB	Asian Development Bank
ADGB	General German Trades Union Federation
AFL	American Federation of Labor
AFL-CIO	American Federation of Labor—Congress of Industrial Organizations
AFPC	Australian Fair Pay Commission
AiG	Australian Industries Group
AIOE	All India Organisation of Indian Employers
AIRC	Australian Industrial Relations Commission
AITUC	All India Trade Union Congress
AKLU	All-Korean Labour Union
ALP	Australian Labor Party
AME	Asian Market Economy
APWPC	*Act Concerning the Promotion of Worker Participation and Cooperation* (Korea)
ARAN	Agenzia per la Rappresentanza Negoziale delle

	Pubbliche Amministrazioni (Agency for Bargaining in the Public Administrations, Italy)
ASAP	Associazione Sindacale Aziende Petrochimiche (Italian Employers' Association of Petrochemical Firms)
AWA	Australian Workplace Agreement
AWIRS	Australian Workplace Industrial Relations Surveys
BCA	Business Council of Australia
BDA	Bundesvereinigung Deutscher Arbeitgeberverbände (Confederation of German Employers' Associations)
BJP	Bharatiya Janata Party (India)
BMS	Bharatiya Mazdoor Sangh (India)
CAGEO	Council of Australian Government Employee Organisations
CAI	Confederation of Australian Industry
CAW	Canadian Auto Workers
CCL	Canadian Congress of Labour
CCP	Chinese Communist Party
CDU/CSU	Christian Democratic Union (Germany)
CEC	China Enterprise Confederation
CFDT	Confédération française démocratique du travail
CFE-CGC	Confédération française de l'encadrement-confédération générale des cadres
CFTC	Confédération française des travailleurs chrétiens (French Confederation of Christian Workers)
CGB	Christlicher Gewerkschaftsbund (Confederation of Christian Unions)
CGC	Confédération générale des cadres (France)
CGIL	Confederazione Generale Italiana del Lavoro (Italian General Confederation of Labour)
CGL	General Confederation of Labour (Italy)
CGPME	Confédération générale des petites et moyennes enterprises (France)
CGPME	Confédération générale des petites et moyennes enterprises (Confederation of Small and Medium-sized Enterprises, France)
CGT	Confédération générale du travail (France)
CIE	Council of Indian Employers
CIL	Catholic Union Confederation (Italy)
CIPD	Chartered Institute of Personnel and Development (UK)
CIO	Congress of Industrial Organizations (USA)
CISL	Confederazione Italiana Sindacati dei Lavoratori (Italian Confederation of Workers' Unions)

CITU	Centre of Indian Trade Unions
CLC	Canadian Labour Congress
CME	Coordinated market economy
CNPF	Conseil national du patronat français
CNTU	Confederation of Trade Unions (see also CSN) (Canada)
COBAS	Comitati di Base
COE	Collectively owned enterprises
CO-industri	Central Organisation of Industrial Employees in Denmark
COLA	Cost of living adjustment
COLSIBA	Latin-American Coordination of Banana Workers
COPE	Committee on Political Education (USA)
CPIM or CPM	Communist Party of India—Marxist
CSN	Confédération des syndicats nationaux (Canada) (see also CNTU)
CSQ	Centrale des syndicats du Québec
CTW	Change to Win (USA)
CtW	Change to Win (Canada)
CWA	Communications Workers of America
DA	Dansk Arbejdsgiverforening (Danish Employers' Confederation)
DBB	Deutscher Beamtenbund (German Civil Service Association)
DC	Democrazia Cristiana (Christian Democrat Party)
DGB	Deutscher Gewerkschaftsbund (German Trade Union Federation)
DI	Erhvervenes organisation (Confederation of Danish Industry)
DME	Developed market economy
DSP	Democratic Socialist Party (Japan)
DTI	Department of Trade and Industry (UK)
EAP	Employee assistance programs
ECM	European Cities Monitor
EFA	Enterprise Flexibility Agreement
EFCA	*Employee Free Choice Act* (USA)
EIP	Employee involvement and participation
EIRO	European Industrial Relations Observatory
EMS	European Monetary System
EOWA	Equal Opportunity for Women in the Workplace Agency
ER	Employment relations

ERISA	*Employee Retirement Income Security Act* (US)
ESDC	Economic and Social Development Commission (Korea)
ETUC	European Trade Union Confederation
EU	European Union
FA	Finansektorens Arbejdsgiverforening (Danish Employers' Association for the Financial Sector)
FDI	Foreign direct investment
FDP	Free Democratic Party (Germany)
FEN	Fédération de l'éducation nationale (National Education Federation, France)
FIE	Foreign investment enterprises
FIOM	Federation of Metalworkers (Italy)
FKI	Federation of Korean Industries
FKTU	Federation of Korean Trade Unions
FLM	Federazione Lavoratori Metalmeccanici (Italian Metalworkers' Union)
FMCS	Federal Mediation and Conciliation Service (USA)
FO	Force ouvrière (France)
FOE	Foreign-owned enterprises
FRG	Federal Republic of Germany
FSU	Fédération syndicale unitaire de l'enseignement, de la recherche et de la culture (France)
FTA	Free trade agreement
FTF	Confederation of Professionals in Denmark
FWA	Fair Work Australia
GATT	General Agreement on Tariffs and Trade
GDP	Gross domestic product
GDR	German Democratic Republic
GFC	Global financial crisis
GFKTU	Daehan Dogrib Chockseong Nodong Chongyeonmyeng (General Federation of Korean Trade Unions)
GHQ	General Headquarters (Allied Powers in Japan)
GUF	Global union federation
HCM	High commitment management
HMS	Hind Mazdoor Sabha (India)
HRM	Human resource management
IAM	International Association of Machinists and Aerospace Workers (USA)
IBT	International Brotherhood of Teamsters (USA)
ICFTU	International Confederation of Free Trade Unions

IFA	International Framework Agreement
IFC	International Finance Corporation
ILIU	Labourers' Union (USA)
ILO	International Labour Organization
INC	Indian National Congress
INTUC	Indian National Trade Union Congress
IR	Industrial relations
ITUC	International Trade Union Confederation
IUF	International Union of Food, Agricultural, Hotel, Restaurant, Catering, Tobacco and Allied Workers' Association (USA)
JCP	Japan Communist Party
JSP	Japan Socialist Party
KCCI	Korean Chamber of Commerce and Industry
KCTU	Korean Confederation of Trade Unions
KCTU	Minjunochong (Korean Confederation of Trade Unions)
KEF	Korea Employers Federation
KFIU	Korea Finance Industry Union
KHMWU	Korea Health and Medical Workers Union
KL	Local Government Denmark
KMWU	Korea Metal Workers Union
KTUC	Cheonnohyp (Korea Trade Union Congress)
LCSMSNS	Law Concerning the Special Measures for Safeguarding National Security (Korea)
LDP	Liberal Democratic Party (Japan)
LH	Ledernes Hovedorganisation (Organisation of Managerial and Executive Staff in Denmark)
LIC	Life Insurance Corporation (India)
LIUNA	Laborers' International Union of North America
LMC	Labour–Management Council
LME	Liberal market economy
LO	Landsorganisationen i Danmark (Danish Confederation of Trade Unions)
MEDEF	Mouvement des entreprises de France
MIT	Massachusetts Institute of Technology
MG	American Military Government (see USAMGIK)
MNC	Multinational corporation
MNE	Multinational enterprise
MoLSS	Ministry of Labour and Social Security (China)
MTIA	Metal Trades Industry Association (Australia)
MWC	Minimum Wage Commission (Korea)
NAFTA	North American Free Trade Agreement

NBS	National business system
NCTU	Cheonkuk Nodongjohab Hyeobuiehyo (Korean National Council of Trade Unions)
NDP	New Democratic Party (Canada)
NES	National Employment Standards
NGO	Non-government organisation
NJCS	National Joint Consultative Committee for Steel Industry (India)
NLRA	*National Labor Relations Act* (USA)
NMW	National minimum wage
NRLB	National Labor Relations Board (USA)
NSSO	National Sample Survey Organisation (India)
OECD	Organization for Economic Cooperation and Development
OT	Ohne Tarifbindung (collective agreements, Germany)
PCI	Communist Party of Italy
PCIRR	Presidential Commission on Industrial Relations Reform (Korea)
PDS	Partito Democratico della Sinistra (Italian Democratic Party of the Left)
PIL	Public-interest litigation
PIRRC	Presidential Industrial Relations Reform Commission (Korea)
PQ	Parti Quebecois (Canada)
PSI	Socialist Party of Italy
PVH	Philips Van Heusen
RMI	Revenue minimum d'insertion
RSA	Rappresentanze Sindacali Aziendali (Italian Firm Union Representative)
RSU	Rappresentanze Sindacale Unitarie (Italian Unitary Union Representative at Firm Level)
SALA	Sammenslutningen af Landbrugets Arbejdsgiverforeninger (Danish Confederation of Employers' Associations in Agriculture)
SCOPE	Standing Conference on Public Enterprises (India)
SDP	Social Democratic Party (Germany)
SDP	Social Democratic Party (Japan)
SEIU	Service Employees International Union
SME	Small and medium-sized enterprises
SMIC	Salarie Minimum Interprofessional de Croissance (France)
SOE	State-owned enterprise

TUC	Trades Union Congress (UK)
TULAA	*Trade Union and Labour Adjustment Act* (Korea)
TUPE	Transfer of Undertakings Protection of Employment (UK)
UAW	Union of Automotive Workers (USA)
UFCW	United Food and Commercial Workers (USA)
UIL	Unione Italiana dei Lavoratori (Italian Union of Labour)
UMP	Union pour un movement populaire (France)
UN	United Nations
UNITE-HERE	Union of Needletrades, Industrial, and Textile Employees and Hotel, Entertainment and Restaurant Employees (USA)
UNSA	Union Nationale des Syndicats Autonomes (France)
UPA	Union professionnelle artisanale (France)
USAMGIK	US Army Military Government in Korea (see AMG)
USS	Union Syndicale Solidaire (France)
USW	United Steel Workers (USA)
VEBA	Voluntary Employee Benefit Association (USA)
VoC	Varieties of capitalism
WC	Works council (Germany)
WCL	World Confederation of Labour
WERS	Workplace Employment Relations Survey
WFTU	World Federation of Trade Unions
WTO	World Trade Organization

Preface

The changes taking place in the international economy have far-reaching implications for the world of work, and have renewed interest in the study of international and comparative employment relations. This book summarises traditions and issues in employment relations in 12 significant market economies: the United Kingdom, the United States, Canada, Australia, Italy, France, Germany, Denmark, Japan, South Korea, China and India, providing interested readers with the background necessary for them to compare employment relations policies and practices across countries.

For the first time, this fully revised edition of the book includes chapters on China, India and Denmark, as well as fully revised and updated chapters on nine countries that have appeared in previous editions. The inclusion of chapters on India and China reflects the growing significance and status of these two large countries in the international economy over the past decade. Denmark has been included because its novel form of employment relations is seen by many as a model for other developed countries in the context of globalisation.

This edition also includes a completely revised and rewritten introductory chapter. This chapter introduces readers to the field of international and comparative employment relations and reviews some of the main debates in the field. It also highlights some of the international dimensions of employment relations.

Each of the country chapters has been written by specially selected country experts. Employment relations traditions and issues are analysed in each chapter using a similar format, with an examination of context—economic, historical, political, legal and social—and the characteristics of the major interest groups—employers, unions and governments. This is followed by a concise summary of the main process of employment relations in that country. Each chapter concludes with a brief discussion of key contemporary employment relations issues and challenges in its featured country.

In this edition, we have placed a particular emphasis on the Varieties of Capitalism (VoC) approach as a framework for understanding the similarities and differences in employment relations across countries. The introductory chapter introduces the VoC approach and discusses its application to international and comparative employment relations. The book contains chapters on at least two countries from each of the main varieties of capitalism that have been identified in the literature, enabling readers to compare employment relations policies and practices both within and across varieties of capitalism.

Earlier editions and the subsequent Japanese, Korean, Chinese and Thai editions of this book were repeatedly reprinted and have been read widely around the world. This book is one of the most extensively prescribed texts in its field internationally. We hope that this new edition will continue to meet the needs of scholars, teachers, students and practitioners who have an interest in international and comparative employment relations.

Despite the difficulties of working across different languages, cultures and disciplines, the contributors have patiently met our requests for updating and redrafting. We are extremely grateful to them for all their hard work. We would also like to thank the many colleagues who read drafts of the chapters and provided comments and suggestions for improvement.

We are indebted to the large number of colleagues from around the world who have provided us with feedback on how they have used previous editions in their courses and have made constructive suggestions for improvement. The improvements in this edition reflect the feedback that we have received from international and comparative employment relations specialists. Over the years, we have also learnt a lot from our students and wish to acknowledge the important role they have played in helping us to refine and improve this book. We would always be glad to hear more feedback.

Compiling a book like this is a complex and time-consuming task. We have been ably assisted by Rawya Mansour and Maryan Wadick, and wish to extend our gratitude to them. Special thanks go to Susan Jarvis for the painstaking job of proofreading and copyediting. Finally, we wish to acknowledge the continued enthusiasm, support and patience of our publishers—Allen & Unwin in Australia and New Zealand, and Sage internationally. Our greatest debt, however, is owed to our families, to whom this book is dedicated.

— Greg J. Bamber
Department of Management, Faculty of Business and Economics,
Monash University, Melbourne, Australia
Email: GregBamber@gmail.com

— Russell D. Lansbury and Nick Wailes
Work and Organisational Studies, Faculty of Economics and Business,
The University of Sydney, Sydney, Australia
Email:nick.wailes@sydney.edu.au; russell.lansbury@sydney.edu.au

CHAPTER 1

International and comparative employment relations: An introduction

Nick Wailes, Greg J. Bamber
and Russell D. Lansbury

THE GLOBAL FINANCIAL CRISIS AND EMPLOYMENT RELATIONS

Dramatic events gripped the world economy after Lehman Brothers filed for bankruptcy in September 2008. This was the largest bankruptcy in US history; Lehman held more than US$600 billion in assets. This precipitated a global financial crisis. We live in an era in which national economies have become increasing interconnected. This is a form of *globalisation*. At least since the 1990s, international employment relations scholars have been considering how globalisation is reshaping the employment relationship across companies, industries and countries. The global financial crisis has increased the priority of this consideration. In 2009, General Motors (one of the world's largest automakers) filed for bankruptcy and announced it would close plants and cut many thousands of jobs in a range of countries; British Airways asked its staff to work for free for a month; and more than 20 million factory workers in southern China lost their jobs and returned to the rural areas from which they had originally come. These examples are repeated in other countries; they illustrate that the global financial crisis and its aftermath have potentially far-reaching implications for employment relations in many countries.

Globalisation in general, and the global financial crisis in particular, raise some fundamental employment relations questions. Will we see major changes in traditional patterns of employment relations as employers and countries deal with the aftermath of this global financial crisis? To what extent will these changes have an impact in particular countries and sectors? Will the global financial crisis accelerate recent trends in employment relations (such as the decentralisation of bargaining, the decline in union membership and the rise of contingent, less stable forms of employment) or will it reverse some of these changes? Will the global financial crisis and its aftermath promote or undermine employee involvement and participation in decision-making at workplaces? When economic growth slows, are workers in developing countries more likely to form unions than they were in the past? Will governments strengthen or dilute legal protections for workers in the wake of the global financial crisis? Will changes in international economic regulations, designed to prevent further turmoil on international financial markets, encourage or erode the propensity of employers to offer decent work?

This book aims to provide interested readers with the background information and some of the conceptual tools they need to help them answer these and many of the other employment relations-related questions raised by the post-2008 turmoil in the international economy. The following chapters, written by leading national experts, provide a concise overview of employment relations in twelve countries. The book includes chapters on four English-speaking countries: the United Kingdom, the United States, Australia and Canada. It includes chapters on four Continental European countries: Germany, France, Italy and Denmark. The last of these is smaller, but its employment relations system, which balances flexibility with security (and may be referred to as *flexicurity*), is often seen by many as a model for other countries in Europe (see Auer 2008). The book also includes chapters on four Asian countries: Japan, Korea, India and the People's Republic of China. The latter are the world's two most populous countries, and in recent years they have come to play an increasingly important role in the international economy.

This chapter provides an introduction to the study of international and comparative employment relations. It discusses some of the benefits and the challenges of adopting an internationally comparative approach to employment relations, provides an overview of some of the frameworks of analysis associated with the comparative literature and introduces readers to the *varieties of capitalism* (VoC) approach, an increasingly influential framework for comparative analysis. Finally, the chapter briefly outlines some of the international dimensions that influence national patterns of employment relations.

WHY STUDY INTERNATIONAL AND COMPARATIVE EMPLOYMENT RELATIONS?

In this book, we are interested in the broad range of factors that shape the relationship between employers and employees and the similarities and differences in these relationships over time and across countries. As Heery et al. (2008: 2) note, industrial relations (IR) scholarship traditionally has tended to focus on three aspects of the employment relationship: the parties to the employment relationship; the processes through which the employment relationship is governed; and the outcomes of these processes. IR has therefore tended to focus on the formal and informal *institutions* of job regulation, including collective bargaining, unions, employer associations and labour tribunals. Human resource management (HRM), on the other hand, has been focused more at the level of the individual organisation, and is concerned with 'the effective overall management of an organisation's workforce in order to contribute to the achievement of desired objectives and goals' (Nankervis et al. 2008: 9–10). HRM has thus tended to focus on issues such as recruitment, selection, pay, performance and human resource development. We believe both perspectives are valuable for understanding the factors that shape the relationship between employers and employees, and therefore adopt the term *employment relations* (ER) to encompass both IR and HRM. On occasions where they are appropriate, however, the terms IR and HRM are also used in this book.

Although the study of employment relations focuses on the regulation of work, it must also take account of the wider economic and social influences on the relative power of capital and labour, and the interactions between employers, workers, their collective organisations and the state. A full understanding of employment relations requires an interdisciplinary approach that uses analytical tools drawn from several academic fields, including accounting, economics, history, law, politics, psychology, sociology and other elements of management studies.

Adopting an *internationally comparative approach* to employment relations requires not only insights from several disciplines, but also knowledge of different national contexts. Some scholars distinguish between *comparative* and *international* studies in this field. Comparative employment relations may involve describing and systematically analysing two or more countries. By contrast, international employment relations involves exploring institutions and phenomena that cross national boundaries, such as the labour market roles and behaviour of inter-governmental organisations, multinational corporations (MNCs) and unions (cf. Bean 1994). This is a useful distinction, but again we incline towards a broader perspective whereby *international* and *comparative* employment relations includes a range of studies that traverse boundaries between countries. This book emphasises an internationally comparative approach, combining comparative and international approaches to the subject.

There are a number of reasons why it is beneficial to study internationally comparative employment relations. First, this area can contribute to our knowledge of employment relations in different countries. One of the consequences of globalisation, with increased levels of cross-border trade and investment, is that IR and HR professionals often need knowledge about ER practices in more than one country (Strauss 1998). A second benefit of the internationally comparative study of employment relations is that other countries may provide models for policy-makers, managers and workers. At various times over the past 50 years, aspects of employment relations in the United States, Sweden, Japan and Germany have been seen as models to emulate. One reason for including Denmark in this book is that its system of flexicurity is seen by some as a potential model for other developed market economies.

Interest in different national models of employment relations is not confined to employment relations scholars. Political scientists have long been interested in how the ways in which employers and workers are organised affect national politics and some economists have focused on the role that labour market institutions play in explaining difference in aggregate economic performance (Freeman 2008: 640).

The third, and for us the most important, reason for the internationally comparative study of employment relations is its potential to provide theoretical insight into the factors and variables that shape the relationships between employers and employees (Bean 1994). Both IR and HRM, as fields of study, have been criticised as overly descriptive and for their apparent inability to develop causal explanations of relevant phenomena (see, for example, Barbash & Barbash 1989; Sisson 1994; Kelly 1998). This view was expressed in Dunlop's famous observation that:

> The field of industrial relations today may best be described in the words of Julian Huxley 'Mountains of facts have been piled on the plains of human ignorance . . . the result is a glut of new material.

Great piles of facts are lying around unutilised, or utilised only in an occasional and partial manner'. Facts have outrun ideas. Integrating theory has lagged far behind expanding experience. The many worlds of industrial relations have been changing more rapidly than the ideas to interpret, to explain and determine them. (Dunlop 1958: vi)

While this tendency towards description has also been noted in comparative employment relations (Clark et al. 1999; Schuler et al. 2002), it has been suggested that comparative research offers significant potential for theoretical development by establishing casual inferences (Shalev 1980; Bean 1994; Strauss 1998). This is because comparison requires the abstraction of concepts from particular contexts. As Kochan (1998: 41) puts it:

Each national system carries with it certain historical patterns of development and features that restrict the range of variation on critical variables such as culture, ideology, and institutional structures which affect how individual actors respond to similar changes in their external environments. Taking an international perspective broadens the range of comparisons available on these and other variables and increases the chances of discovering the systematic variations needed to produce new theoretical insights and explanations.

McLaughlin (2009) provides a good example of the theoretical contribution that comparative analysis can make to the study of employment relations. In light of evidence that the introduction of a national minimum wage (NMW) in the United Kingdom in 1999 has failed to produce anticipated increases in labour productivity, his analysis focuses on the relationship between the NMW and productivity in Denmark and New Zealand. While both these countries have relatively high NMWs, there are significant institutional differences between the two countries. McLaughlin (2009: 343) shows that the productivity-enhancing effects of a NMW in Denmark are closely related to 'high levels of government funding for training . . . [and] that coordination mechanisms between employers and unions at various levels of the economy play a pivotal role', while the absence of equivalent funding and coordination mechanisms in New Zealand helps explain the limited contribution of a NMW to productivity enhancement. By focusing on two countries that both have high minimum wage levels but have experienced different outcomes, McLaughlin's analysis highlights the causal significance of institutional and bargaining arrangements.

5

In another study that illustrates the theoretical potential of comparative analysis, Doellgast (2008) was interested in identifying the factors that explain company-level variations in outcomes of collective negotiations over outsourcing. She does this by examining the process and outcomes of bargaining over outsourcing in six telecommunications companies—three in Germany and three in the United States. Her findings show that, despite differences in national employment relations institutions, there is considerable variation in outcomes within each country and that the success of unions in limiting the scale and scope of outsourcing depends largely on their ability to mobilise critical bargaining resources. In the United States, this involves mobilising external community and political support, while in Germany success rested on the ability of the union to establish effective internal coordination. Doellgast's (2008: 285) conclusion is that, despite national context, 'unions can gain an independent voice in restructuring decisions through using traditional forms of bargaining power in innovative ways'; however, doing so requires 'considerable effort, creative and organised political action'.

WHAT AND HOW TO COMPARE?

While an internationally comparative approach may provide the basis for establishing causal inferences in employment relations research, the act of comparison itself does not necessarily ensure this outcome. One of the challenges of comparative studies is the choice of 'what' and 'how' to compare.

The lack of a common language and terminology may create confusion in comparative analysis. As Blanpain (2010) points out, 'identical words in different languages may have different meanings, while corresponding terms may embrace wholly different realities'. He notes, for example, that the term 'arbitration' (or '*arbitrage*' in French), which usually means a binding decision by an impartial third party, can also signify a recommendation by a government conciliator to the conflicting parties. There can also be difficulties in distinguishing between the law and the actual practice. For example, while Australia formally practised 'compulsory arbitration' from the beginning of the twentieth century at least until the mid-1990s, there was relatively little 'compulsion' in practice and the arbitration tribunals has relied mainly on advice and persuasion (see Chapter 5).

The collection of comparative data also poses challenges for those studying this field. For example, definitions of industrial disputes differ significantly between countries. Conflicts of *right* concern the interpretation of an *existing* contract or award, such as which pay grade applies to a particular individual or group of workers. However, conflicts of *interest* arise during collective bargaining about an apparently *new* demand or claim, such as for a general pay increase or a reduction in working hours. In practice, conflicts of interest are usually collective disputes. In the United States, Sweden and elsewhere, this distinction is important. In France, Italy and certain other countries, conflicts of right are further divided into *individual* and *collective* disputes. The general intention is that different settlement procedures will apply to different types of dispute. In some countries, only conflicts of interest can lead to lawful strikes or other forms of sanction, but conflicts of right should be settled by a binding decision of a labour court or similar tribunal (see Bamber, Sheldon & Gan 2010).

Arguably, the difficulty of collecting genuinely comparable cross-national employment relations measures implies that the contribution of comparative research based on empirical datasets and large-scale national surveys is likely to be limited (see Ryan et al. 2004). Indeed, Whitfield and Strauss (1998) note the particular difficulties associated with the use of large national surveys in comparative research.

Many of the problems associated with comparative analysis relate to the difficulties of establishing *conceptual equivalence* when operationalising comparative research. Linden (1998) distinguishes between *phenomenal equivalence*—where identical measures are used for the same concept regardless of context—and *conceptual equivalence*—where different measures are used for the same concept to reflect differences in contexts. He argues that comparative analysis can only proceed effectively on the basis of conceptual equivalence (Linden 1998: 5–6).

In a similar vein, Locke and Thelen (1995: 340) argue that there are problems associated with comparative analyses which focus on the same issue across countries because these studies 'often assume that the same practice has the same meaning or valence across the various countries'. They argue instead for the use of *contextualised* comparisons that focus on different national 'sticking points' between employers and employees across countries. Thus, for example, they show that whereas unions in the United States resisted the introduction of more flexible work arrangements during the 1980s and 1990s, German unions embraced work reorganisation because they saw it as a way of increasing skills. Locke and Thelen argue that this difference reflects the greater significance of job control for union power in the United States (see Chapter 3). For German unions, they argue, issues of working time and wage flexibility—particularly in the context of

7

German reunificiation—were much more salient and became a source of contention between employers and employees (see Chapter 8).

Effective comparison therefore often requires detailed understanding of each different national context. Strauss (1998) advances the interesting proposition that it is fruitless to seek to design a complete, full-grown comparative theory at this stage of the field's development. Rather, he suggests, it is more appropriate to 'creep towards a field of comparative industrial relations' by developing generalisations and testable hypotheses that explain differences among countries, and that subsequently may provide the basis for developing useful theories. He draws attention to advantages to be gained from studying close pairs of countries with similar economies, cultures and historic traditions. This permits researchers to hold many characteristics constant and examine those that vary between countries.

In fact, it possible to identify two different research designs that enhance the likelihood of establishing causal inferences from comparative research (Skopcol & Somers 1980; Przeworski & Teune 1970). The first, alluded to by Strauss, is known as a *most similar case* research design and involves the comparison of two or more cases that share a number of common features but differ in certain key respects.

There are a number of comparative employment relations studies that exploit similarities between countries to identify potential sources of variation. Rose and Chaison (2001), for example, examine differences in the pattern of union decline in the United States and Canada. Despite the similarities between the countries, union decline has been more rapid and dramatic in the United States than in Canada. Rose and Chaison argue that this difference can be accounted for by differences in the legal systems, which make it easier for US employers to avoid unions, and by closer affiliation between unions and a left-of-centre political party in Canada. There are also a number of most similar case comparisons that focus on Australia and New Zealand. These studies suggest that the differences in employment relations policies that developed in the two countries during the 1980s and 1990s can in part be explained by differences in organisation of employers and unions (Bray & Walsh 1998, Wailes et al. 2003). In New Zealand, a high degree of consensus amongst employers about the need for labour market deregulation and divisions amongst unions made it easier for successive governments to drive through significant reforms to employment relations policy. In Australia, by contrast, division in employer opinion and the existence of a single, strong peak union organisation provided the context for less dramatic change to the traditional employment relations system. The study by McLaughlin (2009), referred to above, is also an example of most similar case research design.

A second comparative research design is known as *most different case* comparison. As its name implies, this approach involves comparison of countries that differ in a number of respects except for the phenomenon under study. While less common, most different case comparisons are likely to produce as many theoretical insights as most similar case comparison. The study by Doellgast (2008) referred to above is an example of a most different case comparison. In her study, despite significant differences between the two countries, she was able to identify a common factor (the ability of unions to mobilise bargaining resources) that helped explain differences in outcomes of negotiations over outsourcing within the two countries.

CONVERGENCE AND DIVERGENCE IN NATIONAL PATTERNS OF EMPLOYMENT RELATIONS

One of the most enduring concerns of comparative employment relations scholars has been assessing the extent to which national patterns of employment relations are either *converging* (becoming more similar) or *diverging* (moving further apart). The original *convergence* thesis was developed by Kerr and colleagues in their book *Industrialism and Industrial Man* (Kerr et al. 1960). Their core proposition is that there is a global tendency for technological and market forces associated with industrialisation to push national employment relations systems towards uniformity or 'convergence'. This conclusion is based on the view that there is a *logic of industrialism*. As more societies adopt industrial forms of production and organisation, this logic creates 'common characteristics and imperatives' across the societies. To accommodate these imperatives, Kerr et al. (1960: 384–92) argue that industrial societies had to develop a means of developing a consensus and employment relations systems which embodied the 'principles of pluralistic industrialism' that played a central role in establishing this consensus. Goldthorpe (1984: 316) describes this as a model of 'evolutionary convergence of all modern and "modernising" societies on one particular form of industrialism: namely, "pluralist industrialism"'.

Figure 1.1 illustrates schematically the logic of industrialism, showing how the various social changes are related to the prime cause: technology. Convergence between advanced industrial societies occurs most readily at the technological level, at workplace

9

and industry levels or at urban levels, and then at national levels. However, Kerr and colleagues do concede that total convergence is unlikely because of the persistence of political, social, cultural and ideological differences. Nevertheless, while the authors acknowledge that there were factors that could mediate the relationship between industrialism and the particular institutions that developed, including the timing of development and the nature of the modernising elite, they also argue that the logic of industrialism tended to override these sources of difference and would produce convergence on a particular set of institutional arrangements of labour market regulation.

Figure 1.1   The logic of industrialism

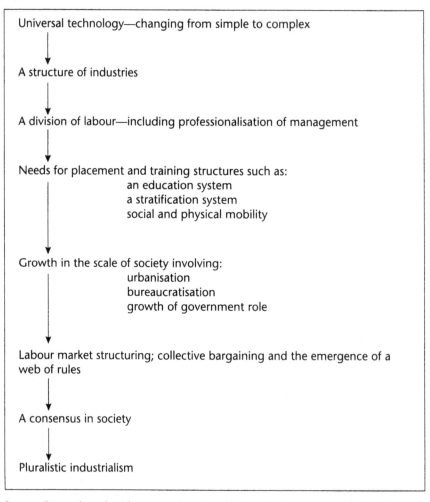

Source: Reproduced with permission from Brown & Harrison (1978: 129)

The convergence hypothesis, based on the logic of industrialism, has been widely criticised. Some accused Kerr and colleagues of *technological determinism*, arguing that even though there may have been strong pressures associated with industrialism and modernisation, this did not necessarily imply that there would be convergence on a single set of societal institutions (Cochrane 1976; Doeringer 1981; Piore 1981; Berger 1996: 2–4). In line with this criticism, Kerr later revisited the convergence hypothesis and argued that the logic of industrialism resulted in a *tendency* towards convergence which may be counteracted by a range of institutional factors (Kerr 1983).

In a notable contribution to the convergence debate, Dore (1973) suggested that while there may be a tendency towards convergence in national patterns of employment relations, the tendency is toward convergence on Japan rather than the United States (the implicit model that underpinned Kerr et al.'s model). Placing less emphasis on technology than Kerr and colleagues, Dore argues that because Japan began to industrialise relatively late (a century after Britain), it was able to learn from the experience of the countries that had already been through the process. He argues that late developers had been able to adopt organisational forms and institutions more suited to industrialisation than those of countries that industrialised relatively early.

A second line of critique of Kerr and colleagues' convergence hypothesis questioned the notion of industrialism itself. *Industrialism and Industrial Man* was one of number of books, including Daniel Bell's (1962) *The End of Ideology* and W.W. Rostow's (1960) *The Stages of Economic Growth*, written during the Cold War that presented the American social, political and economic system as superior to Soviet communism and as a model for other countries to emulate. To this extent, the links drawn between industrialism and a particular set of social and political institutions were prescriptive. The implication was that countries needed to adopt social and political institutions like those of the United States to be able to benefit from modernisation and industrialism (Goldthorpe 1984).

The criticisms of the convergence thesis were largely borne out by the empirical evidence. In the aftermath of the publication of *Industrialism and Industrial Man*, there was a growth of empirical research that set out to test the extent of convergence in industrial relations systems. While some claimed to show evidence of convergence, as Katz and Darbishire (2000: 8) note:

11

> The thrust of . . . much of the comparative industrial relations literature . . . was that there was wide and persistent variation in industrial relations across countries in part due to the influence of nationally specific institutional factors

In the late 1970s and early 1980s, empirical research suggested that, rather than converging, national patterns of employment relations were increasingly *diverging*. Following World War II, there was a prolonged period of economic growth that is often referred to as the 'Long Boom'. As the Long Boom came to an end during the 1970s, growth in the (developing) Third World slowed, conflict between employers and employees began to increase and differences between market societies became more evident (Cammack 1997; Katzenstein 1978; Crouch & Pizzorno 1978). In an influential analysis, Goldthorpe (1984) identified the development of two distinct national patterns of employment relations during this period. He argued that some countries, like Norway, Austria, Germany and Sweden, attempted to increase economic growth and reduce inflation through *corporatist* policies that involved centralised negotiations between employers, unions and, in some cases, the state. In countries like Britain and the United States, by contrast, the traditional labour market institutions (e.g. collective bargaining) were being undermined in an effort to eliminate perceived rigidities in the market. Goldthorpe argued that this was producing a *dualism* in employment relations in these countries, with the workforce separated into core and peripheral employees. The former may remain unionised and within the collective bargaining framework—albeit in a more decentralised mode—while the latter are employed under more individualistic work arrangements characterised by contractual forms of control.

In a similar vein, Freeman (1989) identifies evidence of divergent trends in union membership and density across developed market economies during the 1980s. He argues that, 'far from converging to some modal type, trade unionism . . . traditionally the principal worker institution under capitalism developed remarkably differently among Western countries in the 1970s and 1980s' (1989: 32). Since the 1980s, union density has been maintained at high levels in the Scandinavian countries but declined significantly in other countries, such as the United Kingdom, Australia and the United States. This divergence in density occurred despite common factors such as increasing trade, technological transfer and capital flows between countries, which might have been expected to exert pressures for similarities.

While some employment relations scholars emphasised diversity and divergence of national employment relations systems, others focused on what they saw as common developments across countries. For example, since the mid-1980s there has been a noticeable decentralisation of bargaining taking place in many countries. This has generally involved the locus of bargaining shifting downwards from a national or industry level to an enterprise or workplace level. However, the degree of decentralisation and the means by which changes in bargaining structures occurred have varied between countries. Based on a comparison of experiences in six countries (Australia, Germany, Italy, Sweden, Britain and the United States), Katz (1993) reports many similarities in the process of decentralisation. In each country—except Germany—there was a shift towards decentralisation in the formal structure of bargaining initiated by employers, and a consequent reduction in the extent of multi-employer bargaining. With the exception of Australia (where there was an Accord between the unions and the then Labor government—see Chapter 5), most central union organisations opposed decentralisation of bargaining.

Katz evaluates three hypotheses that have been suggested to explain the trend towards decentralised bargaining: first, shifts in bargaining power from unions to employers; second, the emergence of new forms of work organisation that put a premium on flexibility and employee participation; and third, the decentralisation of corporate structures and diversification of worker preferences. Katz concludes that the second hypothesis is the most convincing on the grounds that labour and management appear to have gained distinct advantages from the work restructuring that accompanied decentralisation. However, shifts in bargaining power, as well as the diversification of corporate and worker interests, are also important contributing factors to the decentralisation process.

Questions of convergence and divergence in national patterns of employment relations were reconsidered in the 1990s by researchers associated with the strategic choice approach at the Massachusetts Institute of Technology (MIT) (see Locke, Kochan & Piore 1995). This research sought to understand the impact on employment relations of increasing international competition and of new production technologies (Kochan et al. 1994; Womack et al. 1990). The research project developed in two stages. The first stage involved identifying developments in the various countries and comparing them (e.g. Kitay & Lansbury 1997). The second phase involved examining employment relations in specific industries in these countries, including: airlines, automobiles, banking, electronics, steel and telecommunications (e.g. Bamber, Gittell, Kochan, & von Nordenflytch 2009; Katz 1997; Kochan et al. 1997; Regini et al. 2000).

While there was evidence of changing employment practices within industries and across countries, such industry studies also highlighted the continued importance of national-level institutional frameworks (see Kochan et al. 1997; Katz 1997; Regini et al. 2000). Katz (1997: 11–23), for example, in summarising the findings of research on the telecommunications industry in ten countries, argues that there are broad similarities across countries in relation to employment security, work organisation, training, compensation and governance. Yet there also remain important national differences.

Building on the MIT project, Katz and Darbishire (2000) examined two industries (car manufacturing and telecommunications) in six countries. They conclude that there was increased diversity of employment patterns across the countries studied. They call this 'converging on divergence' and argue that it was characterised by the spread of four employment patterns, which were low wage, HRM, Japanese oriented and joint team based. However, they also note differences in the distribution of these patterns at the national level, as well as in the extent of variation within countries. They attribute these variations to differences in national-level institutions. In particular, they argue that differences in employment patterns reflected the differential impact of national-level institutions on the degree of centralisation of bargaining, the extent of commonality of processes at a decentralised level and the degree of effective coordination between decentralised bargaining structures. Thus Katz and Darbishire conclude that, despite evidence of divergence, 'the persistence of sizeable country differences in the relative mix of various employment patterns, and the role that national level institutions play in shaping that mix, suggest a continuing influential role for national employment-related institutions' (2000: 281).

GLOBALISATION AND EMPLOYMENT RELATIONS

Issues of convergence and divergence have also dominated debates about the impact of globalisation on employment relations. As Wade (1996) notes, globalisation usually refers to changes in the international economy that are associated with increases in international trade in goods and services, greater flows of foreign direct investment (FDI) and the growth of international financial transactions. These changes include higher levels of interconnectedness in international economic activity.

Several authors, including Hirst and Thompson (1996), as well as Wade, have argued that national economies have become 'internationalised' rather than globalised, and that the pressures associated with globalisation are not as strong as others claim. However, as Perraton et al. (1997) demonstrate, there are contemporary changes in the international economy, which can be usefully summarised by the term 'globalisation'. These include changes in the extent and intensity of international trade, international financial flows and the operations of MNCs. On the basis of this evidence, Perraton et al. (1997: 274) argue that, while:

> the world does fall short of perfect globalised markets . . . this misses the significance of global processes. Global economic activity is significantly greater relative to domestically based economic activity than in previous historical periods and impinges directly or indirectly on a greater proportion of national economic activity than ever before.

One approach to the impact of globalisation on employment relations has emphasised the extent to which globalisation has created common pressures across all countries, and is likely to produce similar employment relations outcomes. We call this the *simple globalisation approach*. This approach assumes that international economic activity has become so interconnected and that the pressures associated with globalisation are so overwhelming that they leave little scope for national differences in economic activity, including employment relations policies and practices (Ohmae 1990). This perspective has tended to be the most prominent in popular debates about the effects of contemporary changes in the international economy on working conditions and the relations between workers and their employers.

In its extreme form, this approach predicts a 'race to the bottom' in terms of wages and other labour standards across most economies and the erosion of nationally specific labour market regimes, including those that may provide for union security or encourage the pursuit of equity as well as efficiency (see, for example, Ohmae 1995).

The *simple globalisation* approach, and particularly the view that globalisation has eroded national policy autonomy, has been criticised widely. Garrett (1998), for example, argues that just because national governments are faced with similar economic pressures, it does not follow that they have no choice over how to respond to these pressures. He supports this argument with evidence to show that there is considerable diversity in monetary and fiscal policy-setting

15

across countries. In line with arguments put forward by Evans (1997) and Weiss (1998), Garrett cites evidence that the pressures associated with globalisation may increase the role the nation state can play in some areas, including the labour market, to ensure the maintenance of international competitiveness.

Criticisms of the simple globalisation approach and evidence of continued diversity in national patterns of employment relations have contributed to the development of the *institutionalist approach*—a second perspective on the impact of globalisation on employment relations. The institutionalist approach suggests that differences in national-level institutions are likely to refract common economic pressures in different ways. As Locke and Thelen (1995) put it, according to this view, 'international trends are not in fact translated into common pressures in all national economies but rather are mediated by national institutional arrangements and refracted into divergent struggles over particular national practices' (1995: 338). Because differences in national-level institutions are relatively enduring, this approach suggests that globalisation is unlikely to lead to a general convergence in national patterns of employment relations (Locke, Piore & Kochan 1995). Rather, it predicts continuity and even increased divergence between national patterns of employment relations. This approach draws on arguments from a variety of disciplines about the independent role institutions play in shaping economic and political outcomes.

Examples of the institutionalist approach in the employment relations literature are studies by Turner (1991) and Thelen (1993) of German industrial relations in a comparative framework. Both argue that the 'dual system' of industrial relations in Germany has enabled German unions to withstand the pressures of globalisation better than their counterparts in the United States and Sweden. Turner (1991) compares the involvement of unions in industrial restructuring in Germany and the United States, and places heavy emphasis on the role that differences in institutional arrangements have played in determining the reaction of employers and workers to international economic pressures. Similarly, according to Thelen (1993), the German system—with national and industry-level bargaining plus separate legally enriched rights for workers at the workplace level—has allowed pressures for decentralised bargaining to be accommodated within the existing institutional configuration. In Sweden, by contrast, the absence of institutionalised rights for workers in the workplace, and the divisions created between blue-collar and white-collar workers by the centralised bargaining system, has meant that pressures for decentralised bargaining could not be accommodated within the existing structure of bargaining.

The importance of differences in national-level institutions for explaining differences in patterns of employment relations is also emphasised by Ferner and Hyman (1998) in their comparative European studies. In particular, they point to the re-emergence of 'societal corporatism' in some European economies during the 1990s as evidence that 'states possess a key role in the reconfiguration of the relations between social regulation and markets (including labour markets)' (Ferner & Hyman 1998: xxi). They also develop the notion that some forms of labour market institutions can adapt to international economic changes better than others. Further support for the institutionalist perspective on globalisation and industrial relations is provided in an empirical study by Traxler et al. (2001), who argue that divergence is likely because 'market pressures affect labour relations institutions indirectly, in that they are processed and filtered by institutions' (2001: 289).

The institutionalist approach represents a useful correction to the simple globalisation model. The focus on the mediating role of institutions helps to explain patterns of persistent national differences and demonstrates that the relationship between globalisation and national employment relations is neither simple nor deterministic. It also points to key variables that play a decisive role in determining distinctive national patterns of industrial relations, many of which may be national in character. In particular, it suggests that to understand the impact of globalisation on employment relations on a particular country, it is important to understand the type of specific details outlined in the national chapters that follow.

While the institutionalist approach provides a correction to the convergence logic of the simple globalisation thesis, there are at least three limitations to this approach. First, by focusing on the role of national-level institutions, the institutionalist approach tends to emphasise differences between countries and struggles to explain common developments across countries with differences in their institutional arrangements (Pontusson 1995). Thus, for example, even though there are significant institutional differences between Britain (Chapter 2), the United States (Chapter 3) and Australia (Chapter 5), each of these countries has experienced significant declines in union membership in recent decades. Second, it is widely acknowledged that institutional approaches have difficulty accounting for change (Streeck & Thelen 2005). In technical terms, institutionalist arguments tend to treat institutions as an *independent* variable and examine how particular institutions (like bargaining systems) affect employment relations outcomes. However, as this book demonstrates, one of the dominant features of employment relations in many countries is the degree of change in the institutions of labour market regulation. Just as important is the extent to which the same set of institutions can produce different outcomes over time. Hassel (2006) for example, demonstrates how, in the context of increased international competition, the traditional institutions of labour market regulation in Germany have produced markedly different outcomes.

THE VARIETIES OF CAPITALISM APPROACH

An important development in comparative analysis has been the emergence of theories of diversity (for an overview, see Deeg & Jackson 2007). We focus on Hall and Soskice's (2001) *Varieties of Capitalism* (VoC) approach because, as Howell (2003: 103) notes, it '[has] achieved a level of theoretical sophistication, explanatory scope and predictive ambition' that has rapidly made it a leading theory in the field. We introduce the VoC approach and assess its potential as a framework for the comparative analysis of employment relations. The VoC and similar approaches are developed from the field of political economy. This framework has much potential for trying to understand and compare patterns of employment relations in different countries (Martin & Bamber 2004). We conclude that a modified form of the VoC approach provides a promising basis for the advancement of internationally comparative employment relations.

As noted in the previous section, there were differences in the policy reactions of market economies to the end of the Long Boom and scholars began to identify different families (or varieties) of market economy (for an overview, see Hamann & Kelly 2008). This project was given added impetus by the rise of neo-liberalism in the 1980s (which was led by President Reagan in the United States and Prime Minister Thatcher in the United Kingdom) and the collapse of Soviet communism at the end of the 1980s. Neo-liberals argued that the economic problems that had beset many market economies during the 1970s and 1980s were the consequence of excessive government interference in the free functioning of markets, including notably the labour market, and pointed to the collapse of Soviet communism as an extreme version of the problems associated with market interference. In reaction to neo-liberal claims that there was one best way to organise a market economy—or, in Mrs Thatcher's famous words, 'there is no alternative'—comparative scholars pointed to different patterns in the social organisation of capitalism. The relatively strong economic performance of Japan and Germany—two countries with very different institutional arrangements to those prevalent in the United Kingdom or the United States—during the 1980s cast doubts over the veracity of neo-liberal claims, as did evidence that the state played a significant role in the rapid economic development of the East Asian Tiger economies like Korea and Taiwan.

In keeping with this tradition, Hall and Soskice (2001) reject the notion that there is one best way to organise a market society and point to the role that institutional arrangements play in shaping how market societies function. Drawing on what they describe as 'the new economics of organisation', they develop a firm-centric theory of comparative institutional advantage. Hall and Soskice (2001: 6–9) argue that, in market economies, firms are faced with a series of coordination problems, both internally and externally. They focus on five spheres of coordination that firms must address:

- industrial relations
- vocational training and education
- corporate governance
- inter-firm relations and
- relations with their own employees.

Hall and Soskice argue that it is possible to identify two institutional equilibria (or solutions) to these coordination problems that produce superior economic outcomes. *Liberal market economies* (LMEs) are those in which firms rely on markets and hierarchies to resolve the coordination problems they face. LMEs are therefore more likely to be characterised by, amongst other things:

- well-developed capital markets
- 'outsider' forms of corporate governance
- market-based forms of industrial relations, with relatively few long-term commitments by employers to workers and
- the use of market mechanisms and contracts to coordinate their relations with supplier and buyer firms.

The United States is the prime exemplar of an LME, but the literature also often includes the United Kingdom, Australia, New Zealand, Canada and Ireland in this category.

The second variety of capitalism identified by Hall and Soskice, *coordinated market economies* (CMEs), includes countries in which firms make greater use of non-market mechanisms to resolve coordination problems internally and externally. In comparison with

LMEs, CMEs are more likely to be characterised by:

- 'patient' forms of capital
- insider forms of corporate governance
- industrial relations systems based on bargaining, and which reflect a longer term commitment to employees and
- the use of non-market mechanisms, such as industry associations, to coordinate relations between firms within and across industries and sectors.

Germany is the prime exemplar of a CME but the literature also often includes other northern European countries, as well as Japan and sometimes Korea, within this category.

Central to Hall and Soskice's argument, and the identification of distinct varieties of capitalism, is the concept of *institutional comp-lementarities*. In the VoC model, institutional complementary refers to two related but separate effects. First, institutions are said to be complementary to the extent that the existence of one enhances the effectiveness of another. Thus, for example, the existence of a cohesive industry association may enhance the economic efficiency of industry-wide collective bargaining. In this sense, institutional complementarily helps explain why two contrasting institutional configurations, LMEs and CMEs, are able to produce superior economic outcomes.

The VoC model also suggests that institutional arrangements are likely to converge on one or other institutional equilibria over time. Thus Hall and Soskice (2001: 18) argue that 'nations with a particular type of coordination in one sphere in the economy should tend to develop complementary practices in other spheres as well' (see also Amable 2003: 54–66). For example, the VoC model suggests that in countries characterised by well-developed capital markets and outsider forms of corporate governance, it is difficult to sustain industrial relations practices that imply a long-term commitment to employees. Over time, there are likely to be pressures for the adoption of more market-based forms of industrial relations. As Gospel and Pendleton (2005) have demonstrated there appear to be close relationships between forms of firm financing and labour management practices.

There is some empirical support for this notion of institutional complementarity, particularly in relation to the link between corporate governance and employment relations. Hall and Gingerich (2004), for example, estimate the impact of complementarities in employment relations and corporate governance on economic growth, drawing on measures of shareholder power, dispersion of control, size of the stock market, level and degree of wage coordination, and labour turnover (Hall & Gingerich 2004: 3). Their results suggest not only that there is a strong degree of institutional congruence across countries (the higher the level of coordination in corporate governance factors, the higher the level of coordination in labour relations factors), but also provide strong empirical support for the assertion that these practices are complementary (each raises the returns to the other) (Höpner 2005).

There are features of the VoC approach, then, that may provide a fruitful framework for internationally comparative analysis of employment relations in general, and an understanding on the impact of globalisation on national patterns of employment relations in particular. First, many of the coordination problems on which the VoC model focuses relate to variables and issues that have long been a concern of employment relations scholars, including industrial relations, skill development and relations with employees.

Second, the VoC approach suggests that it is not possible to understand employment relations issues in isolation and that comparative analysis needs to place changes in employment relations in a broader context. While this insight is consistent with the traditions of comparative analysis, the VoC approach has the added advantage of specifying a limited number of relevant variables. While some have argued that the range of factors that the VoC approach considers is too limited (which is addressed in more detail below), one of the advantages of this approach is that it directs the focus of comparative analysis to a limited number of issues.

In relation to the study of the impact of globalisation on employment relations, the VoC approach overcomes some of the limitations of the institutionalist approach noted in the previous section. By focusing on the interconnections between institutional arrangements, it overcomes the tendency of the institutionalist approach to treat employment relations institutions in isolation. Moreover the firm-centric nature of the VoC approach overcomes the tendency of institutionalist analysis to treat institutions as separate from the social actors who engage with them. In particular, the focus on the coordination problems that individual firms face makes it possible to bring employers back into the analysis of change in employment relations (Swenson 1991).

Further, in contrast to the simple globalisation and institutionalist approaches outlined in the previous section, the VoC approach is able to explain both similarities *and* differences between countries. For example, the VoC framework can help explain why globalisation appears to be associated by significant declines in union density and collective bargaining coverage in some countries (mainly the LMEs) but has not produced identical outcomes in other countries (the CMEs) (for further discussion, see Godard 2005). Indeed, one of the main implications of the VoC approach is that globalisation is likely to have differential impacts on employment relations processes and outcomes across varieties of capitalism (Hamann & Kelly 2008). Thus, while increased international competition is likely to create incentives for firms in LMEs to adopt more market-based employment relations practices (including decentralisation and individualisation of bargaining, individualised payment systems and more contingent forms of employment), the institutional dynamics of CMEs suggest that increased international competition may reinforce, rather than undermine, traditional forms of coordination between employers and employees. Thelen (2000, 2001), for example, argues that the pressures associated with globalisation have reinforced rather than undermined the commitment of German employers to industry-wide bargaining and works councils. The VoC approach also suggests that that pursuing a neo-liberal industrial relations agenda in a CME has the potential to erode, rather than enhance, economic competitiveness. For example, Harcourt and Wood (2007) show how the erosion of employment protections in CMEs has undermined the effectiveness of the vocational training systems that play such an important role in making these economies internationally competitive.

The VoC framework has become increasingly influential in comparative employment relations analysis. It has been used to help explain cross-national similarities and differences in, amongst other things, union membership and density, the gendered nature of labour markets, employee participation and vocational training systems (Frege & Kelly 2004; Lansbury & Wailes 2008; Estevez-Abe 2006; Harcourt & Wood 2007).

Despite the potential benefits of the VoC framework, Hall and Soskice's work has been subject to a number of criticisms. These criticisms suggest that the VoC approach needs to be modified if it is to provide a suitable framework for the comparative analysis of employment relations. One of the main criticisms of the VoC approach is that it does not contain enough variety (Allen 2004). The VoC's focus on only two varieties of capitalism—CMEs and LMEs—has a number of implications. First, it limits the range of countries to which the model can be applied. Hall and Soskice (2001: 21) themselves acknowledge that six European countries—France, Italy, Spain, Portugal, Greece and Turkey—are difficult to accommodate within either the LME or CME category, and they raise the prospect of a Mediterranean variety of capitalism. However, they leave this idea relatively under-developed. Second, the CME and LME categories are so large that the framework has the potential to ignore important differences between countries said to be of the same variety. As the contributions to two volumes edited by Streeck and Yamamura (2001 and 2003) demonstrate, while Japan and Germany are classified as examples of CMEs, there are important differences between them that are overlooked by the VoC approach. Jackson (2001), for example, notes that even though German and Japanese corporate governance arrangements produce similar outcomes, they differ both in terms of the institutional foundations on which they are based and the historical forces that shaped them. Thus, for example, in comparison with LMEs, employees in Japan and Germany have a greater role in corporate governance. However, in the German case workers' corporate governance rights are contained in legislation; this is not the case in Japan.

If the VoC approach is to form the basis of comparative analysis of employment relations, it is important to increase the number of varieties of capitalism to capture differences in the social organisation of market economies. Other comparative scholars have developed models that include more varieties of capitalism. Schmidt (2002), for example, adds a third variety of capitalism to accommodate the statist tradition in France. Hancke et al. (2006) argue for four varieties of capitalism, which they suggest make it possible to extend the model to Eastern European countries. Wailes (2007) introduces the notion of an Asian Market Economy (AME) variety to capture some of the distinctive elements of the social organisation of capitalism in Japan, Korea and China.

A second feature of the VoC framework that has elicited both criticism and debate is what some have described as its *determinism*. This is nicely captured by Crouch (2005: 1):

> The main emphasis of the [VoC approach] . . . was that there was no single form of capitalism . . . But I was increasingly struck by the paradoxical determinism behind this ostensibly liberating message: There were two but only two viable forms of capitalism. Nation states possessed one of the other of these two, the institutions appropriate to which extended in a coherent way across a wide range of economic, political and social areas, determining their economic capacities over most products and types of production. And once a country had a particular set of such institutions, there was very little it could do to change it.

This determinism, and the related difficulty that the VoC approach has in accounting for change, can in part be explained by the fact that the VoC approach is based on *comparative statics*, the comparison of two cases at the same point in time. However, others have suggested that these features are more deeply rooted in assumptions about the nature of social action. Consistent with earlier institutionalist analysis, the VoC approach tends to assume that the behaviour of social actors, such as employers and unions, is largely determined by the institutional context in which they operate (Pontusson 1995; Allen 2004). This implies that once an institutional order is established, social action is *path dependent*. Such a view leaves very little scope for agency, politics and conflict to play a role in shaping social outcomes (Howell 2003).

The determinist tendency of the VoC framework is particularly problematic for scholars interested in examining employment relations issues. First, it has long been understood that issues of material interest and conflict are central to any understanding of the employment relationship. Second, understanding change is one of the most important challenges for students of employment relations. While national employment relations patterns may not be converging towards a single neo-liberal model, there is overwhelming evidence that change is a common feature of employment relations in many countries (see Traxler et al. 2001). Third, even more important than change in the institutions regulating the employment relationship is change in the outcomes produced by these institutions. For example, while some countries have retained centralised bargaining systems, there have been significant shifts in the wage and working conditions outcomes associated with these patterns of bargaining (Hassel 2006). It is not easy to explain such types of change using the VoC approach.

Comparative analysis of employment relations should be based on a less deterministic view of the role of institutions. As Deeg and Jackson (2007: 159–61) note in rejecting the view of path dependence that characterises Hall and Soskice's original work, the comparative capitalism literature has moved away from treating institutions, and the complementarities between them, as determinant of social action. Rather, there is an increasing tendency to emphasise a more complex view of institutions as *resources* that actors can use to help them achieve their aims. This reconceptualisation of institutions as resources not only brings issues of agency, power and conflict to the centre of the analysis but also provides a framework for identifying sources of change (see also Crouch 2005). For example, in a recent seven-country study of the impact of globalisation on employment relations in the automobile assembly industry, Wailes et al. (2009) show that, while there are differences between varieties of capitalism, there is also evidence of considerable within variety diversity. They argue that this within-variety diversity suggests that the agency of managers and workers influences how individual companies in the automobile assembly industry respond to the challenges posed by globalisation.

A third set of criticisms directed at the VoC approach focuses on the relative lack of attention it gives to international factors. As Hancke et al. (2006: 7) note, the VoC approach has a tendency to treat 'nation-states as "hermetically sealed" and [to] neglect the linkages between them'. Hall and Soskice's original VoC model is largely based on a closed economy in which institutions are seen to have relatively homogenous effects within national boundaries. As a result, the VoC approach tends to downplay or ignore the role that international factors play, other than the competitive pressures associated with economic globalisation. This issue is addressed in more detail in the following section.

In this section, we have reviewed the influential Varieties of Capitalism approach and assessed its suitability as a framework for the international comparative analysis of employment relations. We favour a modified version of the VoC approach that includes more varieties of capitalism than Hall and Soskice's original model, adopts a more dynamic and less deterministic view of the role of institutions, and is attentive to connections between countries and the potential role of international factors. Especially if we keep in mind its limitations, the VoC approach offers a promising framework for the internationally comparative analysis of employment relations in an era of globalisation.

INTERNATIONAL DIMENSIONS OF EMPLOYMENT RELATIONS

As this book demonstrates, there are developments beyond the level of the nation state that can impact on national patterns of employment relations. Employment relations in many of the European countries included in this edition are increasingly affected by developments associated with the European Union. In such countries as the United Kingdom, for example, the European Directive on Information and Consultation has resulted in the introduction of—albeit limited—statutory consultation rights for British workers for the first time in history (see Chapter 2). The international dimension is also significant outside of Europe. The decision of the People's Republic of China to join the World Trade Organization (WTO) has also had a significant impact on labour regulation in that country (see Chapter 12).

As noted, one of the potential limitations of the VoC approach is that it tends to downplay the connections between countries and the impact of international factors. However, just as economic activity takes place in a political and social context within national boundaries, international economic activity does not take place in a vacuum (Haworth & Hughes 2003). The aim of this section is to illustrate some of the ways in which the international dimension can influence national-level employment relations practices (see Gumbrell-McCormick 2008).

While their focus is often local or national, employment relations actors can and do operate beyond the level of the nation state. One common view is that labour has been the passive victim of globalisation and that workers and their organisations are nationally bound. This view ignores the long history of international cooperation between labour movements, or *labour internationalism*. It also ignores evidence that workers and their representatives can and do attempt to use the international dimension to support their interests. Ambruster-Sandoval (2005), for example, reviews a number of cases of cross-border mobilisation associated with the contemporary anti-sweatshop movement in the United States. One case on which he focuses is the campaign organised against shirt manufacturer Philips Van Heusen (PVH) in Guatemala between 1992 and 1999. Faced with a repressive labour regime, workers at PVH established ties with United States-based NGOs and US unions to form a transnational activist network. In the early 1990s, US unions used US tariff regulations to file a workers' rights complaint on behalf of PVH workers. As a result, the company was forced to recognise the union but used the Guatemalan labour code to avoid bargaining with it. In 1996, this network staged a coordinated campaign of demonstrations by workers outside the PVH factory in Guatemala and of US based activists encouraging consumers to boycott the company's products in shopping malls and department stores during the busiest shopping period of the year. Concerned about the damage that this campaign was doing to the image of the company's products, PVH entered into collective bargaining with the union. While this victory was short-lived—PVH closed its Guatemala factory in 1998—this example illustrates the extent to which globalisation of production creates opportunities as well as challenges for workers, and shows how the international dimension can play a role in shaping employment relations outcomes.

Wills (1998) argues that globalisation may require labour to rethink its modes of representation and action. Traditionally, one of the ways labour has sought to advance its interests is through collective bargaining with employers. Some have suggested that, with the increasing internationalisation of business, labour needs to pursue opportunities for transnational collective bargaining (that is, collective bargaining between multinationals and their workers in more than one country). However, as Haworth (2005) notes, there are many inherent difficulties and obstacles to transnational collective bargaining that suggest this goal is unlikely to be achieved. These include management hostility to the extension of collective bargaining, fear of loss of sovereignty by national unions, lack of membership support, different national employment relations systems and the lack of an international regulatory framework. Even in the European context, where the conditions for the development of transnational collective bargaining appear to be the most favourable, recent research suggests that genuine European collective bargaining is limited, and where it does occur it more often than not involves companies using 'coercive comparisons' across their operations to place downward pressure on wages and working conditions (Arrowsmith & Marginson 2006).

An interesting development that reflects a change in the way unions have sought to engage with employers in the context of globalisation has been the development of International Framework Agreements (IFAs). IFAs are voluntary agreements on minimum labour standards negotiated between global union federations (GUFs) and multinational corporations. At a minimum, they contain a commitment to freedom of association and the right to collective bargaining. They also provide unions with formal representation at the corporate level of the enterprise. As Riisgaard (2005) notes, this representation at the corporate level offers unions the potential to overcome hostile management at a local level, and this is one of the key features that differentiates IFAs from other voluntary codes of conduct between employers and their workers. IFAs also give the union federation a role in monitoring compliance with the agreement across the company's operations (Egels-Zandén & Hyllman 2007).

While there are still relatively few IFAs, the pace of adoption has accelerated in recent years, with the majority being adopted since 2004 (Papadakis 2008). The first IFA was concluded in 1988 by the French company Danone and the International Union of Food, Agricultural, Hotel, Restaurant, Catering, Tobacco and Allied Workers' Association (IUF). By December 2007, there were 61 IFAs, covering approximately five million workers (for a detailed list, see Papadakis 2008: 101–3). By the end of 2009, more than 70 such agreements were estimated to be in place. While the number of IFAs is increasing, relatively few employers have been willing to enter into such agreements.

Which factors influence the adoption of IFAs? Riisgard (2005) examines the 2001 IFA between Chiquita, a US banana company, and the Latin-American Coordination of Banana Workers (COLSIBA). She found that COLSIBA's success at getting Chiquita to enter into an IFA was closely associated with the high levels of regional coordination within the union federation and the effective development of alliances with NGOs, which were able to put pressure on the company through campaigns focused on consumers. A study by Egels-Zandén (2008) focuses on a European MNC's motivations for entering into an IFA. The literature on voluntary agreements stresses four main factors that may prompt companies to enter into such an agreement: (1) the desire to retain or regain legitimacy with stakeholders, especially consumer groups; (2) the desire to avoid or forestall government interference; (3) ethical reasons; and (4) the desire to exploit potential competitive advantages, such as improvements in supply chain standards. Egels-Zandén's study found little evidence to support any of these factors. Instead, he suggests that the company's decision to enter into an IFA reflected its desire to maintain a good relationship with its enterprise union.

Both these examples suggest that the growth of this form of regulation is likely to be heavily influenced, both by the level of cooperation between different levels of the union movement and by the extent to which unions are able to establish effective relationships with labour-oriented NGOs across national borders.

Another example of the impact the international dimension can have on national patterns of employment relations can be seen in the recent literature on the HR practices of multinational corporations. One of the implications of the VoC approach is that, within a given national institutional framework, employers will tend to adopt similar employment relations practices. There is, however, growing evidence of a diversity of employment relations practices within countries (Katz & Darbishire 2000). An important potential source of this diversity is MNCs. Given the growing size, scale and spread of these companies, the extent to which these firms attempt to reproduce similar employment relations practices across their global operations has the potential to have a significant impact on national patterns of employment relations (Hall & Wailes 2009).

Studies of the employment relations practices of MNCs consistently reveal a strong country of origin effect. Ferner (1997) rejects the notion that this country of origin effect stems primarily for cultural differences between countries and argues instead that the tendency of MNCs to diffuse key employment relations practices across their subsidiaries reflects the extent to which MNCs and their management are embedded in the institutional context of their home countries. Studies of US MNCs operating in Europe, for example, have shown the tendency of these firms to adopt highly centralised HR policies with an emphasis on performance management, workplace diversity and anti-unionism (e.g. see Ferner et al. 2001). Thus, while the transfer of employment relations practices across US MNCs is in part shaped by institutional arrangements in the host country and power relations between corporate headquarters and the subsidiary, they are also influenced by distinctive features of the US national business system, including the structure of capital markets and the dominant form of corporate governance (Clark & Almond 2006).

Ferner and Quintanilla (1998) use a national business system (NBS) approach, which is closely related to the VoC approach, to examine the HR practices of German MNCs. In a sophisticated analysis, they note that while there is evidence to suggest that, in the process of internationalising, German firms have adopted some Anglo-Saxon management practices, 'the consensual thrust of German employment relations . . . has strongly coloured the internationalization process' (Ferner & Quintanilla 1998: 726). Thus they find that German MNCs encourage employee cooperation, make relatively high investments in training and are less likely to use widespread downsizing than MNCs from other countries. Ferner et al. (2001) explore the impact that the NBSs of host countries play in shaping the diffusion of this distinctively German pattern of HR to subsidiaries of two German MNCs in the United Kingdom and Spain. While these two countries were selected as examples of highly regulated (Spain) and highly deregulated (United Kingdom) host countries, Ferner et al. argue that (2001: 124) 'the lack of strong management traditions' in Spain meant that German MNCs have a 'greater degree of managerial choice in their [Spanish] subsidiaries' than is the case in the United Kingdom.

Edwards et al. (2005) explore the phenomenon of reverse diffusion in MNCs. Reverse diffusion refers the transfer of practices by MNCs from foreign subsidiaries to their operations in their country of origin, and is an issue of particular strategic importance because it relates to the ability of MNCs to learn from their operations. Edwards and colleagues initially assume that in theory there might be substantial reverse diffusion by US MNCs from their operations in the United Kingdom. Nevertheless, drawing on five case studies, they find in practice only very limited evidence of reverse diffusion. They argue that this reflects the constraints that key features of the US NBS place on diffusion. Thus, for example, they attribute the failure of one of their cases to adopt a system of broadband skills development involving teamwork to established practices of union avoidance in the parent company (2005: 1277). Indeed, one of the few examples of reverse diffusion took place in a parent company located in a 'right to work' state, where union avoidance was less of an issue.

Research on the international activities of unions and the diffusion of HR practices in MNCs suggest that the institutional matrix of national systems is not as complete as the VoC approach tends to assume (Wailes 2008). These examples imply that, in order to understand employment relations developments fully, students should consider the connections between countries rather than focusing only on one particular country.

The globalisation of the international economy has in part been underpinned by changes in the formal rules of international trade, which allow for increased access to markets and put fewer constraints on international trade. These changes, often referred to as *trade liberalisation*, have been introduced through bilateral and multi-national free-trade agreements (FTAs). Multilateral trade liberalisation began in the 1940s, with the negotiation of the General Agreement on Tariffs and Trade (GATT) and culminated in the formation of the World Trade Organization in 1996. The WTO is a United Nations agency. Its aim is to promote free trade and to provide mechanisms for the resolution of trade disputes between member countries (see Wilkinson 2002a).

During this process of trade liberalisation, there has been considerable debate as to whether these trade agreements should include reference to minimum labour standards. Historically, the International Labour Organization (ILO) has been the main agency for developing and enforcing international labour standards (Engerman 2003). The ILO was founded in 1919 under World War I peace treaty, and in 1946 became the first specialist agency of the newly formed United Nations.

Since its inception, the ILO has been involved in promoting international labour standards through the use of Conventions and Recommendations. Conventions, once ratified by member states, are meant to be legally binding, while recommendations are advisory standards that are designed to assist member states to apply a convention (whether ratified or not) to their local setting. These instruments deal with a wide range of issues, including: (1) fundamental human rights such as freedom of association, equality of treatment and the abolition of forced labour; (2) occupational health and safety; (3) working conditions; (4) social security and workers' compensation;

(5) labour administration; (6) migrant workers; and (7) the specific needs or circumstances of particular occupational groups. Collectively, these standards are referred to as the International Labour Code.

As Wilkinson (2002b) notes in the lead-up to the formation of the WTO, the United States (supported by France) sought the inclusion of minimum labour standards in the new rules of world trade. This is commonly referred to as the *social clause*. This occurred because US policy-makers argued that without enforceable minimum labour standards, American (and French) workers would be faced with unfair competition from countries where there are no protections against child labour and other practices. One of the main sources of opposition to the social clause came from developing countries, which argued that minimum labour standards would be used as a form of non-tariff barrier and would be used to limit their access to the markets of developed economies.

Under these circumstances, it was agreed that the WTO would defer making a decision on labour standards and other 'additional items' until after its formation. Despite consistent campaigns by labour movements from developing and developed countries, and an increasingly prominent anti-globalisation campaign, in a ministerial statement issued after its meeting in Dohar in 2000, the WTO reaffirmed the view that there was no need for direct inclusion of labour standards in the rules of the WTO or for social items to be the grounds for trade disputes between countries (see Hughes and Wilkinson 1998; Wilkinson 2002b, 2002c). Wilkinson (2002c: 20) argues that:

> the closure of the labour standards debate within the WTO, coupled with the ILO's exclusion from the contemporary system of global political governance, ensures that organised labour lacks an appropriate political voice [in these increasingly important international organisations] . . . Given that within these circles a consensus has emerged on the divorce between trade and work rights, labour's role in the contemporary global economy remains precarious.

However, in rejecting the inclusion of labour standards in the rules of international trade, the WTO recognised the ILO 'as the competent body to set and deal with these standards and we affirm our support for its work in promotion them' (WTO Singapore Ministerial Declaration 1996, cited in Hughes 2005: 416). Hughes (2005) argues that the social clause debate created the conditions for a significant change in the strategic direction of the ILO, as it sought to re-establish its relevance in an era of globalisation.

The first sign of this new strategy was the 1998 *Declaration on Fundamental Principles and Rights at Work and its Follow-up*. This declaration summarises what the ILO regards as universal and core labour standards (see Table 1.1). Importantly, because it was adopted as a Declaration, these core labour standards are meant to be binding on member countries, irrespective of whether or not they have ratified the associated conventions. The follow-up contained in the Declaration commits member states that have not ratified the relevant conventions to report in their progress towards implementation.

Table 1.1   Core labour standards

Fundamental principle	Relevant convention
Freedom of association and the effective recognition of the right to collective bargaining	87 (Freedom of Association and Protection of the Right to Organise) and 98 (Right to Organise and Collective Bargaining)
The elimination of all forms of forced or compulsory labour;	29 (Forced Labour) and 105 (Abolition of Forced Labour)
The effective abolition of child labour	138 (Minimum Age) and 182 (Worst Forms of Child Labour)
The elimination of discrimination in respect of employment and occupation	100 (Equal Remuneration) and 111 (Discrimination, Occupation and Employment)

Source: ILO (2009)

The ILO'S Decent Work Agenda, developed under the leadership of the current head of the ILO, Juan Somavia, seeks to build on these core labour standards. Its aim is the achievement of 'decent work for all by promoting social dialogue, social protection and employment creation, as well as respect for international labour standards' (ILO, 2009). The principles of the Decent Work Agenda are contained in the Declaration on Social Justice for a Fair Globalization, which was adopted by the General Assembly of the ILO in June 2008. As Hughes (2005) notes, the Decent Work Agenda is an attempt to both extend the ILO agenda in recognition of the growth of non-traditional forms of work and to integrate its programs within a single conceptual framework.

The ILO's shift in strategic direction has not achieved unanimous support. For example, a former ILO official asserts that 'the Declaration . . .weakened the ILO by making even the core standards subject only to monitoring by means that were strictly promotional, that could include offers by the ILO for technical assistance to improve implementation' (Standing 2008: 367). Standing argues that the focus on promoting a relatively small number of conventions at the expense of many important labour standards and rights contained in other conventions contradicts the ILO's core mission and the principles upon which it was established. He objects to the shift away from an emphasis on positive rights and their enforcement towards a mode of 'soft regulation' that he regards as largely ineffective. He criticises the ILO's shift away from its traditional mode of enforcing labour standards and its increasing involvement in the notion of voluntary codes of conduct and various forms of self-regulation. Standing also questions whether the ILO and the International Labour Code has a future.

While Standing's criticisms may be over-stated, they do highlight the extent of change taking place in the international regulation of employment relations. Hassel (2008) argues that these changes have resulted in the emergence of a new regime of global labour governance. Unlike Standing, however, she suggests that this new regime may produce some positive outcomes.

Hassel (2008:232) traces the shift away from a state-based system of rights enforcement towards a more private self-regulatory set of standards contained in codes of conduct (including the UN Global Compact that covers more than 2500 firms), charters of corporate social responsibility, IFAs and other voluntary agreements. She argues that, notwithstanding the lack of a legal framework of global regulation and enforceability, patterns of local self- regulation, norm-setting and international codes can lead to higher expectations of the behaviour of firms that operate transnationally. She suggests also that this also becomes an indirect form of regulation. In particular, she argues that international firms with high labour standards have strong incentives to ensure that other firms—particularly their competitors—comply with the standards to which they have committed, and will therefore be more likely to enter into alliances with NGOs and governments and to advocate the adoption of higher standards and the improved monitoring of outcomes.

The implication of Hassel's argument is that, despite a shift in the global regime of labour regulation towards private self-regulation, the international dimension is likely to continue to influence and place bounds on the ER practices that companies adopt across all national economies. Therefore, as Giles (2000) suggests, employment relations students should continue to consider international dimensions.

CONCLUSIONS

This chapter has provided an introduction to the internationally comparative study of employment relations. It argued that the emerging Varieties of Capitalism (VoC) approach, appropriately modified, provides a promising framework for the internationally comparative study of employment relations. In particular, the VoC approach—which examines the broader institutional context within which patterns of employment relations develop—has the potential to account for similarities and differences in national patterns of employment relations. A VoC approach that includes more than two types of market economy, adopts a dynamic view of institutions and is attentive to the possible interconnections between countries would provide an especially fruitful basis for the development of internationally comparative study of employment relations.

The remaining chapters in this book are written by experts on each country. They provide concise introductions to employment relations in these economies. The countries included represent different forms of market economy (as shown in Table 1.2). Four (the United Kingdom, United States, Canada and Australia) are liberal market economies (LMEs) and three (Germany, Denmark and Japan) can be seen as coordinated market economies (CMEs). There are chapters on five European economies, including two (Italy and France) that are neither LMEs nor CMEs. Italy is often treated as an example of a Mediterranean variety of capitalism, whereas France is described by some as an example of statist form of capitalism (see Amable 2003; Schmidt 2002). There are also chapters on four prominent Asian economies (Japan, South Korea, China and India). The latter two are important emerging economies.

Table 1.2 Categories of economies included in this book

Liberal market economies	Coordinated market economies	European developed economies	Asian developed economies	Asian emerging economies
United States	Germany	United	Japan	China
United	Denmark	Kingdom	South Korea	India
Kingdom	Japan	Italy		
Canada		France		
Australia		Germany		
		Denmark		

As noted at the beginning of the chapter, globalisation is having a profound influence on the way work is regulated in every economy in the world. In this chapter, we have argued that, if properly designed and conducted, comparative analysis has the potential to not only enhance our understanding of the world around us, but also to generate insights into the factors that shape employment relations outcomes in our own work situation, country and region. The following chapters are designed to provide some of the background information necessary for readers to start comparing employment relations across countries. They aim to facilitate comparison between similar countries and also comparisons between different types of economies. Hence we hope that this book can help contribute to a greater understanding of the forces that are reshaping our working lives.

CHAPTER 2

Employment relations in Britain

Mick Marchington, Jeremy Waddington and Andrew Timming

Britain has a total population of around 59 million people and an employment rate of nearly 80 per cent. Whilst most men work full time, the proportion of women working part time is still high—at over 40 per cent—which is significantly higher than the European Union (EU) average. Temporary employment has grown marginally since the early 1980s, and now constitutes about 6 per cent of the workforce, while the number of employment agencies has grown sharply, with more than one million people employed as agency workers (DTI 2007). The rate of people classifying themselves as self-employed is more than double that of the late 1970s (now about 13 per cent). The proportion of workers claiming to work from home has also grown substantially, but this figure is potentially confusing as it includes people who spend any part of their time working away from the office (Kersley et al. 2006). Migrant workers have become a more common feature of the British labour market, particularly among low-wage earners (McGovern 2007).

As well as compositional shifts in the labour force, there have also been major shifts in the sectoral distribution of workers. Britain has relatively fewer people employed in agriculture than any other OECD country, less than a quarter of its other civilian employees work in manufacturing and the remainder (nearly 75 per cent) work in services. There has been a greater decline in its 'industry' category since 1970 than in that of any other OECD country. In spite of the relative growth of services, there was a steep rise in unemployment, from 1.2 per cent of the working population in 1965 to nearly 12 per cent by 1986;

at that time, Britain had a higher unemployment rate than most of the other countries discussed in this book. Levels of unemployment fell during the 1990s and in the early part of this century, but have recently started to rise again, so by the end of 2008 unemployment had grown to about 6 per cent of the labour force. In terms of gross domestic product (GDP) per capita—an approximate indicator of labour output—Britain ranks in the lower half of industrialised market economies. The rate of inflation has been steady for much of the period since the mid-1990s at around 2 to 3 per cent; however, following the financial crisis in late 2008, this rose to over 5 per cent—largely due to higher energy prices. It is forecast to decline due to recessionary pressures.

British politics has been dominated by two parties since 1945. The Conservative Party's support is strongest amongst the business and rural communities. By contrast, the Labour Party's support is traditionally strongest in urban working-class communities, though this has broadened. In 2008 and 2009, support for the governing Labour Party was lower than it had been for years, and in May 2010 Labour was replaced by a Conservative-Liberal Democrat coalition government with David Cameron as Prime Minister. The Green Party gained its first M.P. There are several other political parties, nationalist parties in Scotland and Wales, all of which have increased their representation in recent years. Increased devolution of powers to Scotland and Wales modified certain provisions in these countries.

There has been much change in employment and industrial relations in Britain over the last two decades. Successive Conservative governments over the period 1979–97 set the tone with their radical step-by-step reform of industrial relations law, labour market deregulation and attempts to foster a competitive 'enterprise culture'. Labour governments after 1997 have continued to promote increased private sector involvement in the public sector through a variety of initiatives, with potentially significant implications for employment relations. However, as with other broader socio-economic trends, this changed in late 2008 and substantial state support was provided for the banking sector. Whether this is akin to nationalisation is a moot point.

There is little doubt that the landscape of British employment relations has changed substantially over the last three decades, although the Workplace Employee Relations Survey (WERS) panel data shows that this has been much less pronounced in 'older, continuing' than in new workplaces. We now move on to review industrial relations parties and processes, and consider three areas of growing relevance.

THE INDUSTRIAL RELATIONS PARTIES

Unions

As Britain was the first country to industrialise, many unions can trace their roots back to before the mid-nineteenth century. The earliest enduring unions were formed exclusively by and for skilled craft workers. Widespread unionisation of semi-skilled, unskilled and female manual workers began in the late nineteenth century. Before World War II, the majority of unionised white-collar workers were employed in the public sector. It was only after about 1960 that substantial numbers of private sector white-collar workers were unionised. Although there were 1348 UK unions in 1920, by 2008—principally as a result of mergers—there were only 193 unions. Union membership is concentrated: the fourteen unions with over 100 000 members account for 85.3 per cent of the total membership and the three largest trade unions represent 50.6 per cent (Certification Officer 2008).

The British union movement was instrumental in the establishment of the Labour Party in 1906. Party political activity was seen as a necessary complement to the industrial activities of the unions, particularly after a series of adverse legal judgments meant that new legislation was required to re-establish union rights. Today, individual unions may affiliate with the Labour Party, contributing to its funds through a 'political levy' on members, from which individuals may 'opt out' if they wish. Since the mid-1980s, the Labour Party leadership has increasingly 'distanced' the party from the unions, the voting power of unions at the annual conference of the party has been reduced and victories secured by the unions against the leadership of the party at conference have been ignored. This distancing from the unions by the Labour Party coincided with a greater proportion of party funds being secured from business. The future character of this relationship remains to be seen, as funding for the Labour Party from business has declined and the party is again more reliant than in the post-1997 period on funding from the unions.

The level and density of unionisation has fluctuated since World War II. Three broad post-war phases can be identified. First, between 1948 and 1968 membership grew from 9.3 million to 10.2 million, but tended to lag behind employment growth. During this period, union density fluctuated between 41.9 per cent and 44.9 per cent (Bain & Price 1983: 40). Second, membership grew markedly in the 1970s, as (particularly white-collar) workers were attracted into unions. Membership grew from 9.7 million in 1968 to an all-time high of 12.6 million in 1979, when density peaked at 55.8 per cent

(Waddington 1992). The onset of the third phase in 1979 coincided with the election of a Conservative government led by Margaret Thatcher, the policies of which prompted the decline of employment in manufacturing to accelerate and led to a serious economic recession in the early 1980s. The sharp rise in unemployment contributed to reduced union membership, which also continued to decline as later periods of employment growth were concentrated in private sector services where unions found it difficult to organise. Union density declined continuously during the 1980s and 1990s. Between 1979 and 2008, union membership fell by five million members to 7.6 million (Certification Officer 2008), and between 1979 and 2007 density fell from 55.8 per cent to 28 per cent (Mercer & Notley 2008).

Within the labour force, there are marked variations in union density. Non-manual workers have constituted an increasing proportion of total union membership, and are now more likely to be unionised than manual workers. By December 2007, union density was 59 per cent in the public sector, where 58.6 per cent of all union members were employed. Union density in the private sector was 16.1 per cent, with 21.8 per cent organised in manufacturing. For the sixth consecutive year, union density among women (29.6 per cent) was higher than among men (26.4 per cent). Full-time workers were more likely to be unionised (30.1 per cent) than their part-time counterparts (21.9 per cent), and workers over the age of 50 were more likely to be members (35.2 per cent) than workers aged less than 25 years (9.8 per cent) (all data from Mercer & Notley 2008).

Although there is no agreement regarding the relative effects of the forces that promoted the decline in unionisation, it is generally accepted that external influences such as macro-economic context, the changing composition of the labour force, management resistance and workplace practices, and state policy all had adverse effects on unionisation (Mason & Bain 1993; Metcalf 1991). In addition, issues internal to unionism have contributed to the decline. Included among internal issues are inadequate recruitment programs, whether inadequacy is measured in terms of resources allocated or practices implemented (Voos 1984; Kelly 1990), union failure to deliver benefits effectively for employees (Bryson & Gomez 2005; Metcalf 2005), the commitment of senior officers to reform (Undy et al. 1981) and the failure to reform union policy, practices and government to 'fit' with the interests of potential members (Hyman 1999; Dølvik & Waddington 2005). What is clear, however, is that the election of a Labour government in 1997 was not associated with a significant boost in unionisation. The terms of the new recognition procedure laid down in the *Employment Relations Act* 1999 were seen as enabling managers to resist unionisation (Gall 2003; Ewing et al. 2003). Although more recent data suggest that the number of new recognition agreements was increasing, they tend to be concentrated in areas where unions are established and barely outnumber de-recognition cases (Gall 2004; Blanden et al. 2006).

Concurrent with the decline in unionisation was a decline in strike activity. From a peak of 3906 strikes resulting in almost 11 million working days lost in 1970, the number of strikes had fallen to 116 in 2005, resulting in 157 000 working days lost (Beardsmore 2006). Associated with the decline in strike activity was a shift in the reasons for strikes, with 'defensive' strikes assuming a greater prominence throughout the 1990s. Wages and pay-related issues still underpinned more than half of all strikes after 1999, however. The decline in strike activity in Britain is steeper than elsewhere due to the restrictive legislation enacted by the Conservative governments during the 1980s (Elgar & Simpson 1993); subsequent Labour governments did not repeal the legislation.

Britain has one main union confederation: the Trades Union Congress (TUC), which was established in 1868. In 2008, a total of 58 unions representing almost 6.5 million union members were affiliated with the TUC. The TUC has never had a direct role in collective bargaining, and is afforded relatively little constitutional authority over affiliated unions. Historically, the TUC has undertaken three primary purposes: the lobbying of governments; the provision of services to affiliated unions; and the adjudication of disputes between affiliated unions. The scope of the TUC as a lobbying organisation increased during and after World War II, when the political influence of the TUC increased and it convened union representation on many tripartite bodies and quasi-governmental agencies (Goodman 1994). After 1979, however, many tripartite institutions were dismantled and the TUC effectively was excluded from the 'corridors of power', with the result that the influence of the TUC diminished to its lowest level since the 1930s. The return of a Labour government in 1997 was accompanied by a more distant relationship between the TUC and government than under previous Labour governments, as the government sought to establish a closer alliance with business than its Labour predecessors had enjoyed (Waddington 2003). The TUC has regenerated aspects of the lobbying role *vis-à-vis* the European Union. The TUC still provides a wide range of services to affiliated unions, although many of the larger affiliates are no longer reliant on services from the TUC and tend to provide them in house. The role of the TUC in adjudicating disputes between affiliated unions has also diminished as the number of disputes has declined.

The loss of political influence, combined with the absence of constitutional authority over affiliated unions, led to a major review of TUC activities in 1994, the outcome of which was that the TUC jettisoned much of its committee structure with the intention of becoming more of a campaigning organisation (Heery 1998). A wide range of campaigning initiatives have resulted, two of which are prominent. The first centred on the establishment of the Organising Academy, at which representatives from affiliated unions were trained in organising techniques (Heery et al. 2003). The purpose of the Organising Academy was to encourage a wider range of unions to pursue organising campaigns as a means to reverse the pattern of membership decline. The range of initiatives taken and techniques employed under the rubric of organising is vast (Heery et al. 2000). However, while there have been some notable successes arising from organising initiatives, they are barely sufficient to match membership losses sustained elsewhere. A second prominent campaign highlighted the establishment of partnerships with 'good' employers. Partnership initiatives were intended to exploit mutual interests between employees and employers on a range of issues and assumed union concessions on work flexibility in return for commitments from employers on job security. Relatively few companies signed up to partnership agreements in the complete form envisaged by the TUC; many of those who did were in the throes of restructuring (Heery 2002; Martinez Lucio & Stuart 2005).

Management, employers and their associations

The Confederation of British Industry (CBI), formed in 1965, is the peak employer body in Britain. It is an important lobbyist of the British government and EU agencies but, like the TUC, it does not participate in collective bargaining. It claims to represent the views of 200 000 employers covering approximately half the workforce in the United Kingdom (Marchington & Wilkinson 2008: 83). Although the smaller Institute of Directors grew in influence during the 1980s, it is no longer significant in terms of industrial relations activities.

Historically, associations of employers played an important part in shaping the British voluntarist system of industrial relations (Rollinson & Dundon 2007). Initially at the local level and then (more importantly) at the national level, they acted as representatives for employers in each industry, reaching agreements with unions over recognition, dispute procedures, and the substantive terms and conditions across member companies. They offered forms of mutual defence against union campaigns and to some extent took wages 'out of competition' among British employers competing in the same product market. There were many signs in the 1950s and 1960s that the agreements to which employers' associations were signatories were losing their regulatory effectiveness. The growth of workplace-based incentive payment and job evaluation systems, the escalation of overtime working and the broadened scope of joint regulation into what were notionally areas of management prerogative were led by workplace-based union shop stewards.

The number of employers' associations has declined from more than 1350 in 1968 to just 80 in 2008 (Certification Officer 2008). Employers' associations typically offer one or more sets of services to their members: (1) collective bargaining—typically little more than the setting of frameworks, which the parties at local level then add to in order to address their own specific problems and issues; (2) assisting with dispute resolution by providing, along with recognised trade unions, an independent role in trying to resolve 'failures to agree' at company level; (3) providing members with specialist advice about new legislation and answering queries about workplace matters; and (4) representing members' views, either at employment tribunals or to government and the European Commission. Although there are some exceptions, employers' associations have moved to the periphery of industrial relations, offering legal, advisory, training and other services, and are generally shadows of their former selves.

The period since the 1980s has seen greatly enhanced employer power and freedom of action, driven by higher levels of competition in product markets and reductions in unionism. While employer objectives in the labour field continue to focus on control, productivity improvement and cost reduction, the mix of strategies and balance of methods is diverse—which is not surprising given the relative lack of influence employers' associations have within a liberal market economy. Many could be described as using pragmatic/opportunist (Purcell & Sisson 1983) management styles, strongly influenced by attempts to cut costs and remain in business; this is especially characteristic of small employers or those whose industrial relations style is largely determined by the power of 'lead' firms in sectors such as food retailing or vehicle manufacture (Edwards & Ram 2006). Not all employers utilise a strictly cost-driven strategy, especially those that compete on the basis of product or service quality, and rely on human capital to achieve competitive advantage (Marchington & Wilkinson 2008).

Managements have aimed for greater levels of flexibility and employee commitment, with many developing direct employee involvement and participation (EIP) techniques and associated HRM practices. They have also introduced performance-related pay linked to performance appraisals. Experience of redundancy has also been widespread. There has been a growth in direct investment in manufacturing and financial services by American, European, Japanese and more recently Chinese, Indian and Middle Eastern companies. The employment practices of such multinational companies have had a significant influence on British workplaces (Pulignano 2006).

One-third of workplaces with ten or more employees have a personnel or HR specialist, and well over half have access to a specialist either in the workplace or at a higher level in the organisation. Not surprisingly, the likelihood of a personnel presence at workplace level is greater in larger workplaces and organisations. More than 60 per cent of private sector workplaces have a personnel/HR presence on the board of directors, although this figure varies between sectors and with size of organisation, and is more prevalent in those organisations that recognise unions (Kersley et al. 2006: 64). Membership of the professional body (the Chartered Institute of Personnel and Development) has risen nearly tenfold since the 1970s, to more than 130 000 in 2008, and it is now by far the largest body for personnel specialists in Europe and second only to the US equivalent worldwide. Associated with this is an increased interest in how the HR function can contribute to strategic decisions via what is called a 'business partner' role (Ulrich & Brockbank 2005; Francis & Keegan 2006).

Nevertheless, there is a threat to the future of the personnel function, both from line managers and from specialist consultancy firms, outsourcing and shared service operations. In many enterprises, line managers undertake a greater range of human resource activities (Purcell & Hutchinson 2007), and in some cases this has led to the break-up of specialist internal functions (Reilly et al. 2007; Marchington & Wilkinson 2008). The fragmentation of management support for employment relations is likely to accelerate as employers face sustained pressures to reduce costs, focus on their core business and increase contracting out to other firms (Marchington et al. 2005).

The principal employee relations responsibilities of HR/IR specialists remain concerned with issues such as grievance and discipline handling, recruitment and selection, staffing and employee consultation (Kersley et al. 2006: 48). It is also clear that there has been a significant growth in the incidence of HR practices aimed at engendering employee commitment and promoting high performance. The WERS survey indicated, for example, that almost three-quarters of core employees were involved in teams at work, though it is less clear how much influence these had over work-related decisions (Kersley et al. 2006: 91). Significant questions remain, however, about the extent to which such policies are fully embedded within organisations (Cox et al. 2006) and whether their use is strategically based or merely pragmatic.

THE ROLE OF THE STATE

Industrial relations researchers have traditionally characterised the British state as 'voluntarist' because of its comparatively low level of legal regulation of employment. But that characterisation is increasingly anachronistic. Historically speaking, 'the British state has in fact been a central actor in the construction, maintenance, and reconstruction of industrial relations institutions' (Howell 2005: 3). It is only with regard to employee rights that the state has generally—albeit not entirely— abstained from intervention.

Legal reforms of industrial relations

The Industrial Revolution in Britain laid the groundwork for, simultaneously, an unprecedented drive on the part of workers toward unionisation and, starting with the *Combination Acts* of 1799 (Orth 1991), a heavy-handed response to unionisation on the part of the state. At the turn of the twentieth century, the voluntarist framework began to take shape. Rather than affirming a set of positive rights for employees, the state opted for a system of immunities for unions from various areas of criminal and civil law. This process was consolidated by the 1906 *Trade Disputes Act* (Wedderburn 1986), which served as the foundation of union law until the 1980s.

The principal features of voluntarism included: (1) non-legally binding collective agreements; (2) voluntary union recognition by employers; (3) a relatively low level of formalisation of industrial relations structures; and (4) a light, voluntary framework of state-provided supplementary dispute resolution facilities, with no governmental powers to order the suspension of industrial action or impose cooling-off periods. This *laissez-faire* approach to regulation was supported by both unions and employers.

From the post-war period through the 1970s, unionisation increased while Britain's economic performance concurrently weakened. In order to reverse the decline, industrial relations reform was high on the political agenda. Although the Donovan Commission (1968) had argued for a continuation of voluntary reform in its report, in subsequent years successive governments resorted to legislation. An example was the Conservatives' 1971 *Industrial Relations Act*, which sought to weaken the ability of workers to strike (Rideout 1971). Following the US model, this ill-fated Act also aimed, *inter alia*, to make collective agreements legally enforceable contracts. The unions boycotted much of the Act and few employers used it, thereby rendering it largely ineffective. Most of the legislation, apart from the unfair dismissal provision, was repealed by Labour in 1974.

Margaret Thatcher's Conservative government, bent on smashing the unions, swept to power in 1979. Fairbrother (2002) highlights this point in time as a transition away from traditional voluntarism and towards a neo-liberal interventionist state. Among the host of reforms implemented during successive Conservative governments has been legislation aimed at limiting the ability of unions to organise lawful industrial action, narrowing traditional union immunities from legal action, outlawing secondary strike action, imposing a secret ballot prior to industrial action, prohibiting the closed shop and removing statutory procedures to facilitate union recognition, thus making it much more difficult for unions to consolidate and extend union membership. In addition, the new laws intervened prescriptively in internal union governance.

Looking at the big picture, the post-1997 Labour governments did not change the fundamental framework of industrial relations law introduced by the Conservatives, though they eased some details, such as arrangements for the deduction of union dues, and introduced a new mechanism for unions to secure recognition from employers (Simpson 2000). There was also a successful move in 1999 to introduce a national minimum wage in order to tackle low pay. In addition to these indigenous initiatives, Blair's opt-in to the Maastricht Social Protocol strengthened statutory employment rights, in some measure, surrounding representative participation structures, working time regulations, equal opportunities, non-discrimination, redundancy protection and health and safety provisions, among other areas in which European Union directives have been transposed into British labour law (Deakin & Morris 2005). Thus it can be concluded that, in recent times, there has been a real shift from voluntarism towards juridification in the regulation of the employment relation in Britain, at least in terms of minimum rights and standards.

Economic policies

The economic policies of the British state have evolved dramatically, especially since the post-war period. Immediately following World War II, demand-side economics, based on state-directed income redistribution and a commitment to full employment, was the order of the day. This Keynesian consensus came to an abrupt end with the election of the Conservatives in 1979. The Thatcher government opted for mainly supply-side solutions to managing the economy by adopting both monetarist policies and fiscal restraint and by exerting more control over public sector pay. These reforms were accompanied by a deregulation of the economy and flexibilisation of the labour market. Ultimately, the defeat of inflation became the dominant priority, and on this measure it could be argued that the Conservatives were more or less successful (Matthews & Minford 1987).

In 1997, the election of Labour led to a number of policy changes (Dickens & Hall 2006), but the Tories' preoccupation with inflation was central to Blair's, and later Brown's, handling of the economy. For a full decade, inflation rates in Britain remained low, comparatively speaking. The Labour government devolved the ability to set interest rates to the independent Monetary Policy Committee of the Bank of England and set an annual target of no more than 2.5 per cent (later 2 per cent). Inflation breached 3 per cent in 2007, however, just as financial markets and the broader economic outlook in Britain began to deteriorate. The following year, the post-2008 global financial crisis threatened to spill over into a recession, all within the context of rising inflation. It remains to be seen how the Cameron–Clegg government will handle the crisis and what effect it will have on wages and employment. However, the Cameron government is cutting public expenditure severely and may take a tougher stance in industrial disputes.

Dispute resolution

The British state has provided conciliation and arbitration services as a supplement to voluntary collective bargaining and disputes procedures since the end of World War II. These services were initially offered in 1945 by the Personnel Management Advisory Service (later the Industrial Relations Service and then Commission on Industrial Relations) within the Ministry of Labour (Kessler & Purcell 1994), but in 1975 the Wilson government established the independent Advisory, Conciliation and Arbitration Service (ACAS) through the *Employment Protection Act*. Since then, ACAS has been governed by a tripartite council, which consists of employer and union nominees with a balance of independent members. By these means, successive governments have sought to distance themselves from the direct settlement of particular industrial disputes, though their influence as an interested party in the public sector is still important.

ACAS services are publicly financed and include conciliation in complaints by individuals over alleged breach of statutory employment rights (its principal and hugely expanded activity) as well as in collective disputes. It also offers information on employment matters and advice to the parties on all aspects of employment relations and policies. ACAS officials carry out individual and collective conciliation and advisory work, but they appoint independent experts (often academics) to act as ad hoc mediators and arbitrators. Unlike the position in many other countries, arbitration is neither compulsory (as was the case in Australia) nor legally binding (as in North America and Australia). Although ACAS was established by Labour, it continued under the Conservatives—though the latter did curtail the use of arbitration in the public sector, cut ACAS's role in conducting inquiries and remove its earlier responsibility to promote the growth and reform of collective bargaining (Goodman 2000).

For instance, ACAS received 896 requests for collective conciliation in 2007–08, of which over 90 per cent were resolved (ACAS 2008). That same year, the ACAS national helpline received 885 353 telephone inquiries and staff made almost 2000 advisory visits (ACAS 2008). In addition to conciliation and arbitration, ACAS also produces its own research on employee relations and offers training and development programs for managers and employee representatives. For example, ACAS Equality and Diversity Services offers workplace training aimed at preventing disputes before they erupt. As a result of their activities, 76 per cent of firms 'introduced or amended a specific or general equality and diversity policy or procedure' (ACAS 2008: 22). The organisation thus plays an important role in ensuring that worker–employer relations in Britain are fair, an issue that will be addressed again at the end of the chapter.

The public sector

The state plays an important role as a direct or indirect employer for a substantial proportion of the labour force (in 2008, nearly one-quarter of all workers in Britain were employed in the public sector), and less directly through its influence as an exemplar to other employers. Throughout much of the twentieth century, the government aimed to be a 'good' employer by encouraging union membership and offering broadly comparable terms and conditions and generally more secure employment *vis-à-vis* the private sector. The election of Margaret Thatcher in 1979 again marked an important turning point.

Between 1979 and 1997, the public sector was transformed as successive Conservative governments sought to limit public expenditure and reduce both the role and size of the state. The most dramatic change was the privatisation of publicly owned corporations (telecommunications, airlines, coal, steel and the railways), as well as utilities. In principle, the aim of privatisation was to inject competition into these industries, and thereby improve efficiency and productivity. An obvious effect was a reduction in public sector employment from 30 per cent to 22 per cent of the labour force (Winchester & Bach 1995). Furthermore, strict cash limits and projected efficiency gains were built into forward budgets to restrain public sector pay settlements to lower than inflation rates in many cases (Beaumont 1987). Public sector strikes—for example, the steelworkers in 1980 and the coalminers in 1984—were resisted and access to arbitration was withdrawn or restrained.

Deregulation was also introduced into many areas by the Conservatives—for example, in public transport systems, local authorities and the National Health Service. Many civil service functions were reorganised into more autonomous and accountable executive agencies, and other areas were subjected to substantial reductions in employment and 'market testing' (Stewart & Walsh 1992). Local authorities were required, under 'best value' provisions, to put some services out to tender with the private sector, and public–private partnerships were subsequently introduced into local governments and National Health Service Trusts with major implications for employment relations (Rubery et al. 2002; Grimshaw et al. 2002). This process was meant to institute private sector values and practices into the public sector. In practice, it resulted in a fragmentation of work across organisational boundaries (Marchington et al. 2005), the implications of which are addressed below.

As with legal reforms and economic policies, after 1997 Labour governments broadly retained many of the Conservative initiatives to transform public sector industrial relations by continuing to push for an injection of competition and prudent fiscal policies. Furthermore, in order to deliver on election promises of improved public sector performance, there was a push for the introduction of performance-related pay, especially in teaching and health care.

INDUSTRIAL RELATIONS PROCESSES

The terms and conditions that regulate levels of pay, working time, methods of working and procedures for resolving differences between workers and employers are central to the employment relationship. They can be established in various ways, including legal enactment, management decisions—with or without employee consultation— and collective bargaining between unions and employers. Collective bargaining has diminished in coverage and scope, and in many cases managements now set terms and conditions directly rather than bargaining with unions. Towers (1997) refers to the vacuum left by the contraction of collective bargaining (and the general absence of a mandatory system of employee consultation) as the 'representation gap'.

Collective bargaining

Collective bargaining has a long history in Britain. Industrial-level bargaining developed in several industries in the late nineteenth century and in others through 'joint industrial councils' soon after World War I. By the early 1920s, multi-employer bargaining for manual workers was well established, and industry-level negotiations were encouraged by successive governments as a way of establishing orderly industrial relations. Although there were exceptions, centralised negotiations across entire industries generally left little room for workplace bargaining.

   In some industries during World War II, and in several industries after the war, shop stewards increasingly became involved as workplace bargainers, supplementing the industry-wide negotiations conducted between national union officials and representatives of employers' associations. This development occurred because centralised agreements could not specify workplace rules in sufficient detail and the power of shop stewards increased as labour markets tightened, resulting in what became known as 'wages draft'. The Donovan Royal Commission, set up in 1965 to examine 'the industrial relations problem', argued for workplace bargaining to be formalised, as this would weaken the influence of multi-employer national negotiations and at the same time remove the so-called 'disorder' created by uncoordinated in-company agreements. To the extent that employers and unions took this advice, single employer bargaining received a significant boost and from the mid-1970s collective bargaining was decentralised throughout much of the private sector.

In 1970, collective bargaining covered approximately 70 per cent of the workforce, but it has since declined to around 27 per cent, with management setting pay unilaterally at 70 per cent of workplaces (Kersley et al. 2006: 179). Furthermore, the percentage of workplaces engaging in collective bargaining over pay fell from 30 per cent in 1998 to 22 per cent in 2004 (Kersley et al. 2006: 182). There are sizeable variations between sectors, with the public sector having the highest coverage (83 per cent) and private sector services the lowest (14 per cent). The shape and character of collective bargaining also vary considerably between workplaces, in relation to the level at which bargaining takes place, the size and structure of the unit of employees covered by any agreement, and the scope of the subjects determined by joint regulation (Kersley et al. 2006: 179–80). The contraction in the scope of collective bargaining since the early 1980s has led some to suggest that union involvement in the regulation of workplace industrial relations had been 'marginalised', and that many collective bargaining arrangements are 'hollow shells' as managers refuse to negotiate with their union counterparts (Marchington & Parker 1990).

Very little multi-employer bargaining remains in the private sector and it is also weakening in the public sector. Moves towards single unionism and to single-table bargaining (whereby all recognised union negotiate together) accelerated after 1990. In 2004, a single union was recognised in just under half of workplaces with union recognition, just less than one-third recognised two unions and around one-fifth recognised three or more. Single-table bargaining occurred in 60 per cent of workplaces at which more than one union was recognised (Kersley et al. 2006: 123). In practice, the number of managements who refuse to recognise unions for the purpose of collective bargaining is increasing. The WERS surveys show that the number of workplaces that recognised union(s) for collective bargaining declined from 66 per cent in 1984 to 39 per cent in 2004 (Blanchflower et al. 2007). The coverage of collective bargaining and the extent of union recognition for bargaining from management in Britain are thus now lower than elsewhere in Western Europe.

Employee involvement and participation

Interest in employee involvement and participation (EIP) has waxed and waned over the past century, with surges of activity at times when employers felt they were under threat from labour and a loss of impetus when this threat receded (Ramsay 1977). This is illustrated by a growth in participation through profit sharing in the late nineteenth century and joint consultation during and just after World War I (1914–20) and World War II (1940s), and an increase in the number of worker directors through the TUC and the Bullock Committee of Inquiry during the 1970s. The most recent growth of interest and activity has occurred under the EIP label since the 1980s, and it differs substantially from earlier variants. It tends to be individualist and direct (as opposed to collective and through representatives), it is initiated unilaterally by management and it is directed at securing greater employee commitment to and identification with the employing organisation. EIP has grown without much pressure from employees or unions, but with some legislative support for employee share ownership, profit-related pay, and information and consultation.

The growth in EIP is apparent from data taken from successive WERS surveys. Millward et al. (1992: 166) note that 'management initiatives to increase EIP were made with rising frequency throughout the 1980s', a trend that continued throughout the 1990s. Cully et al. (1999) indicate that four of the top five 'new management practices and EI schemes' were forms of direct EIP. By the time of the WERS survey (Kersley et al. 2006), team briefing had taken even greater hold (over 90 per cent of workplaces claimed to practise it), along with more systematic use of the management chain for disseminating information within organisations. In contrast, joint consultative committees (JCCs) had become less widely used; they were present in just 14 per cent of workplaces (down from 20 per cent in 1998), though the decline in JCCs beyond the workplace was much less sharp. This picture is reinforced by case study data (Marchington & Cox 2007), and it is now argued that direct EIP is more effective than union-based and indirect EIP (Bryson 2004).

Direct EIP takes several distinct forms: (1) downward communi-cation from managers to employees via techniques such as team briefing and employee reports; (2) upward problem-solving designed to tap into employee knowledge and opinion through practices such as quality circles and suggestion schemes; and (3) task participation, in which individual employees are encouraged or expected to extend the range and type of tasks undertaken at work, via practices such as job rotation, job enrichment and teamwork (Kelly 1982; Appelbaum et al. 2000). There is also financial involvement, which aims to link part of an individual's rewards to their own performance and/or that of the unit or enterprise as a whole. These include profit sharing and various employee share ownership schemes, and *WERS 2004* estimated that just over 20 per cent of workplaces had one of these schemes (Kersley et al. 2006: 191), covering three million workers.

Although direct EIP has grown considerably since the 1980s, representative participation has not disappeared altogether. Although it was felt JCCs were unlikely to survive the development of strong shop steward workplace organisation in the 1960s, they re-emerged during the 1970s before declining again since the 1980s (Kersley et al. 2006). They remain more extensive in the public than the private sector, in larger workplaces than smaller, and where unions are recognised than where they are not. Their decline is principally due to changing structural and sectoral composition of workplaces, in particular to the falling number of larger establishments. WERS panel data (Millward et al. 2000: 111) suggest that JCCs were rarely introduced as an alternative to unions, and direct EIP was equally likely to be found in workplaces where management actively encouraged unions as in those where it did not.

CURRENT AND FUTURE ISSUES

Fairness at work

An increasingly important topic in employment relations is the idea of fairness at work. We take a broad definition of fairness to include absolute and relative pay, fair treatment of immigrants, gender equality in the workplace, and bullying and harassment. Each of these topics can be subsumed under the larger debates surrounding dignity at work (Hodson 2001), as can questions about worker voice.

The issue of low pay in Britain has been rising in prominence, especially since the Conservative government abolished wages councils in 1993 in the name of promoting labour market flexibility. In 1997, the incoming Labour government established the tripartite Low Pay Commission, which resulted in the introduction of a national minimum wage two years later. One of the key aims in implementing the minimum wage was to 'make a positive contribution to fairness' (Grimshaw 2009). Recent evidence suggests that the minimum wage has not only decreased the number of low-paid workers in Britain, but it has also done so without imposing labour market rigidities (Grimshaw 2009). In this case, the promotion of fairness at work in the form of a statutory minimum wage can be seen in positive sum terms for workers, unions and employers.

Labour was arguably less successful on the pressing issue of relative pay. Income inequality, which skyrocketed during the Thatcher and Major governments, was at historically unprecedented levels when Blair came to power in 1997 (Sefton & Sutherland 2005). After then, if anything, there was a slight rise in the distribution of earnings (Brewer et al. 2007), all in spite of Labour's efforts to reduce inequality. So, even though levels of pay rose, the increases were relatively greater at the top end of the spectrum. Also worth mentioning is that, as noted above, inequality in the workplace was institutionalised under Labour in the implementation of performance-related pay in the public sector. At a micro level, performance-related pay leverages structured inequality in order to promote productivity (Armstrong 2002). Although inequities in reward structures can potentially serve as a motivating force, they can also create problems such as alienation and higher levels of turnover.

Another important trend was the acceleration of immigration since 1997. It is estimated that net immigration to the United Kingdom quadrupled after the election of Labour (Somerville 2007). A significant proportion of these newcomers were economic and temporary migrants from Eastern Europe (Dustmann & Weiss 2007). Such massive demographic changes posed a real threat in relation to racial and ethnic discrimination at work and also new challenges for Britain's trade unions in terms of recruiting black and ethnic minority members and responding to competing visions of social inclusion (Martinez Lucio & Perrett 2009). In 2007, the Equality and Human Rights Commission was established to document and combat discrimination, broadly defined. It is currently conducting research on migrants' experiences with inequality in Britain.

Gender equity has been on the political agenda since the *Equal Pay Act* 1970, but since progress on this front has been slow, it lost none of its contemporary relevance under Labour. Though the implementation of the national minimum wage went some way towards closing the gender gap to an extent (Grimshaw 2009), it is still the case that women are disadvantaged in the workplace and under-represented in the upper echelons of many firms. In the light of the continuation of these gendered hierarchies, it makes sense that feminism and feminist approaches ought to play a more active role in 'mainstream' industrial relations in order to capture more accurately the complexities of employment beyond social class (Holgate et al. 2006).

Of growing importance within the context of the emerging fairness at work debate in Britain is the issue of workplace bullying and harassment (Hoel & Beale 2006). This topic clearly intersects with low pay and inequities in reward structures (inasmuch as they generate disparate power relations), the fair treatment of immigrants (since they are often the targets of abuse) and gender inequalities (because women are often subjected to sexism in the workplace). The sources of bullying include co-workers (Vartia & Hyyti 2002), customers (Bishop et al. 2005) and managers (Hoel & Beale 2006). Though the issue of bullying is often perceived in relation to physical violence, it has a psychological component to it as well. Future research in the area of bullying and harassment is justified not only by a moral imperative, but also by the idea that respect in the workplace is good for productivity (Appelbaum 2008).

The industrial relations consequences of EU membership

When the United Kingdom joined the then European Economic Community (EEC) in 1973, employers—led by the CBI—were generally in favour of UK participation, whereas much of the trade union movement was opposed to the entry of the United Kingdom. Since 1973, most employers' organisations have supported the economic aspects of European integration in the form of the development of the Single European Market, although there is no uniform position among employers towards the adoption of the euro. In contrast, the extension of the European social policy agenda has been resisted by most employers' organisations. While positions towards the EEC shifted among the unions after 1979, the turning point in relations with the EEC was the address by the President of the European Commission, Jacques Delors, to the Annual Congress of the TUC in 1988. After this address, the majority position within the union movement was in favour of deeper European economic integration coupled with a more wide-ranging social dimension. The policies of Thatcher's Conservative governments influenced the shift in the union position on two counts. First, the exclusion of trade unionists from engagement with government and the restrictive legislation enacted by the Thatcher administration limited the political room for manoeuvre for unionists. Second, the growing social agenda of the EEC offered industrial relations opportunities that were not available domestically, while the opt-out from the Social Protocol of the Maastricht Treaty (Social Chapter) by the Conservative administration in 1992 threatened to exclude unionists from these benefits. The shift in position among unionists was thus driven by a desire to gain access to the benefits of social policy measures that might override the absence of domestic measures.

The Labour government elected in 1997 reversed the UK opt-out from the Social Chapter, thereby committing the country to a range of social polices including the directive on European works Councils

(94/45/EC). More generally, however, the Labour government sought to retain the competitive advantages it perceived as arising from the form of regulation enacted by the previous Conservative government, particularly regarding labour flexibility. To this end, the Labour government, supported by employers' organisations, campaigned against the adoption of the directive on Information and Consultation (2002/14/EC), withdrawing its opposition only when other member states withdrew from the blocking minority; introduced a wide range of exceptions and derogations to the working time regulations, and does not favour a revision of the directive on European works councils that would include more specific definitions of information and consultation. The faltering progress of European social policy and the increasing prominence of neo-liberal policy objectives within the European Commission (Hyman 2005) has also led many British trade unionists to reassess their position towards the EU. The failure to ratify the EU Charter of Fundamental Rights and the openly neo-liberal proposals advanced in the Bolkestein directive on the liberalisation of services exemplifies the current trend.

In addition to a raft of legislation on a wide spectrum of health and safety matters, influential legislation originating from the EU that impinges on UK labour law and industrial relations is concentrated in two broad fields: individual employment rights, and information and consultation rights.

The voluntarist tradition informed much industrial relations practice before 1960. While this tradition was weakened by the enactment of legislation that restricted managerial authority in areas such as recruitment, equality, job termination, redundancy payments and unfair dismissal during the 1960s and 1970s (Anderman 1986), its impact remains evident insofar as the scope of individual employment rights is narrow relative to other countries of Western Europe. Since the reversal of the UK opt-out from the Social Chapter in 1997, a range of new rights that originated from the EU have been enacted, prominent among which are those covering the regulation of working time, a right to urgent family leave, a right to parental leave, a right to equal treatment for part-time workers and protection for fixed-term contract workers. The final pair of rights resulted from framework agreements concluded between the social partners at European level. The floor of individual employment rights is thus being extended in consequence of EU membership and the commitment to the Social Chapter.

A second area in which EU legislation has impinged on UK industrial relations practices is information and consultation. The directives on

European works councils (94/45/EC), extended specifically to cover the United Kingdom by directive (97/74/EC), and on Information and Consultation (2002/14/EC), coupled to the European company statute (Regulation No. 2157/2001) and its accompanying directive on the involvement of employees in European companies (2001/86/EC), constitute a wide-ranging network of provisions that operate at national and international levels. Initially, the opt-out from the Social Chapter excluded United Kingdom-based companies from a requirement to comply with the directive on European works councils. The voluntary option allowed by the provisions of the directive for the two years from September 1994 was sufficiently attractive for many United Kingdom-based companies to establish European works councils. To date, however, no United Kingdom-based companies have adopted European company status. Similarly, the response to the Information and Consultation Regulations (the UK transposition of the directive on Information and Consultation) has been muted among employers, trade unions and employees (Hall 2006). The shift from a single channel to a dual system of representation in the United Kingdom, made possible by the directive, is thus something for the future (Davies & Kilpatrick 2004).

Employment relations across networked organisations

In recent years, the concept of employment relations has become blurred and fragmented due to the growth of networks. This is now a significant aspect of the British scene, due to privatisation and to increases in subcontracting between private sector firms that choose to seek cost reductions by outsourcing some of their existing work (Legge 2007). This links with both of the themes we have just examined. With fairness at work, it relates to workers in supplier companies being treated less well than their counterparts in client or lead organisations. Its link with EU membership is that many of the directives, such as those connected with information and consultation, low pay and working time, impact upon the experience of work for those working for subcontractors or agencies. This also raises concerns that the way in which employment relations, HRM and law are defined fails to allow for a proper theorisation of multi-employer networks. This is particularly pertinent when the terms and conditions of workers employed by one firm are heavily influenced, or even determined, by another employer—as with agency workers or subcontractors further up the supply chain (Purcell et al. 2004; Marchington et al. 2005; Coyle-Shapiro et al. 2006). In these cases, the internal employment relationship between employer and employee is no longer a simple (and relatively closed) matter, but is shaped by the contractual and power relations between clients and subcontractors/agencies. Clients can in effect set wages and shape patterns of work organisation of those employed on their premises, as well as collective bargaining and EIP. Three examples will illustrate how the passage of risk along the chain and down the hierarchy can impact on employment relations at supplier firms.

Employment security is affected explicitly when work is transferred from a client to a supplier. In some cases, the people undertaking the work in the first place are transferred—say, from a public sector body to a private sector employer that has won the contract to provide these services. In these situations, workers are likely to get some protection from the Transfer of Undertakings Protection of Employment (TUPE) Regulations, at least for a period of time. But TUPE is limited in coverage, and over a period of time its influence declines, with the result that transferred staff frequently end up with worse terms and conditions than they would have had if they were still employed by the original employer (Marchington et al. 2005). In other cases, merely the work is transferred and then there are no legal protections for staff employed to do this work. Consequently, they tend to have much lower levels of employment protection due to harsher policies adopted by the new employer or the agency, or because they are treated less favourably in the event of a future redundancy. However, even if agency workers are not actually made redundant they may experience greater levels of insecurity (Purcell et al. 2004).

The second example is pay and benefits. It is likely that workers employed by a subcontractor working at other sites receive lower levels of rewards than those employed by the core employer; indeed, many employers see that as the major attraction of contracting work out. Problems can also arise if workers from different organisations are employed alongside one another on the same team, but are paid different rates. At the airport studied by Rubery et al. (2004), baggage handlers were employed by a range of different firms on a variety of contracts. Some had been taken on initially by the local council (public sector) and enjoyed protected conditions while they remained in employment. A second group comprised seasonal staff paid substantially less than the original workers, while a third group had been subcontracted from another firm and were paid a different rate again. All three sets of workers did precisely the same work but received different benefits, and not surprisingly tensions arose between them.

Finally, the fragmentation of work has implications for employee voice, either through reduced (or no) access for these workers to union recognition and collective bargaining, or in not being allowed access to EIP practices at the workplace. Not only are there logistical problems for unions in trying to organise groups of workers employed by different organisations, there are also issues to do with worker solidarity. It is hardly surprising that those working for the core firm will feel antagonism to those employed—typically on lower rates of pay—by a subcontractor. Moreover, the issues that concern permanent staff are likely to be different from those on temporary contracts, something that holds true irrespective of occupation (Grimshaw et al. 2003). Similar problems arise if staff from different organisations work alongside each other but are given differential access to communications and involvement forums or may even be denied access to an intranet that provides information that contributes to work quality/customer service.

CONCLUSIONS

Over the last 30 years, the British industrial relations system has undergone substantial change. Union density is now around half of its peak in 1979 and unions are struggling to find a clear identity for the twenty-first century, both in their international and workplace profiles, and in their traditional links with the Labour Party. Much will depend upon the success of the 'organising' model in generating increases in union membership, the direct and indirect impact of the recognition legislation, and the ability of partnership to deliver improvements for workers as well as for employers. There are specific challenges for unions in the much-reduced public sector, and there are signs of growing discontent with increasing private sector involvement in public services.

Despite increased juridification, the absence of a strong and centrally regulated system of employment relations has meant that employers have been relatively free to set or negotiate terms and conditions at levels they deem to be appropriate for their own competitive circumstances. There appears to be a growing bifurcation of employer approaches along the lines of 'contract or status' (Streeck 1987), with some employers adopting policies of high commitment management (HCM) whereas others opt for a cost minimisation model. It is also apparent from *WERS 2004* that trade union representation and HRM can and do coexist.

The role of the state in industrial relations has also been subject to change. In some respects, it has lessened in line with declines in the size of the public sector, while expanding in others through an increased legal regulation of many areas of employment practice. Much of this has been driven by EU legislation, especially in strengthening individual employment rights. At the same time, an increased range of statutory rights exercised via individual complaints to tribunals poses a potential threat to employers and unions who, for the most part, have managed recently to maintain a relatively consensual state of affairs in Britain.

The most recent era in British industrial relations has introduced new issues that will affect future developments—fairness at work, the role of EU legislation and new organisational forms. Despite the picture of relative calm that appears to be portrayed by low levels of industrial action, it is also abundantly clear that employment relations in Britain continue to be characterised by tensions and contradictions. Managing these issues will remain a major task for employers, trade unions and governments alike.

A CHRONOLOGY OF BRITISH EMPLOYMENT RELATIONS

1780–1840	Period of primary industrialisation.
1799–1800	*Combination Acts* provide additional penalties against workers' 'combinations'.
1811–14	'Luddites' begin smashing machines.
1824–25	Repeal of *Combination Acts*.
1834	'Tolpuddle martyrs' transported to Australia for taking a union oath.
1868	First meeting of TUC.
1871	*Trade Union Act* gives unions legal status.
1891	Fair Wages Resolution of the House of Commons.
1899	TUC set up Labour Representation Committee, which became the Labour Party in 1906.
1906	*Trades Disputes Act* gives unions immunity from such liability, if acting 'in contemplation or furtherance of a trade dispute'.
1913	*Trade Union Act* legalises unions' political expenditure if they set up a separate fund, with individuals able to 'contract out'.
1926	General strike and nine-month miners' strike.
1927	Subsequent legislation restricts picketing and introduces criminal liabilities for political strikes.
1945–51	Election of Labour government leads to repeal of 1927 Act; nationalisation of the Bank of England, fuel, power, inland transport, health, steel, etc.
1968	Donovan report advocates voluntary reform of industrial relations.
1971	*Industrial Relations Act* legislates for reform; most unions refuse to comply. It also introduces the concept of 'unfair dismissal'.
1974	A miners' strike precipitates the fall of the Conservative government.
1974	*Trade Union and Labour Relations Act* replaces the 1971 Act, but retains the 'unfair dismissal' concept, sets up ACAS and signals a new Social Contract.
1974	*Health and Safety at Work Act*.
1975	*Employment Protection Act* extends the rights of workers and unions; *Equal Pay Act* implemented.
1976	*Race Relations Act*.

1979	'Winter of discontent' followed by election of Conservative government led by Mrs Thatcher.
1980–92	*Employment Acts* restrict union rights to enforce closed shops, picket and strike, weakening the rights of individual employees.
1984	*Trade Union Act* requires regular secret ballots for the election of officials, before strikes, and to approve the continuance of political funds.
1984–1985	Miners' strike.
1988–90	*Employment Acts* remove all legal support for closed shops, further restricting unions and their scope for invoking industrial action.
1991	UK opts out of Social Chapter of Treaty of Maastricht.
1993	EC establishes a single European market.
1997	Labour government, led by Tony Blair, elected with a large majority; Labour re-elected in 2001 and 2005. National Minimum Wage introduced and *Employment Relations Act* introduces new union recognition provisions.
2005	Information and Consultation Regulations come into force.
2007	Equality and Human Rights Commission established (combines the activities previous undertaken by the Commission for Racial Equality, the Disability Rights Commission and the Equal Opportunities Commission.
2010	Hung parliament for the first time in over 35 years leads to formation of a Conservative-Liberal Democrat coalition government, led by David Cameron.

CHAPTER 3

Employment relations in the United States

Harry C. Katz and Alexander J. S. Colvin

In accord with the relatively strong role that market forces have played in American economy history, the United States has long been noted for a high degree of diversity in the conditions under which employees work. Yet in recent years the amount of labour market diversity has increased markedly, spurred in part by the share of the labour force represented by unions continuing to decline (from a peak of 35 per cent in the early 1950s to 20 per cent in 1983 and to 12 per cent in the early twenty-first century) (Bureau of Labor Statistics 2008a).

Diversity also appeared because, while union representation declined, parts of the American labour movement engaged in revitalisation efforts. Thus, although facing continuing difficulties in organising new members, the American labour movement has been engaged in innovation and experimentation. Diversity was also apparent in collective bargaining outcomes as, although many workers and unions lost devastating strikes or were forced into severe concessions, at least some other unions were winning significant contractual gains, at times as a result of innovative collective bargaining strategies.

As shown by its GDP of US$14 294 billion (Bureau of Economic Analysis 2008) and its labour force of 154.7 million (Bureau of Labor Statistics 2008b), the American economy is the largest of any considered in this book. Because of the size of the US economy and its important role in global political affairs, the United States has played an important role in the development of other national systems.

THE HISTORICAL CONTEXT

American skilled craftsmen started to form unions even before industrialisation, which began in the 1790s.[1] The skilled trades nature, practical goals and economic strategy of these early pre-factory unions had a lasting legacy in American unions (Sturmthal 1973). Yet, from the time of the American revolution in 1776, there has also been an element of radical egalitarianism in the US labour movement. Also, in the early years of the nineteenth century many workers were attracted to various utopian schemes (Foner 1947).

The widespread establishment of the factory system in the 1850s and 1860s brought into the industrial system large numbers of rural women and children, and many immigrants from Ireland, Britain, Germany and other countries. These early factory workers did not unionise. This may have been partly because their pay was generally comparable to American farm earnings and higher than those of factory workers in Europe. It may also be that the high rate of worker mobility to other jobs and considerable social mobility hindered the development of the solidarity among workers that would have facilitated the widespread organisation of unions (Lebergott 1984: 373, 386–7; Wheeler 1985). In addition, as often occurred later in US history, vigorous repression of unionisation by employers, both directly and through government action, inhibited unionisation (Sexton 1991).

In spite of these difficulties, skilled craftsmen did form national unions in the 1860s. These pragmatic 'business' unions quickly drove competitors from the field, and in 1886 the craft unions organised on a national basis into a peak organisation, the American Federation of Labor (AFL) (Taft 1964).

Around 1900, building on a large home market made accessible by an improved transport system, large corporations achieved dominance in American industrial life. These complex, impersonal organisations required systematic strategies for managing their workers. Responding to this need, Frederick Taylor, the father of 'scientific management', and his industrial engineer disciples gained a powerful influence on the ideology and practice of management in the United States (Hession & Sardy 1969: 546–7). These ideas were widely accepted before they became influential in Europe and other parts of the world. By declaring 'scientific' principles for the design of work and pay, the Taylorists undermined the rationale for determining these matters by power-based bargaining by unions. Added to this difficulty for the unions was the continuing vigorous opposition of the capitalists, who had enormous power and high prestige (Sexton 1991).

The craft unions survived and prospered in the early part of the twentieth century, partly because of cooperative mechanisms put into place during World War I and their patriotic support of the war. Yet by the 1920s a combination of the influence of Taylorism, employer use of company-dominated unions as a union-substitution device, tough employer action in collective bargaining, widespread use of anti-union propaganda by employer groups and a hostile legal environment had reduced even the proud and once-powerful craft unions to a very weak position, although unions in a few industries such as railroads and printing continued to have some success.

It was not until the 1930s, during the Great Depression, that US unions first arose as a broadly influential and seemingly permanent force. Then, for the first time, they penetrated mass production industry, organising large numbers of factory workers. A fateful conjunction of circumstances led to this. Working conditions and pay had deteriorated. There was a changed political environment with the election of Franklin D. Roosevelt as President in 1932. A wave of strikes, many of which were successful, took place in 1933–34. The *Wagner Act* 1935 gave most workers a federally guaranteed right to organise and strike for the first time. Under these conditions, the strategy of mass campaigns by unions organised not by craft but by industry (United Automobile Workers, United Mine Workers, United Steel Workers) and united in a new labour movement—the Congress of Industrial Organizations (CIO)—led to unionisation of cars, steel, rubber, coal and other industries (Bernstein 1970; Wheeler 1985).

In the 1940s and 1950s, the unions continued to grow, although federal legislation of this period restricted and regulated them. It was during this time that they developed the collective bargaining system, with the support of the War Labor Board, which institutionalised collective bargaining and related dispute-resolution mechanisms due to the need for wage (and price) stabilisation and uninterrupted war production. The post-World War II period saw general prosperity and improving standards of living accompanied by industrial peace. Union automatic wage increases (cost of living adjustment, or COLA, clauses) in major industries contributed to the rise in living standards during this period. A wave of organising in the 1960s and 1970s, led by school teachers, transformed government employment in many parts of the country into a sector with strong unions.

THE MAJOR PARTIES

In the United States, all of the participants in the employment relations system retain some influence. However, it is the employers that have generally been the most powerful of the actors and, as will be argued below, it is the employers that are becoming increasingly dominant.

Employers and their organisations

As large corporations expanded in the twentieth century in the United States, structured and bureaucratic 'internal labour markets' appeared within those 'primary sector' enterprises. This included well-defined job progressions and formal pay and fringe benefit policies (Doeringer & Piore 1971; Jacoby 1985). Jobs found in the union sector, even in industries such as construction that faced substantial cyclical economic volatility, led the way in developing structured and high-pay employment practices.

Yet the United States also retained more unstructured employment practices, often in smaller or rural firms, where pay was lower and administered in a less formal manner. Furthermore, job progressions, dispute-resolution procedures and other employment practices were also relatively informal and of lower quality in these 'secondary sector' enterprises, especially when compared with the work practices found in large private or public sector employers.

Employers' organisations are relatively unimportant in the United States (Adams 1980: 4). In contrast to many other countries, there have never been national employers' confederations engaging in the full range of industrial relations activities. There have, however, long been employers' organisations that have the mission of avoiding the unionisation of their members' employees. The National Association of Manufacturers was formed for this purpose in the nineteenth century. In addition, many regional Chambers of Commerce include union avoidance in their activities. These employer groups and others engage in anti-union litigation, lobbying and publicity campaigns.

In contrast to the relative weakness of employers' organisations, management consultants and law firms that represent employers play important roles in the United States. Management consultants are active in advising employers on human resource policies. For example, in wage-setting, employers commonly rely on consulting firms to supply information from compensation surveys. Management consultants, along with management-oriented law firms, also engage in the lucrative business of educating employers in techniques of union avoidance.

The unions

The US labour movement is generally considered an exceptional case because of its apolitical 'business unionism' ideology, focusing rather narrowly on benefits to existing members. The most convincing explanations for this are historical (Kassalow 1974). First, there is no feudal tradition in the United States, which has made the distinctions among classes less obvious than in much of Europe. Second, US capitalism developed in a form that allowed fairly widespread prosperity. Third, the diversity of the population, divided particularly along racial and ethnic lines, has hampered the organisation of a broad-based working-class movement. Fourth, the early establishment of voting rights and free universal public education eliminated those potential working-class issues in the nineteenth century. Fifth, social mobility from the working class to the entrepreneurial class blurred class lines, creating a basis for the widely held belief in the 'log cabin to White House' myth. In consequence, the labour movement has seldom defined itself in class terms. Additionally, the historic experience of unionists was that class-conscious unions (i.e. those that assumed the 'burden of socialism') tended to be repressed by the strong forces of US capitalism (Sexton 1991).

American unions have relied upon collective bargaining, accompanied by the strike threat, as their main weapon. This strategy has influenced the other characteristics of the labour movement. It has provided the basis for an effective role on the shop floor, as the day-to-day work of administering the agreement requires this. It has required unions to be solvent financially in order to have a credible strike threat. It has resulted in an organisational structure in which the power within the union is placed where it can best be used for collective bargaining— the national union, the regional or the local union, depending on the locus of collective bargaining (Barbash 1967: 69).

Centralisation of power over strike funds in the national union has been a crucial source of union ability to develop common rules and to strike effectively. It has facilitated, and perhaps even required, an independence from political parties that might be tempted to subordinate the economic to the political. It is one reason why there is a relatively low total union density, as collective bargaining organisations need to have a concern about density only as it pertains to their individual economic territories.

Although unions have emphasised collective bargaining, they have also engaged in politics. Their political action has for the most part taken the form of rewarding friends and punishing enemies among politicians and lobbying for legislation. They have avoided being involved in the formation of a labour party. The American Federation of Labor-Congress of Industrial Organizations' (AFL-CIO) Committee on Political Education (COPE) and similar union political agencies are major financial contributors to political campaigns, most frequently in support of Democratic Party candidates. The goals of such political activity have often been closely related to unions' economic goals, being aimed at making collective bargaining more effective. However, the labour movement has also been a major proponent of progressive political causes such as laws on civil rights, minimum wages, plant-closing notice, social security and other subjects of benefit to citizens generally.

The structure of the labour movement is rather loose compared with that of other Western union movements, as the national unions have never been willing to cede power over the function of collective bargaining to the AFL-CIO. The AFL-CIO is a federation of national unions that includes a substantial share of union members. The AFL-CIO serves as a national-level political and public relations voice for the labour movement, resolves jurisdictional disputes among its members, enforces codes of ethical practices and policies against racial and sex discrimination, and is US labour's main link to the international labour movement.

Two major changes have occurred in the AFL-CIO in recent years. In 1995, there was an unprecedented election challenge for the federation's presidency by John Sweeney. As president of the Service Employees International Union (SEIU), Sweeney successfully organised a coalition of union leaders within the federation's member unions and defeated the chosen successor of the previous president who had retired as a result of the Sweeney-led challenge. In an effort to address the decline in union density, the Sweeney administration of the AFL-CIO has emphasised organising new membership through a variety of new initiatives. The most innovative of these measures are described in more detail later in this chapter. Although the Sweeney administration entered office as a reform movement, divisions continued among the national unions around issues such as political and organising strategies. These divisions came to a head in 2005 when a group of major national unions withdrew from the AFL-CIO and formed a new union federation called Change-to-Win. This split in the labour movement and the formation of Change-to-Win will be described in more detail later in this chapter.

Within the labour movement, the national unions have been described as occupying the 'kingpin' position (Barbash 1967: 69).

They maintain ultimate power over the important function of collective bargaining, in large part through their control of strike funds. The national unions can establish and disestablish local unions. They can also withdraw from the national federations if they wish, as happened with the formation of Change-to-Win.

Continuing a trend that began in the early 1980s, several mergers and proposals for mergers among national unions have occurred. Recent examples of mergers include the combination of the two largest textile unions. In addition, many small independent unions have begun to choose to be absorbed into national unions, further consolidating the union structure of US unionism (McClendon et al. 1995).

The local unions perform the day-to-day work of the labour movement. They usually conduct bargaining over the terms of new agreements and conduct strikes, although in some industries national unions do this. They administer the agreement, performing the important function of enforcing the complex set of rights that the collective bargaining agreement creates. Social activities among union members take place at the local level, where there is a union culture (Barbash 1967: 26–41).

Government

The rapid increase in public sector unionisation in the 1960s and 1970s was probably the most important development in the US labour movement since the 1930s. Teachers led the way as they successfully protested about declines in their salaries and benefits relative to those of other workers. Rapid expansion in public sector union membership and militancy followed.

In the mid-1970s, a taxpayers' revolt emerged and slowed the gains of public employee unions—although union representation as a share of the total public sector workforce held steady. Then, in the mid-1980s, teachers and other public-employee groups benefited from public concerns over the inadequacy of public services and saw their bargaining power rebound. In the 1990s, calls to reinvent the public sector led to diverse strategies that ranged from downsizing and privatisation to efforts to bring empowerment and a quality focus to public service provision.

Federal, state and local government employees are excluded from coverage under the *National Labor Relations Act* (NLRA). Separate legal regulations govern collective bargaining in each of these sectors. Federal employees received the rights to unionise and to negotiate over employment conditions other than wages or fringe benefits through Executive Order 10988, signed by President Kennedy in 1962. In 1970, as part of its effort to reform the postal service, Congress provided postal employees the right to engage in collective bargaining about pay, hours and working conditions. Then, in 1978, Congress replaced the executive orders of President Kennedy (and a related order of President Nixon) with the first comprehensive federal law providing collective bargaining rights to federal employees. Subsequently, collective bargaining in the federal sector has been regulated by the Federal Labor Relations Authority. Responsibility for impasse resolution is vested in the Federal Services Impasse Panel. The panel may use mediation, fact-finding or arbitration to resolve disputes. The right to strike is prohibited.

As of 2006, all but nine states had legislation providing at least some of their state or local government employees with the rights to organise and to bargain collectively. Twenty-four states have passed comprehensive laws that cover a range of occupational groups; the others that have not yet enacted public sector bargaining laws are primarily in the south. With the help of favourable state laws the public sector became the most heavily unionised sector with slightly more than one-third of employees organised (Bureau of Labor Statistics 2008a).

In addition to its role as an employer, the US government has two other main roles in industrial relations: the direct regulation of terms and conditions of employment and regulation of the manner in which organised labour and management relate to each other.

The direct regulation of terms and conditions of employment was limited to the areas of employment discrimination, worker safety, unemployment compensation, minimum wages and maximum hours, and retirement (Ledvinka & Scarpello 1991). In 1964, the government prohibited discrimination in employment on the grounds of race, colour, sex, religion or national origin. This law was subsequently strengthened and broadened to prohibit discrimination against disabled workers.

Unusually, compared with other developed market economies (DMEs), disputes involving employment laws in the United States are resolved through the general court system, rather than through specialised labour courts or employment tribunals. This means that employment law enforcement in the United States reflects the nature of American litigation, being a system with relatively high procedural complexity and requiring long periods of time for dispute resolution, while at the same time producing awards that are at times remarkably large in comparison to those of other countries. The combination of high process costs, great variability in outcomes and potential for major damage awards results in employment litigation being a major concern for employers in the United States (Colvin 2006).

From the 1980s onwards, there was a great deal of legislative activity in the broad field of employment relations, in part to fill gaps created by the weakening influence of unions. Legislative initiatives in the areas of minimum wages, termination of employment, race and sex discrimination in employment, pensions, health and safety, plant closing, drug testing, discrimination against disabled workers, polygraphs (lie-detector machines), and family and medical leave have all attracted attention and produced a plethora of new laws. At the same time, the general rule of employment in the United States continues to be that of employment-at-will, meaning there is no requirement for just cause for dismissal or any general entitlement to reasonable notice or severance pay on dismissal.

Unemployment benefits are provided for on a state-by-state basis, but with some federal control and funding. They involve payments to persons who have become involuntarily unemployed and are seeking work. The duration of payments is less than in most other countries. Federal and state wage and hour laws provide for a minimum level of pay and a premium pay rate for overtime work, although many workers are excluded from the coverage of these laws.

Retirement benefits are regulated in two main ways. First, through the social security system, employers and employees are required to pay a proportion of wages into a government fund. It is out of this fund that pensions are paid by the government to eligible retired employees (*Social Security Act*). The second way in which the government controls pensions is by regulation of the private pension funds that are set up voluntarily by employers. The *Employee Retirement Income Security Act* 1974 (ERISA) requires retirement plans to be financially secure, and insures these plans. It also mandates that employees become permanently vested in their retirement rights after a certain period. In recent years, ERISA's provisions focusing on defined benefit retirement plans are increasingly being bypassed with the growth of defined contribution plans that are not subject to as extensive regulation (Salisbury 2001).

Government regulation of the private sector labour–management relationship consists largely of a set of rules through which these actors establish, and work out the terms of, their relationship. Through the *National Labor Relations Act* (NLRA) of 1935, as amended in 1947 and 1958, government provides a structure of rules establishing certain employee rights with respect to collective action.

The process and rules established by law for union certification and bargaining in the private sector represent one of the more unusual features of US labour–management relations. The NLRA specifies a multi-step organising process ordinarily culminating in a secret-ballot election by employees to determine whether they want union certification. The objective of the law regulating union representation elections is to ensure employees have a free choice. To achieve this objective, the National Labor Relations Board (NLRB) determines the appropriate voting unit, conducts the secret ballot election, certifies the union as the exclusive bargaining agent for the unit when the union achieves a majority of the votes cast, and rules on allegations of unfair labour practices such as employer retribution against employees who support the union. When the union is victorious in the election, the NLRB issues a certification that requires the employer to bargain in good faith with the union. The union has the same obligation.

Much controversy has focused on whether or not the election process is working in accordance with the original legislative intent. This has led to a continuing debate over the adequacy of laws protecting workers' rights to form and join unions. The Commission on the Future of Worker–Management Relations (Dunlop Commission), reporting in 1994, reached the conclusion that the labour laws should be changed to facilitate union organising. Little has come to date from these and other related recommendations to reform US labour laws, however—in part because most employers remain reasonably satisfied with the outcomes of the present legal framework. The return to Democratic Party control of Congress and the Presidency in 2009 raises the prospect of renewed attention to labour law reforms, such as the proposed *Employee Free Choice Act* (EFCA) designed to remove barriers to union organising.

The government plays a very limited role in the collective bargaining process in the private sector. Although it requires 'good faith' bargaining efforts, government generally takes a 'hands-off' position—with the notable exception of the railroad and airline industries, which are covered by separate legislation—in influencing contract outcomes achieved between labour and employers in private sector collective bargaining.

THE MAIN PROCESSES OF EMPLOYMENT RELATIONS

In the *non-union sector*, employers have devised a set of management practices to determine pay and conditions of work systematically. In terms of pay, a combination of job evaluation and individual performance evaluation systems is widespread. The range of possible pay rates to be paid to workers in, say, a clerk's job is determined by an assessment of the worth of the job to the firm (i.e. job evaluation). A particular employee is assigned a pay rate within this range depending upon seniority, performance or other factors. In addition to pay, fringe benefits such as health insurance, pensions, vacations and holidays are determined by company policy. All of this is done with an eye to the external labour market, with total compensation having to be adequate to attract and keep needed workers (Gomez-Meija et al. 1995).

In the *union sector*, the structure of collective bargaining is highly fragmented, and this fragmentation is increasing. As is the case in many other DMEs, trends discussed in more detail below suggest the locus of collective bargaining is shifting downward towards the enterprise or workplace level (Katz 1993). Single-company or single-workplace agreements are the norm in manufacturing. Most collective bargaining takes place at such levels. Even where there are company-wide agreements, as in the car industry, substantial scope is left for local variation.

While the government plays only a very limited role in determining collective bargaining agreements in the private sector, mediators employed by the national government through the Federal Mediation and Conciliation Service (FMCS) are active in the negotiation of new agreements, and their work is generally popular with the parties. In negotiations involving government employees, some state laws provide for binding arbitration of unresolved disputes over the terms of a new agreement. This is especially common where the government employees involved, such as fire fighters or police officers, are considered to be 'essential' such that a work stoppage involving those employees would do substantial harm to the public. Interest arbitration of the terms of a new agreement is rare in the private sector.

Although there is considerable variety in collective bargaining agreements (contracts), the majority share certain features. Most are very detailed. Agreements generally cover pay, hours of work, holidays, pensions, health insurance, life insurance, union recognition, management rights, the role of seniority in determining promotions and layoffs, paid time off, and the handling and arbitration of grievances. Most agreements have a limited duration, usually of one to three years.

In both the private and public sectors, nearly all agreements provide a formal multi-step grievance procedure that culminates in rights arbitration. The formal procedure specifies a series of steps through which the parties can settle disagreements about the application and interpretation of an existing collective bargaining agreement. The procedures are almost always capped by the provision for an independent arbitrator to be selected jointly by the union and the employer. Compared to most DMEs, the emphasis on formal grievance arbitration represents one the more unusual features of employment relations in the United States. A substantial body of private 'law' has grown up through arbitral decisions, providing employment relations with a set of norms that are often used in the non-union sector as well as the union sector. Decisions of arbitrators historically have been treated by the courts as final, binding and unappealable (Feuille & Wheeler 1981: 270–81).

In 1991, through its decision in the *Gilmer* case, the Supreme Court allowed statutory employment rights claims to be solved in arbitration. This spurred the spread of 'alternative dispute-resolution' procedures, particularly in the non-union sector, to settle disputes over matters such as dismissals or racial discrimination. In 2001, further impetus to so-called employment arbitration was provided by the Supreme Court's *Circuit City* decision. Some analysts charged that the replacement of court procedures with private justice violated employee rights (Stone 1996). Employment arbitration has proven attractive for many employers because it allows them to avoid the uncertainties and risk of large awards in the litigation system. Research suggests that employment arbitration procedures cover more employees in the United States than are represented by unions (Colvin 2007; Lewin 2008). What is less clear is whether employment arbitration will simply serve as a substitute for litigation or will represent a more substantial change in the nature of employment relations in non-union workplaces in the United States.

The 2000s: Growing pressures on employment relations

The 2000s saw a combination of growing pressures on the US employment relations system, yet relatively limited changes in response to these pressures. Polarisation in both incomes and collective bargaining continued to intensify. Growing cost pressures on health care and retirement benefits dominated many collective bargaining relationships. Pressures from globalisation became particularly acute, even though exports of goods constitute only 12 per cent of US GDP—smaller than any other OECD country (Economic Report of the President 2001). The relative lack of importance of exports to the economy reflects the large US home market, which creates considerable potential for self-sufficiency. However, international trade and investments have become increasingly important to United States-based MNEs. The wage and other cost control pressures resulting from increased international competition have led to more aggressive management behaviour towards unions. Regional trade pacts, particularly the North American Free Trade Agreement (NAFTA), helped spur further globalisation.

Benefit issues emerged as a key topic for collective bargaining in the 2000s. Due to the US system, in which most working-age individuals and retirees under 65 years of age receive health insurance through employer-provided plans, health insurance is a major labour cost item for many employers. As health-care costs grew rapidly in the 1990s and 2000s, significantly outpacing overall inflation, this put increasing pressure on employer cost structures. Employers sought to control cost increases through measures such as requiring employees and retirees to pay larger portions of premiums, reducing benefits and increasing co-pays. Whereas these changes could be introduced unilaterally for non-union employees, employer attempts to negotiate similar measures for unionised employees often produced major tensions in collective bargaining. One of the largest labour disputes of the 2000s, the five-month strike by 70 000 grocery store workers in Southern California in 2003–04, stemmed in large part from employer efforts to reduce health-care costs and benefits (Katz et al. 2007: 215).

Retirement benefits were also a major issue in collective bargaining, particularly for industries such as autos and steel that had sizeable retiree 'legacy' costs dating from earlier decades when they supported much larger workforces. In the steel industry, the steelworkers' union negotiated an agreement with employers and the federal government to transfer retiree benefit obligations on to a Voluntary Employee Benefit Association (VEBA). In the auto industry, the efforts of General Motors to lower its retiree health care costs led to a major strike in 2007 and eventually resulted in an agreement whereby General Motors, Ford and Chrysler were scheduled to transfer their retiree health insurance obligations to a union-run VEBA from 1 January 2010 (Bureau of National Affairs 2007). The Union of Automotive Workers (UAW) came under further pressure to reduce benefit (and wage) costs when General Motors and Chrysler received federal 'bail-out' funds in late 2008 in an effort to forestall their bankruptcy.

Globalisation continues to be a major force affecting the US economy. The trade deficit reached a record level of $753 billion in 2006 (US Census Bureau 2008). Outsourcing was a growing concern in employment relations—particularly in the service sector, which previously had been more insulated from international competition.

For example, in 2004 two major service sector unions, the Service Employees International Union (SEIU) and the Union of Needletrades, Industrial, and Textile Employees and Hotel, Entertainment and Restaurant Employees (UNITE-HERE), launched a joint plan to address outsourcing of service work through organising outsourcing firms and creating alliances with unions in other countries. In 2006, the Communications Workers of America (CWA) negotiated an agreement with AT&T to bring back offshored technical service support jobs (Katz et al. 2007: 395). At the political level, organised labour has been active in lobbying for the inclusion of labour rights provisions in trade agreements.

Despite these various pressures, the US employment relations system remained relatively stagnant in the 2000s. No major new pieces of labour or employment legislation were passed at the federal level, reflecting President Bush's pro-business administration. It also reflected the business communities' general satisfaction with its power position, and the lack of political strength of labour and its allies. Some innovations occurred at the state level, such as California's enactment of the first paid maternity leave program in the United States, albeit with a relatively low six-week paid leave benefit. With the return of Congress to Democratic Party control in 2006, expectations for new policy initiatives increased.

Efforts continue to enact the labour movement's major labour law reform initiative, the *Employee Free Choice Act* (EFCA). The EFCA was a key aspect of the Democratic platform in the 2008 elections, raising the possibility of further action in this area under the post-2008 Obama Administration and with increased Democratic majorities in the US Congress (Bureau of National Affairs 2008). The EFCA's major provisions, which are modelled on some features of Canadian labour law, involve allowing unions to organise through card-check recognition, speed the processing of unfair labour practice charges involving dismissals, increasing penalties on employers who unlawfully discharge employees, and providing for interest arbitration if the parties are unable to negotiate a first contract. Although the EFCA would remove some of the major impediments to union organising and potentially increase union membership levels, the ultimate effects of the Act (if it were to pass) on union membership and power remain unclear. In addition, the Act would represent a relatively limited change in the nature of the US labour–management relations system. In particular, it would not change the relatively decentralised and adversarial nature of the US collective bargaining system or the lack of mandated consultative or participatory structures in US employment relations.

CHANGING EMPLOYMENT RELATIONS

The non-union sector has continued to grow in the private sector as management has aggressively resisted union organisation and taken advantage of new technologies and relatively lax enforcement of labour laws to shift work within or outside the United States, or rely on outsourcing or 'contingent labour' to meet competitive pressures and union organising efforts.

Union revitalisation

Faced with a growing non-union sector, since the mid-1990s the labour movement has initiated innovative efforts to stimulate new organising. Union organisers have been elected to leadership positions in several unions. National unions and the AFL-CIO have begun to spend more on organising, and innovative organising tactics—including efforts to organise on a community or regional basis outside the NLRB procedures—have been launched (Turner et al. 2001).

One of the purposes of the AFL-CIO organising initiatives is to diffuse throughout the labour movement some of the successful organising strategies used by affiliated unions. Unions such as UNITE-HERE and the SEIU have had above-average success in their organising. The campaigns of these unions use young, well-educated organisers and involve extensive direct communication with prospective members and links to community groups such as churches.

This approach to organising has been labelled a 'rank-and-file' style, and contrasts with more top-down traditional organising that relied on appointed organisers and formal communication strategies. Rank-and-file organising also tries to modernise and broaden the issues around which employees are attracted to unions by confronting childcare, equal pay and other issues that are of concern to the current workforce. Research suggests that this method of union organising has been more successful than traditional methods in the private sector (Bronfenbrenner 1997).

During the 1990s and early 2000s, there was little evidence of any widespread effect from these new organising initiatives as union membership rates continued to decline, reaching a low of 12 per cent in 2006. However, in 2007, union membership numbers increased by 311000—the largest increase in over 25 years—and the union membership rate increased slightly (Bureau of Labor Statistics 2008a). Although the percentage increase was very small (0.1 per cent), it is noteworthy that this was the first year in which the US union membership rate had increased since the 1950s. Preliminary estimates indicate that the union membership rate increased further in 2008 (Milkman & Kye 2008). While it is too early to tell whether this trend will continue, it is worth noting that the declining manufacturing unions now represent a smaller proportion of the US labour movement than at any time in the past. By contrast, the growing service sector unions such as SEIU and UNITE-HERE, where much of the new organising activity has been concentrated, represent a larger portion of organised labour in the United States.

Division in the AFL-CIO and the formation of the Change to Win Coalition

Declining union membership rates has been accompanied by divisions within the labour movement about how best to rebuild union strength. In 1995 John Sweeney was elected as President of the AFL-CIO on a reform platform challenging the existing direction and leadership of the AFL-CIO. A decade later, a new group of union leaders in turn emerged to challenge the Sweeney administration leadership of the AFL-CIO and propose a new direction for the labour movement. In 2001, the Carpenter's Union had withdrawn from the AFL-CIO over disagreements about the pace and nature of change inside the labour movement. By 2004, a number of major unions began issuing calls for changes in the AFL-CIO to devote greater resources to organising and to encourage the merger of smaller unions to form larger, more powerful unions (Katz et al. 2007: 146–9).

During 2005, conflicts over the future direction of the AFL-CIO came to a head. In May 2005, four major unions—the SEIU, UNITE-HERE, the International Brotherhood of Teamsters (IBT), and the Laborers' Union (LIUNA)—issued a joint proposal for reforms of the AFL-CIO. These reform proposals focused on three main areas. First, they argued that greater resources needed to be devoted to organising activity. To encourage this, they proposed that half of the dues paid to the AFL-CIO by any unions that were active in organising be rebated. Second, they argued that many existing unions were too small to devote adequate efforts to organising. The reforms proposed designating 'lead unions' for organising particular industries, crafts or employers and encouraging the merger of smaller unions to form larger unions. Third, they argued that the AFL-CIO was devoting too much of its political activities to getting candidates of one political party, the Democrats, elected. Instead labour's political efforts should be focused on building the labour movement and worker power, including supporting pro-labour Republican or third-party candidates.

The executive committee of the AFL-CIO rejected the proposed reforms and instead adopted a counter-proposal offered by President Sweeney. Among the objections to the proposed reforms were concerns that shifting resources away from political activities and towards organising would undermine the ability to get more pro-labour candidates elected, and pushing for merger of smaller unions would deny workers freedom of choice in representation.

In June 2005, the four dissenting unions, along with the United Food and Commercial Workers (UFCW), announced the formation of a new organisation, to be called the Change to Win Coalition (CTW). At the beginning of the July 2005 convention of the AFL-CIO (which ironically was supposed to be a celebration of the 50th anniversary of the formation of the federation by the merger of the formerly competing AFL and CIO), both the SEIU and Teamsters announced they were leaving the AFL-CIO, soon to be joined by the other members of the CTW Coalition. In September 2005, the founding convention of the CTW Coalition was held in St Louis, Missouri, signalling that for the first time in half a century there were now two different major labour federations in the United States. In addition to its initial five members, the CTW Coalition was also joined by the Carpenters Union and the United Farm Workers. Together, the seven unions in the CTW Coalition represent some six million workers, compared with the nearly nine million workers represented by unions that were still members of the AFL-CIO.

Supporters of the CTW Coalition argue that with the decline in unionisation levels, a new, more dynamic and innovative union movement is needed and that the existing AFL-CIO federation was unable to provide this. By contrast, critics of the split have argued that dividing the labour movement into two competing federations will undermine the strength and unity of the movement. Some supporters of the existing AFL-CIO leadership have argued that the split is really a dispute about leadership and control of the labour movement. Much noted has been the split between John Sweeney, who was president of SEIU before assuming the leadership of the AFL-CIO, and Andy Stern, the most prominent leader of the CTW Coalition, who took over as president of SEIU following Sweeney in 1995.

One major concern following the split was that the two federations would compete with each other and be unable to work together on issues of common interest to unions. However, the initial experience has been that the two organisations are able to work together in some areas, such as on some political campaigns.

What are the implications of this dramatic split in the labour movement? For the labour movement, a danger is that its voice in the political realm will be weakened by such a division. This is a concern that has been strongly articulated by critics of the split amongst unions that have stayed within the AFL-CIO. As United Steelworkers President Leo Gerard commented at the time of the split: 'Today is a tragic day because those who left the house of labor are weakening our house, and shame on them' (Bureau of National Affairs, 2005). At the same time, there have been competing union federations at earlier points in American history. Indeed, the most dramatic growth in union membership occurred during the period from 1935 to 1955 when the labour movement was split into competing AFL and CIO federations. The initial Change to Win Coalition Statement, issued in June 2005, harkened back to precisely that experience in invoking the historical example of the formation of the Committees for Industrial Organization in the 1930s to organise the new mass production industries of the time. Whether the CTW will be able to fulfil a similar role in the future, and also whether there may be some future equivalent of the 1950s merger of the competing AFL and CIO, are important issues that remain.

Variation in employment practices

Economic pressures have induced a substantial increase in the amount and nature of the variation in employment practices. Some of the increased variation has been spurred by a decline in unionisation and the differences between the union and non-union sectors. Perhaps most striking is the fact that, even within the union and non-union sectors, variation has been increasing through the spread of a diverse array of employment practices. Another divergent aspect of collective bargaining is that union representation is much more substantial in the public sector, where the union density was about 36 per cent versus 7.5 per cent in the private sector in 2007 (Bureau of Labor Statistics 2008a).

A key factor promoting variation in employment relations has been a substantial decline in the level of unionisation and growth in various types of non-union employment. The density of unionisation in the United States never approached the higher levels found in many other countries. As a result of a lower level of unionisation, and the limited influence of other constraints on managerial behaviour, the United States generally has had a relatively large low-wage employment sector. Nevertheless, there were other non-union firms that chose to pay more, often as part of employment strategies that followed either bureaucratic, human resource management or Japanese-oriented employment patterns.

The downward trend in unionisation increased the variation in employment conditions given that, where it existed, unionisation brought a high degree of standardisation in employment conditions. Job-control unionism put a high premium on contractual rules and pattern bargaining, linking contractual settlements within and between industries (Katz 1985: 38–46). In contrast, a common feature of non-union employment systems has been procedures that relate pay and other employment terms to individual traits and organisational goals. The result has been much higher variation in employment practices across individuals, companies and industries compared with union employment systems.

COLLECTIVE BARGAINING INITIATIVES

Unions have struggled in recent years to extend their membership and maintain their influence in unionised settings. To do so, unions have made significant changes in the process and outcomes of collective bargaining, including corporate campaigns and the linking of collective bargaining to organising and political strategies. While corporate campaigns historically had been used sporadically by the US labour movement, the use and intensity of these campaigns increased in the 1990s and later as unions struggled to find ways to counteract the power advantages management had gained through factors such as the availability of outsourcing, globalisation and the use of permanent striker replacements (Block et al. 2006).

Corporate campaigns are characterised by the use of media, political, financial, community and regulatory pressures to build bargaining power. The United Steel Workers (USW) have been particularly aggressive in developing these tactics and have successfully used corporate campaigns in disputes with the Ravenswood Aluminum Corporation (Juravich & Bronfenbrenner 1999) and, after their merger with the United Rubber Workers, in the Bridgestone dispute (settled in 1996). Unions painfully learned through lost strikes at Phelps Dodge (Rosenblum 1995) and International Paper (Getman 1998) that corporate campaigns had to be well developed and started early in order to succeed.

The revitalisation efforts of the Communications Workers of America highlight the advantages of a triangular agenda linking organising, politics and collective bargaining (Katz et al. 2000). In such a triangulation strategy, union activities in any one of these three spheres interact with and complement activities in another sphere. It is, for example, through novel language won in collective bargaining agreements in the telecommunications industry (with the Regional Bell phone companies) that the CWA gained card check recognition and employer neutrality in representation elections, key parts of the union's organising initiative. Similarly, the CWA has linked political actions towards public agencies that regulated pricing and access in the telecommunications industry with efforts to strengthen the union's strike leverage (and win more at the collective bargaining table).

The labour movement will have to find ways to extend triangulation linkages into the international arena. The expansion of international trade and the accelerated expansion of MNEs extend the market internationally. In his classic analysis of early union formation among American shoemakers, John R. Commons (1909) explained that, as the extent of the market expanded, to counteract 'competitive menaces' and retain bargaining power, unions at the beginning of the twentieth century shifted to a national structure. This provided a structure of representation that was parallel to the emerging national structure of markets.

The problem confronting labour movements all over the globe is that they need cross-national unionism, but their efforts to create such unionism face substantial barriers. These barriers include divergent interests (i.e. each labour movement wants the employment) and national differences in language, culture, law and union structure. Yet unions will need to find an international parallel to the sort of domestic sphere linkages being pursued by the CWA. There are some recent signs of increased international activity among US unions. Several cases where American unions have engaged in cross-national pressure campaigns involve NAFTA provisions (Katz et al. 2007: 390–1). The United Steelworkers, which has significant membership in Canada as well as the United States, announced an alliance with two major British unions, partly in response to the increasing dominance of the steel industry by multinational employers. However, union gains from such international alliances in the United States are limited and the barriers remain daunting.

While it is important to note the extent of innovative bargaining strategies being developed by unions, unions still successfully use traditional collective bargaining pressure tactics such as strikes (or strike threats) to make gains. One example is the bargaining involving machinists represented by the International Association of Machinists and Aerospace Workers (IAM) at Boeing, where the machinists used bargaining leverage due in part to a sizeable back order of planes and the limited ability Boeing had to shift the production of its technologically complex products to alternative sites to gain a favourable contract (though these contract gains came after a long strike).

Pay is perhaps the most important employment outcome, and there is clear evidence of growing earnings variation (Levy & Murname 1992: 1333). While increasing income inequality is a trend common to many countries, the increase is particularly large in the United States. There is growing evidence that a mixture of market and institutional factors (most importantly the low level of unionisation and decentralised structure of collective bargaining) have caused income inequality to rise and help explain why the rise in equality is so large in the United States (Blau & Kahn 1996).

The decentralisation of collective bargaining structures

While there were diverse outcomes in collective bargaining, there were also significant changes underway in the structure of US collective bargaining, perhaps the most important of which is decentralisation (Katz & Darbishire 2000). Until the early 1980s, the structure of bargaining affecting unionised employees was a mixture of multi-employer, company-wide and plant-level bargaining (Kochan et al. 1994). After that, however, the structure of collective bargaining began to decentralise as formally centralised structures broke down, the locus of bargaining shifted to the plant level within structures that maintained both company- and plant-level bargaining to some degree, and pattern bargaining weakened. Differing corporate strategies and product market pressures resulting in diverging interests among once-similar firms also contributed to this decentralisation.

Simultaneously, there has been a shift to plant-level, and away from company-wide, collective bargaining agreements. In many cases, such as the tyre and airline industries, this involved the negotiation of local pay and/or work rule concessions. Often these negotiations included whipsawing by management, with local unions and workers being threatened with the prospect of a plant closing if adequate concessions were not granted (Cappelli 1985; Kochan et al. 1994: 117–27). In some cases, concessions on work rules have been accompanied by new arrangements that provide extensive participation by workers and local union officers in decisions that had formerly been made solely by management. With increasing frequency, work rule bargaining has come to involve a decision about whether or not to implement a joint team-based approach or involve disputes that arise during the implementation of that type of work organisation.

Even where company-level collective bargaining has continued, greater diversity in collective bargaining outcomes has appeared across companies. This diversity has replaced the pattern bargaining that informally had served to centralise bargaining structures to the multi-employer level. In the aerospace and agricultural implements industries, for example, pattern bargaining weakened and significant inter-company variation in wages and other contractual terms emerged (Erickson 1992, 1996; Block et al. 2006).

There was even wider variation appearing in work practices across companies and industries in light of the uneven spread of work reorganisation. Some plants adopted team systems of work while others did not. Wide differences appear in the form and role of any work teams. In some places, there was much bargaining at the plant and work group level, involving team systems, pay-for-knowledge and other contingent compensation mechanisms, and changes in work time arrangements (Kochan et al. 1994: 146–205). More direct communication between managers and workers also spread in many parts of the union sector. The increased role for localised bargaining and work-rule adjustment contributed to the emergence of a 'participatory' employment system in a number of unionised settings. Perhaps the most elaborate service-sector example of a participatory employment pattern is the Kaiser Permanente–AFL-CIO partnership (Katz et al. 2007: 324; Bureau of National Affairs 2000).

Yet in some workplaces, employee and union participation in business decisions or other forms of work restructuring have been limited. Even some renowned examples of worker and union participation, such as that in GM's Saturn division, failed (Rubinstein & Kochan 2001). Osterman (2000: 186) finds that while the overall incidence of innovative work practices increased, the rate of penetration of work teams actually fell during the period he studied. Applebaum and Batt (1994) provide a rich description of the diversity of work practice changes and an insightful analysis of why there has been sluggishness and variation in the diffusion of new work practices.

CONCLUSIONS

Diversity in employment relations is growing as a product of the growth in non-union employment and the variety of union and non-union employment practices. The breakdown of pattern bargaining across enterprises and industries in the union sector, and the spread of contingent forms of pay and associated greater reliance on individualised rewards, are all contributing to increased variation in work rules and pay. The changes in pay practices have contributed to the unusually large increases in income inequality in the United States.

While team systems have spread and operate as a critical part of the employment systems in some firms, more traditional forms of work organisation continue in other firms. Decentralisation, more direct management–employee communication and increased employee (and union) involvement in business decisions all have contributed to the wide variation of work practices.

There is also wide variation in the tenor of recent collective bargaining. In some companies, heightened conflict has appeared, while in others partnerships have been forged. Some workers suffered greatly as management took advantage of a power imbalance provided by globalisation and the growth of non-unionised enterprises. In other contexts, unions used innovative bargaining or traditional strike leverage to make gains.

Unions have shown a willingness to cooperate with workplace changes that attempt to increase productivity and product/service quality where the innovations also include attention to the union's goals. As such, consistent with US 'business unionism', the collective bargaining process has shown flexibility in responding to competitive pressures. The challenge faced by the labour movement is to find ways to combine collective bargaining successes and revitalisation efforts to further promote high-end employment outcomes and limit the growth of low-wage employment patterns and income inequality.

A CHRONOLOGY OF US EMPLOYMENT RELATIONS

1794	Federal Society of Cordwainers founded in Philadelphia—first permanent US union.
1828	Working Men's Party founded.
1834	National Trades Union founded—first national labour organisation.
1866	National Labor Union formed—first national 'reformist' union.
1869	Knights of Labor founded. This is a 'reformist' organisation dedicated to changing society, which nevertheless was involved in strikes for higher wages and improved conditions.
1886	Formation of the American Federation of Labor (AFL), a loose confederation of unions with largely 'bread-and-butter' goals. Peak of membership of the Knights of Labor (700 000 members), which then began to decline.
1905	Formation of the Industrial Workers of the World—the 'Wobblies'—an anarcho-syndicalist union.
1914–22	Repression of radical unions because of their opposition to war, and during 'Red scare' after the Russian Revolution.
1915	Establishment of the first company-dominated union, Ludlow, Colorado.
1920s	Decline and retrenchment of the American labour movement.
1932	Election of Franklin D. Roosevelt as President—a 'New Deal' for unions.
1935	*National Labor Relations Act* (Wagner Act) gives employees a federally protected right to organise and bargain collectively. Formation of Congress of Industrial Organizations (CIO), a federation of industrial unions.
1935–39	Rapid growth of unions covering major mass production industries.
1941–45	Growth of unions and development of the collective bargaining system during the war.
1946	Massive post-war strike wave in major industries.
1947	Enactment of Taft-Hartley Act, prohibiting unions from certain organising and bargaining practices.

1955	Merger of AFL and CIO to form the AFL-CIO.
1959	Landrum-Griffin Act, regulating the internal operations of unions.
1960	New York City teachers' strike—the beginning of mass organisation of public employees.
1962	Adoption of Executive Order 10988 by President John F. Kennedy, providing for limited collective bargaining by federal government employees.
1960–80	Growth of unionism of public employees. Decline in union density in the manufacturing sector.
1977–78	Defeat of Labor Law Reform Bill in Congress, as employer movement in opposition to unions gains strength.
1980	Election of President Ronald Reagan—new federal policies generally adverse to organised labour.
1981	Economic recession.
1988–89	Federal legislation on drugs, lie detectors, plant closing, minimum wages. Court decisions on drug testing and termination of employment.
1991	Federal legislation prohibiting discrimination against disabled workers. Federal legislation strengthening employment discrimination laws.
1991	Through the *Gilmer* and related decisions, the Supreme Court allows statutory employment rights disputes to be resolved through (private) arbitration. Alternative dispute resolution then spreads, particularly in the non-union sector.
1991–92	Extended economic recession.
1992	Election of President Bill Clinton. A more labour-friendly national Administration comes to power.
1992–2000	Sustained economic growth with low unemployment, low inflation and limited real wage growth.
1994	The Commission on the Future of Worker–Management Relations (Dunlop Commission) recommends that a number of changes be made in the nation's labour laws, but these recommendations are ignored by the US Congress.
1994	Republicans win Congressional elections. A very conservative Congress comes into being.
1994	NAFTA removes tariff and other trade barriers among the United States, Canada and Mexico.

1995	Increases in the minimum wage voted by Congress.
1995	John Sweeney elected president of the AFL-CIO spurring accelerated union revitalisation.
2000	George W. Bush elected President in an extremely close election. Republicans subsequently gain control of the Senate and House.
2001	Economic recession; 9/11 terrorist attacks.
2002–07	Slow economic recovery with limited real wage and job growth.
2005	Change to Win split from the AFL-CIO.
2006	Democrats win Congressional elections.
2008	Barack Obama elected President. Democrats expand majorities in Congress.

CHAPTER 4

Employment relations in Canada

Mark Thompson and
Daphne G. Taras

Employment relations in Canada rest on several fundamental characteristics. A large proportion of the labour force is subject to the influence of collective bargaining, either directly or indirectly, and there is strong legal protection for collective bargaining. There are traditions of adversarialism and moderate levels of strike activity. The structures of employment relations are less centralised than in other nations. While Canada has incorporated employer, union and public policies that originated in the United States, it has produced a distinctive employment relations system.

On a comparative basis, Canada is a liberal market economy and its employment relations display the characteristics of that model. Firms rely on hierarchies and markets; bargaining structures are decentralised and unions are not generally key participants in economic and labour policy-making.

THE HISTORICAL, POLITICAL AND SOCIO-ECONOMIC CONTEXT

Canada's federal system of government is one of the most decentralised in the world, vesting authority for most employment matters in the ten Canadian provinces. Federal authority is mostly limited to regulation of the federal civil service and employment within national industries, such as inter-provincial transport. Approximately 8.4 per cent of Canadian workers fall within this domain. Although this decentralisation has led to considerable public policy experimentation, all jurisdictions have similar labour legislation.

Into this already complex mix is added the history and traditions of French Canada, with the province of Quebec having social, economic and legal traditions that are distinct from those of the rest of North America. Quebec is the second most populous province in Canada, after the neighbouring Ontario. The strong nationalism of many Quebec residents (*Quebecois*) has reinforced the already powerful decentralising forces within Canada. Canada is well known as a bilingual and bicultural nation; however, the country is regionally fractured into the primarily French-speaking province of Quebec and parts of adjacent provinces, and the primarily English-speaking provinces, known colloquially as the 'Rest of Canada'.

Immigration continues to be important. Immigrants have accounted for 80 per cent of labour market growth in recent years (Statistics Canada) and almost 20 per cent of all Canadians are immigrants. After World War II, Europe—especially Britain—was the biggest source of immigrants. From the 1960s onwards, the pattern of immigration shifted to developing countries, especially (South-East) Asian nations. By 2006, China (including Hong Kong) was the largest source of immigrants. Recent immigrants lack the tradition of working-class activism displayed by earlier European immigrants.

Simultaneously, the relatively conservative political tradition of the United States has been a powerful model for Canadians. These influences, combined with a Westminster parliamentary political system (and its acceptance of minor political parties), have combined to produce a value system which incorporates US-style individualism in a liberal market economy with the traditions of collectivism as found in European coordinated market economies.

Politically, Canada has a multi-party system reflecting regional interests. For decades, the country was dominated by a rivalry between two parties—the Liberals and Conservatives—with a powerful third party, the New Democratic Party (NDP), able to achieve some of its left-of-centre agenda when it occasionally held the balance of power. Since the 1930s, the Liberals have dominated federal politics, occasionally forming a minority government or yielding power to the Conservatives. The Liberals are a pragmatic and reformist party, with a traditional base of support in Quebec and Ontario. The Conservatives are a right-of-centre party, usually drawing votes from the Eastern and Western regions. The Conservatives won large majorities in 1984 and 1988 and formed minority governments in 2006 and 2008. While they had a market orientation and a preference for small government, the Conservative governments did not embrace the social and economic policies of either the Thatcher government in Britain or the Reagan administration in the United States. Political parties that govern for long periods of time may alternate between conservative and liberal economic policies.

Canadian elections in the 1990s dramatically changed the nature of party politics. In a stunning reversal of fortune, the Conservatives were almost eliminated from Parliament in the 1993 election and struggled to rebuild the party to its former level of support during the rest of the decade. The NDP, with a social-democratic philosophy and strong union support, traditionally had held a small number of parliamentary seats and 15 to 20 per cent of the popular vote. It too lost much ground in 1993. Although the New Democrats regained their share of the popular vote after 2001, they remained on the margin of federal politics. A significant proportion of voters turned their allegiance from these three parties to regionally-based new parties. In the 1990s, a pro-independence party from Quebec, Bloc Quebecois, and a conservative party from the Western provinces, Canadian Alliance, both gained substantial representation in Parliament.

Referendums held in Quebec in 1980 and 1995 favoured remaining in Canada, but the margin in the 1995 vote was small. In the late 1990s, the Canadian Alliance Party became the official opposition in Parliament, with an agenda of extreme fiscal and social conservatism. In 2003, the Western province-dominated Conservative Party united the right-wing elements by absorbing the Canadian Alliance Party, and it strengthened its political base as a party. The Conservative Party became the official opposition. Three years later, in 2006, it formed a minority government and was re-elected in 2008.

As the provinces have exclusive jurisdiction over labour relations for over 90 per cent of the labour force, provincial politics are significant. Each province has a distinct political culture, reflecting regional differences in the various economies of Canada, immigration patterns and political attitudes. None of the federal parties is strong in all the provinces, and solely provincial parties have governed in three provinces: Quebec, Saskatchewan and British Columbia. While the NDP has never gained power in the federal arena, it has won elections in four provinces. However, it has almost no support in Quebec, where a pro-independence Parti Quebecois (PQ) takes similar positions on social and economic issues.

A review of provincial labour policies reveals that the labour movement receives more favourable treatment when a pro-labour party wins provincial government, even if the party seldom achieves majority status. By 2010, either the NDP or the PQ was the official opposition in four provinces and governed in two.

While Canada has a standard of living equal to the more prosperous nations in Western Europe, it depends heavily on the
production and export of raw materials and semi-processed products—
petroleum, minerals, food grains and forest products. Although
Canada enjoys a comparative advantage in the production of most
of these commodities, their markets are unstable and primary
industries do not generate substantial direct employment. There
is a large manufacturing sector in Ontario and Quebec; however,
manufacturing accounts for only 16 per cent of the gross domestic
product and has experienced sharp declines in recent years. Due to
Canada's lack of a large domestic market, it signed a free trade agreement (FTA) with the United States in 1988 and the North American
Free Trade Agreement (NAFTA) with Mexico and the United States
in 1994. The immediate impact of free trade was to accelerate the
integration of the manufacturing sector into a larger North American
economy. Levels of activity in traditional industries, such as textiles
and furniture, fell substantially, while other sectors, such as car
manufacturing and chemicals, initially expanded until caught up in
the 2008 economic destabilisation.

Canada usually exports approximately 34 per cent of its gross
national product and imports approximately 32 per cent. The United
States accounts for approximately 78 per cent of Canada's exports.
By contrast, trade with Mexico is negligible. Apart from proximity and
a natural complementarity of the two economies, Canadian–American
trade relations are encouraged by extensive US ownership in many
primary and secondary industries, as well as the free trade agreements.

Canada has a mixed economy, with active roles for the public
and private sectors, often in the same industries. Public enterprises
typically emerged for pragmatic reasons—provision of an essential
service, development of natural resources or the preservation of jobs.
Thus Canadian federal and provincial governments once owned many
public utilities, transport and communications companies. When
privatisation of public assets became a trend in the mid-1980s, federal
and provincial governments disposed of natural resources, transport and infrastructure companies, in addition to smaller holdings.
Subsequently, the trend abated—although some provinces enter partnerships with private firms to build and operate new facilities.

From 2000 to late 2008, the Canadian economy performed well.
The most pressing fiscal problem of the 1990s was the elimination of
government deficits. Canada achieved a 32-year low in unemployment
in 2007, with a rate of 5.8 per cent. A boom in natural resources after

2000 contributed to falling rates of unemployment, as Table 4.1 shows. The development of 'unconventional' oil (extracted from sand and shale by techniques similar to mining) in the province of Alberta was a major factor in Canada's economic performance. This relatively labour-intensive technology and the remote location of these operations attracted workers from other regions, reducing unemployment rates nationally.

While economic growth did not cause an increase in inflation, income differentials among Canadians were wider than in preceding decades. Comparatively, Canadian income differentials are higher than Europe and lower than the US, partly as a result of government income transfers. One of the balancing acts of government policy is the exchange rate. A high Canadian dollar increases citizens' purchasing power for foreign goods, but a low Canadian dollar reduces the unemployment rate. The Canadian dollar has fluctuated sharply in recent years. It fell to a low of approximately 63 cents to the US dollar in 2003 and then fluctuated between 79 and 96 cents to the US dollar thereafter.

During the inflationary periods of the 1970s, governments intervened directly to reduce pressure on prices. Between 1975 and 1978, the federal government and nine of the ten Canadian provinces imposed an anti-inflation program, which fell most heavily on public sector workers and their unions. Although opinions differ about the impact of the program, the rate of inflation declined during this three-year period and the rate of wage increases fell even more sharply. However, labour and management resented the restrictions in the program, and therefore it was not extended.

During the recession of 1982, federal and provincial governments again imposed temporary public sector wage controls to reduce government spending. In the following decade, Canada experienced slow economic growth. After 2000, Canada's inflation rate of less than 2.5 per cent was among the lowest of any industrialised nation and the Bank of Canada has aimed for a 2 per cent inflation rate.

Government efforts to deal with economic problems are restricted by the nation's political structure. As with Australia, Canada is a confederation with a parliamentary government. The ten provinces hold substantial powers over industrial relations, with only a few industries—principally transport and communications—under federal authority. The provinces, often led by Quebec, have not only resisted any efforts to expand federal powers, but gradually have gained greater powers at the expense of the federal authorities.

Table 4.1 Earnings, prices and unemployment

Year	% change in wages—major collective agreements	CPI annual rate of change (from previous year)	Annual rate of unemployment
1974–78	11.4	9.2	7.1
1979–83	9.8	9.7	9.0
1984–88	3.8	4.2	9.6
1989	5.3	5.1	7.5
1990	5.6	4.8	8.1
1991	3.6	5.6	10.3
1992	2.1	1.4	11.3
1993	0.6	1.9	11.2
1994	0.3	0.1	10.4
1995	0.9	2.2	9.5
1996	0.9	1.5	9.7
1997	1.5	1.7	9.0
1998	1.7	1.0	8.2
1999	2.2	1.8	7.6
2000	2.5	2.7	6.9
2001	3.1	2.5	6.8
2002	2.9	2.2	7.5
2003	2.5	2.8	7.6
2004	1.8	1.8	7.2
2005	2.3	2.2	6.8
2006	2.5	2.0	6.3
2007	3.3	2.2	6.0
2008	3.2	2.6 (Oct.)	6.2 (Oct.)

Source: Statistics Canada, *Special 2000 Labour Day Release* and (2002) 'Fact-Sheet on Unionization', *Perspectives on Labour and Income.* Statistics Canada Labour Force Survey tables, HRSDC 'Indicators of Well-Being'. Average Wage Settlements for 2003–08 from HRSDC Annual Wage Settlements, <www.hrsdc.gc.ca/en/labour/labour_relations/info_analysis/wages/settlements/yearly.shtml> (accessed 21 November 2008)

A fundamental change in Canadian political life occurred in 1982. The Liberal government produced the nation's first written constitution, which included a Charter of_Rights and Freedoms. The Charter guarantees certain fundamental freedoms, including freedom of association, thought, belief, opinion and expression. The Charter applies to federal and provincial governments and most public bodies. It does not, however, apply to the private sector, including private employers.

Initially, the Charter had little impact on employment relations. Courts ruled that it did not apply to the parties in private sector employment relationships, even if they operated under a legal regime to protect collective bargaining. In a dramatic reversal of earlier decisions, the Supreme Court of Canada ruled in 2007 that the Charter protected collective bargaining as an institution, and courts should be guided by international standards in interpreting that right. This decision is discussed in greater detail below.

THE PARTIES IN EMPLOYMENT RELATIONS

Unions

The Canadian labour movement has displayed steady, though unspectacular, growth since the 1930s, despite long-standing patterns of disunity. The number of employees covered by union bargaining arrangements was over four million at the start of the twenty-first century, constituting 29 per cent of paid non-agricultural employees in 2008 (Statistics Canada, 2008). While absolute numbers of employees represented by unions continued to grow, increases in the labour force grew more rapidly, so union density declined moderately since 1984, in contrast to the United States. This membership was divided between two national centres and a large number of unaffiliated unions. The Canadian density figure reflects growth in female union members and a high union density rate in the public sector. Other than the public sector, the greatest penetration of unionism is in primary industries, construction, transport and manufacturing. In the late nineteenth and early twentieth centuries, Canadian unions were established first in construction and transport—mostly on a craft basis. During the 1930s and 1940s, industrial unionism spread to manufacturing and primary industries, without including white-collar workers in the private sector. Since the late 1960s, the major source of union growth has been the public sector. First public servants, then health and education workers, joined unions. Professionals—notably teachers and nurses—had long been members of their own associations, and these transformed themselves into unions as their members' interest in collective bargaining grew. Public sector employees are almost four times more likely to belong to unions as private sector workers. In 2007, over 19 per cent of Canadian workers were classified as belonging to the public sector. Table 4.2 shows the relative rate of unionisation by industry, sector, gender, age, work status and province.

Table 4.2 Union membership by selected characteristics

	Density %*
By industry	
Education	68
Public Administration	68
Utilities	67
Health Care and Social Assistance	53
Transportation and Warehousing	42
Construction	31
Manufacturing	28
Information, Culture and Recreation	25
Natural Resources	20
Management, Administration and Support	13
Trade	13
Finance, Insurance, Real Estate and Leasing	9.7
Accommodation and Food	7.4
Professional, Scientific and Technical	4.3
Agriculture	3.5
Other	10
By sector	
Public	72
Private	17
By gender	
Men	29
Women	30
By age	
15–24	13
25–44	30
45–54	38
55+	35

By work status

Full-time	31
Part-time	23

By province

Newfoundland	37
Prince Edward Island	30
Nova Scotia	29
New Brunswick	27
Quebec	36
Ontario	27
Manitoba	36
Saskatchewan	33
Alberta	22
British Columbia	31

* Union density is measured as the percentage of Canadian workers who are members of unions. This 'membership' figure is slightly lower than the number of Canadians who are 'covered' by collective agreements, as some Canadians are not union members (e.g, due to religious exemptions) but are represented by unions. In 2007, Canadian density measured by membership was almost 30 per cent. Measured by coverage, it was almost 32 per cent

Source: Statistics Canada (2007)

There are approximately 250 unions in Canada, ranging in size from less than 100 members to almost half a million members. Two-thirds are affiliated with one of the central confederations, with the remainder—principally in the public sector—independent of any national centre or in Quebec. The fifteen largest unions contain 59 per cent of all members. Mergers have created 'mega' unions, concentrating union membership in fewer and larger organisations. Table 4.3 lists the various unions, their sizes and their affiliations. Various union philosophies are represented. Most of the old craft groups still espouse United States-style apolitical 'business unionism'. A larger number of unions see themselves fulfilling a broader role, and actively supporting the NDP and various social causes. A few groups, principally in Quebec, are highly politicised and occasionally criticise the prevailing economic system from a socialist perspective. Rhetoric aside, though, the major function of all unions is collective bargaining.

Table 4.3 Labour organisations with largest membership

Name and affiliation—unions with membership over 60 000	Number of members
Canadian Union of Public Employees—CLC	548 880
National Union of Public and General Employees—CLC	340 000
United Steel, Paper and Forestry, Rubber, Manufacturing, Energy, Allied Industrial and Service Workers International Union—AFL-CIO/CLC	280 000
National Automobile, Aerospace, Transportation and General Workers Union of Canada (CAW Canada)—CLC	265 000
United Food and Commercial Workers Canada—CtW/CLC	245 330
Canadian Teachers' Federation	219 000
Public Service Alliance of Canada —CLC	166 960
Ontario Teachers' Federation (1)—CLC	155 000
Communications, Energy and Paperworkers Union of Canada—CLC	150 100
Canadian Federation of Nurses—CLC	135 000
Fédération de la santé et des services sociaux—CSN (CNTU)	117 130
Ontario Public Service Employees Union (2)—CLC	113 500
Teamsters Canada—CtW/CLC	108 510
Service Employees International Union— Canada—CtW/CLC	86 860
Elementary Teachers' Federation of Ontario—CLC	71 690
Alberta Union of Provincial Employees—Ind	69 000
Canadian Police Association	66 800
Laborers' International Union of North America—CtW	65 000
FTQ Construction—CLC	61 600
BC Government and Service Employees' Union (2)—CLC	61 564
Ontario Secondary School Teachers' Federation—CLC	60 700
Fédération des syndicats de l'enseignement—CSQ	60 000

Note: Change to Win (CtW) was created in September 2005 by a number of American international unions disaffiliated from the American Federation of Labor and Congress of Industrial Organizations (AFL-CIO)

Source: Strategic Policy, Analysis, and Workplace Information Directorate, Labour Program, Human Resources and Social Development Canada

The role of US-based 'international' unions is a special feature of the Canadian labour movement. Most of the oldest labour organisations in Canada began as part of American unions—hence the term 'international'. Cultural and economic ties between the two countries encouraged the union connection, while the greater size and earlier development of US unions attracted Canadian workers to them. For many years, the overwhelming majority of Canadian union members belonged to such international unions, which often exerted close control over their Canadian locals. But the spread of unionism in the public sector during the 1960s and 1970s brought national unions to the fore, as internationals were seldom active among public employees. Since the 1970s, many Canadian unions have seceded from internationals. This reflected a perception of inattention to Canadian workers' needs, the protectionism of American unions and a wave of Canadian nationalism. Due to these factors, the proportion of international union membership declined from more than 70 per cent in the mid-1960s to less than 28.5 per cent in 2006. The Canadian experience illustrates the difficulties unions face in exerting effective transnational action.

Despite this cross-border history, there is one area in which Canadian unions enjoy a distinct advantage over their United States-based counterparts. The majority of Canadians who are represented by unions are required to pay union dues, whether they desire to be members of unions or not. This prevention of free-riding is required by labour statutes in most Canadian jurisdictions under an arrangement popularly known as the 'Rand Formula'. Hence, there is no equivalent of the 'right to work' movement that has greatly weakened the ability of US unions to organise and function.

The most important central confederation is the Canadian Labour Congress (CLC), representing almost 72 per cent of all union members belonging to 98 national and international union affiliates. Members of CLC affiliates are in all regions and most industries. It is the principal political spokesperson for Canadian labour, but is weaker than confederations in many other countries. It has no role in bargaining, for instance; nor does it have any substantial powers over its affiliates, unlike confederations in Germany and Scandinavia. The CLC's political role is further limited by the constitutionally weak position of the federal government (its obvious contact point) in many areas the labour movement regards as important, such as labour legislation, regulation of industry or human rights. In national politics, it has supported the NDP. The poor electoral record of the NDP federally further weakens the CLC's political role. The CLC has chartered federations in each province to which locals of affiliated unions belong. Some of these bodies wield considerable influence in their provinces.

The second-largest congress is the Confederation of National Trade Unions (CNTU, or CSN in French) representing 6.4 per cent of all union members, most located in Quebec. It began early in the twentieth century under the sponsorship of the Catholic Church as a conservative French-language alternative to the predominantly English language secular unions operating elsewhere in Canada and in Quebec. As Quebec industrialised during and after World War I, members of the Catholic unions grew impatient with their lack of militancy and unwillingness to confront a conservative provincial government. As part of a rapid change to a secular society, the Catholic unions severed their ties to the Catholic Church, abandoned their former conservatism and moved into the vanguard of rapid social change in Quebec. Since then, competition has prevailed in the Quebec labour movement, and the CNTU has probably become the most radical and politicised labour organisation in North America. It has supported Quebec independence and adopted left-wing political positions. Because of the union's history, current political posture and the large provincial public sector in Quebec, CNTU membership is concentrated heavily among public employees.

Management

The majority of unionised firms grudgingly accept the role of unions, and open attacks on incumbent unions are rare. In industries with a long history of unionism—for example, manufacturing or transport—unionism is accepted as a normal part of the business environment. However, non-union enterprises energetically strive to retain that status, some by matching the wages and working conditions in the unionised sector, others by combinations of paternalism and coercion. Some enterprises have union substitution policies, which replicate many of the forms of a unionised work environment with grievance procedures, quality circles or mechanisms for consultation. Management-influenced forms of employee representation for non-union workers are not illegal as in the United States. Almost 20 per cent of Canadian non-union workers have a formal non-union employee representation plan at their workplaces, and of those workers more than half—that is, 10 per cent of workers—are covered by that representation plan. Thus, although the number of workers represented by unions is slightly more than 29 per cent, the number of workers who experience some form of collective representation is considerably higher.

The high degree of foreign ownership in the Canadian economy affects the economy generally, but seldom affects industrial relations directly. About 25 per cent of the assets of all industrial enterprises are foreign owned, chiefly by MNEs. About 75 per cent of foreign investment comes from US MNEs. Foreign ownership affects strategic managerial decisions, such as product lines or major investments. But there appears to be little impact by non-Canadians on industrial relations decisions in unionised sectors. Foreign owners prefer to remain in the mainstream of industrial relations for their industries rather than imposing corporate policies.

Consistent with Canada's liberal market economy, employers do not rely on organisations for employment relations functions, although the degree of organisation varies among regions. No national group participates directly in employment relations; rather, several bodies present management viewpoints to government or the public. Since most employment relations law falls under provincial jurisdiction, no industries have national bargaining structures under provincial legislation. In two provinces, Quebec and British Columbia, local conditions and public policy have encouraged bargaining by employers' associations formed specifically for that purpose. Elsewhere, single-plant bargaining with a single union predominates, except in a few industries with many SMEs, such as construction, long-shoring or trucking, where multi-employer bargaining is common.

Canadian employers favour limited roles for government in the economy, including deregulation of their own activities. They prefer unilateral control over the employment relationship and accept unions grudgingly. After 2000, a wave of corporate acquisitions changed the face of the Canadian economy. Foreign firms, including MNEs based in developing nations, purchased dozens of large Canadian companies, including iconic unionised firms.

Government

The government in Canada has a dual role in employment relations—it regulates the actors' conduct and employs about 19 per cent of the labour force, directly and indirectly.

There is extensive government regulation of union-management relations, though it rests on an assumption of voluntarism. Each province, as well as the federal government, has at least one Act covering employment relations and employment standards in the industries under its jurisdiction. Employment standards legislation generally sets minima for such areas as pay or holidays, reflecting the liberal market economy in Canada. In a few areas, notably maternity leave, the law has led most employers. Enforcement of these laws often is weak.

Although the details vary considerably, union–management legislation combines many features of the US *National Labor Relations Act* (Wagner Act) and an older Canadian pattern of reliance on conciliation of labour disputes. Each statute establishes and protects the right of most employees to form unions and sets out a procedure by which a union may demonstrate majority support from a group of employees to obtain the right of exclusive representation for them. Unionisation typically occurs at the level of the workplace, again reinforcing the decentralised structure of Canadian employment relations. The employer is required to bargain with a certified union. A quasi-judicial labour relations board administers this process and enforces the statute, although the legislation often specifies the procedural requirements in detail.

Legislation imposes few requirements on the substance of a collective agreement, though the exceptions are significant and expanding. Canadian laws prohibit strikes during the term of a collective agreement, while also requiring that each agreement contain a grievance procedure and a mechanism for the settlement of mid-contract disputes. Despite these restrictions, about 15 per cent of all stoppages occur while a collective agreement is in force. Most of these stoppages are brief and seldom attract legal action.

Separate legislation exists federally and in most provinces for the public sector. These statutes may apply to government employees and to quasi-government employees, such as teachers or hospital workers. They are patterned after private-sector labour relations acts except for two broad areas. The scope of bargaining is restricted by previous civil service personnel practices and broader public policy considerations. In a majority of provinces, there are restrictions on the right to strike of at least some public employees. Police and fire fighters are the most common categories affected by such limits, but there is no other common pattern of restrictions. Employee groups without the right to strike have access to a system of compulsory arbitration. While a statute requires arbitration, the parties normally can determine the procedures to be followed and choose the arbitrator.

THE PROCESSES OF EMPLOYMENT RELATIONS

The major formal process of Canadian employment relations is collective bargaining, with union power based on the ability to strike. Joint consultation is sporadic. Health and safety legislation in all jurisdictions requires joint consultation on those subjects for all but the smallest employers. The parties have initiated consultation outside of any legislative framework in about a quarter of enterprises covering such subjects as product quality, technological change or performance. Other formal systems of worker participation in management are rare, although in an era in which employee involvement systems have become popular more collective agreements have developed novel clauses reflecting this thrust, including some relaxation of strict work rules, multi-skilling and cross-crafting, pay for education and training, and so on. Arbitration of interest disputes is largely confined to the public sector.

Collective bargaining

Collective bargaining is decentralised. The most common negotiating unit is a single establishment—single union, followed by multi-establishment single union. Taken together, these categories account for almost 90 per cent of all units and more than 80 per cent of all employees. Company-wide bargaining is common in the federal jurisdiction, where it occurs in railways, airlines and telecommunications, and in provincially regulated industries concentrated in a single province, such as car or lumber manufacturing.

Despite the decentralised structure of negotiations, bargaining often follows regional patterns. National patterns in bargaining are rare. Instead, one or two key industries in each region usually influence provincial negotiations. In larger provinces, such as Ontario and Quebec, heavy industry patterns from steel, paper or cars often predominate.

The results of bargaining are detailed, complex collective bargaining agreements. Few of the terms are the result of the law; negotiated provisions typically include pay, union security, hours of work and holidays, layoff provisions and miscellaneous fringe benefits. Grievance procedures are legal requirements and invariably conclude with binding arbitration. In addition, there are often supplementary agreements covering work rules for specific situations or work areas. Seniority provisions are prominent features in almost all collective agreements, covering layoffs, promotions or transfers, with varying weight given to length of service or ability.

Given the detail in collective agreements and the parties' preference for litigation, rights arbitrations are frequent and legalistic. In turn, this emphasis on precise written contracts often permeates employment relationships.

Strikes and settlement methods

Another outcome of collective bargaining is labour stoppages, the most controversial feature of Canadian industrial relations. In most years, Canada has lost more working days due to industrial disputes than any other country in this book. From 1986 to 1995, Canada's strike rate was about 2.5 times higher than the average of the 24 nations of the Organization for Economic Co-operation and Development (OECD). There have been frequent allegations—never really proven—that labour unrest has hindered the nation's economic growth. Like other industrialised nations, Canada experienced a steady decline in strikes during the 1990s. Nevertheless, in this decade Canada still lost more working days than any country in this book, although the total time lost usually is below 0.1 per cent of time worked.

Historically, strike levels have moved in cycles. There was a wave of unrest early in the twentieth century, another around World War I, a third beginning in the late 1930s and a fourth in the 1970s. The latest wave abated in 1983, and most measures of disputes have fallen sharply since then. By international standards, the two salient characteristics of Canadian strikes are their length and the concentration of time lost in a few disputes (see Table 4.4). Involvement is medium to low (3 to 10 per cent of union members annually), and the size of strikes is not especially large (350 to 450 workers per strike on average). The largest five or six strikes typically account for 35 per cent of all days lost. In recent years, the average duration of strikes has been 12 to 15 days. These characteristics have not been explained fully.

Conciliation and mediation efforts have long been features of Canadian collective bargaining. There are two models. A tripartite board may be appointed and given authority to report publicly on a dispute. Alternatively, single mediators function without the power to issue a report. In most jurisdictions, participation in some form of mediation is a precondition for a legal strike. Although elements of compulsion have diminished, more than half of all collective agreements are achieved with some kind of third-party intervention.

Apart from the public sector, compulsory arbitration of interest disputes is rare. However, there may be special legislation to end particular disputes in public sector or essential service disputes.

103

Table 4.4   Work stoppages in Canada involving 500 or more
            workers

Period	Total number	Workers Involved	Person-days not worked	% of estimated working time
2008*	10	19 126	113 822	–
2007	27	49 172	1 243 190	0.03
2006	11	27 583	260 230	0.01
2005	41	179 482	3 645 060	0.10
2004	37	236 843	2 396 003	0.07
2003	26	56 730	1 076 560	0.03
2002	31	142 089	2 273 000	0.07
2001	44	189 240	1 296 960	0.04
2000	44	112 468	779 410	0.02
1999	56	127 372	1 415 010	0.04
1998	63	214 847	1 631 460	0.05
1997	32	237 246	2 855 740	0.09
1996	32	250 406	2 484 250	0.08
1995	39	125 531	993 430	0.03
1994	29	55 283	736 470	0.03
1993	25	73 757	498 680	0.02
1992	44	121 831	1 145 810	0.04
1991	36	218 377	1 452 400	0.05
1990	66	226 665	3 520 150	0.12

* 2008 data reflect January–June

Source: <www.hrsdc.gc.ca/en/labour/labour_relations/info_analysis/work_
stoppages/index.shtml> (accessed 21 November 2008)

Back-to-work laws are unpopular with the labour movement and have contributed to the politicisation of employment relations in some areas. In the public sector, interest arbitration is common. Arbitrators are usually chosen on an *ad hoc* basis from among judges or professional arbitrators, who are usually lawyers or academics. The process is legalistic without the use of sophisticated economic data. When collective bargaining first appeared in the public sector, there were concerns that compulsory arbitration would cause bargaining to atrophy. Experience has demonstrated that collective bargaining and compulsory arbitration may be able to coexist successfully, though the availability of arbitration does reduce the incidence of negotiated settlements.

CURRENT AND FUTURE ISSUES

The future of collective bargaining is being questioned in most DMEs. In large measure, this debate revolves around the ability of unions to retain, or even expand, their traditional bases of strength in heavy industry and blue-collar occupations. Though union density in these industries has fallen in Canada, it has not declined in absolute numbers and is still twice as high as that of the United States, for instance. However, Canadian unions have had difficulties similar to their counterparts elsewhere in extending their membership base into the more rapidly growing areas of the service sector and technologically advanced industries. As employment shifts from the goods-producing sectors to services, the historic base of collective bargaining gradually shrinks as a proportion of the labour force. For example, from 1976 to 1998 the proportion of Canadians employed in the bastion of traditional unionism, the goods sector, fell from 32 to 22 per cent. Compared with the non-union employers, the organised elements of the labour force have played a leading role in the expansion of employee rights and improvements in pay and conditions of employment. If collective bargaining becomes confined to declining sectors of the economy, this leading role also will diminish.

This dilemma was exacerbated by sharp declines in Canadian manufacturing employment provoked by the global financial crisis of 2008. Thousands of jobs in that sector, especially in the automobile industry, disappeared when US auto makers cut production. By the end of 2008, the full effects of these changes were still unclear. However, since the 1930s, the leading private sector unions in Canada have been based in heavy manufacturing. These organisations produced innovations in terms and conditions of employment, were heavily involved in politics and constituted a large percentage of provincial federations. It is unlikely that they will be able to retain their influence in the face of severe economic changes.

Years before the 2008 crisis, centres of collective bargaining were under pressure from foreign competition and deregulation, factors common among DMEs. Canada has long relied heavily on foreign trade, so foreign competition is not new. Tariff barriers were reduced slowly in the 1960s and 1970s and more rapidly after the FTA took effect in 1989. The Canadian manufacturing sector, aided by a depreciating currency, responded well to these challenges. The decentralised structure of collective bargaining seems to have facilitated adaptation to economic change. Exports rose steadily, while manufacturing employment was stagnant. These developments were sources of stress for employment-relations institutions, but changes were incremental.

Similar results occurred after deregulation. Governments deregulated product markets in most of the transport and communications sectors in the 1980s and 1990s. In addition, several public enterprises in these sectors were privatised. Employment in the unionised firms in these industries shrank while new competitors were largely non-union. These developments occurred gradually and generally did not provoke disputes.

The immediate future of collective bargaining will be a function of the actions of governments and managers in the face of union economic and political power. Federal and provincial governments continue to respect the legitimacy of collective bargaining and an active labour movement. A review of labour relations in federally regulated industries completed in 1995 found strong support for the institution of collective bargaining among the employment-relations parties, for instance. Legislation and other public policies reflect that commitment, even when most right-of-centre political parties govern. Occasional efforts by right-wing governments to change the legal framework of collective bargaining have failed to upset the basic features of the system.

On balance, it appears that the legislative support for collective bargaining will not change markedly across Canada. However, there is little political support for reform that would appreciably strengthen union power. Given Canada's tilt towards a more right-wing agenda, a more likely scenario is further modest reductions in unions' legal position without a wholesale dismantling of the collective bargaining regime.

Management and collective bargaining

After the 1980s recession, Canadian employers faced similar market forces to their private sector counterparts in other DMEs to reduce costs: foreign trade, increased domestic competition in services and deregulation. Public sector employers were required either to limit or reduce labour costs. The FTA with the United States and NAFTA added to competitive pressures. Many employers responded to these changes by initiating layoffs, which dramatically reduced employment in many industries. The use of part-time and casual workers rose substantially. But there was no general movement to escape unionism.

In industries where unionism was well established, a combination of tradition and legal forces induced Canadian employers to work within the collective bargaining system to meet competitive pressures. Militant anti-unionism is not a popular public position among Canadian employers, although many managers privately express hostility to labour organisations. Major employers' organisations usually advocate cooperative relations with unions and have not called for a deregulation of labour markets. At the company level, surveys of industrial relations and human resource managers show little interest in unseating incumbent unions, although resistance to the spread of unionism may have strengthened.

Legal restrictions on employer tactics make de-unionisation very difficult, and protections for unionism are effective. Employer success in bargaining has diminished pressures for structural changes. The decentralisation of bargaining structures in the private sector, driven by employers, effectively put wages into competition. Negotiated changes in work rules have been frequent, and in the mid-1990s wage freezes and concession bargaining became more common. In a few industries, the parties have negotiated collective agreements with terms as long as six years, typically incorporating wage freezes followed by modest wage increases coupled with employment guarantees for most bargaining unit members. With low rates of inflation, it is difficult for unions to bargain for anything other than very modest pay increases.

At the workplace level in unionised industries, radical reorganisations of work and the implementation of work systems based on high levels of employee commitment have been limited, due to both union resistance and lack of management commitment. Labour generally is concerned that these initiatives have the effect, and perhaps the goal, of reducing workers' support for their unions. Where initiatives have been introduced, the failure rate is relatively high. However, many employers are seeking to move away from the traditional adversarial system of employment relations, especially in manufacturing. Increased consultation and communication by managers with their unions is a common development, for instance. There have been many modest changes in work practices, often outside of formal collective bargaining. However, the lifespan of many of these initiatives appears to be limited.

It is unclear just how much Canadian employers' acceptance of collective bargaining in the face of difficult economic conditions is due to legal protections for unions and collective bargaining and how much it relates to a philosophical agreement with the legitimacy of these institutions. If employers are merely obeying the law, then support for collective bargaining obviously is subject to changing political and legal circumstances. If the support for collective bargaining is cultural, then industrial relations institutions will probably survive and evolve gradually.

Industrial disputes

Historically, the most important issue in Canadian industrial relations has been the incidence of strikes, described above. After a period of frequent strikes in the 1970s and early 1980s, by most measures strike levels fell sharply after 1982, as the economy suffered a severe recession and unemployment rose. The decentralised structure of collective bargaining and reductions of employment in manufacturing virtually eliminated large strikes in the private sector in the 1980s. Most large strikes in the 1990s and after 2000 occurred in the public sector. Despite public concern about strikes, there have been few efforts to deal with their underlying causes or even to understand them better.

Public policies to reduce the incidence of industrial disputes fall into two models. The choice of the models is largely based on the political orientation of the government in power. One is to encourage consultation. During the 1970s and 1980s, several governments took initiatives directed at establishing labour–management consultation as practised in Western Europe. In cases of large-scale layoffs, joint labour–management committees (in union and non-union workforces) were mandated. Later the federal government sponsored tripartite sectoral committees to deal with the effects of restructuring. These committees function well, and their number has expanded slowly, but there still is no evidence that cooperation at this level of the employment-relations system affects the parties' actions at other levels.

Every province requires joint health and safety committees in most workplaces. In unionised organisations, such committees are an avenue of influence outside of collective bargaining. These committees operate in large workplaces, and stoppages or serious disputes over health and safety are rare. However, employers resist vigorously any initiatives to strengthen the statutory authority of health and safety committees. Mandating labour–management cooperation represents a sharp departure from the North American traditions of a limited role for government in the workplace and the maintenance of a clear distinction in collective representation between the unionised and non-union segments.

A second model for dealing with labour unrest has been to impose legislative controls on the exercise of union power. Conservative governments frequently amend legislation to make certification of unions more difficult. When left-of-centre parties take control, they do the opposite. As in Britain and other countries, even though governments in these jurisdictions may legislate against unions, most large employers seem to be reluctant to openly advocate such laws against their workers or the unions that represent them. There is little groundswell of support that would seriously threaten the legitimacy of the current collective bargaining regime, and public opinion supports the institution.

Public sector employment relations

The public sector is the area of Canadian employment relations most subject to change. From the mid-1960s through the 1980s, mature systems of collective bargaining developed in all provinces and the federal government. Beginning with the 1982 recession, governments in several jurisdictions addressed budgetary shortfalls by restricting public sector pay levels. In general, governments dealt with their fiscal problems by legislation rather than bargaining. By 1987, legal restraints had been removed. Early in 1991, the federal government led another round of restrictions on public sector bargaining and compensation. By 1995, a majority of all provinces had imposed restrictions on public sector bargaining as part of programs of fiscal restraint.

One of the most comprehensive restraint programs was the misnamed 'Social Contract' in Ontario. In 1993, an NDP government attempted to negotiate substantial reductions in compensation with more than 100 public sector bargaining agents. When negotiations failed, the government threatened to impose cuts legislatively if agreements were not reached. Under pressure, nearly all unions agreed to cuts in labour costs that did not entail reductions in rates of pay. Compulsory unpaid holidays, for example, became a common feature in the Ontario public sector. These policies split the Ontario labour movement, which had supported the government, generally on public versus private sector lines. The vigorous action by an NDP government marked a shift in the politics of restrictions on public sector collective bargaining. No longer were severe policies regarded as aberrations of right-wing governments. This made it easier for more conservative regimes to impose similar or more severe controls. For example, in 1994 the province of Alberta cut public sector salaries by 5 per cent and cut funding of most social services, including those in health care and education. The split in the Ontario labour movement contributed to the election of an anti-union Conservative government.

Public sector unions protested all the restraint programs, but generally in vain. Governments found that restricting public sector wages and bargaining rights was politically popular. Reliance on legislation or other means to impose freezes or reductions have brought into question the commitment of Canadian governments to collective bargaining systems enshrined in many statutes. Under these circumstances, unions' responses to government initiatives are likely to be political. In the 1980s, public sector unions in Quebec, Ontario and British Columbia (the three most populous provinces) organised major demonstrations and work stoppages that exerted pressure on governments to moderate their policies. A major national strike by a federal public sector union with a tradition of moderation showed that public sector workers could be mobilised when they faced restrictions they regarded as unfair. In the end, however, the government employers prevailed. Led by the federal government, deficit reduction became a dominant theme in the nation's political orthodoxy. Federal government employment fell substantially, and several provincial governments also cut employment as well as pay. In such conditions, the unions could do little to resist these losses.

One of the harshest examples of policies directed against public sector workers and their unions was in British Columbia in 2001. A newly elected right-wing government (misnamed 'Liberal') removed many provisions from public sector collective agreements, mandating contracting out of health sector jobs and the lay-off of over 10 000 employees. The provincial government made no effort to consult with the unions affected by these changes and passed the enabling legislation quickly. Union members demonstrated to no avail. Similar, though less severe, legislation applied to teachers in the public school system.

The health care unions launched a challenge to the law under the Charter of Rights and Freedoms. In a 2007 decision, the Supreme

Court of Canada held that the government had violated the Charter, reversing an earlier line of cases. The legislation in question was not eliminated, but the court extended the protections of the Charter to collective bargaining and stated that the principles in ILO standards should govern the application of this protection in the future.

Years will pass before the full implications of this decision are known. But it is clear that the court has barred the more severe legislation affecting collective bargaining in the public sector.

Apart from legislative action, the practice of free collective bargaining at the level of the federal and provincial governments has been undermined substantially. The frequency of back-to-work legislation in the 1990s through the mid-2000s put unions on notice that they could not defy government fiscal policies at the bargaining table. A pattern developed whereby governments made offers, normally consistent with the economic climate, and then imposed these terms on public sector unions.

Political role of the labour movement

Although many unions and union leaders are active in partisan politics, the labour movement has been unable to define a political role for itself. Officially, the CLC supports the NDP, but this alliance has presented problems. Federally, the NDP has been unsuccessful in raising its share of the popular vote (and legislative seats) beyond about 20 per cent and the labour movement has been unable to deliver large blocs of votes to the federal NDP. Electoral finance reforms in 2003 and 2005 led to the elimination of campaign contributions from either corporations or unions, and individual contributions were capped at a maximum of $1000. Now parties receive government funding proportionate to the votes cast for them, supplemented by party-based fundraising campaigns under new limits.

The liberal market economic model, with limited use of consultation with labour on economic and social policies is more firmly entrenched than ever before. Overall, the political role for labour federally is limited and shows no signs of expanding. Future gains in the status of labour may come through the courts.

Provincially, the situation is different. The NDP has governed in Ontario and three western provinces. Labour's political role is better defined when the NDP is a viable option provincially. However, the labour movement's partisan position provincially risks making labour issues more political and subject to sharp variation after changes of government. Quebec unions have supported independence for the province and have enjoyed great political influence when pro-separatist parties have governed Quebec. Politically, Quebec resembles a coordinated market economy more than other regions in Canada, and labour has a role in major policy deliberations.

The aftermath of the Social Contract in Ontario sharpened labour's dilemma. Public sector unions withheld all support for the NDP in the 1995 election, contributing to the NDP's defeat. This experience revealed that the labour movement had no alternative to the election of the NDP. Punishing the NDP improved the electoral chances of more anti-labour parties. In provinces where the NDP is a viable alternative to the governing party, labour has a voice—although not always a strong one— in public policy, including public sector employment relations.

The state of employment relations is affected by a trend in Canadian society to individualise workers' responsibilities and risks. Canada is not unique in this regard. The Canadian tendency is one of a series of small actions, driven by the same overriding objectives found in other countries. Employers prefer labour to be a commodity— flexible, already trained, but easily disposable. Long-term employment relationships are no longer an expectation of the labour market, and employees are instructed to manage their own careers. Employment systems have increasingly used performance-based pay, and pension plans have changed from defined benefit plans to defined contribution plans. Hours of work have been increased, and the pay premium to unionised workers has been reduced. Wages have been put into competition where production can be moved. When labour shortages appeared after 2000, federal and provincial governments established programs to import thousands of temporary and vulnerable migrant workers from developing countries rather than allowing market forces to raise the wages of domestic workers substantially. Employers use technology to monitor the behaviour of individual employees more closely. Within several industrial sectors, including parts of construction, meatpacking, trucking and logging, de-unionisation has been effected through contracting out, decentralisation of bargaining and deregulation. Service sector employers with multiple branches prevent union inroads by matching negotiated conditions.

Governments have not increased statutory rights for workers in any major way for more than a decade. Enforcement of employment standards is weak at best, and employers have little risk of being charged or punished for evading the law. Even in policy areas where there has been a tradition of labour involvement, such as apprenticeships and health and safety, the role of organised labour is no longer valued highly.

These policies, public and private, have undermined the strength of the labour movement. By 2008, Canadian income differentials were greater than at any time since the 1920s. Neither of the major federal parties, the Liberals and the Conservatives, even pretends to advocate for labour rights. The NDP has been able to exercise only limited influence in opposing these tendencies, mostly at the provincial level. Few Canadians look to unions as an effective agent that might address weaknesses in the Canadian society or economy.

CONCLUSIONS

A major change in the trajectory of Canadian employment relations is unlikely. The employment relations system itself displays few of the overt signs of structural changes found in other DMEs. Unlike the United States, unionism and collective bargaining have not been subjected to an attack by management. By contrast with Britain, it is rare—though not unheard of (such as in Ontario in 1996)—for governments to undertake a sustained anti-union campaign. The labour movement has legitimacy in Canada. It has close ties with the women's movement and consumer groups, for instance. The labour movement is recognised as the spokesperson for workers in economic and social consultations. But the status of organised labour as a factor of production or a major consideration in public policy is being undermined steadily.

Canada's record of moderate economic growth, punctuated by commodity-based booms and busts, provides scant support for politicians or employers who wish to blame collective bargaining or unionism for the economy's performance. The collective bargaining system has responded successfully to most of the changes in economic conditions. There is not much evidence of militancy among Canadian workers of late, which might change if job security is endangered by the global meltdown of 2008. The lack of perceptions of crisis in employment relations has stifled debate over the broader questions of worker representation outside of the traditional strongholds of unions and the conditions of Canadian workers generally. Unless the global economic crisis that began in 2008 creates a direct assault on the stability of the Canadian labour market, the recent pattern of incremental adaptation seems destined to continue.

A CHRONOLOGY OF CANADIAN EMPLOYMENT RELATIONS

1825	Strike by carpenters in Lachine, Quebec for higher wages.
1825–60	Numerous isolated local unions developed.
1867	Confederation—Canada became an independent nation.
1872	Unions exempted from criminal and civil liabilities imposed by British law.
1873	Local trade assemblies formed the Canadian Labour Union, the first national labour central.
1886	Trades and Labour Congress (TLC) formed by 'international' craft unions.
1900	Department of Labour established under the *Conciliation Act*. William Lyon Mackenzie King named first Deputy Minister. First issue of *Labour Gazette* published.
1902	'Berlin Declaration', TLC shunned unions not affiliated to international unions.
1906	Canadian chapter of Industrial Workers of the World founded.
1907	*Canadian Industrial Dispute Investigation Act*—first national labour legislation, emphasised conciliation.
1908	Under the *Government Annuities Act*, the federal Department of Labour administers a plan to help individual Canadians provide for their old age.
1909	*Labour Department Act* creates a separate labour portfolio in the federal government. William Lyon Mackenzie King becomes the first Minister of Labour.
1919	Winnipeg General Strike—most complete general strike in North American history. International Labour Organization established with Canada a founding member.
1921	Canadian and Catholic Confederation of Labour formed; Quebec federation of Catholic unions.
1927	All-Canadian Congress of Labour founded.
1930	*Fair Wages and Eight-Hour Day Act* for workers in the federal jurisdiction; Great Depression leads to the

	passage of the *Unemployment Relief Act* for a system of relief payments to provinces and municipalities.
1935	Following the *National Labor Relations Act* (Wagner Act) in the United States, there are demands for similar Canadian legislation.
1937	Auto workers' strike at General Motors, Oshawa, Ontario establishes industrial unionism in Canada.
1939	TLC expels Canadian affiliates of US Congress of Industrial Organizations (CIO).
1940	CIO affiliates join All-Canadian Congress of Labour to form the Canadian Congress of Labour (CCL); Unemployment Insurance Commission comes under the direction of the federal Department of Labour.
1944	Order-in-Council PC 1003 guarantees unions' right to organise (combining principles of the US Wagner Act with compulsory conciliation). Imposes a legal obligation upon the employer and the employees' bargaining agent to negotiate in good faith; many provinces begin extending PC 1003 to their own labour relations situations or drafting similar legislation between the late 1930s and mid-1940s.
1948	*Industrial Relations and Disputes Investigation Act.* Collective bargaining rights are firmly established in law; Canada Labour Relations Board created in the federal jurisdiction.
1949	Miners in Asbestos, Quebec, strike in defence of law, initiating a 'quiet revolution' in Quebec.
1956	Merger of TLC and CCL to form the Canadian Labour Congress (CLC).
1958	Full-time workers in the federal jurisdiction are guaranteed two weeks of paid vacation per year under the *Annual Vacation Act.*
1960	Canadian and Catholic Confederation of Labour severs ties with the Catholic Church to become the Confederation of National Trade Unions.
1965	Canada Labour (Standards) Code establishes minimum standards for hours of work, wages, vacations and statutory holidays for workers in the federal jurisdiction.
1967	Federal government gives its employees bargaining rights; other jurisdictions follow suit.

1975	Federal government imposes first peacetime wage and price controls.
1977	*Canadian Human Rights Act* is passed, forbidding discrimination against certain groups.
1982	Federal government enacts Charter of Rights.
1984	Protection from sexual harassment is added to the Canada Labour Code.
1986	Joint employer–employee safety and health committees in the workplace are required under the Canada Labour Code. *Employment Equity Act* passed to deal with issues of discrimination.
1987	Charter of Rights and Freedoms (enacted in 1982) takes effect.
1991	Legislated pay freeze imposed on federal government employees.
1994	North American Agreement on Labour Cooperation between Canada, the United States and Mexico. Commits countries to protection of labour standards and enforcement of their own labour laws.
2001	Government of British Columbia removes major sections of collective agreements in the health sector, causing thousands of lay-offs.
2007	Supreme Court of Canada declares collective bargaining by public employees protected by the Constitution by overturning most actions of the British Columbia government in 2001.

CHAPTER 5

Employment relations in Australia

Russell D. Lansbury and Nick Wailes

Australia was colonised by the British, has a wealth of mineral and energy resources and is sparsely populated. In 2008, Australia had a population of 21 million people and a GDP of over US$1 trillion. Out of its total civilian employment of approximately 10 million people, 75 per cent are employed in services, and 20 per cent in manufacturing and construction, Australia's economy, however, remains highly dependent on export earnings from mining and agriculture, which employs only 5 per cent of the total workforce.

Strong economic growth from the middle of the 1980s to 2007, and a reduction in real wages, enabled the labour market to expand and reduced the rate of unemployment. However, deteriorating economic conditions in the late 1980s and early 1990s resulted in a rise in the unemployment rate to 11 per cent in the period 1991–93. With a tightening of government economic policy and a sharp downturn in 1990–91, inflation fell to 1 per cent in 1992–93, but after this began to rise again and reached 4.5 per cent by 2008 amid growing concerns about deterioration of the world economy.

While unemployment remained below 5 per cent from the mid-2000s, it began to rise again with the international economic crisis in 2008. The structure of employment has changed radically in recent years, with a decline in full-time permanent work and the expansion of various kinds of non-standard forms of employment. This has occurred as a result of increases in casual work, temporary jobs, outsourcing and the use of agencies and other labour market intermediaries. As Burgess and Campbell (1998) have noted, the majority of all new jobs created during the 1990s were casual, while part-time jobs represented the fastest-growing area of employment.

THE LEGAL, ECONOMIC AND POLITICAL BACKGROUND

Australia achieved federation in 1901. When the former colonial governments agreed to establish the Commonwealth of Australia, the new federal government was given only a limited jurisdiction over employment and industrial relations. Under the Constitution of the Commonwealth of Australia (1901), the federal government was empowered to make industrial laws only with respect to 'conciliation and arbitration for the prevention and settlement of industrial disputes extending beyond the limits of any one State' (Section 51, para. xxxv). However, the scope of federal powers over industrial relations and other matters gradually expanded, particularly after World War II.

From the late 1980s, there were major changes to the Australian system. In 1988, the Labor government replaced the *Conciliation and Arbitration Act* 1904 with the *Industrial Relations Act* 1988. The name of the Commonwealth Conciliation and Arbitration Commission was changed to the Australian Industrial Relations Commission (AIRC), but its functions remained largely the same. More significant changes were introduced in the *Industrial Relations Reform Act* 1993 (the *Reform Act*), the *Workplace Relations and Other Amendments Act* 1996 (the

Table 5.1   Selected economic variables

Year	Real GDP (% change)	Inflation (% change in CPI)	Unemployment (% of workforce)
2001–02	3.9	2.8	6.3
2002–03	2.8	2.7	6.1
2003–04	3.8	2.5	5.5
2004–05	2.3	2.5	5.1
2005–06	2.8	4.0	4.9
2006–07	3.2	2.1	4.3
2007–08	3.7	4.5	4.2

Sources: ABS 5204.0 *Australian System of National Accounts* (for various years); ABS 6202.0 *Labour Force Australia* (for various years); ABS 6401.0 *Consumer Price Index* (for various years)

Workplace Relations Act) and the *Workplace Relations Amendment Act* 2005 (*Work Choices Act*). The 1993 *Reform Act*, introduced by the Labor government, made it possible to certify non-union collective agreements in the federal jurisdiction for the first time (Bennett 1995). Furthermore, this Act incorporated a right to limited industrial action during the designated 'bargaining period', and thus introduced to Australia the distinction between disputes of 'interest' and 'rights'.

The election of a Liberal–National Coalition government in 1996, after thirteen years of Labor government, heralded further changes to the industrial relations system. The *Workplace Relations Act* 1996 attempted to limit the power of the Australian Industrial Relations Commission, and for the first time made it possible to register individual contracts, known as Australian Workplace Agreements (Pittard 1997; McCallum 1997). Despite attempts by the Howard government to further deregulate industrial relations, a hostile Senate (upper house) blocked further legislative reform until the government was returned with a majority in the Senate in 2005.

The *Work Choices Act* 2005 contained reforms that previously had been rejected by the Senate and introduced fundamental changes to the Australian industrial relations system. Key objectives of the reform package were the creation of a single national system for labour market regulation, expansion of Australian Workplace Agreements (AWAs) that could replace awards, increased restrictions on union activities and a reduced role for the Australian Industrial Relations Commission. The *Work Choices Act* established a new body known as the Australian Fair Pay Commission to establish and adjust minimum rates of pay, exemption from unfair dismissal laws for small to medium sized businesses with fewer than 100 employees, the introduction of five new minimum employment conditions and the removal of the no disadvantage test whereby workplace agreements could previously only be certified if employees were no worse off 'overall' compared with a relevant award.

The *Work Choices Act* proved to be highly controversial, and contributed to the loss of government by the Coalition parties in the 2007 federal election. The union movement launched a high-profile campaign called 'Your Rights at Work', which included television and newspaper advertising and online petitions. The Act imposed significant new restrictions on unions entering workplaces to organise workers and negotiate on their behalf. However, the union campaign against Work Choices emphasised job insecurity and highlighted the removal of rights of workers employed in firms with fewer than 100 employees to appeal against unfair dismissal. The unions gathered

119

strong support from church and community leaders who also spoke out strongly against the 'excesses' of the government's new workplace laws. Although the federal government eventually reintroduced a 'fairness test' for all new agreements, it proved to be too late to blunt the unpopularity of the reforms (Cooper & Ellem, 2008).

One of the most significant aspects of the *Work Choices Act* was changing the constitutional foundation for federal industrial relations legislation from the conciliation and arbitration power to the corporations power. Among other things, this allowed the federal government to directly set minimum terms and conditions of employment without recourse to the making of awards in the settlement of an industrial dispute. Despite challenges from state governments that the law was unconstitutional, the High Court upheld the new law and opened the way for the federal government to exclude state laws, with some specific exceptions. However, despite the federal government extending its powers over industrial relations laws, about 15 per cent of Australian workers are not employed in trading and financial corporations, and are therefore not covered by the Act. Yet the High Court ruling significantly extended the jurisdiction of the federal government in this field.

After Labor's election victory in November 2007, Prime Minister Kevin Rudd and Deputy Prime Minister and Minister for Employment Julia Gillard pledged that the new government would implement a 'fair and balanced' industrial relations policy under the banner of 'Forward with Fairness'. However, as the detail of the policy was revealed, critics argued that it appeared to be 'more a retreat from the excesses of Work Choices than a fundamental recasting of industrial relations' (Hall 2008: 376)

Labor's ability to 'rip up Work Choices' (as it had promised to do) and pass new legislation was limited by the fact that the Coalition parties and independents controlled the Senate. Hence the new government moved cautiously and engaged in prolonged consultation with all interested parties, including the business community. It introduced a transition Bill that disallowed new AWAs and provided for interim statutory individual agreements, listed new legislated national employment standards and ordered the AIRC to begin the process of award modernisation. The main features of the *Fair Work Act* 2009 were as follows:

- Fair Work Australia (FWA) was established as the new employment regulator, replacing six existing bodies including the Australian Industrial Relations Commission. The office of the Fair Work

Ombudsman was established to promote and enforce compliance with the new workplace laws.

- Individual statutory agreements such as AWAs were abolished but individual common law contracts of employment were permitted.
- Ten new National Employment Standards (NES) were established to set minimum conditions for all workers covered by the national system. The NES included provisions for annual leave, personal leave, flexible work arrangements for parents, notice of termination and redundancy pay.
- A new system of 'modern awards' was introduced to provide an additional safety net for most employees.
- Unfair dismissal protection was broadened to cover all workers in enterprises with fewer than fifteen full time equivalent positions. Employees are only excluded if dismissed during a qualifying period of service (generally twelve months in a small business and twelve months in larger enterprises).
- Enterprise flexibility clauses were introduced to allow employees earning more than $100 000 per year to be on arrangements not based on an award.
- Employers and unions are now required to bargain in good faith, although parties are not required to reach an agreement. However, FWA is permitted to make a workplace determination where a party ignores a good faith bargaining order.
- FWA is empowered to settle disputes between parties where there is protracted industrial action which is causing damage to people or the economy.
- No distinction is made between union and non-union agreements but an agreement now requires the approval of employees. A union that has acted as a bargaining agent during negotiations may apply to FWA to be covered by the agreement.
- Union officials are given rights to enter workplaces to hold discussions with employees provided that they hold a permit issued by FWA and that they abide by certain conditions of that permit.
- There is provision for the making of single or multi-purpose agreements, subject to obligations to bargain in good faith, and a test that requires each employee to be better off overall than they would under an applicable award.

The federal government proposed that that both the system of 'modern awards' and the National Employment Standards come into operation on 1 January 2010. Although the government did not hold a majority in the Senate and required support by minor parties to secure the legislation, the Liberal and National Parties declared 'in-principle' support for Labor's proposed changes on the basis that it had secured a mandate in the federal election of 2007. However, division of opinion emerged within the opposition parties as to which parts of the legislation they should agree with or oppose, which led to confusion about their policies after the demise of Work Choices.

THE MAJOR PARTIES

Unions

The establishment of the arbitration system encouraged the rapid growth of unions and employers' associations. By 1921, approximately half of the Australian labour force was unionised. Union density has fluctuated; during the Depression of the early 1930s, it dropped to around 40 per cent. The 1940s witnessed a steady increase in density and a peak of 65 per cent was achieved in 1953.

As in Britain, unionism originally developed on a craft basis; however, with the growth of manufacturing, general and industrial unions became more common. The basic unit of organisation for the Australian union is the branch, which may cover an entire state or a large district within a state. Workplace-level organisation tends to be informal, but shop-floor committees and shop steward organ-isations exist, in both the blue-collar and white-collar sectors (see Peetz 1990).

Union membership in Australia has steadily been declining over the past two decades or more (see Table 5.2). Union density fell from 49 per cent in 1990 to 19.5 per cent in 2007. The reasons for the decline of union membership are complex and varied. A study by Peetz (1998: 82) concluded that 'a reasonable estimate is that around half of the decline in union density in the decade to 1992 can be explained by . . . [structural] factors'. These include changes in the structure of the economy, which has seen contraction of employment in manufacturing, a sector in which unions traditionally have been well organised, and the growth of the service sector, in which unions have been weaker. A related change has been the decline in full-time employment and the rise of non-standard employment. Yet these phenomena have characterised most advanced industrialised countries, not all of which have experienced as much decline in membership as Australian unions. Other factors contributing to the decline of unionism include the growing anti-unionism amongst employers and the removal of institutional arrangements enshrined under the centralised system of arbitration (such as de facto compulsory unionism), which artificially inflated union membership numbers. It has also been suggested that the unions' policies may have contributed to the decline in union membership (see Peetz 1998).

The main confederation for manual and non-manual unions is the Australian Council of Trade Unions (ACTU). It was formed in 1927 and covers around 95 per cent of all unionists. The ACTU expanded considerably following its merger with two other confederations that formerly represented white-collar unions: the Australian Council of Salaried and Professional Associations (ACSPA) joined the ACTU in 1979 and the Council of Australian Government Employee Organisations (CAGEO) followed in 1981.

Under the direction of the ACTU, strategies aimed at reversing membership decline have been put in place by Australian unions in recent years. During the 1990s, the union movement focused on restructuring and amalgamations, which resulted in the merger of 360 federally registered unions into 20 industry-based 'super unions'. The rationale for the creation of these unions was that it would release resources for improved provision of services to members. While the strategy was successful in changing the structure of Australian unions and reducing their number, it did not halt the decline in membership density.

Table 5.2   Recent changes in trade union membership

Year	Trade union coverage (% of workforce)	% change from previous year	Public sector coverage (as a proportion of trade union membership)	Private sector coverage (as a proportion of trade union membership)
2002	23.1	−1.4	46.5	17.7
2003	23.1	0	46.9	17.6
2004	22.7	−1.8	46.4	17.4
2005	22.4	−1.3	47.2	16.8
2006	20.3	−10.3	42.6	15.2
2007	19.5	−4.1	44.1	15.1

Source: ABS 6310.0 *Employee Earnings, Benefits and Trade Union Membership Australia* (for various years)

The strategy adopted by the union movement after the election of the Coalition government in 1996, and the demise of the Accord, was to focus on the principles of 'organising'. Unions have been encouraged to build workplace activism, develop alliances with the broader community and strengthen their capacity for strategic campaigning. The objective is that unions should redefine themselves as more auto-nomous and less dependent on the state. In 1994, the ACTU initiated an 'organising works' program, based partly on the experience of US unions, in order to build their organising skills and capacities of the Australian union movement and to give effect to an 'organising model'. At the ACTU Congress in 2000, a new strategy was launched, Unions@Work, which emphasised the central role of the organising model in building a more inclusive, social movement approach to unionism, and thereby increasing membership (Cooper 2000).

After the defeat of the ALP in the 2004 federal elections, when it was apparent that the Howard government would use its majority in the Senate to introduce radical industrial relations reforms that previously had been blocked by Labor and the minor parties, the ACTU initiated a campaign under the slogan 'Your Rights at Work: Worth Fighting For'. As part of this campaign, the ACTU also organised a series of National Days of Action to publicise 'Your Rights at Work' in capital cities; these attracted crowds of up to 250 000 people. Considerable funds were also expended on advertisements in all the media as well as posters. The union movement mobilised large numbers of its members to campaign against the Howard government in marginal electorates and contributed significantly to the government's defeat in 2008 (Cooper & Ellem 2008).

Employers' associations

The early growth of unions in Australia encouraged the development of employers' associations and led them to place greater emphasis on industrial relations functions than their counterparts in some other countries. Numerous employers' associations have a direct role or interest in industrial relations (Plowman 1989). However, there is variation in the size and complexity of employers' associations, from small, single-industry bodies to large organisations that attempt to cover all employers within a particular state. In 1977, the Confederation of Australian Industry (CAI) was established as a single national employers' body, almost 50 years after the formation of the ACTU. In 1983, a group of large employers set up the Business Council of Australia (BCA), partly as a result of their dissatisfaction with the ability of the CAI to service the needs of its large and diverse membership. Membership of the BCA comprises the chief executive officers of Australia's largest corporations, which has given it a high profile and significant authority when it makes pronouncements on matters such as employment relations.

Disunity and fragmentation have been ongoing problems for employers' bodies. Since the mid-1980s there have been several important secessions from the CAI. These included large affiliates such as the Metal Trades Industry Association (MTIA) in 1987 and the Australian Chamber of Manufacturers (ACM) in 1989. One repercussion has been employers airing different viewpoints at events such as National Wage Case hearings. In 1992, the CAI attempted to present a more united front and to attract back former affiliates by merging with the Australian Chamber of Commerce to form a new organisation, the Australian Chamber of Commerce and Industry (ACCI).

There were further changes in employer representation after the election of the pro-business Liberal and National Coalition government in 1996. One major development was the trend of employer associations shifting from providing industrial advocacy and introducing a range of fee-based services for members. This shift can in part be said to reflect the decline of the centralised bargaining system, and the need for advocacy. Sheldon and Thornthwaite (1999) argue that this produced growing competition between employers' organisations for members and encouraged the consolidation of employers' associations. Most notable amongst these was the 1998 merger of the MTIA and ACM to form the Australian Industries Group (AiG).

During the 2007 election campaign, schisms occurred within the ranks of the employers' bodies. The ACCI and the BCA strongly defended Work Choices and criticised the policy platform of the Labor Party, arguing that any 'roll-back' of Work Choices would risk an upsurge of industrial disputes and that a Labor government would be captive to union interests. The ACCI criticised the Coalition government when it introduced a 'fairness test' during the 2007 election campaign in an attempt to deflect criticisms that it policies were unduly harsh. However, the ACCI was a key organiser of an employer-funded advertising campaign, under the banner of the National Business Action Fund Limited, in which nineteen employer associations sought to defend the government's industrial relations reforms (Hearn MacKinnon 2008). While a supporter of the Work Choices regime, the AiG declined to contribute funds to the ACCI/BCA-led employer advertising campaign and declared that it was a non-partisan employers' organisation. After its election victory, the

125

Labor government appointed the AiG chief executive, Heather Ridout, to a number of advisory committees to represent employers while the other employer associations were less favourably treated.

Government

The powers of the federal government over industrial relations, as noted previously, were limited under the Constitution until the High Court's ruling on the corporations power in 2007. The lack of legislative power, particularly over prices and incomes, had frustrated federal governments of all political persuasions.

The Howard coalition government hastened the move to a more deregulated employment relations system through its *Workplace Relations Act* 1996. The main policy changes in the Act included a reduction in the role and importance of awards, which would be limited to an enforceable safety net of minimum wages and conditions; new arrangements for enterprise bargaining, which included individual agreements without union intervention; and removal of restrictions on the use of particular types of labour and hours of work. Although the minor parties holding the balance of power in the Senate forced a number of amendments to the government's original Bill, the principal reforms were retained in the new Act.

The election victory of 2004, which delivered majorities to the Howard Coalition government in both the House of Representatives and, from 2005, the Senate, opened the way to the most radical industrial relations reforms in Australia since 1904. Although the Howard government had advocated 'deregulating' the labour market, Work Choices was a most ambitious attempt to 'reregulate' industrial relations. It represented a comprehensive attack on arbitration, unions and collective bargaining that even took many employers by surprise. In fact, a number of larger employers in major industries, such as automotive manufacturing, rushed to make agreements with their unions under the pre-Work Choices legislation because it gave them greater freedom and scope to include matters that were important to them but were excluded under the new regime.

Despite the unpopularity of Work Choices in the wider electorate, which assisted the ALP to victory in the 2007 federal election, the Rudd Labor government proceeded very cautiously with changes to the legislation. Nevertheless, the effects of the Howard government's use of the corporations power have given subsequent federal governments greater power to legislate on industrial relations.

EMPLOYMENT RELATIONS PROCESSES

Historically, the Australian system of conciliation and arbitration was based on the assumption that the processes of conciliation would be exhausted before arbitration was undertaken. The system of arbitration was compulsory in two senses. First, once engaged, it required the parties in dispute to submit to a mandatory procedure for presenting their arguments. Second, tribunal awards were binding on the parties in dispute. Awards specified minimum standards of pay and conditions which an employer must meet or else face legal penalties. However, unions and employers were free to negotiate above these minimum standards. It is necessary to distinguish between the formal provisions of the arbitration system and the way it worked in practice. In reality, there has always been a considerable amount of direct negotiation between the parties. Agreements directly negotiated between employers and unions coexist with or take the place of arbitrated awards. When these agreements were ratified by the Commission, they were known as 'consent awards' and could deal comprehensively with the terms and conditions of work in particular workplaces or supplement existing agreements. In this way, awards were more flexible in practice than they appeared to be in a formal sense.

There was considerable growth of informal direct bargaining in Australia during the 1970s (Niland 1976). While this was halted by attempts by the Commission to control wages in the early 1980s, by the late 1980s there were attempts to foster more collective bargaining within limits set by the Commission (McDonald & Rimmer 1989). The trend towards greater decentralisation of employment relations processes increased during the 1990s in response to economic recession and growing political pressures. The *Industrial Relations Reform Act* 1993 extended the scope for enterprise bargaining by reducing the ability of the Commission to vet union negotiated enterprise agreements and by introducing Enterprise Flexibility Agreements (EFAs). These allowed workplace agreements to be negotiated in non-unionised workplaces. The Commission retained a role in ensuring that the terms and conditions of EFAs did not disadvantage employees when compared with the relevant award. However, EFAs laid the foundation for AWAs, which were introduced by the Howard government after its election in 1996.

This tendency was further enhanced by the legislative reforms of the Howard government. A key element of these reforms was the introduction of Australian Workplace Agreements (AWAs), which enabled (and sought to encourage) employers to enter into individual (non-union) contracts with their employees. While the Rudd Labor government has abandoned AWAs, and has established a new regulatory body, Fair Work Australia, it has continued to emphasise the role of collective bargaining but has not reverted to compulsory arbitration.

THE SETTLEMENT OF DISPUTES

One of the principal motivations behind the introduction of compulsory arbitration was to render strikes unnecessary. The 'rule of law' provided under arbitration was supposed to displace the 'barbarous expedient of strike action' (Macintyre & Mitchell 1989). For many years, the *Conciliation and Arbitration* Act contained a provision making strike activity illegal and subject to penalties. Although this provision was removed in 1930, Australian workers in the federal system were granted a qualified and limited right to strike only in 1993.

The 1993 *Reform Act* provided unions and employers with a period of immunity from common law and secondary boycott actions associated with strikes and lockouts. Under this Act, either party could notify the other of its intention to use industrial action during the designated bargaining period. The Commission could intervene and make use of its traditional arbitral functions if it believed that the parties were not acting in good faith, if there was little likelihood of an agreement being reached or on the grounds of public interest. In seeking to resolve the dispute, parties engaging in unlawful strikes could be fined as well as have their awards suspended or cancelled. The Howard government maintained a limited right to strike during the designated bargaining period in its *Workplace Relations Act* 1996, and strengthened the Commission's powers to address illegal industrial action, prohibited the payment and acceptance of pay or wages for workers when involved in strike action and restored secondary boycott provisions to the *Trade Practices Act*, with substantial fines for breaches.

Another older sanction, used sparingly by tribunals, has been to deregister a union that has acted in defiance of a tribunal order. Since deregistration has tended to be difficult and complex, tribunals have generally hoped that the threat of this sanction would be sufficient. However, threats made little impact on the Builders Labourers' Federation, deregistered in 1986; its members were quickly absorbed by other unions, leaving only the shell of a once-powerful union.

During the 1980s and 1990s, average working days lost through disputes per 1000 employees were halved. Beggs and Chapman (1987) argue that while changing macro-economic conditions played a part in this absolute and relative decline in the impact of industrial stoppages, so did the Accord. While the Australian strike rate in 2000 was above the OECD average, it was much lower than in the previous decade and almost ten times lower than in 1980. However, it is doubtful whether the reduction in industrial disputation in Australia can be ascribed to activities of the Howard government, as the decline in strike activity began during the previous Labor government's period in office.

There has been an increase in the use of employer-initiated industrial action to support non-union agreements among private sector employers (Ellem 2001). Several high-profile disputes have been sparked by employers attempting to introduce non-union agreements in areas such as mining and the maritime industries, which traditionally were strongly unionised (Briggs & Cooper 2006). Such employers have been actively seeking to eliminate unions from their operations and activities by the use of lock-outs, a tactic that increased significantly under the Howard government (Briggs 2005).

The *Work Choices Act* 2005 further eroded the role of the Australian Industrial Relations Commission (AIRC) in dispute settlement by removing its compulsory arbitral power. Although it might have been expected that a Labor government would restore the role of the AIRC, the arbitral powers of the Commission were subsumed by Fair Work Australia and it could only intervene where there was a breakdown or intractable wage negotiations between employers and unions, or where industrial action was causing significant economic harm to the parties.

THE DETERMINATION OF WAGES

The arbitration system led to the development of a relatively centralised wages system in Australia. This has been achieved by increasing the influence of the federal tribunal over key wage issues, despite constitutional limitations. The federal tribunal initially became involved in fixing a minimum wage in 1907 when it described the 'basic wage' as being intended to meet 'the normal needs of an average employee, regarded as a human being living in a civilised community'. The basic (male) wage was set at a level sufficient to cover the minimum needs of a single income family unit of five and became the accepted wage for unskilled work. The rate for women workers was set at 57 per cent of the basic wage. The custom of wage differentials (margins) for skills was formalised in the 1920s, based largely on historical differentials in the metal and engineering trades (Hancock 1984).

The Commission and its predecessors thus began to regulate wages and differentials through decisions on the 'basic wage' and 'margins' at National Wage Case hearings. These were much-publicised rituals and occurred at regular intervals, usually with one National Wage Decision per year. The employers, unions (through the ACTU) and governments (at federal and state levels) each made submissions to the Commission, which later handed down its decision.

The dominant feature of Australian wage determination from 1983–96 was a social compact called the Price and Incomes Accord (the Accord), originally negotiated between the ALP and the ACTU prior to the 1983 election (Accord Mk 1) and renegotiated seven times between 1985 and 1996 (Accords Mk 2–8). Under the Accord, the government and the ACTU presented a joint submission to the National Wage Case. For most of this period, with the notable exception of Accord Mk VI in 1990/1, the Commission largely accepted these proposals and introduced wage principles designed to give them effect.

In its initial stages, the Accord led to centralisation of wage determination in Australia. The first Accord was essentially a voluntary incomes policy in which the ACTU pledged the union movement to making no extra claims in wage bargaining in return for the reintroduction of wage indexation. For its part, the government pledged—among other things—to introduce a range of reforms to the taxation system, to increase the 'social wage' and to implement a range of industry policies (Lansbury 1985; Rimmer 1987).

The election of the Howard government in 1996 ended the Accord and its role in shaping wages policy. The *Workplace Relations Act 1996* further decentralised wage determination in Australia. This Act retained the award stream and the mechanism of safety net adjustments but reduced the ability of the AIRC to vet outcomes of non-union enterprise agreements and also introduced AWAs, which are a new non-union individual stream of wage bargaining.

This continued decentralisation of wage bargaining led to further wage dispersion in Australia. In 1997, the AIRC established a federal minimum wage across industries and occupations set at the lowest level of the Metal Industries Award. However, minima continued to fall behind average weekly earnings, and in 2000 the basic federal minimum weekly rate for adult full-time workers was 46 per cent of average weekly earnings, compared with 58 per cent for females. Indeed, wages dispersion in Australia increased at a faster rate than in most Continental European member nations of the OECD.

Under Work Choices, the responsibility for setting minimum wages passed from the Australian Industrial Relations Commission to the

Australian Fair Pay Commission (AFPC), which had the power to determine its own processes and procedures for setting minima. Although the AFPC was expected it to adhere strictly to government policy, it surprised the union movement by initially setting more generous minima than advocated by the Howard government. However, the AFPC did not have the independence of the AIRC and the initial appointments tended to reflect the political preferences of the Howard government. Its decisions focused mainly on macroeconomic considerations rather than the broader principles followed by the AIRC. The Rudd Labor government replaced the AFPC with a Minimum Wages Panel under Fair Work Australia.

CURRENT ISSUES

Unemployment and working hours

After experiencing full employment and labour shortages for much of the past decade, the official unemployment rate in Australia rose from 4.3 per cent in mid-2008 to 5.3 per cent in mid-2009 and was expected to continue to rise due to the recession caused by the global financial crisis. However, the government's economic stimulus package was credited with keeping the unemployment rate to 5.3 per cent (by February 2010). At the same time, the CPI declined from 4.5 per cent to 2.0 per cent from 2008 to 2009. The participation rate also declined from 65.3 per cent to 64.7 per cent during this period. The rising levels of unemployment have put downward pressure on wages and conditions. Employers tend to prefer to hire workers on temporary contracts during difficult economic times, and often switch to casual or part-time workers. Unions find their bargaining powers are reduced and their membership levels decline. The results of rising levels of unemployment include deepening inequality and increased levels of debt.

Under-employment is also a growing problem, as many workers are employed for fewer hours and at levels below their qualifications and skills. Studies have revealed that a high proportion of part-time workers desire more hours of work, often in order to maintain their standard of living. Conversely, as full-time workers are expected to work longer hours, often without receiving overtime pay for the extra hours worked, many want fewer hours. Recent data reveal that one in five workers is employed for more than 50 hours a week and full-time workers are at work for an average of 44 hours per week. Almost 30 per cent want to work fewer hours each week.

The Rudd government has included 'the right to request flexible working arrangements' as one of the ten new National Employment Standards (NES). This provision allows parents of a child under school age to request a change in working arrangements to care for the child, such as changes in hours of work, patterns of work and location of work. Eligibility for the provision is limited to employees who have twelve months' service with an employer and long-term casual employees. However, an employer can refuse a request on 'reasonable business grounds', and the employee has no avenue of appeal. Concerns have been expressed by academics and other interested parties that employers should be required to consider requests seriously, that compliance mechanisms need to be strengthened and that employees should have the right to appeal (Charlesworth & Campbell 2008). British experience suggests that these provisions will be confined to women unless a 'universal care-giver/worker model is adopted which encourages and facilitates both men and women to work part time and spend time in care work' (Himmelweit 2007).

Gender equality at work

Women comprise 48 per cent of the paid workforce in Australia, and labour force participation rates for women (15–65 years of age) are 58 per cent compared with men's participation rate of 72 per cent. While Australia's female participation rates are not as high as those of many other comparable developed economies, they have gradually been increasing in recent years. However, women have not fared as well as men in the labour market, as their wages have been lower, they have been concentrated in low-paid areas of work, and they have been disadvantaged in terms of entitlements such as paid leave for illness and holidays.

The gender pay gap has remained at around 16 per cent in recent years, although there are differences between state and industry sectors (see Preston & Jefferson 2007). In the past, major advances to achieving pay equity came from test cases in the AIRC, where wage increases were achieved through the application of equal pay principles. However, these advances were stalled after the passage of the *Work Choices Act* 2005. Furthermore, changes introduced by Work Choices had a negative impact on women, particularly in relation to unfair dismissal and job security, and to receiving fair and correct pay (Pocock et al. 2008). Enterprise bargaining had only limited success in promoting pay equity, as many women were located in industries and jobs that provided little bargaining power, such as retailing and hospitality. The plight of female workers, their low pay, job insecurity and lack of adequate child care were highlighted by the ACTU campaign against Work Choices (Muir 2008).

The new *Fair Work Australia Act* 2009 promised to improve the situation for women at work. According to the ACTU, it would 'remove any doubt that the pay equity principle is not limited to where the "same" work is done but clearly includes "similar" work' (ACTU 2008: 16). The new legislation enabled FWA to make orders requiring equal remuneration for work of equal or comparable value. This replaced the more limited provision of 'equal remuneration for work of equal value'. Applicants seeking an equal remuneration order would not need to prove that discrimination had caused the gender pay gap. This removed the high threshold of proving that discrimination had occurred, as was required by the previous *Workplace Relations Act*, which had discouraged any successful equal remuneration case from being conducted at the federal level (Smith & Lyons 2006: 28).

The *Fair Work Act* also introduced a new multi-employer bargaining stream for low-paid employees, in recognition of the fact that low-paid employees often lacked the skills and bargaining power to engage in effective enterprise bargaining. FWA has an obligation to facilitate agreement making for low-paid employees and to guide them through the agreement-making process. Unlike other bargaining streams, FWA is able to enforce good-faith bargaining provisions to progress bargaining for low-paid employees and also make determinations. It was estimated that up to 20 per cent of the workforce would be eligible to engage in this bargaining stream, many them women.

Australia's lack of a universal and comprehensive paid maternity leave scheme has been a subject of considerable discussion in recent years (see Baird & Charlesworth 2007). A confusing mix of arrangements has existed in the private and public sectors of the economy, which resulted in around 55 per cent of the female working population having no access to paid maternity leave. Only about one-third of mothers at work actually use paid maternity leave (Whitehouse et al. 2006), and just under half of all organisations with 100 or more employees provide paid maternity leave according to the Equal Opportunity for Women in the Workplace Agency (EOWA 2008) Furthermore, it is estimated that only around 22 per cent of current enterprise agreements include a paid maternity leave clause.

However, the Rudd government announced in the 2009 federal budget that it would introduce eighteen weeks of parental leave from 2011 for working parents with primary care responsibility for a newborn child.

Employee participation in decision-making

There has been continuing debate about the degree to which employees have influence over decisions that affect them in the workplace. Evidence from the Australian Workplace Industrial Relations Surveys (AWIRS) in 1990 and 1995 revealed that the proportion of workplaces with joint consultative committees increased from 14 to 33 per cent during this period, although they were more prevalent in large workplaces with 500 or more employees. However, when managers were asked whether they had consulted workers about important changes that had affected their workplaces during the previous year, only 29 per cent responded positively and only 18 per cent said that employees had a significant input into decisions (Morehead et al. 1997: 244).

The merits of statutory mandated works councils as a means of employees gaining greater influence in decision-making at the enterprise level continue to be debated (Gollan et al. 2002). McCallum (1997) argues that legislation is needed to strengthen 'industrial citizenship' and give employees the right to participate in workplace governance. He proposes the establishment of electoral works councils in enterprises with 100 or more employees. These councils would consult with employers on a wide range of issues including the introduction of technological change, rostering agreements and amenities (see also McCallum & Patmore 2002).

Opposition to works councils in Australia has been based on concerns that there is an absence of preconditions that would enable them to function as effective vehicles for collective representation and social protection. Buchanan and Briggs (2002) argue that the resurgence of managerialism and employer militancy, and a lack of commitment among employers to 'social partnership' strategies, mean that works councils are likely to entrench managerial prerogatives rather than reverse the 'representation gap' left by declining unionisation. Their view is that works councils should be considered only after there have been measures implemented to address deepening inequalities and rebuilding of coordinated bargaining structures and collectivism. Yet there is a growing concern, even among union leaders, that it is necessary to look beyond traditional union and workplace structures 'to secure for employees a genuine democratic right to information and consultation' (Combet 2003). Simply waiting for a revival of union membership will forego an opportunity to introduce alternative forms of employee voice and representation, which would strengthen the role of workers in decision-making within the enterprise, such as statutory works councils (Lansbury & Wailes, 2003; Lansbury 2009).

CONCLUSIONS

The 1990s were a period of significant change in Australian employment relations as the shift towards a more decentralised form of labour market regulation, begun by a Labor government, gained increased momentum under a Liberal–National Coalition government. By the turn of the new century, the emphasis was on individualistic rather than collectivist approaches to employment relations, in which industrial tribunals played a diminished role and unions increasingly were marginalised. There was less consensus between employers, unions and government about future directions of employment relations than had existed under a more centralised system in the past. With the decline of unionisation, employers' organisations became less powerful and employers advocated more enterprise-based approaches to employment relations. Employers continued to place greater emphasis on human resource strategies with a diminished role for unions. While there was increased involvement of employees in informal participation activities, employers were reluctant to establish more formal mechanisms of joint consultation with employees. Unions attempted to arrest their decline in membership by focusing more directly on organising and strengthening representation at the workplace level.

The unpopularity of the *Work Choices Act* played a key role in the election of the Rudd Labor government in 2007. Labor's 'Forward with Fairness' policy on industrial relations promised to restore unfair dismissal rights to workers in enterprises with fifteen or more employees, end AWAs and introduce good-faith bargaining by employers with unions. A new industrial relations body, Fair Work Australia, assumed most of the responsibilities of the existing labour market institutions, including the arbitral powers of the AIRC. Concerns were expressed by unions that the Rudd government intended to retain key aspects of the *Work Choices Act* that restricted unions' access to workplaces and their ability of unions to undertake industrial action, except in limited circumstances. By basing their legislative reforms on the corporations power rather than the more limited industrial relations power in the Australian Constitution, the Howard government greatly expanded the influence of the federal government over labour market regulation. This was embraced by the Rudd Labor government, which also sought to establish a unified system and reduce the role of the states and their industrial relations tribunals. Hence the Work Choices legislation introduced fundamental changes in the Australian industrial relations system, which will continue to have long-term consequences for the future.

A CHRONOLOGY OF AUSTRALIAN EMPLOYMENT RELATIONS

1788	European settlers arrive in New South Wales, with separate British colonies established subsequently.
1856	Building unions win recognition of the eight-hour day. The Melbourne Trades Hall Council is formed.
1879	First Inter-Colonial Trade Union Conference.
1890–94	The Great Strikes. Following defeat by combined employer and colonial government power, unions found Labor Parties in each colony.
1901	Commonwealth of Australia founded.
1904	Commonwealth Conciliation and Arbitration Court established under the *Commonwealth Conciliation and Arbitration Act*, with powers of legal enforcement.
1907	The *Harvester Case* establishes the principle of the basic wage above which the court could award a margin for skill.
1927	Founding of the Australian Council of Trade Unions (ACTU).
1929	The Conservative government is defeated in a federal election in which proposals to weaken powers of the Conciliation and Arbitration Court are a major issue.
1956	Following the *Boilermakers' Case*, the Arbitration Court is disbanded. The Conciliation and Arbitration Commission set up with arbitral functions, and the Industrial Court with judicial responsibility.
1972	A federal Labor government is elected after 23 years of Liberal Coalition government.
1975	Wage indexation introduced; Labor government defeated.
1981	Wage indexation abandoned.
1983	Hawke Labor government elected. ALP-ACTU Prices and Incomes Accord becomes the lynch-pin of government policy. Return to centralised wage fixation and full wage indexation. Formation of Business Council of Australia.
1985	Report of the Committee of Review of Australian

	Industrial Relations Law and Systems (the Hancock Report).
1988	Elaboration of structural efficiency principle; reforms to the federal *Industrial Relations Act*.
1989	Award restructuring; domestic airline pilots' dispute.
1991	National Wage Case decision in October condones shift to more enterprise bargaining. Paul Keating replaces Bob Hawke as Prime Minister.
1992	Further movement towards decentralisation of bargaining, including amendments to the federal *Industrial Relations Act.*
1993	Keating Labor government re-elected for an unprecedented fifth consecutive term of Labor government.
1994	The *Industrial Relations Reform Act* 1993 comes into operation and extends the scope of enterprise bargaining.
1996	Election of Liberal–National Party Coalition government led by John Howard.
1997	The *Workplace Relations and Other Legislation Amendment Act* 1996 is proclaimed.
1999	The Howard government's attempts to introduce further industrial relations reforms through the More Jobs Better Pay Bill is rejected by the Senate.
2001	The Liberal–National Party Coalition government led by John Howard is elected for a further three-year term.
2005	The Liberal–National Party coalition government, led by John Howard, is elected for a record third term with a majority in the Senate.
2006	The *Workplace Relations Amendment (Work Choices) Act* 2005 comes into force.
2007	A Labor government, led by Kevin Rudd, is elected in an election in which industrial relations reforms feature strongly.
2009	The Rudd government's *Forward with Fairness Act* is passed by the Senate with minor amendments.

CHAPTER 6

Employment relations in Italy

Lucio Baccaro and Valeria Pulignano

The Italian employment relations system traditionally has baffled comparative scholars, who have had a hard time placing it into cross-country classificatory schemes—both those issuing from the literature on corporatism and, more recently, those based on the Varieties of Capitalism literature (Hall & Soskice 2001). Italy has seemed to lack the institutional and organisational features (e.g. social-democratic dominance of government, highly centralised interest associations) once considered conducive to corporatist policy-making, yet corporatist agreements were often attempted and sometimes surprisingly agreed upon. Also, while the Italian industrial relations system appeared to share several features with 'coordinated market economies'—for example, centralised bargaining—the absence of a well-developed apprenticeship system specialising in the production of industry-specific skills and of cooperative institutions at the workplace level, like the German works councils, made it a mixed case that did not fall clearly into either the 'liberal' or the 'coordinated' camp (Thelen 2001).

Within Italy, the tone of the academic debate has often been one of engaged critique, if not reproach. Italian industrial relations has appeared chaotic, poorly institutionalised and not sufficiently mature when compared with the industrial relations of other advanced countries. For a long time, the main problem has been perceived to rest with the Italian unions' militancy and political divisions, and with their unwillingness to compromise on a much-needed policy of centralised wage moderation. The absence of a clear set of agreed-upon rules has also frequently been singled out as a significant factor. The failure of national agreements in the early 1980s, and the decentralisation of collective bargaining that ensued, provided empirical support for these critical views.

Beginning with the early 1990s, the situation of Italian employment relations changed dramatically. With a series of centralised agreements, governments, unions and (to a lesser extent) organised employers spearheaded a new era of social pacts and collaborative policy-making in Europe. The architecture of collective bargaining was thoroughly reformed in 1993, and the linkages across bargaining levels became much more rational and institutionalised than they had ever been before.

The main argument of this chapter is that since the early 1990s the Italian industrial relations system has been evolving (by no means linearly) towards a new kind of corporatism (Rhodes 1996, 2001; Streeck 2000; Baccaro 2007). The unions have been involved in all the major policy-making decisions of the last fifteen years, even though they have sometimes disagreed among themselves about the desirability of specific measures. However, centralised negotiations have produced few of the redistributive and decommodifying outcomes that once characterised Scandinavian corporatism. The new corporatism that has emerged in Italy, as well as in other countries, has mobilised societal support for an austerity-based economic policy based on moderate wage growth and tightly controlled public expenditures, while economic inequality has been allowed to increase. While the recent Italian economic woes (stagnating economic growth, growing inequalities and a widespread sense of economic insecurity) have many causes, the new Italian corporatism possibly has contributed to them by enforcing a multi-year policy of wage restraint. Additionally, the Italian corporatism has done nothing to stem the erosion of the union's organisational strength. The unionisation rate has declined steadily since the early 1980s, and current density rates in the private sector (estimated to be less than 20 per cent) make one wonder whether, with labour so weak where it matters most—among the workers—corporatism has become an empty shell.

The remainder of this chapter is organised as follows. We begin with an historical reconstruction of Italian industrial relations until 1992, a year we regard as a watershed. We then examine the actors and the process of employment relations respectively. We conclude with an overview of current and future challenges.

THE DEVELOPMENT OF ITALIAN EMPLOYMENT RELATIONS PRIOR TO 1992

The trajectory of Italian employment relations after World War II was strictly linked to the evolution of the Italian political system as a whole. In 1944, union groups of different ideological orientations (Communists, Socialists, Catholics and others) joined ranks and established a unitary union confederation, the Confederazione Generale Italiana del Lavoro (CGIL). The unions' organisational structures were reconstituted almost from scratch and were populated by party personnel who often lacked specific union experience (Romagnoli & Treu 1981; Turone 1992).

With the onset of the Cold War, the unity of anti-fascist forces vanished, both at the governmental and the union level. The left-wing parties (Communist Party, Socialist Party and the smaller Action Party) were pushed out of government in 1947, and a coalition of Christian Democrats and smaller centrist parties ruled. In 1950, both the Catholic faction and the republican/social democratic factions quit the CGIL to establish independent union confederations: the Confederazione Italiana Sindacati dei Lavoratori (CISL) and the Unione Italiana dei Lavoratori (UIL), respectively.

In the 1950s, Italian trade unions were particularly weak. Businesses took advantage of the slack labour market to purge their factories of union activists (Pugno & Garavini 1974; Accornero 1976). Unionisation rates declined dramatically. In the metalworking sector, for example, the unionisation rate collapsed from 60 per cent in 1951 to 20.3 per cent in 1960 (Pizzorno et al. 1978: 295).[1] Furthermore, collective bargaining was almost completely centralised at the national level.

The prevalence of centralised collective bargaining was the result of several factors. Centralisation was in the interests of Confindustria, the major business association, because it tightly linked labour costs in the most dynamic industrial sectors to the economic conditions prevailing in more backward sectors, like agriculture. Also, trade unions lacked the organisational infrastructure needed for decentralised collective bargaining. Their plant-level representation structures were either weak or non-existent. Even where they were present, they were scarcely effective. Furthermore, the CGIL regarded organisational centralisation with suspicion because it feared that decentralised structures would either develop into company unions or would become too autonomous, and hence endanger the Communist Party's control over the working class (Cella 1976; Garavini 1976).

The 1950s were instead golden years for organised business (Locke 1995: 71). Due to the centralisation of collective bargaining, wages lagged below productivity in these years (Salvati 1984). Strikes were rare, and when they occurred their motivation was predominantly political (Bordogna & Provasi 1989: 297–82). Wage moderation and labour quiescence contributed to create the preconditions for the low-cost, export-oriented strategy of economic growth from which emerged the economic miracle of the late 1950s and early 1960s.

Italian industrial relations changed dramatically in the 1960s. Labour market conditions became much more favorable to labour, especially in the northwestern parts of the country. Also, the political alliance between Christian Democrats and Socialists—which led to the emergence of a series of centre-left governments, as well as theological innovations introduced by the Council Vatican II that encouraged dialogue between Catholics and Marxists—eased many of the ideological tensions that had divided the labour camp in previous years. With the diffusion and consolidation of Fordist models of work organisation in large firms, trade unions began devoting far more attention and resources to negotiating work conditions at the shop-floor level than had previously been the case.

With the so-called 'Hot Autumn'—a massive wave of strikes initiated by popular demonstrations over pension reform in 1968, which continued during the 1969–72 collective bargaining round—political divisions within the Italian labour movement were overcome from below (Pizzorno et al. 1978; Sabel 1982). In many industrial plants, especially in the metalworking industry, the three union confederations embraced unity of action. In 1972, there was a partial reunification of the Italian labour movement with the establishment of the so-called Federazione Unitaria CGIL-CISL-UIL. This unitary federation did not replace the old union confederations. Rather, it sought to create closer links among them through various coordination structures (Lange & Vannicelli 1982).

The Hot Autumn introduced a number of innovations in collective bargaining. Campaigns for the unification of blue- and white-collar job classification schemes, the abolition of territorial differences in wage levels, demands for equal wage increases for all workers regardless of skill levels, improvements in health and safety conditions, and reductions in the speed and duration of work were all promoted in these years.

During this period, the national industry federations were able to absorb and generalise the most innovative practices introduced in large industrial establishments, and consequently considerably increased their power (Romagnoli & Treu 1981: 165–97; Santi 1983). The metalworking federations of CGIL, CISL and UIL, together with the unitary Federazione Lavoratori Metalmeccanici (FLM), acted as vanguards for the whole labour movement (Golden 1988). They consistently practised unity of action and used their power to push for higher wages, limit overtime, regulate lay-offs, restrict internal mobility and slow down the pace of work.

The Hot Autumn overturned virtually all the social, political and economic patterns established in the post-war period. Its repercussions on the Italian strategy of export-led development were, however, disastrous. Between 1970 and 1974, unit labour costs increased 59.5 per cent. Inflation rates jumped from 5 per cent in 1970 to 21.2 per cent in 1974, also due to the first oil shock. Italy became the advanced industrialised country with the highest levels of industrial conflict (Bordogna & Provasi 1989: 285). Squeezed between higher wages, shorter work weeks and more stringent labour regulation, firm profits dropped sharply (Barca & Magnani 1989: 27–38). Consequently, Italy's competitiveness on international markets deteriorated sharply. In just a few years, Italy's current balance turned from positive (3.1 per cent in 1968) to negative (–1.7 per cent in 1973). According to OECD estimates, Italy lost ten market-share points in 1973 alone (OECD 1984: 31).

In the mid-1970s, a general consensus emerged among Italian political-economic elites that union demands and industrial conflict were imposing unbearable costs on the Italian economy. Even confederal union leaders began worrying that the unions' strategy of the preceding few years, based on simultaneous grass-roots mobilisation at the factory level and national mobilisation for social reforms in the political arena, was undermining the viability of the Italian economy (Lama 1976: 83–149). With the worsening of Italy's economic crisis in the second half of the 1970s, the three major union confederations, CGIL, CISL and UIL, embraced a new strategy, which became known as the 'EUR Policy'. With it, they agreed to moderate wage demands and limit industrial conflict in exchange for participation in national policy-making (Lange & Vannicelli 1982).

In 1977, a first tripartite agreement entailing minor labour concessions was negotiated. In exchange for these concessions, the unions obtained from government a series of legislative measures aimed at correcting sectoral imbalances through planning measures, promoting job creation and (it was hoped) rekindling the process of economic growth. The concrete results achieved by these legislative provisions were, however, minimal. Overall, this early combination of union moderation and industrial *dirigisme* failed to live up to expectations.

Notwithstanding this early failure, national-level negotiations continued in the early 1980. In 1983, a tripartite agreement cut wage indexation (*scala mobile*), imposed a series of wage ceilings on sectoral collective bargaining negotiations and banned plant-level wage negotiations for eighteen months. In 1984, government proposed the renewal and updating of the previous tripartite pact by cutting wage indexation again (Carrieri 1985; Regini 1985). This government proposal met with a lot of opposition from within the Italian labour movement. Unions in some of the largest enterprises mobilised against it. In the end, the Italian unions split along partisan lines: CISL and UIL supported the agreement, while the CGIL refused to sign it. Faced with union division, the government implemented the accord through an executive order. One year later, the Communist Party promoted an electoral referendum to abrogate the government's decree. The communists within the CGIL campaigned for the abolition, while the CISL and UIL, as well as the socialists within the CGIL, stood by the government's side. The results of the referendum favoured the pro-government factions but led to the demise of unity of action among the three union confederations. The Federazione Unitaria was dismantled.

The failed agreement of 1985 and the ensuing referendum seriously undermined relationships among the three confederations. The structure of collective bargaining was decentralised. Even industry agreements lost much of their previous role (Locke 1992). The demise of centralised bargaining was only a temporary phenomenon, however. Indeed, this type of agreement returned to dominate the scene in the early 1990s. Before analysing these more recent developments, however, the next section examines the actors of the Italian employment relations system.

THE PARTIES IN EMPLOYMENT RELATIONS

Density trends

Italy's interest representation system appears remarkably fragmented in comparative perspective, and organisations are divided on both functional and political lines. The most important employer association is Confindustria. This organisation represents all kinds of enterprise interests. However, also due to a weighted system of voting, the interests of large enterprises generally predominate (Vatta 2007).

Traditionally, two different strategic orientations vie for power within Confindustria: on the one hand there are the interests of large firms, who often face strong and militant unions at the company level, and hence are generally not prejudicially against keeping some form of dialogue with unions at the national level. On the other hand, there are small and medium enterprises, which generally face weaker unions at the workplace level, and hence favour a more muscular approach to industrial relations and labour market policy. In 2001, the President of Confindustria was elected on a platform emphasising the need to strengthen the voice of small and medium enterprises. The result was a shift in the organisation's policy away from national tripartite negotiations and towards greater support for governmental attempts to introduce flexibility in hiring and firing, including through unilateral measures (Baccaro & Simoni, 2004).

Reliable data on representation and density are notoriously hard to come by for employer organisations. In 2002, Confidustria declared that the total number of workers employed by its affiliates was 4 280 085 (Vatta 2007: 218). In the same year, the total number of dependent employees in industry (including construction) and services was 15 398 000. This corresponds to a density rate of 28 per cent. However, the density rate would probably be much higher if one were to take into account only the employees of non-craft companies (Vatta 2007).

Aside from Confindustria, there are other specialised employer organisations in Italy, representing small enterprises, companies operating in the retail and service sectors, craft-based companies (which have a special legal status) and cooperatives. Organisations representing retail and service companies, craft-based companies and cooperatives are divided along party lines, with one organisation being closer to the left-of-centre political camp and the other leaning towards the other camp. While these additional employer associations increasingly participate in national negotiations, their ability to shape the strategy of the employer camp as a whole in these negotiations is limited, and they generally follow the line dictated by Confindustria.

As far as unions are concerned, traditionally the attention of scholars has focused on the three major union confederations, CGIL, CISL and UIL. There are, however, several other organisations which claim to represent workers in particular sectors or skill categories. Data on these other organisations' membership are, however, sparse and often unreliable. If one were to take their self-reported membership figures at face value, the unionisation rate in Italy would have to be doubled if not more.

Figure 6.1 plots aggregate union density rates for the three major confederations against time from 1960 to 2006. It shows that after peaking at about 50 per cent of the workforce in the late 1970s (after the Hot Autumn mobilisations), union density has been more or less steadily declining ever since. Despite falling density rates, union membership has grown constantly, thanks to the steady increase (until 2005) in the number of retired workers affiliated to the three confederations. Unionisation of retired members is favoured by the presence of semi-public institutional arrangements, known as *patronati*, which process the workers' applications for retirement and in exchange persuade workers to join the pensioners' unions.

Self-reported membership data generally over-estimate union density rates in a particular country, as revealed by comparing data based on administrative sources and on labour market surveys for those countries in which both are available.[2] According to self-reported membership counts, in 2006 the unionisation rate for the three confederal unions was slightly below 33 per cent (Giacinto 2007). However, according to survey data, the estimated *total* union density rate among active workers in 2008 was lower, at 29 per cent

Figure 6.1   Union density, CGIL-CISL-UIL percentage

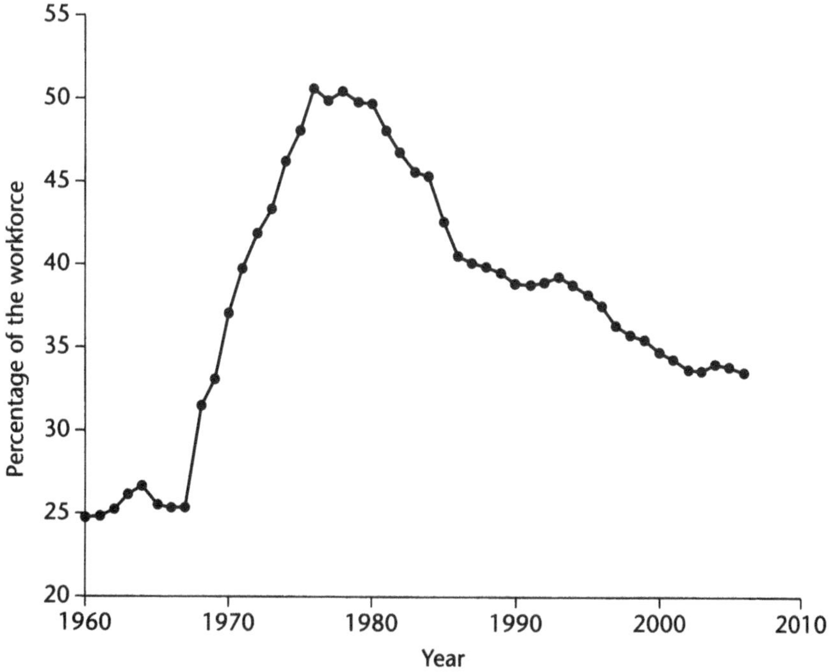

Source: Courtesy of Jelle Visser, University of Amsterdam

145

(see Table 6.1). This rate included union members affiliated to all union organisations, and not just the three major confederations, CGIL, CISL and UIL. These data are based on a representative sample of about 1600 dependent workers 18 and older and retirees, stratified by labour market status (active/retired), gender and geographical area of residence.[3] The density rate among retired workers was estimated to be 28 per cent. The three main confederations, CGIL, CISL and UIL, organised an estimated 81 per cent of all union members, and thus were by far the most representative organisations according to these data.

Table 6.1 Union density rates by labour market status percentage

	Non-members	*Members*
Retired	72	28
Active	71	29
Total	71	29

Note: Row proportions: n = 1 525
Source: Authors' estimates using unpublished survey data, courtesy of the IRES-CGIL

The union density rate by sector was estimated to be only 19 per cent in the private sector in 2008, based on the above-mentioned survey data (see Table 6.2). At 44 per cent, the estimated density rate was instead considerably higher in the public sector (see Table 6.3). Interestingly, the latter estimate was not very different from officially certified data: 46.46 per cent in 2002 according to Aran, the public agency in charge of collective bargaining in the public sector (see above).[4] Incidentally, these official data make it clear that non-traditional confederations largely overstate their claims to representation.

Table 6.2 Union density rates, private sector percentage

	Non-members	*Members*
Retired	65	35
Active	81	19
Total	74	26

Note: Row proportions: n = 948
Source: Authors' estimates using unpublished survey data, courtesy of the IRES-CGIL

Table 6.3 Union density rates, public sector percentage

	Non-members	Members
Retired	80	20
Active	56	44
Total	68	32

Note: Row proportions: n = 577
Source: Authors' estimates using unpublished survey data, courtesy of the IRES-CGIL

The survey data also permit an evaluation of the unions' attractiveness among age cohorts (see Table 6.4). Unsurprisingly, the estimated density rate for workers between 18 and 34 was only 19 per cent—that is, considerably lower than the one for more mature workers.

Table 6.4 Union density rates by age profile percentage

	Non-members	Members
Up to 34	81	19
35<age<54	66	34
More than 54	71	29
Total	71	29

Note: Row proportions: n = 1 525
Source: Authors' estimates using unpublished survey data, courtesy of the IRES-CGIL

It should be emphasised that the survey data should be taken with a pinch of salt, as they could be marred by sample error. However, they are in line with officially certified data, and thus appear to be reliable. They paint a picture that is considerably bleaker than the one transpiring from previous scholarly work, including our own (Baccaro et al., 2003). With a density rate of 19 per cent in the private sector, a clear difficulty in organising young workers (also due to the diffusion of contingent work among these age cohorts) and a constant replacement of active with retired members within the union ranks, the prospect of unions ceasing to be significant labour market actors in the near future no longer seems far-fetched.

ORGANISATIONAL STRUCTURES

The organisational structures of employer and worker organisations match each other: both Confindustria and the three confederal unions have both vertical, industry-based organisational structures and horizontal structures. In the case of the CGIL, the most important horizontal structure is the local Camera del Lavoro (Labour Chamber). The other confederations have similar entities. The Camera's jurisdiction approximately corresponds to that of Italian provinces. The unions' vertical structures link the enterprise level, provincial industry organisations and national industry federations. In 2008, thirteen industry federations were affiliated with the CGIL (nineteen in 1985), nineteen federations were affiliated with the CISL (seventeen in 1985) and eighteen were affiliated with the UIL (28 in 1985). As in other countries, over time there has been a tendency towards consolidation of the industry federations through mergers (Ebbinghaus 2003b). Aside from this trend, the organisational structure of the unions has remained more or less stable above the workplace level, while it has changed considerably at the workplace level itself. Indeed, this has been the area in which the most interesting organisational innovations have emerged over time.

The organisational model of the early post-war years was that of the Commissione Interna (internal commission). This had been the structure of workplace representation prevailing in the pre-fascist period, and employers' and workers' representatives reintroduced it in 1943 through a national agreement. It was not formally a union body, had no bargaining prerogatives and could not call strikes. It was instead a small parliament in charge of ensuring smooth relations between workers (both union and non-union) and companies. Its functions ranged from consultation to monitoring the implementation of collective agreements signed by external trade unions. However, because in the early post-war years free trade unions had not yet been established, the internal commissions were in some cases assigned bargaining rights as well.

With the Hot Autumn wave of strikes, workplace structures changed dramatically. The internal commissions were replaced by the Consigli di Fabbrica (factory councils), composed of workers' delegates elected by and directly accountable to small homogeneous worker groups. Simultaneously, a major legislative reform, the Workers' Statute (Law 300) of 1970, authorised the so-called 'most representative' unions to set up workplace representation structures (Rappresentanze Sindacali Aziendali, or RSA) and benefit from a number of paid leaves for union activities. The Workers' Statute never defined how exactly 'most representative' was to be determined, and for a long time it was simply presumed that the three main confederations were to be considered as such.

The synthesis between the organisational model embedded in the Workers' Statute and the one emerging from the workers' struggles was reached pragmatically: the three confederations recognised the Factory Councils as their own and attributed to them the institutional benefits to which they were entitled by virtue of their 'most representative' status under the law. Thus the Factory Councils became union structures, but at the same time represented all workers in a workplace.

However, this synthesis had its own downside. In particular, the lack of boundaries between worker councils and trade unions made the model viable only insofar as the three union confederations shared the same strategic view and operated in unison. Also, the absence of clear rules concerning the election and re-election of representatives left the door open to a possible bureaucratic involution of the Councils. When in 1984 the three confederations broke up over the issue of wage indexation reform, relationships deteriorated at both the national level and the workplace level. In some cases, the unitary Factory Councils were dismantled and each organisation established its own RSA. In other cases, Factory Councils were not renewed for several years, thus jumpstarting a heated debate about the lack of union democracy in Italy (Baccaro 2001).

Different reform initiatives were launched in the late 1980s and early 1990s. In 1993, the three union confederations and the employers settled on the so-called Rappresentanze Sindacale Unitarie (RSU). Like the Factory Councils, the RSU were both union bodies and organs of general worker representation. Unlike the Factory Councils' delegates, however, RSU members were elected by the workers at large, and no longer chosen by homogenous groups. To ensure institutional continuity between external unions and internal workplace structures, also at the request of employers, it was established that two-thirds of RSU representatives were to be elected by all workers in a workplace, while one-third were to be appointed by the most representative unions, which would in this way almost certainly be assured control over these structures.

The creation of the RSU allowed the main union confederations to set workers' representation on a more solid and predictable footing, and to rely on a more reliable base to negotiate change and regulate employment relationships on the shop floor (Pulignano 2006).

The RSUs became the formal bargaining agents at company and local levels on issues explicitly referred to in national agreements; also, the RSUs were attributed consultation and information rights, which concurred to identify them as formal bodies of employees' participation and therefore an important instrument for union democracy (Carrieri 1995).

The introduction of the RSU spurred a wave of union elections in Italian workplaces. The CGIL, CISL and UIL obtained close to 95 per cent of the workers' votes in most cases, except in the case of a limited number of well-identified skill groups (e.g. locomotive engineers). In 1997, the RSU was extended by law to the public sector. The so-called Legge Bassanini mandated the regular election of workplace representatives in the Italian public sector and imposed the official counting of membership data.[5] The purpose of these dispositions was the measurement of union representation. Those unions that passed a threshold of 5 per cent (calculated as the average between electoral votes and quota of membership cards) were designated as 'representative', and were therefore allowed to participate in collective bargaining in the various public sector compartments (e.g. schools, ministries, municipalities) and sign collective bargaining agreements that were binding for all workers. The official data gathered by Aran, the public agency in charge of public sector industrial relations, revealed that the fragmentation of trade union representation was in some cases extreme—for example, in the health-care sector workers were affiliated to 68 different organisations. This fragmentation notwithstanding, CGIL, CISL and UIL together organised 71 percent of all union members in the public sector. The number of votes that they obtained in the first RSU election was slightly lower (68 per cent), but still considerable.[6]

Notwithstanding several legislative attempts to institutionalise the election of workplace representatives in the private sector as well, the RSU remained a private and voluntary affair in the private sector. Consequently, beginning with the mid- to late 1990s, the RSUs were found to display some signs of fatigue (Carrieri 1997). At the core of their difficulties were a lack of unity among the three main confederations, the limited diffusion of company bargaining and non-renewal of the elected representatives.

Overall, the results of the RSU elections bolstered the confederal unions' claim to general representation of Italian workers and, for some time at least, contributed to re-legitimate and re-energise them (Carrieri 1995, 1996). However, as examined above, they did not prevent a serious erosion of union density—so serious as to make it doubtful at this point whether the unions will continue to be an important private sector actor in the future.

THE PROCESS OF EMPLOYMENT RELATIONS

The national level

Italy is a country in which peak-level neo-corporatist deals have for years been deemed particularly unlikely. This was not for lack of trying, however: beginning in the late 1970s, there had been various attempts at national-level negotiations between government and the social partners.

The crux of the problem seemed to lie in the organisational and institutional structure of the Italian actors, which lacked—or so it was argued—the centralised organisational capacities needed for corporatism to succeed (Tarantelli 1986; Cella & Treu 1989). One element that, in retrospect, was especially important in determining the early failures had to do with strategy rather than structure: a sizeable portion of the Italian union movement was unwilling (and not just unable) to commit itself to a policy of wage restraint.

This situation was to change dramatically in the early 1990s. Two factors facilitated the re-emergence of centralised bargaining. The first was economic: in the early 1990s, Italy found itself faced with a serious economic crisis. As a result of both constant nominal exchange rates (due to the fact that the lira was tied to the European Monetary System, or EMS) and positive inflation differentials between Italy and all major international competitors, real exchange rates had experienced a constant appreciation since 1985. This dampened exports and increased import penetration, thus causing persistent current account problems. Eventually, speculative attacks spurred by perceptions of non-sustainability of the lira's nominal parity *vis-à-vis* stronger EMS currencies pushed the Italian currency out of the EMS in September 1992 (Vaciago 1993).

The second factor was political: the old political party system, which had both shaped and constrained relations among collective actors, disappeared in the space of a few years. The Italian Communist Party changed its denomination in 1989, officially pledged allegiance to parliamentary and reformist methods of action, and applied for membership in the Socialist International, the international association of social democratic parties. In early 1992, a wave of corruption scandals, known as Tangentopoli (Bribeville) shook all major governmental parties including the Christian Democrats and the Socialists. Both parties went through a tremendous legitimation crisis and were dismantled. Their place was taken by a new coalition of centre-right political parties hegemonised by Silvio Berlusconi, a media tycoon.

The concomitance of both political and economic crisis provided the Italian confederal unions with a major opportunity to impose themselves on the national political sphere as the senior partners of 'emergency' governments. Indeed, the governments of 1992, 1993 and 1995 were, from the point of view of parliamentary support, extremely weak governments, devoid of clear parliamentary majorities and (as in the case of the 1993 and 1995 executives) composed of independent 'technicians' formally unaffiliated with any political party. At the same time, the range of tasks these governments had to perform was daunting. First, it was important to avoid sparking a new inflationary spiral through the nominal devaluation of the lira. For this, wage moderation was indispensable. Second, since the state of the Italian public finances was disastrous (the public deficit hovered around 10 per cent of GDP between 1992 and 1993 and public debt peaked at 125 per cent of GDP in 1994), the government could not use counter-cyclical (Keynesian) policies. Instead, Italy's economic authorities needed to engage in fiscal consolidation—a set of policies that is generally quite unpopular, as it involves cuts in public expenditures and/or increases in taxes (in Italy, it involved both)—while at the same time trying to preserve social cohesion and peace.

The three confederal unions were uniquely placed to provide the support and collaboration governments needed. First, unlike other major socio-political actors in Italy (e.g. the employers and the politicians), they emerged from the Tangentopoli wave of scandals virtually unscathed. Second, due to the deep transformations that occurred in the political party structure, the unions' political sponsors either had disappeared or were for the first time in Italy's post-war history sitting together as partners in the same centre-left coalition. This political rapprochement generated close unity of action among the three confederations. Between 1992 and 1998, a series of peak-level bargaining agreements was negotiated by the three confederal unions and the Italian governments, with or without (as in the case of the 1995 pension reform agreement) the Confindustria.

In July 1992, in an ill-fated attempt to stave off expectations of a forthcoming devaluation of the lira, a tripartite agreement brought about the abolition of wage indexation. In addition, enterprise-level bargaining was also temporarily banned. Another centralised agreement was signed in July 1993. This confirmed the abolition of wage indexation, linked industry-level wage increases to the government's macro-economic targets, and introduced a two-tier structure of collective bargaining, at the industry and company level.

In 1995, government and unions (but not the employers) negotiated a comprehensive reform of the pension system. This introduced a simulated funded system in the long term (with benefits proportional to paid contribution), but only marginally attacked acquired rights. The 1996 tripartite 'Pact for Labour' introduced a moderate flexibilisation of the rules regulating flexible and contingent forms of labour. In 1998, the so-called 'Christmas Pact' confirmed the structure of collective bargaining on two levels established in 1993 and introduced a contractual obligation for government to consult with the social partners on all social policy issues and even to devolve decision-making authority to the social partners.

At the end of the 1990s, the newly emerged corporatist system seemed well on its way to institutionalisation, and there was even talk of embedding it in the Italian Constitution (Carrieri 1997). Also, the three main confederations seemed very close to merging into a single organisation. However, this opportunity was missed: the CGIL and the CISL in particular had different views on a number of key issues, such as union democracy (with the CISL opposing widespread use of worker referenda and the CGIL favouring it) and the decentralisation of collective bargaining (with the CISL being much more open than the CGIL). These differences had led in some cases to agreements signed only by the CISL and the UIL but not the CGIL.[7]

In turn, Confindustria became increasingly disenchanted with tripartite negotiations and, on the eve of national elections in 2001, struck a strategic alliance with the center-right coalition. The new government's labour program emphasised labour market deregulation, criticised concertation as a rite that blocked much-needed structural reform, and underscored the need to move from job protection to employability (Biagi et al. 2002). In 2002, another tripartite agreement was signed. This time, however, the union front split. These tripartite negotiations started with the ambitious objective of boosting employment creation with a comprehensive reform of both employment protection legislation and economic shock absorbers. Eventually, however, the scope of the agreement shrank and the proposed text ended up exchanging the promise of tax reductions for a less rigid regulation of individual dismissals. The CGIL refused to sign this agreement and called for workers to mobilise in opposition. This call was largely heeded and the policy reform stalled. As a result, the government never implemented the new rules on dismissals that it had negotiated.

Corporatist policy-making returned in full splendour in 2007. The opportunity was once again a pension reform. While the reform of 1995 had fundamentally altered the future structure of the system, it had had only a limited impact on the transition phase affecting workers who had matured pension rights under the old regime. To prevent a short-term increase in pension expenditures, in 2004 the centre-right government unilaterally increased the minimum age for seniority-based pensions. However, it postponed the introduction of the reform to 2008 in order to avoid political problems with its base. The new centre-left government abolished the unilateral reform and negotiated with the unions a gradual increase of the minimum age for seniority-based retirement. Leftist parties in the government opposed the agreement and appealed to Italian workers to reject it. As had previously occurred both in 1993 and 1995, the three confederations organised a massive campaign of information among the workers, followed by a binding referendum. The workers approved the agreement by an overwhelming proportion and thus contributed to bolster both the unions and the government's credibility.

In 2008, the centre-right coalition returned to power. Strategic divisions among the three confederations resurfaced and the unions split again. The crux of the matter this time was the updating of the 1993 agreement and the reform of the collective bargaining structure. This was a topic that had been tabled repeatedly in the past, including during the 1998 negotiations, but that had never been dealt with due to the parties' inability to converge on a mutually agreeable solution. The January 2009 agreement confirmed the 1993 articulation of collective bargaining on two levels (industry and company), but introduced some changes to the old regime. All the major employer organisations signed the agreement and so did the CISL and UIL, but not the CGIL. The CGIL's refusal was motivated by the agreement's inadequate protection of the wages and salaries' purchasing power.

While the incisiveness of the early pacts is largely gone (Carrieri 2008), the parties continue to negotiate national-level agreements well into the twenty-first century, following what has by now become a predictable pattern: when the centre-left coalition is in power, all three confederations share responsibility for the final agreement; when the government is in the hands of the centre-right coalition, the CISL and UIL (as well as the other union confederations) sign, while the CGIL digs its heels in. The CGIL seems to find it difficult to negotiate agreements with a government it does not trust.

Retrospectively (and counterfactually), it could be argued that without the centralised agreements of the 1990s, Italy's political economic situation would be much worse than it currently is: the country would not have joined the single European currency, inflation would be higher, the currency would be an easy target for speculative attacks, and the public deficit would have grown due to higher interest rates, thus adding further pressure to an already restrictive fiscal policy. At the same time, the resurgence of tripartite negotiations did nothing to prevent continuous erosion of the unions' representation capacity among active workers, especially in the private sector. Also, and perhaps more importantly, by introducing and sustaining a multi-year policy of wage restraint, it may have contributed to what is currently being presented in the Italian public debate as a true and proper emergency: wage incomes that are insufficient to cover normal expenditures and basic needs of an average family, especially in large metropolitan areas.

The industry level

The industry-level contract has historically had a symbiotic relationship with enterprise bargaining, even though the two contracts have often vied for primacy. After the Hot Autumn, enterprise bargaining (in large firms) became the channel through which the most interesting collective bargaining innovations emerged, and the role of the industry contract was to generalise and diffuse them (Cella & Treu 2009). In the 1980s, there was a trend towards collective bargaining decentralisation, which Italy shared with all other advanced countries (Katz 1993; Katz & Darbishire 2000), and the industry agreement lost some of its significance (Locke 1992). However, with the tripartite agreement of 1993, it was restored to its focal place (Regalia & Regini 1998).

The 1993 agreement introduced a clear division of labour across bargaining levels. Something similar had been attempted with the tripartite agreement of 1983, but it had been short lived. Collective bargaining was to be conducted at both the industry level (every four years in the case of normative clauses, every two years as far as wage and salary conditions were concerned) and the enterprise (or territorial) level (every four years). The role of the industry agreement was to homogenise the working conditions of the employees belonging to a specific productive sector. As far as remuneration was concerned, industry-level negotiations had the function of keeping inflation expectations in check by tightly linking wage increases distributed at the industry level with the expected inflation rates decided by the government.[8] Also, they would guarantee purchasing power stability by compensating *ex post* for any positive difference between anticipated and actual inflation. Even in this case, the adjustment would be net of terms of trade changes. In other words, if the delta between predicted and actual inflation had been caused by a rise in import prices, real consumption wages would be allowed to fall.

By its very institutional design, the 1993 agreement had the potential to cause a decline of the wage share in Italy. Indeed, productivity increases were supposed to be no longer redistributed at the industry level, but only at the enterprise or territorial level. Hence, unless the coverage rate of enterprise bargaining increased dramatically, wages would grow less than productivity. To obviate this situation, from 2006 the metalworking contract began to include an additional (small) wage element, paid to workers to whom only the industry contract applied.

The collective bargaining structure introduced in 1993 represented a delicate equilibrium among different interests and views (Mascini 2000). This has made it very difficult to reform it, notwithstanding repeated attempts. In principle, the employers have been against collective bargaining at two levels, and have argued for a single bargaining level. Initially, they favoured the industry contract but over time they have shifted to the enterprise contract. The unions have vocally defended the complementary nature of both the industry and the enterprise level of bargaining, and argued for the need to retain both. When push has come to shove, however, the CISL and the UIL have proven willing to experiment with institutional solutions increasing the weight and importance of decentralised levels, while the CGIL has cast itself in the role of defender of the industry contract.

Divisions on the proper role of the industry level do not just pit different organisations against one another but often also reflect specific sectoral traditions and peculiarities. For example, the chemical sector agreement of May 2006 attributed greater autonomy to company-level bargaining and even introduced an opting-out clause for companies in distress. It was a very different situation when it came to the January 2008 metalworking contract, which in many ways recentralised labour relations at the industry level. A significant innovation was introduced only for craft-based companies in March 2004. For these companies, the role of compensating differences between anticipated and actual inflation was moved from the national to the regional level of bargaining. This reduced the importance of the industry agreement.

After years of fruitless discussion and failed negotiations, the January 2009 national agreement explicitly set out to reform the architecture of Italian collective bargaining. Hailed as a historic event, it did not fundamentally alter the existing system. Rather, it confirmed the dual structure introduced by the 1993 accord, increased the duration of industry-level agreements from two to three years, linked industry-level wage increases to an EU-wide predictive index rather than to Italy's expected inflation, reiterated that decentralised bargaining should take place only on issues explicitly delegated by the industry contracts and should not concern topics already negotiated at other levels, and affirmed the need for government to increase the diffusion of decentralised bargaining by introducing special tax advantages. Given the vagueness of some commitments, and given that the largest union confederation (the CGIL) did not sign it, this accord is unlikely to have ended the debate on collective bargaining reform in Italy.

The company level

In this domain, too, the 1993 social protocol represented a landmark. It did two key things. First, it established the RSU—that is, a new system of workplace representation which, at least for some time, reinvigorated and re-legitimised the Italian confederal unions. Second, for the first time in Italian history it introduced a series of rules regulating decentralised bargaining. These were contractual rather than legal rules, thus institutionalisation was weaker than it could have been. However, compared with the previous situation, in which decentralised bargaining had depended on voluntary recognition and on the balance of power between the parties, the 1993 accord was an important step forward.

As argued above, the 1993 protocol attributed an important role to enterprise-based bargaining and was in many ways premised on greater diffusion of enterprise bargaining than the previous status quo. Did company bargaining really become more prevalent?

The answer to this question is somewhat speculative: some studies are available, but they are based on specific sectors and/or geographic areas, are limited to enterprises of a particular size (e.g. with at least 50 employees) or lack a longitudinal dimension. Their results are often not comparable. A survey conducted in 1995–96 by the Italian statistical agency ISTAT, based on a representative sample of private-sector enterprises with at least ten employees, estimated that company bargaining involved only 10 per cent of relevant enterprises and covered 39 per cent of private-sector employees (ISTAT, 2002). Based on various sources of data, Rossi and Sestito (2000) concluded that company bargaining in 1995–97 had been less diffuse than in 1988–89 and approximately as diffuse as in 1985–86. There had been a peak of enterprise-based bargaining in 1996, presumably as a result of the 1993 accord, but it had not been sufficient to bring the coverage rate back to previous levels. Overall, the time trend was negative. The propensity to negotiate at the enterprise level was strongly positively correlated with company size (see also Bordogna 1997, 1999) and company-specific union density. Hence the decline in decentralised bargaining appeared to be due both to a decline in average size and to a decline in union density. This analysis also showed that there had been no increase in the relative importance of wage increases negotiated at the enterprise level. Instead, increases decided unilaterally by management had become more important. However, the type of wage increases negotiated seemed to have changed in the direction indicated by the 1993 agreement. Wage bargaining at the enterprise level had concerned mostly the so-called 'variable wage' and had been linked to the company's productivity or profitability (Pulignano 2007). Overall, in those companies in which there had been negotiations, enterprise bargaining had been used to negotiate more flexible working conditions and to establish workplace partnerships.

A more recent analysis of decentralised bargaining trends confirmed the findings reported above and revealed that bargaining propensity had declined between 1998 and 2006 for a sample of private enterprises with at least 100 employees. The decline had been greater for companies of smaller size (CNEL 2007). Thus it looks as though institutionalisation of enterprise negotiations in 1993 did not increase the diffusion of this form of bargaining. Two forces possibly operated at cross-purposes: on the one hand, the 1993 protocol provided unions with a 'right to access', so to speak, that was previously unavailable; on the other hand, due to the decline of density rates, unions were increasingly unable to act on such a right.

Labour relations in the public sector

The year 1993 was crucial for employment relations in the public sector as well. That year, a union–government agreement, translated into law (Law 29/1993), introduced the principle of autonomy in collective bargaining. The main goal was to 'privatise' public sector employment relations—that is, make them more similar to the private sector ones. Employment relations in the public sector are currently formally regulated via collective agreements. Before this reform, there had been informal collective bargaining, especially after the introduction of a previous reform in 1983—the so-called Legge Quadro (Framework Law). However, the agreements needed to be translated into law to be valid.

The reform created an autonomous agency, the Agenzia per la Rappresentanza Negoziale delle Pubbliche Amministrazioni (ARAN). This agency is a technical organ with organisational and managerial autonomy, reporting directly to the central government. It is legally responsible for all national collective bargaining in the public sector. It also oversees the equal application of the collective employment contracts and, upon request, assists with specific needs of the administration involved.

The impetus for the establishment of an independent agency came from the perceived need to correct some of the unintended consequences of the 1983 reform. This had effectively introduced collective bargaining in the public sector, but had created little incentive for the employer not to give in easily to union demands. In the public sector, it was argued, there was a situation of 'pluralism without market' (Bordogna 1994): the parties were more or less free to negotiate the terms of the employment relation; however, due to the multiple protections enjoyed by public sector employees and the particular electoral constraints of the public sector employer, they had little incentive to settle on reasonable terms. In particular, unlike the private sector, unions that pushed their demands too far did not risk seeing their members lose their jobs to the competition and managers who settled too generously faced little risk of demotion. In the mid- to late 1980s, public sector collective bargaining had contributed to both wage inflation and growing public sector deficits because politicians had been unable to resist the explosive wage demands put forward by small and extremely militant professional unions—the so-called Comitati di Base (Grassroots Committees) or COBAS, particularly in the school and railway bargaining units. With the creation of ARAN, public sector collective bargaining was constrained by tight budget limits imposed by the government.

In 1997, another law, the so-called Legge Bassanini, integrated the previous legislative reform. It further extended contractualisation by abolishing some remaining constraints to decentralised negotiations. Currently, the structure of public sector collective bargaining is similar to that obtaining in the private sector (regulated by the 1993 protocol). Accordingly, decentralised bargaining takes place under the coordination and within the limits indicated by national industry agreements, which are different for the various branches of the public administration (e.g. schools, health care services, central government, etc.). Administrative units are, at least in theory, allowed to use their own funds in second-level negotiations to reward and motivate their personnel. However, the adding of a new layer of decentralised collective bargaining does not seem to have had appreciable effects on the productivity of the administrations involved and the quality of the services provided.

It is not clear what effects the various reforms have had. The wage spirals that were observed in the late 1980s have disappeared, but this may be due to the fact that the macroeconomic situation of the country is now considerably different. Some important progress has been made with regard to the qualitative aspects of negotiations—for example, the number of job classifications has been cut and now wage increases are more strictly tied to tasks and responsibility, as opposed to being simply linked to automatic career progression. Moreover, new forms of labour flexibility have been introduced, such as part-time, fixed-term contracts and teleworking.

One clear benefit of the new regime has been the sorting out of the system of union representation. As argued above, the Legge Bassanini introduced clear criteria for the determination of the unions' representation, based on a mix of electoral results and membership. The official data on membership and electoral support made available by ARAN have made it clear that the claims put forward by the grassroots committee and other professional unions in the late 1980s and early 1990s that they were the true representatives of Italian workers were largely overstated. There is indeed a crisis of union representation in Italy, but it manifests itself in a general decline, not in the substitution of established organisations with new ones.

CURRENT AND FUTURE ISSUES

This chapter has argued that the main trend in Italian employment relations has been the emergence since 1992 of a new type of corporatism, one that involves the social partners in virtually all major economic policies but produces few, if any, of the redistributive, egalitarian and decommodifying outcomes of the classic Scandinavian corporatism of the old days. Indeed, and more controversially, the chapter has argued that the Italian corporatism may have contributed to the current economic crisis (stagnating growth rates, more disperse wage and income distributions and a pervasive sense of economic insecurity) by introducing and enforcing a multi-year policy of wage restraint.

Specifically, this outcome has been the result of the particular way in which the crucial tripartite agreement of 1993 regulating collective bargaining structure has been implemented. This agreement was very important, and commentators were right to call it an historic event.

The new system attributed a new role to the industry-level contract—that of guaranteeing purchasing-power stability—and established that productivity increases should be distributed at the enterprise level. This made perfect sense in a country used to very high inflation rates and highly inertial inflationary expectations (Tarantelli 1986). The problem was that most private sector workers were only covered (directly or indirectly) by the industry contract, and that the second level of bargaining became *less*, not more, pervasive over time. In these circumstances, the institutional structure of collective bargaining created a situation in which wages were highly likely to grow more slowly than productivity.

To illustrate that the argument is at least plausible, Figure 6.2 plots the wage in efficiency units over time. This is (roughly) a measure of unit labour costs, keeping factor proportions (labour/capital) constant. A growth in the index indicates that wages grow faster than (technologically warranted) labour productivity, and vice versa. The graph shows that between 1973 and 1991, the wage in efficiency units first grew and then returned more or less to the same level. From 1992 on—that is, with the abolition of wage indexation and the onset of the new Italian corporatism—there was a sustained period of decline, which was not simply a cyclical phenomenon. In the early 2000s, wages again began to grow faster than productivity.

Figure 6.2 Wages in efficiency units

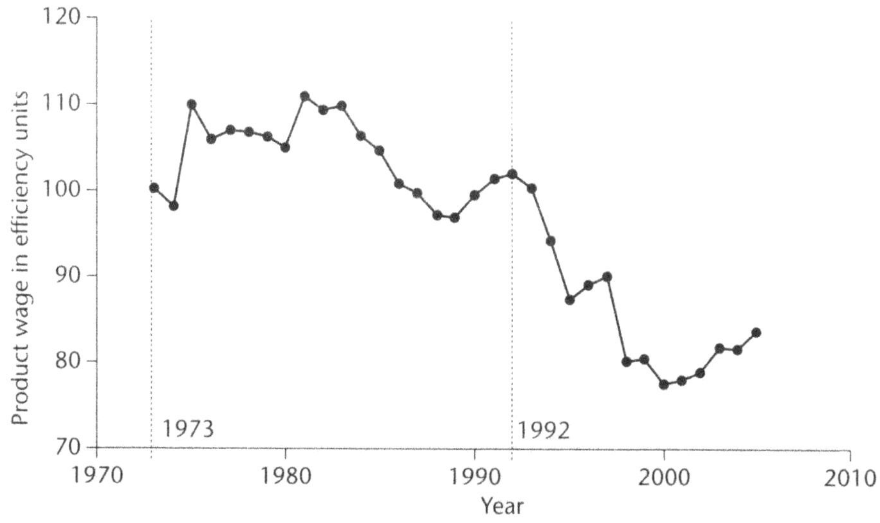

Source: AMECO Database of the European Commission, DG ECFIN

Figure 6.3 plots wage shares of GDP over time for the four largest European economies. In 1992, Italy's wage share was the same as Germany's and larger than France's. Between 1992 and 2000, the wage share in Italy declined much faster than elsewhere. Both graphs suggest that something in the Italian system of wage determination built a gap between wage and productivity dynamics in the 1990s.

Wages that grow less than productivity—that is, falling unit labour costs—may not necessarily be a bad thing, as they imply that cost competitiveness improves. For example, wage moderation did wonders for the Irish economy, at least until the late 1990s, and was a key factor in bringing about the 'Celtic Tiger' (Baccaro & Simoni 2007). The Irish economy imploded in the late 2000s, due to the consequences of a giant real estate bubble and associated banking crisis. However, there is a fundamental difference between an economy like the Irish one and the Italian economy. In the Irish economy, foreign demand is much more important than domestic demand; in Italy the opposite holds. In Italy, as in every large country, the export-benefiting effects of cost competitiveness may be dominated by the recessionary effects of shrinking domestic demand (Carlin & Soskice 2009).

Obviously not all Italian problems stem from the employment relations system. Faini and Sapir (2005) have offered an interesting

Figure 6.3   Wage shares of GDP in large European economies

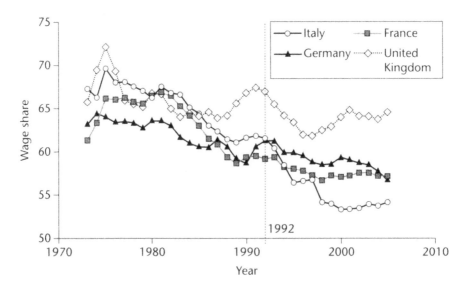

Source: AMECO Database of the European Commission, DG ECFIN

analysis focusing on comparative advantage and sectoral specialisation. According to their argument, Italy has been hit in the face by globalisation, which implies greater economic integration with developing countries, particularly China. Unlike other European countries, Italy is specialised in labour-intensive sectors, and thus competes head to head with China and other developing countries. Also, while other European countries have upgraded their productive structure in the 1990s and moved towards higher value-added markets, Italy is the only country to have become even more specialised in traditional sectors. This phenomenon points to some historic weaknesses of the Italian economy—for example, low investments in R&D, prevalence of small firms and inefficient public services. However, it also hints at a role that the employment relations system could have played and did not play: that of acting as a 'beneficial constraint' (Streeck 1997). If unit labour costs fall dramatically, if the low road is not sealed off, managers and entrepreneurs have fewer incentives to upgrade.

The main present and future challenge for the Italian employment relations system, as well as for the Italian economy as a whole, is that of addressing the current wage emergency, and associated with it the prevailing sense of insecurity. In Italy's public discourse, it is often argued that wages cannot grow if productivity does not grow. This is true, but as the analysis above has shown, wages have grown considerably less than productivity throughout the 1990s. Addressing this fundamental distributive issue will require a reform of collective bargaining institutions. Current reform projects focus on strengthening the second bargaining level. This is unlikely to lead to an equitable distribution of productivity gains short of a dramatic boost in company-level bargaining. This boost is unlikely to happen because one of the key determinants of decentralised bargaining is the local strength of the union, and that has been declining for several years. Additional institutional mechanisms will probably be necessary.

There is, then, the microeconomic problem of rekindling productivity growth. This will require reforms of the educational system, the skill development system and industry policy. Upgrading the Italian productive structure to enable it to weather the challenges of globalisation is unlikely to happen through the invisible hand: it will require the targeting of particular sectors and the deliberate building of capacities. Employment relations can contribute to this policy mix, particularly by addressing inefficiencies in the public sector and by increasing the quality of public services.

Finally, there is the problem of labour's organisational strength. At present, Italy's organised labour is in the enviable position of being granted access to all major policy-making tables. However, its capacity to push its own goals at these bargaining tables may be waning because density rates have been falling for the past 30 years or so. Institutional access without social power may amount to little. The trajectory of second-level bargaining provides an illustration: the 1993 agreement gave unions, for the first time, an opportunity to negotiate regularly every four years. However, because there were fewer unionised workers around to act on it, this opportunity went largely unheeded.

A dramatic reversal in union density is unlikely. Unions are declining everywhere, both in liberal and coordinated market economies—possibly for structural reasons (e.g. crisis of Fordist organisations, fragmentation of the productive structure, deindustrialisation, diffusion of new typologies of contract). The only countries that, at least until the mid-1990s, managed to buck the trend were the Ghent ones. The recent literature on union revitalisation notwithstanding, so far no recipe has produced consistently good results.

The Italian unions still maintain remarkable mobilisation capacities, their density rates are still considerable (especially in comparative perspective) and their legitimacy is bolstered by their generally good performance in workplace elections. Nonetheless, with less than 20 per cent coverage among private sector workers, they seem to be on their way to becoming a marginal labour market actor. If these trends continue—and at this point there are all sorts of reasons to think they will—employment relations scholars are well advised to start reflecting on what a world without unions would look like, and which new institutions and social forces will emerge to take up the crucial role—embedding a market economy—that they historically have played.

A CHRONOLOGY OF ITALIAN EMPLOYMENT RELATIONS

1848	First printing workers' associations. Ad hoc development of craft unions.
1850s	Mutual aid societies, localised cross-class unions dominant union form.
1861	Reunification of Italy ('Il Risorgimento'). Spurs diffusion of unionism.
1868	First city-wide general strike, in Bologna.
1870s	Class-conscious but local and sectional 'Leagues of Resistance' supplant mutual aid societies as dominant model. Multi-unionism at work.
1880s	Growth of local union organisation and socialist organisation, particularly in northern agricultural areas.
1891	First *camere del lavoro* (labour chamber) in Milan (based on French model) as worker and union-controlled local labour exchange. Horizontal, inclusive, localist unionism. *Rerum Novarum* (papal encyclical) fosters Catholic labour movement activism.
1892	Formation of the Socialist Party of Italy (PSI). Federation of *camere del lavoro*.
1900	Industry union of railway workers.
1901	Socialists active in formation of Federterra (Agricultural Workers' Union Federation), Italy's largest and most influential union, the FIOM (Federation of Metalworkers), and other important industry unions.
1902	First local, all-industry employers' federation (Monza).
1906	General Confederation of Labour (CGL), composed of *camere del lavoro* and industry unions.
1910	Confindustria, national employers' confederation.
1918	Formation of Catholic Union Confederation (CIL).
1919	People's Party (Catholic).
1920	First national industry collective agreement, for gas workers.
1921	Communist Party of Italy (PCI).
1922	Mussolini and Fascist Party seize power.
1925	Fascist government abolishes freedom of association, bans all non-fascist unions. Strikes and other forms of union action are forbidden.

1943–45	Liberation of Italy, starting from southern Italy: many strikes in northern Italy against fascist regime and Nazi occupation. Final liberation, 25 April 1945.
1944	Pact of Rome (anti-fascist forces) for creation of single, non-party union confederation (CGIL).
1945–48	Coalition government of anti-fascist parties.
1946	National referendum abolishes monarchy for republic.
1948	New constitution guarantees rights to union freedom and to strike. Democrazia Cristiana (DC) wins parliamentary majority and excludes PCI and PSI from government. Catholics leave CGIL to form Confederazione Italiana Sindicati dei Lavoratori (CISL). Start of decades of intense political rivalry among unions and their decline.
1949	Social Democrats and Republicans leave CGIL and later form UIL. Subsequently, PCI increasingly controls CGIL.
1959	Law passed (*ergo omnes*) allowing legal extension of collective agreements to the entire sector.
1962	Protocol between metalworkers' unions and ASAP and Intersind (public sector employer associations) for enterprise level collective bargaining.
1968–73	Long wave of intense industrial conflict including 1969 'Hot Autumn' (*autunno caldo*). Unions gain and entrench workplace presence. Factory councils (*consigli di fabbrica*), a new horizontal forms of workplace representation. Workers' Charter (*Statuto dei diritti dei lavoratori*) advances protection of employee and union rights at work. Formalises new phase of Italian employment relations: union ascendancy at all levels. Employers under siege.
1972	Unified union federation CGIL-CISL-UIL.
1975	Economy-wide agreements between Confindustria and CGIL-CISL-UIL on wage indexation (*scala mobile*) favour lower-paid employees. Start of decade of tripartism.
1976–79	PCI supports DC government at time of economic crisis and domestic terrorism but without governmental participation.
1980	FIAT dispute. Revolt of FIAT technicians and super-

	visors against union policy ('March of the 40000'). Metalworking unions vanquished. New phase: employer ascendancy and union crisis.
1983	Tripartite agreement on labour costs and wage indexation. New law formalises collective bargaining in public employment.
1984	Inconclusive tripartite negotiations on wage indexation lead to collapse of CGIL-CISL-UIL federation. Government decree codifies agreement with CISL and UIL.
1987–89	Rise of rank and file committees (*Cobas*) challenge leading role of union confederations in the public sector.
1990	First legislative protection from unfair dismissal for employees in 'micro' enterprises (fewer than fifteen employees). Law restricting strikes in public sector essential services. Tripartite agreement abolishes *scala mobile* (wage indexation).
1992	Tripartite central agreement reshapes incomes policy, bargaining structure, union workplace representation structures and rights. New phase: more institutionalised employment relations.
1994	First Berlusconi (right-wing) coalition government elected, soon collapses.
1996–2001	Centre-left governments with leading role for the Partito Democratico della Sinistra (PDS) (ex PCI). Structural changes and reforms to employment and labour market policies, welfare and collective bargaining via tripartite 'social pacts' that subsequently gain legislative form.
1998	Italy achieves criteria for entry into European monetary union. 'Christmas Social Pact' confirms the 1993 Central Agreement and new forms of decentralised concertation.
2001	Berlusconi's right-wing coalition regains power again after seven years in opposition. New Berlusconi government presents 'Libro Bianco' on more labour market flexibility for employers.
2002	'Pact for Italy' on competiteveness and social inclusion, but CGIL refuses to sign. Includes a

	partial temporary abolition of the application of the Workers' Charter for new hiring in smaller firms.
2006	Razor-thin electoral victory of the centre-left coalition in parliamentary elections. The new government is supported by an unsteady coalition of centrist, reformist and radical left parties.
2007	Tripartite reform of pensions and social shock-absorbers.
2008	The centre-left government implodes and Berlusconi's right-wing coalition returns to power.

CHAPTER 7

Employment relations
in France

Janine Goetschy and Annette Jobert

The population of France in 2008 was estimated to be 63.8 million, approximately 12.9 per cent of the combined national populations of the 27 members of the European Union. In 2008, life expectancy in France was 77.5 years for men and 84.4 years for women, well above the EU average. The French birthrate was among the highest in the EU, with nearly two children per woman. The total population is expected to grow, while the old-age dependency ratio could evolve more favourably than for the EU as a whole. However, as with other EU countries, France faces the challenges presented by an ageing population. Prospective studies estimate that France will have a population of 70 million by 2050, with one in three inhabitants aged over 60 years, compared with one in five in 2005.

France is the world's sixth largest economic power in terms of gross domestic product. Approximately 66 per cent of France's trade is within the European Union. While France remains the leading agricultural producer and exporter in Europe, its technology sectors, such as telecommunications and pharmaceuticals, as well as its luxury-goods industry, are also major assets. France is the world's second largest recipient of direct foreign investment.

Despite the absence of severe recessions in recent decades, France's economic growth rate has remained low during this time. Between 1993 and 2007, the average growth rate was approximately 2.1 per cent. Many factors account for this situation: a low participation rate among both the young and those over 55 years of age; insufficient reforms in labour market structure and economic policies; relatively short annual working time; the difficulties faced by small and medium-sized enterprises (SMEs) to survive and develop; under-resourced university systems; barriers to competition and limited access to the professions (see Attali 2008).

In 2006, the French workforce was estimated to be 25 million (13 million men and 12 million women). The labour market participation rate was 63 per cent (EU average 64.5 per cent). The participation rate has risen due to the increase in female employment, from 37 per cent in 1963 to 58 per cent in 2006. By contrast, the employment rate for young people aged between 15 and 24 years has been in decline for the past 25 years (29 per cent in 2006), largely due to a rising school retention rate. The participation rate among those aged between 55 and 64 years is also low (37.6 per cent in 2006). As with international trends since the 1970s, the forms of employment in France have changed substantially. In 2006, temporary employment represented approximately 13.5 per cent of the total French labour force, with 17.2 per cent engaged in part-time employment.

Since the 1980s, there has been high unemployment in France, resulting in the development of government-run employment and training schemes. Unemployment impacts significantly on the most vulnerable groups in society: young people and those aged over 50 years; manual workers rather than white-collar workers; the unskilled rather than the skilled; and women rather than men. Long-term and youth unemployment has recently increased, yet French unemployment overall remained at between 8 and 9 per cent in the period 1996–2006 (Freyssinet 2006).

Before the advent of the Fifth Republic in 1958, politics in France was more volatile than it was in most of the other European countries discussed in this book. After various changes during the past decade, the main political parties in France are currently the Union pour un movement populaire (UMP), mainly Gaullists, two small centrist parties which are broadly towards the right of the political spectrum, as well as the Communist Party, the Socialist Party and the Greens, which are all to the left of centre. The extreme right, which was influential in the mid-1980s, was weakened by the defeat of its leader in the 2002 presidential election. On the other hand, the extreme left, while only a minority, has grown in influence over the past decade.

Between 1958 and 1981, France was governed by right-wing governments. The Socialists made a decisive gain in 1981, with the election of François Mitterrand, who served two terms as President, from 1981 to 1995. Since 1995, France has been governed by both the right and the left political parties as well as coalition parties. Jacques

Chirac, from the right, was President of the Republic from 1995 to 2007. In 2007, Nicolas Sarkozy, also from the right, was elected President. François Fillon, the Prime Minister appointed by President Sarkozy, formed a government of the right that also included ministers from the left, the centre and the civil society. President Sarkozy has indicated that he intends to modernise many aspects of French society, including the economy, social welfare, employment, immigration, legal affairs and the justice system, as well as reducing the size of the public sector. President Sarkozy supported the nomination of a French Socialist, Dominique Strauss-Kahn, as head of the International Monetary Fund (IMF). He also attempted to play a leading role during the French term of the European Union Presidency in 2008 by establishing both new European and world financial systems in order to confront the 2008 financial crisis. Within the Eurogroup, which represents the countries belonging to the EU Monetary Union, President Sarkozy pleaded for a less restrictive Growth and Stability Pact.

THE INDUSTRIAL RELATIONS PARTIES

The industrialisation and urbanisation of France occurred during the mid-nineteenth century, which was later than in Britain. Strikes by French workers were permitted in 1864, although it was then illegal for workers to form unions. However, many informal unions were organised at a local level during this period and unions became legal in 1884.

Some features of contemporary French unions reflect their history and ideological complexity. The prominence of anarchists and revolutionary socialists within the French labour movement, combined with the often paternalistic or reactionary attitudes of employers, has heavily influenced the development of French employment relations. This helps to explain the traditional lack of mutual recognition between the employment relations parties (the social partners) and the interventionist role played by the French state in industrial and social matters.

The unions

The French union movement has been characterised by pluralism, rivalry and fragmentation on the one hand, and the paucity of financial and organisational resources on the other (Mouriaux 1994; Moss 1980; Andolfatto & Labbé 2006). These structural weaknesses have been particularly apparent since the 1970s. Union membership has long

171

been declining in France. Membership was approximately 23 per cent of the French workforce in the mid-1970s, 14 per cent in 1985 and had declined to 10 per cent by the mid-1990s. Union membership was estimated to be less than 8 per cent in 2007.

France has five national union confederations:

1. the Confédération générale du travail (CGT)
2. the Confédération française démocratique du travail (CFDT)
3. the Force ouvrière (FO)
4. the Confédération française des travailleurs chrétiens (CFTC) and
5. the Confédération française de l'encadrement-confédération générale des cadres (CFE-CGC).

The Confédération générale du travail (CGT), the oldest French confederation, was established in 1895 (Dreyfus 1995). With the 1906 *Charter of Amiens*, the CGT adopted an anarcho-revolutionary program, with members wary of both political parties and political action. Interestingly, in the same year, the British union movement turned in the opposite direction and formed the Labour Party. The friction between the anarchist and social-reformist members led to a major split in the CGT in 1921, with an expulsion of the Marxists. While the two wings reunited during the 1936 Popular Front, another split occurred in 1939 after the Germano-Soviet pact. A further reunification took place during the Resistance of World War II. However, another split occurred in 1948 when the minority group rejected Marxism, as well as the strong ties between the CGT and the Communist Party, and established the current Force ouvrière (FO). With the end of the Cold War and the collapse of the Berlin Wall in 1989, the independence of the CGT *vis-à-vis* the French Communist Party has grown. The 40th CGT Congress, held in 1999, was a turning point for CGT strategy. Without renouncing industrial action and class struggle, the CGT announced that it would support negotiation with employers and the state in the future. As a result, the CGT has since improved its relationship with the Confédération française démocratique du travail (CFDT). Between 1976 and 1990, the CGT lost two-thirds of its members. However, since the mid-1990s, the CGT's membership has increased and in 2007 it was estimated to have more than 600 000 members (Andolfatto 2007). As with the other national confederations, the CGT is organised into both industry federations and in geographically based local unions. The CGT is especially active in public enterprises, such as railways, gas and electricity supply, where employees are protected by special statutes. In the private sector, the CGT is strongest in the metal industry. While the majority of CGT members were once manual workers, this group now represents 42 per cent of the membership and the number of white-collar employees, technicians, engineers and middle-management members has increased. Women account for 23 per cent of CGT membership and two-thirds of the membership is aged over 60.

The CGT was a member of the World Federation of Trade Unions (WFTU) and held the post of WFTU Secretary General continuously from 1947 until 1978. In the 1992 elections for the ratification of the Maastricht Treaty, the CGT supported the 'no' vote. During the 45th WFTU Congress in December 1995, the CGT decided to leave the WFTU in order to improve its chances of joining the European Trade Union Confederation (ETUC), to which it was admitted in 1999. The CGT's admission to the ETUC was also a result of its change of attitude *vis-à-vis* EU integration. However, during the campaign for the European Constitutional Treaty in 2005, following internal dissent among the membership, the CGT made a different choice from other important unions and the ETUC, by recommending the 'no' vote.

The Force ouvrière (FO) was established in 1948 in reaction to Communist interference in the CGT (Dreyfus et al. 2003). The FO claims to be the true heir of the CGT's traditional policy of political independence and is staunchly anti-communist. Although the ideological tension between the CGT and the FO declined after the end of the Cold War, a degree of friction remains. The FO membership has been declining since the mid-1980s, and was estimated to have approximately 300 000 members in 2008. The FO is strongest among white-collar workers, particularly technical and professional groups in the public sector. The FO has traditionally included diverse political elements, and in the 1990s internal conflict led some members to defect to the Union Nationale des Syndicats Autonomes (UNSA). The FO regards collective bargaining as its main activity, and fiercely defends long-established social rights. Some of these rights are threatened by ongoing government and employer reforms, especially with regard to pensions and health-care entitlements.

On the international level, the FO joined the anti-communist International Confederation of Free Trade Unions (ICFTU) at its inception in 1949, and has been an affiliate of the ETUC since it began in 1973. FO policy has long supported European integration. However, since the late 1980s the FO has been critical of the EU as an instrument for economic integration and the free circulation of capital. In 1992, the FO did not provide any voting guidelines to its delegates during the vote on the ratification of the *Maastricht Treaty*. However, in 2005 the FO supported the 'no' vote on the EU Constitutional Treaty reform.

Christian-affiliated unionism began in 1919 with the formation of the Confédération française des travailleurs chrétiens (French Confederation of Christian Workers) (CFTC). Its main objective was to promote peaceful collaboration between capital and labour in accordance with the social doctrine of the Catholic Church, in particular Pope Leo XIII's 1891 Encyclical *Rerum Novarum*. The CFTC split in 1964, with the minority group retaining both its religious orientation and the CFTC title. Support for the CFTC continues among miners, Christian school teachers and health workers. Current CFTC membership is estimated at approximately 100 000. The CFTC emphasises the development of contractual relations and the defence of the family. As a member of both the World Confederation of Labour (WCL) from its inception, and the ETUC since 1990, the CFTC supports the development of a 'Social Europe' and voted for the ratification of the Maastricht Treaty in 1992.

Following the CFTC split in 1964, the majority group formally abandoned its affiliation with the French Catholic Church and formed the Confédération française démocratique du travail (CFDT) (Georgi 1995). In the 2000s, the CFDT lost almost 10 per cent of its membership due to its support for the 2003 government pension reforms. CFDT membership was estimated to be between 600 000 and 700 000 in 2007 (Andolfatto 2007).

In 1970, the CFDT adopted a form of socialist-Marxist ideology, with elements of 'Gramscism' and supported workers' control. However, after 1979 the CFDT altered its ideological stance and instead emphasised union adaptation to economic change, worked to establish closer links with its rank-and-file membership and aimed to develop closer links with the reformist unions. While the CFDT favours the independence of political parties, it also encourages constructive dialogue with government and employers. Its links with the CGT were strengthened during negotiations for the implementation of the 35-hour week in 1998. The CFDT experienced some factional conflict in the 1990s. Compared with other French unions, the CFDT has a more equal representation in the both private and public sectors, and also includes the highest proportion of women members (40 per cent), many of whom are in the health and commerce sectors.

At the international level, the CFDT is a member of ETUC and has played an active role in building a Social Europe. Some of its previous leaders have held key posts in several EU institutions during the 1980s. In 1978, the CFDT left the WCL and joined the ICFTU. It supported the 'yes' vote during the EU Constitutional Treaty reform.

The Confédération générale des cadres (CGC) was formed in 1944. The Confederation changed its name in 1981 to Confédération française de l'encadrement-confédération générale des cadres (CFE-CGC), to better reflect its changing membership: managers, engineers, sales representatives, supervisors, technicians and commercial agents. By the early 2000s, the CFE-CGC had 80,000 members and currently competes with both the CGT and the CFDT for members. The goals of the CFE-CGC focus on increasing management participation, maximising salaries and protecting their interests in relation to tax and social security. The CFE-CGC claims to be independent of any political party.

The five French union confederations are known at the national level as 'representative unions'. This identity was granted by public authorities in 1966 on the basis of five criteria, the most important being independence from employers. This conferred on the unions some exclusive rights, such as the nomination of candidates in the system of employee representation within the firm, representation on governmental and other consultative bodies, and collective bargaining. Such rights were not dependent on actual union presence within firms or demonstrable union membership. This system remained unchanged until 2008.

The Fédération de l'éducation nationale (National Education Federation, or FEN) is an important specialist union that represents the education sector. The FEN decided to remain independent at the time of the CGT split in 1948. The FEN recruits members and represents staff in most state educational institutions. In 1992, the FEN expelled two left-wing federations, which consequently led to the creation of the Fédération syndicale unitaire de l'enseignement, de la recherche et de la culture (FSU). Seriously weakened, the FEN sought alliances with other groups, mainly in the civil service, which led in 1993 to the foundation of the Union Nationale des Syndicats Autonomes (UNSA). UNSA, which has approximately 130 000 members, has yet to obtain official recognition as a nationally representative union. In 1999, UNSA became a member of the ETUC. It has built a close relationship with the CFDT.

The FSU rejects the collaborative attitude of FEN and has resisted successive government reforms of the educational system. It has approximately 150 000 members.

In addition to these confederations, a looser group of unions called 'the group of ten' was formed in 1981 and gathered the ten autonomous unions active in the public sector (representing areas such as police). Originally 'the group of ten' had a corporatist orientation. However, it became more left wing when joined by the 'Sud group of unions' from the postal and telecommunication sectors. This grouping of unions subsequently changed its name to Union Syndicale Solidaire (USS), with the aim of developing a unionism that was closer to citizens, supported anti-globalisation movements and defended immigrants, as well as citizens without identity papers and the homeless. The influence of the USS, with 80 000 members, is very limited. There are also several other 'autonomous' sector-specific unions, such as air traffic controllers, train drivers, truck drivers and journalists. These unions are called 'autonomous', as they have no affiliation with the larger groups, which are legally defined as 'representative'.

WHY IS UNION MEMBERSHIP DECLINING?

The restructuring of the French economy, high unemployment levels and the increased flexibility of labour contracts have resulted in scepticism among younger workers as to the purpose and value of union membership. Reasons suggested for the decline of union influence since the 1980s include employers' preference for direct dialogue with employees, inadequate union responses to new challenges, a gap between union leaders and rank-and-file membership, and union fragmentation and rivalry.

Broader support for the French union movement has weakened over time for the following reasons:

1. Closed-shop practices were prohibited in order to safeguard workers' rights to join a union. There are, however, some de facto closed shops in sectors such as shipping and printing.
2. As a legacy of their anarcho-syndicalist roots, French unions have traditionally sought to maintain an active core of 'militant' organisers, rather than to recruit a stable mass membership. This also explains why French unions have rarely become large bureaucratic organisations, like those in Germany. The role of militant organisers was to foster strikes and encourage or support political action, rather than engage in collective bargaining with employers, thus making it difficult to demonstrate clear bargaining results to union members. This factor might become less important in the future following the 2008 industrial relation reforms.
3. All wage-earners benefit from any improvement won by the unions; once ratified, a collective agreement applies to all employees, whether unionised or not.
4. In general, no specific welfare benefits accrue to French union members, unlike in some other countries.

5. Employers have often opposed any extension of union influence and have used paternalistic practices, particularly in the numerous SMEs; however, this *situation has slowly changed over time.*

6. Finally, the fragmentation of unions on ideological and political grounds hampered the recruitment and retention of members. As Reynaud (1975) commented, France presents a situation where union pluralism has coexisted with open competition between unions. Thirty years later, Pernot (2005) confirmed this situation and added that both union competition and rivalry had weakened unions further. However, Pernot considered union competition to be an intrinsic and enduring feature of French unionism.

Low union membership in France results in poor financial resources and inadequate organisational infrastructures, in comparison with unions in some other European countries. The financial resources of French unions are strained, as membership fees are paid irregularly. On average, union members pay only half the required annual fees and union fees are relatively low, being on average less than 1 per cent of a member's wage.

Nevertheless, unions do have more political and industrial influence than their low membership implies. Unions play an important role in collective bargaining and in representative elections, partly due to the electoral voting system. Unions also play a role in public tripartite or bipartite institutions, transforming unions into public service agencies (Rosanvallon 1988). However, there has been a recent increase in membership of both the Confédération général du travail (CGT) and the Confédération française des travailleurs chrétiens (CFDT). This seems to be associated with the strategic *rapprochement* between the two confederations, facilitated by the adoption of joint positions regarding the reform of 'representativeness rules' and improved social dialogue between the industrial relations parties.

THE REPRESENTATIVE STATUS OF UNIONS

The 'representative status' for unions has been subject to considerable debate since 1998, when the 'Aubry Law' introduced the 35-hour working week, which was intended to make state aid to unions conditional. In order to benefit from state support, unions were required to obtain a majority of votes at works council elections or to be ratified by employees through a referendum. This new requirement was a major departure from previous French labour law, as it invalidated practices whereby a collective agreement was valid if a union had 'representative status', even if signed by only one union and representing a minority of the workforce. These changes to the law were supported by the CGT and CFDT, which defended 'the majority principle' in the case of collective bargaining at sector and company level. However, the FO, CFTC and CGC were opposed to any change of rules that threatened their negotiating power (Bevort & Jobert 2008).

In April 2008, following a period of negotiation between five union confederations and three employer confederations, the social parties reached 'a joint position' concerning 'union representation, the development of social dialogue and the financing of unions'. An agreement was signed by the unions CFDT and CGT and the employer groups Mouvement des entreprises de France (MEDEF) and Confédération générale des petites et moyennes enterprises (CGPME). This joint position has led to a change in the criteria for determining union representation (Bevort 2008). In order to achieve representative status, a union must obtain, at both plant and company level, a minimum of 10 per cent of votes at the first ballot.

Following the 2008 agreement, there is a transitional period when at least 8 per cent of the ballot is required before unions will be considered to be representative at industry level. The right to negotiate is subordinate to and dependent upon being recognised as representative. To be valid, an agreement must be signed by one or more unions, gaining at least 30 per cent of the combined votes at the elections and without opposition from non-signatory unions. The 'joint position' also prescribes the measurement of the electorate and the financing of unions. It aims to provide greater transparency. Most observers have highlighted the importance of this common position, and consider it to be a genuine breakthrough in the French social partnership. By deciding to base representativeness on employee votes within the company, the social partners have aimed to firmly anchor union action within the company and to increase the unions' legitimacy. By these reforms, unions are seeking to become closer to wage earners and to renew the dynamics of social dialogue. This 'joint position' was supported by legislation in 2008.

These new rules could also foster a different process of union reconfiguration and alliances. Indeed, in order to survive, the smaller organisations will have to either merge or set up alliances. For example, UNSA and CFE-CGC have begun to work together more closely.

The employers

By contrast with the plurality of the various union confederations, employers have been united in their national confederation, the Conseil national du patronat français (CNPF) (established in 1946), which became the Mouvement des entreprises de France (MEDEF) in 1999. Employers began to organise in the early nineteenth century and established their first formal national association in 1919, which was the forerunner of the CNPF. MEDEF represents more than three-quarters of all French enterprises. However, MEDEF members differ in terms of their size and sectoral interests, diversity of capital ownership and range of management origins. Unlike its counterparts in Britain and Germany, the CNPF engaged in negotiation on broad issues from the late 1960s, although wages and working hours were excluded, with rates of pay being determined at the industry level.

The post-1973 economic crisis stimulated important changes in the employers' strategy. The employers' objective at the micro level was to increase the flexibility of labour contracts rather than reduce their workforce. The French government created a new law on redundancies in 1976, which required administrative permission by the state prior to the implementation of redundancies. This law was abolished in 1986.

Another strategy, introduced by employers at the end of the 1970s, was flexible working hours. The average length of the working week varied and could be calculated on a yearly basis until the 1990s. This strategy contributed to developments such as weekend work, shiftwork and flexible working hours, although this trend slowed somewhat after the introduction of the 35-hour working week through the Aubry Law in 1998. In the mid-1980s, the CNPF launched a campaign to increase wage flexibility.

Since 1977, the CNPF has exhorted managers to pursue an active social policy at plant level and to facilitate the implementation of more flexible practices. The election of Ernest Seillière as president of CNPF in 1997 resulted in increased conflict with both the government and the unions, reflecting the CNPF's fierce opposition to the Aubry Law. The CNPF saw the 35-hour week as disastrous to business costs and detrimental to job creation. In 1999, the CNPF changed its name to MEDEF.

French employers considered state intervention to have reached its zenith with the adoption of the 35-hour law and the state's increasing interference with some of the social protection agencies, which are jointly managed by unions and employers. In 2000, MEDEF proposed labour relations reforms to the unions and suggested eight issues to be negotiated: unemployment insurance and social inclusion of youth; pension schemes; occupational health and safety issues; the social protection system (sickness and family benefits); vocational training; the role of management; gender equality; and collective bargaining.

By the end of 2003, four issues had been discussed and agreed upon with most of the unions: unemployment insurance; occupational health and safety; collective bargaining and lifelong training. However, the CGT only signed the agreement on lifelong learning.

The election of Laurence Parisot as the first female president of the MEDEF in 2005 was not only of great significance in itself but also reflected the search for a new balance between the various industry federations, outweighing the traditional importance of the metal industry federation among employer groups. The new president, the ex-CEO of an opinion poll agency, was elected with the support of the major service federations. In contrast to her predecessors, Laurence Parisot's attitude towards unions and social dialogue has been one of greater openness, and she undertook to launch multi-industry bargaining on labour market reforms and representation rules. The Confédération générale des petites et moyennes enterprises (Confederation of Small and Medium-sized Enterprises, or CGPME), founded in 1944, is a rival employers' organisation, which nevertheless shares a common history with MEDEF and the two groups often work together. Two-third of the enterprises which belong to CGPME have fewer than 50 employees. Since the 1970s, public authorities have adopted a number of measures to encourage the growth of small to medium sized businesses.

The Union professionnelle artisanale (UPA) is another employer organisation composed of 850 000 small enterprises and craft industry enterprises, employing 2.7 million workers.

Although SMEs were traditionally important to the French economy, large companies have had a more prominent role since the late 1950s.

The state

State intervention is important in French employment relations (Howell 1992; Crouch 1993). This reflects the traditional reluctance of unions and employers to use voluntary collective agreements. Traditionally, unions have pressed for new laws when the left has been in the ascendancy: in 1936 with the Popular Front; in 1945 with Liberation at the end of World War II; in 1968 following the student riots and general strike in May; and in 1981 with the election of the Mitterand Socialist government.

Since the late 1960s, there has been a close link between the formulation of French industrial law and the outcomes of collective bargaining. Industrial laws have been based on the results of previously negotiated agreements or on earlier discussions between employer and industrial relations parties and the state. Moreover, the state increased the social partners' autonomy by transforming the legal framework for collective bargaining in 1971 and 1982 (Goetschy 1995; Mesh 1995).

The state and public authorities are also major employers, with approximately five million civilian employees working in the public service areas of central administration, hospitals, and local and regional government. As an employer, the state also exerts great influence on pay settlements in the private sector. The state influences wage levels through legislated increases and index-linked adjustments of the national minimum wage (known as the Salarie Minimum Interprofessional de Croissance, or SMIC). Unlike its British counterpart, the SMIC is adjusted according to the price index of consumer goods, when the latter has risen by 2 per cent. Moreover, the government can also raise the SMIC independently of the consumer price index. From a legal viewpoint, the SMIC should not constitute a basis for remuneration packages as a whole; however, it inevitably leads to an increase in all wages.

From the 1980s onwards, successive governments from both right and left have taken a vast array of measures aimed to reduce unemployment, especially to help the young and long-term unemployed find work. After 1988, the Socialist government of Prime Minister Michel Rocard introduced a 'minimum integration income', the Revenue minimum d'insertion (RMI), which was intended to assist the most vulnerable to gain work. By the late 1980s, the government had abandoned its expectation that unemployment would disappear with economic recovery and believed that a continuing significant level of unemployment was unavoidable.

The 1997 election of Prime Minister Lionel Jospin's leftist government brought major changes to French employment policies. First, the Jobs for Young People program was established, under which 350 000 community and public sector jobs were to be created by 2002. The program aimed to provide unemployed youth with five years of full-time contracted work in areas of high social need, such as education, family welfare, the arts and the environment. The government subsidised 80 per cent of participants' wages, which had to be at least equivalent to the national minimum wage (SMIC). Second, the introduction of the 35-hour week law known as the 'Aubry Law' dominated the Jospin government's social policy. Introduced in two stages in 1998 and 2000, the laws were to become effective within two years for enterprises with more than 20 employees and within four years for smaller enterprises. Social partners, at both sector and enterprise level, were encouraged to negotiate collective agreements that would maintain wages and support recruitment, while not undermining competition. Government subsidies were paid to enterprises willing to sign such agreements in advance of the law's implementation deadlines. In the case of enterprises in which union delegates were unwilling to negotiate, wage earners or workplace delegates were 'mandated' by representative union organisations to engage in negotiations. The introduction of a compulsory 35-hour week, applicable to all French industries, was harshly criticised by the MEDEF, which argued it would lead to a destabilisation of the industrial relations system.

However, the new law gave a decisive boost to collective bargaining at sectoral and enterprise levels, where approximately 48 000 agreements on working hours were signed between 1999 and 2001. By mid-2001, 50 per cent of full-time employees in firms with more than ten employees were working less than 36 hours per week. Opinion is divided as to the success of these agreements. According to the Ministry of Employment, these agreements enabled both the retention and creation of a total of 347 000 jobs. This figure is contested by the law's opponents, who consider that increased employment was primarily due to economic growth. While wage levels in general have been maintained, working time has been reduced in numerous enterprises due to work reorganisation, as well as more flexible working hours through 'annualisation' of hours (a trend that most unions had initially opposed). Subsequently, in 2002, the right-wing government of Jacques Chirac legislated to make the 35-hour week law less constraining for small and medium-sized enterprises.

Employee representation within enterprises

Successive French governments have established a range of representative bodies at the enterprise level, in some cases in response to particular social events. Workplace delegates (*délégués du personnel*) were instituted by the Popular Front in 1936; works councils (*comités d'entreprise*) were established in 1945 following Liberation at the end of World War II and workplace union branches (*sections syndicales*) were set up after May 1968. To summarise the role of these bodies, workplace delegates deal with individual employee grievances; works councils deal with workplace consultation; and union branches and stewards represent their unions and participate in collective bargaining at the workplace.

French workplace delegates are not union representatives, unlike shop stewards or workplace delegates in English-speaking countries. However, in practice a majority of workplace delegates are elected on a union 'platform'. Delegates must be elected every four years by all staff in enterprises with ten or more employees. The 1982 Auroux Law stipulates that delegates may also be elected in those workplaces with fewer than ten employees, where several firms operate on a common site, such as a building site or commercial centre, and if there are at least 50 employees in total. Most of the private sector is covered by this law.

Workplace delegates deal with individual claims for wages, working conditions, the implementation of labour law and collective agreements. Workplace delegates may also refer to a government labour inspector in cases where there is disagreement. The number of delegates elected varies according to the size of the firm. The employer must meet delegates collectively at least monthly. To fulfil their duties, delegates are allocated fifteen paid hours per month.

Since 1993, firms with between 50 and 199 employees have been able to choose a single representative structure rather than two, with workplace delegates taking over the work council representatives' role. Many firms have chosen the option of a single representative structure.

Works councils are required in all firms employing at least 50 employees. However, these councils have little real decision-making power, except in relation to welfare issues. Works councils do have the right, however, to be informed and consulted on the general management of a business, particularly in relation to the number and organisation of employees, working hours and employment conditions.

Every three months, French employers are required to inform the works councils of the state of their companies: orders, output and finances. Employers must also provide employment data, including details of any short-term contracts and subcontracting work, and to justify the use of such measures. Once a year, employers must submit written reports to the works councils, covering all business activities: turnover, losses or profits; production; substantial capital transfers; subcontracting; the allocation of profits; subsidies received

183

from the state or other public authorities and their disbursement; investments; and salaries. Works councils may choose to consult accountants in order to interpret these reports. Further, on an *ad hoc* basis, works councils must be informed and consulted on all changes in the economic or legal organisation of companies—for example, in case of sales or mergers. Moreover, works councils must be informed and consulted prior to the implementation of large projects involving the introduction of new technologies, when there might be consequences related to employment, qualifications, wages, training and working conditions. In firms of more than 300 employees, experts can be consulted for advice. In 2000, new rights were awarded to work councils in relation to takeover bids and were part of a wider Act concerning 'New Economic Regulations'. In 2002, the *Social Modernisation Act* stipulated that 'social plans' should reflect the new emphasis on redeployment measures as an alternative to redundancy and strengthened the work councils' information rights on redundancies. This requirement was further strengthened by the 2005 *Social Cohesion Act*.

Works councils are required to consider issues such as profit-sharing arrangements and changes to working hours, and agreement must be reached before implementation. The works councils are composed of the employee representatives and employers, or employers' deputies. The employers chair the meetings, which are held at least monthly. Each representative union can appoint a union observer to the works council. To fulfil their duties, each employee representative can use 20 paid working hours per month. The works councils can create sub-committees to examine specific problems. Health, Safety and Improvement of Working Conditions Committees are compulsory in firms with at least 50 employees. Firms with at least 300 employees are required to set up an employee training committee. Many employers initially resisted works councils, but most now accept their legitimacy.

Since 1968, there have also been workplace union delegates in parallel to the representative bodies. According to the law, workplace union delegates are appointed by the local union branch. However, the designated union delegate must be an employee working in the firm. Each union appoints its own union delegates, with their number varying according to the size of the firm. Union delegates can collect dues during working hours, use notice boards, distribute leaflets and organise monthly meetings (to be held outside working hours). All employee representatives are legally protected against dismissal. It is unlawful to hinder a representative or the various representative institutions.

The representative institutions are not a coherent system, but have grown in an *ad hoc* way. Moreover, due to the complex and occasionally imprecise legal framework, there is some confusion over roles, not least because individual representatives may fulfil several functions.

A major innovation of the 1982 Auroux Law was the establishment of a group committee within large French-registered multi-plant companies. The function of such committees is to receive information about the financial and employment situation within the group at least once a year. With the national implementation of the 1994 EU directive on European Works Councils, which defined information and consultation rights for employees in multinational firms, the role of group committees has become less relevant.

According to research published by the Ministry of Employment in 2007, unions are present in only 38 per cent of private sector companies with more than 20 employees. This varies, however, according to the size and age of the firm and the length of time a firm has been established (DARES 2007).

Employee participation and collective bargaining

The 1981 election of the Mitterand Socialist government brought a different political and legal perspective to collective bargaining, which was outlined in the *Report on the Rights of Workers* by the Minister of Labour, Jean Auroux (1981). The *Employee Participation Act* of February 1982 gave employees the right to withdraw from dangerous working conditions, without stopping workplace machinery. The Act was further extended in August 1982 to give employees the right to make decisions on the content and organisation of their work and, more generally, their working conditions. The Act prescribed that employees' views should be expressed 'directly' and 'collectively' on these matters *(groupes d'expression directe)*. Both the Act and other 1982 ordinances gave priority to collective bargaining. The search for a new balance between state intervention and collective bargaining was a hallmark of President Francois Mitterrand's post-1981 reforms.

The 1982 *Collective Bargaining Act* contained regulations aimed at both improving and innovating the French industrial relations system. For example, in firms with established union branches, employers were obliged to annually negotiate pay and working hours. Since 2001, compulsory bargaining at plant level has been extended to include issues such as equal employment rights for both men and women, sickness benefits and employee saving schemes, as well as a requirement for anticipatory manpower management and skill planning (every third year for companies with more than 300 employees). However, there is no obligation to reach an agreement and the employer's decision is final. Unlike in the United States, there is no requirement in France to bargain 'in good faith'. Plant-level bargaining has greatly progressed since the beginning of the 1980s, and has gained autonomy *vis-à-vis* the law and industry-level bargaining. Approximately 25 000 agreements are finalised annually in the private sector. Traditional bargaining points, such as wages, working time and trade union rights, have expanded due to legal requirements to include issues such as employee savings accounts. Negotiations can also be conducted by elected employee representative bodies, but only in specific circumstances. Trade unions, aware of the importance of employees' interests being well-represented in plant-level bargaining, negotiate 80 per cent of agreements in firms with established union branches. However, plant-level bargaining has serious shortcomings, as 84 per cent of the agreements are signed in companies with more than 50 employees—which excludes half the total wage earners who are employed in small enterprises. Hence it is important to maintain industry-level bargaining, as it covers wage earners in all sectors of the economy.

While important reforms have been made to facilitate greater decentralisation, collective bargaining remains important at the industry level. This is despite the opposition of some employers to high levels of labour market regulation (Jobert 2000). Collective agreements are generally negotiated at the industry level for an unspecified period. Collective agreements establish the basic labour relations rules for a given industrial sector. Moreover, subsequently these rules can be extended by the Minister of Labour to apply to all French workers. This explains why virtually all wage earners in France are covered by a collective agreement. Labour laws also impose regular bargaining on wages and job classifications, equal opportunities and lifelong learning. In firms with more than 300 employees, it is compulsory to negotiate working conditions, provisional human resources planning and qualifications.

After a decline in the 1970s and 1980s, multi-industry bargaining increased in importance in the 1990s. The aims of multi-level bargaining are to achieve agreement on matters such as unemployment benefits, complementary pensions, lifelong learning, employment and alleviating hardship at work. Multi-industry agreements sometimes result from government initiatives that aim to foster social partnership in industrial relations and social protection matters. Since January 2007, the government has been required to consult with representative social partners prior to introducing legal reforms relating to work, employment and lifelong learning. In recent years, multi-level bargaining has gained a greater political dimension, as it involves major national and European public policy issues with important social consequences. The developments in multi-level bargaining reflect the changes in union and employer organisations, as well as in alliances, ideological positions and strategies. Both the CGT and the FO have been reluctant to sign multi-industry agreements, especially with regard to changes in the unemployment benefit system. Three major multi-industry agreements have been ratified since 2000.

First, the 2003 agreement on lifelong learning, signed by all social partners, substantially reformed lifelong learning regulations by granting employees a maximum of 20 hours of training per year, which can be accumulated over six years. French employers have been obliged by law to financially contribute to staff training, This reform was inspired by Jacques Delors, then adviser to Gaullist Prime Minister Jacques Chaban-Delmas. In 2003, the employer contribution increased to 1.6 per cent of the wages bill for enterprises with ten or more employees and to 0.55 per cent for those enterprises with fewer than ten employees.

Second, the 'modernisation of the labour market' agreement, signed in 2008 by all social partners except the CGT, enables a labour contract to be varied by mutual agreement between the employer and the employee, and enables the latter to benefit from redundancy and unemployment benefits. The agreement introduces a new fixed-term contract for engineers and middle management (*cadres*) who complete a given project with a duration of 18 to 36 months. In exchange for this increased flexibility, wage earners can obtain unemployment benefits after only one year of employment, and some of their social rights (linked to the enterprise) can be transferred when they cease their employment.

Third, a multi-industry agreement has been ratified concerning the rules governing both the validity of agreements. As well as the three collective bargaining arenas (multi-industry, industry level and enterprise level), the industrial relations system also includes national social-protection institutions, some of which are jointly managed by the employers' associations and the five representative unions. These social-protection institutions include social security funds (health, pensions, family allowances), supplementary pension funds, unemployment insurance and vocational training for employees. State involvement in collective bargaining varies according to the issue at stake. Since the 1980s, there have been serious problems in all areas of the social welfare system, reflecting the weakness and rivalry of unions, as well as the social partners' inability to undertake reforms without state intervention.

Representative elections

The support for individual unions can be gauged by both their formal membership and from the results of 'social' elections, such as those for the representatives of works councils and industrial tribunals (Conseils de Prud'hommes).

The works council election results for 2005–06 revealed that, in total, the five representative unions obtained nearly 69.2 per cent of the votes (see Table 7.1). Since 1999, the share of votes obtained by each of the five union confederations has remained stable. However, there has been a slight increase on behalf of the autonomous unions. Hence the unions have a much higher degree of support than might be inferred from their low membership. The number of non-unionised candidates contesting representative elections increased between 1985 and 1995, but has subsequently declined. The participation rate for works council elections remains at more than 60 per cent (63.8 per cent in 2005 and 2006); however, there has been a small decline of 3 per cent since the late 1990s.

The industrial tribunal elections represent another indicator of union support. These tribunals are composed of councillors from the firms, and are responsible for resolving individual grievances between employees and employers. The councillors are elected every five years by all employees and employers. Table 7.1 reveals that, although the CGT has remained the leading confederation, its support has declined since 1979. The most striking result of those elections is the continuing increase in the abstention rate, which reached 74 per cent in 2008 compared with only 37 per cent in 1979. However, when comparing these results, it must be kept in mind that the two union representative elections have different voting constituencies. The industrial tribunals have a much larger electorate than that of the works councils.

INDUSTRIAL DISPUTES

The right to strike is guaranteed by the French Constitution, with qualifications. Since 1963, public-sector unions have had been required to give five days' notice before a strike. However, there is little legal regulation of strikes in the private sector. French courts distinguish

Table 7.1 Results of works council elections

	1995–96	1997–98	1999–00	2001–02	2003–04	2005–06
Participation rate	66 200	65 800	64 500	64 600	64 800	63 800
CFDT	21 100	21 300	22 900	22 700	21 200	20 300
CFE-CGC	6 100	6 100	6 000	5 800	6 300	6 500
CFTC	4 800	5 000	5 500	5 800	6 400	6 800
CGT	21 700	22 400	23 000	23 500	23 400	22 900
CGT-FO	12 200	12 100	12 300	12 700	12 600	12 700
Other unions	6 800	6 500	6 500	7 000	7 300	8 200
Non-unionised	27 300	26 600	23 800	22 500	27 800	22 600

Source: DARES, *Premières informations,* October 2008, no. 40.3

between legal and illegal strikes. In the private sector, a strike is legally defined as a 'stoppage of work'. Hence other actions, such as industrial sabotage, working to rule or slowing production, are unlawful. A lawful strike must be concerned with 'industrial relations issues'. Despite legal constraints on 'sit-ins', such actions are permitted when their primary aim is to seek negotiations with employers, rather than merely to disrupt output. Nevertheless, excessive disruption of output through strikes is illegal, and lock-outs are also generally illegal. Following many years of discussion without resolution, the obligation to maintain 'a minimum service' in the case of public sector strikes is now law. An Act proclaimed on 21 August 2007 aims to prevent or minimise conflicts in the public service sector and to provide alternative measures organising the sector in the event of land-based public transport strikes. In these transport sectors, a preliminary negotiation period of eight days must precede a union's notification of a forthcoming strike. Issuing of preventive notice has long been compulsory. Employees who intend to participate in strikes must inform management of their involvement 48 hours before the strike commences. If a strike continues for eight days, any one of the parties involved is entitled to organise a secret ballot among employees to decide whether the strike should be extended. However, the result of this vote is not binding. Further, the enterprise in which the strike takes place must decide, after consultation with its clients, which transport lines will remain in operation in order to limit traffic disruption as much as possible. These regulations governing the conduct of strikes have led to fierce debate among the unions. At the

189

same time, industry and employers who were hoping for more stringent measures to be adopted were also disappointed.

Although there is limited French legislation governing strikes, there are elaborate procedures for the settlement of disputes, including conciliation, mediation and arbitration. However, these procedures are rarely put into practice. While industrial disputes tend to be unpredictable, they are short lived. This is due to the fact that French unions have few financial reserves and generally do not grant strike pay (a legacy of the anarcho-syndicalist tradition). Moreover, France loses relatively few working days due to stoppages when compared with Italy and a number of English-speaking countries.

When comparing strikes over a longer period, the following trends can be noted (Shorter & Tilly 1974). First, compared with the 1970s, there has been a significant decline in the number of working days lost since the 1980s. On average, there were more than three million days lost per year in the 1970s, 1.5 to 2 million days lost per year in the 1980s and less than a million days lost per year in the 1990s. The above statistics concern market sector strikes for both privately and publicly owned companies. However, the general picture changes little when civil servants are included. The years 1995 and 2003 were both exceptional, with 5.8 and 4.4 million days lost respectively in private and public sectors. Second, the proportion of 'generalised conflicts' (multi-employer strikes) decreased significantly in the 1980s and 1990s to between approximately 10 and 15 per cent of the level of such strikes in the 1970s. Strikes in the public sector accounted for approximately 45 per cent of strikes in the late 1980s and early 1990s, and represented two-third of strike days during recent years (Bevort & Jobert 2008). Some of the public sector strikes were characterised by the establishment of rank-and-file 'coordination groups' to organise strikes alongside or in opposition to official union channels, such as those representing administration workers and nurses. These coordinated activities reflected the deficiencies of French unions. In the public sector, claims were made to increase pay and to improve working conditions, career opportunities and human resources policies. Certain sectors, such as public and private transport, are particularly strike prone. Fears of the likely privatisation of the public sector, resulting from EU liberalisation directives, to a large extent explain the number of strikes occurring in these sectors (Denis 2005).

An increasing number of employment issues have caused more recent strike action, and it is very difficult to precisely attribute causation, as many disputes involve multiple issues. Nevertheless, the negotiations on the 35-hour week generated an increased number of strikes. In 1998, a quarter of the strikes were *apparently* about working time issues, whereas wages and employment matters *apparently* precipitated only half the total number of strikes. By the mid-2000s, wage claims were again the major cause of strikes. There were also a growing number of disputes due to restructuring and plant closures in MNEs, which were widely publicised by the media.

In December 1995, there were strikes against Prime Minister Alain Juppé's proposed reforms to align civil servants' pensions with those of the private sector and to end the more favourable pension schemes enjoyed by some employees in the public sector, such as railway workers. As a result of these strikes, the Juppé Plan was withdrawn. However, most of these proposed reforms were introduced subsequently by successive governments.

While there has been a decline in the number of traditional strikes, new forms of conflicts have emerged, such as work-to-rule and go-slow practices, demonstrations and the drafting of petitions (DARES 2007). Such forms of protest and micro-conflicts, while not yet well recorded, have become significant features of recent industrial disputes (Groux & Pernot 2008).

CONCLUSIONS

French unions have continued to have low membership, despite labour legislation that has tended to improve their position, especially under the recent governments. Nevertheless, the steep fall in union membership between the late 1970s and the early 1990s appears to have ceased for the time being, and there has been a slight growth in membership in recent years. Following the 1995 strikes, internal and external rivalries increased and further weakened French unions. However, the end of the Cold War and the CGT's decision to join the ETUC helped to improve the relationship between the two largest unions, the CFDT and the CGT. Their joint positions regarding both the representative role of unions and social dialogue issues have improved their relationship.

A number of factors have made the unions' role difficult in recent years. These include competitive pressures, the increasing number of mergers and takeovers, industry restructuring, the expansion of the service sector, changes in the labour market, high unemployment, the growth of flexible labour contracts, proactive employers' policies and unsuccessful union strategies. French employment relations remain characterised by a great contrast between stakeholders. On the one hand, there are the large companies, in which unions are active participants in company-level bargaining and where they are able to exercise their rights. On the other hand, unions and representative institutions are rarely present in SMEs, which makes company-level bargaining impossible. The reforms undertaken by governments or implemented through collective agreements have not fundamentally altered this situation (Goetschy 1998). This is largely due to the opposition of a proportion of employers who continue to regard the presence of unions in their enterprises as having a negative effect.

Nevertheless, the unions have exercised greater influence than their low membership density might imply. Strikes still occur and cause significant disruption to public services, such as transport, education, health care and postal services. Union resistance is one of the reasons France, in comparison with other EU countries, has not yet fully reformed its pension and health-care systems. This also explains the delay in the privatisation of French public utilities, such as gas, electricity, post and railways, despite the requirements of the EU internal market program.

Despite the changes of government, there has been continuity in employment relations policy in certain areas of political and social life. For example, the decentralisation policies introduced by the Socialists in 1983 has been continued by both right and left governments. There has also been continuity of education and training policies, as well as of employment policies, such as the reduction of indirect labour costs. Nevertheless, the introduction of the 35-hour week continues to cause conflict between employers and unions.

In 2003, the French government undertook a reform of the civil service pension system, similar to the 1983 reform of the private sector pension system. Despite efforts by governments to achieve economic liberalisation, wage earners and most unions remain committed to the state's continuing strong regulatory role in employment relations. This commitment is illustrated by the July 2008 Act on social democracy and working time.

However, the 2008 Act, while maintaining the 35-hour legal working week as a standard, allows for the renegotiation of this provision at plant level in terms of overtime, compensatory rest time, daily payment for the *cadres* and work time organisation. This Act led to a gradual dismantling of an important part of the French labour code in the area of work time organisation, achieved without the government's prior consultation with social partners. The 'transposition' of the 2008 Act has led to severe controversy, as the signatory unions (CGT and

CFDT) considered themselves betrayed by the government, while the employers group (MEDEF) supported the government's decision. The non-signatory unions (FO, CFTC and CFE-CGC) considered the CGT and CFDT unions to have been 'trapped'. This case illustrates the fragmentation of French unionism and the prominent role of the state in employment relations. Until the respective roles and responsibilities of both the state and the social partners are more clearly defined, it will be difficult to develop an autonomous and strong social dialogue in French employment relations.

A CHRONOLOGY OF FRENCH EMPLOYMENT RELATIONS

1791	The *Chapelier* law forbids strikes and unions, but not employers' associations.
1821	Building industry employers' association is established.
1830s–40s	Many illegal combinations of workers and some collective agreements.
1864	Abolition of Le Chapelier Law.
1871	Paris Commune.
1884	Unions entitled to organise on a craft or industry basis, but not at enterprise or plant level.
1895	Confédération général du travail (CGT) established
1906	Anarcho-syndicalist Amiens Charter asserts the CGT's independence from political parties.
1919	The Confédération française des travailleurs chrétiens (CFTC) established following the 1891 *Rerum Novarum* Capital and Labour Encyclical of Pope Leo XIII.
1919	First national industrial employers' confederation founded.
1936	Election of the Popular Front coalition of socialists, communists and radicals. Many strikes and sit-ins. Collective agreements between the employers' association and the reunited CGT. Major social reforms enacted/initiated: paid holidays, the Bill on collective bargaining, the 40-hour legal working week, the introduction of employee delegates at work sites.
1944	The Confédération generale des cadres (CGC) established.
1946	The Conseil national du patronat français (CNPF) established as the main employers' association.
1948	Creation of the Force ouvrière (FO), following a split within the CGT.
1950	Law on collective bargaining and the establishment of a minimum wage system.
1964	A majority of CFTC members vote to form the secular Confédération française démocratique du travail (CFDT). A minority of members reject this decision and remain within the CFTC.

1968	Events of May precipitate a general strike; workplace union branches permitted.
1971	Amendment to 1950 Act to permit plant-level bargaining.
1976	New Redundancy Law enacted.
1981	President François Mitterrand's socialist-communist coalition forms government. Aroux Laws enacted, including the *Employee Participation Act* and the *Collective Bargaining Act*. Retirement age reduced from 65 to 60 years.
1987	New Redundancy Act repeals the earlier requirement for prior administrative approval; new flexible working hours law introduced.
1988	Socialist government returns to power after two years' absence. Bill passed regarding minimum integration income (*Revenu minimum d'insertion*).
1993	A right-wing coalition government takes office under Prime Minister Édouard Balladur; President Mitterrand continues in his post.
1995	Jacques Chirac elected President. Major public-sector strikes against policies of Prime Minister Alain Juppé's government.
1997	Election of left-wing government, headed by Prime Minister Lionel Jospin.
1998	New laws (the Aubry Law) introduce the 35-hour week.
1999	The main employers' confederation (CNPF) is replaced by the Mouvement des Enterprises de France (MEDEF).
2000	Industrial relations reforms (*Refondation Sociale*) launched by MEDEF.
2001	The *Social Modernization Act* strengthens the information rights of works councils on redundancies.
2003	Major reform of the general pension system in both the private and public sectors.
2004	Government's 'social cohesion plan', supporting employment, housing and anti-discrimination.
2005	*Social Cohesion Act*.
2007	Nicholas Sarkozy (right-wing) elected President of the Republic. August Bill.

CHAPTER 8

Employment relations in Germany

Berndt K. Keller and Anja Kirsch

THE HISTORICAL, LEGAL AND SOCIO-POLITICAL BACKGROUND

After the destruction caused by World War II, the West German economy recovered so fast that the 1950s and 1960s came to be known as the 'economic miracle' (*Wirtschaftswunder*). West Germany quickly developed into the strongest economy in Europe and one of the leading nations in world trade. The high-productivity, high-added-value and high-wage model of production based on a highly skilled workforce lasted until the mid-1970s. When the Bretton Woods system of fixed but adjustable exchange rates collapsed in the early 1970s and the two oil crises in the mid- and late 1970s led to sudden drastic increases in crude oil prices, the West German economy stagnated and even declined. Unemployment rose rapidly and the 'golden age' of the economic miracle came to an end.

The economy recovered in the mid- to late 1980s when West Germany achieved record export surpluses and additional jobs were created in new areas of employment. The German model (*Modell Deutschland*), with its strong unions and employer associations negotiating compromises in political processes of coordination, was a fairly successful solution for the difficult challenges of modernising and rationalising the economy. However, unemployment remained relatively high and persistent, averaging about 8 per cent.

Since 1990 and the end of the Cold War, the unification of the Federal Republic of Germany (FRG—*Bundesrepublik Deutschland*)

196

and the German Democratic Republic (GDR—*Deutsche Demokratische Republik*) has caused many problems. The rapid integration of the socialist East German centrally planned economy into the capitalist West German social market economy (*soziale Marktwirtschaft*) has created unique and enduring challenges. In the early 1990s, after the relatively short 'unification boom' in the West, unified Germany experienced high unemployment and the most severe economic crisis since World War II. Since the mid-1990s, the rate of economic growth has been low and unemployment—particularly long-term unemployment—has remained high.

Politically, West Germany, and since 1990 unified Germany, have experienced a high degree of continuity and stability. Between 1949 and the late 1960s, the conservative Christian Democratic Union (CDU/CSU) was in power, in most cases in coalition governments with the Free Democratic Party (FDP). In the period between 1969 and 1982, coalition governments forged between the Social Democratic Party (SPD) and the FDP ruled the country and changed the system of employment relations in various regards. Between 1982 and 1998, the CDU was back in power, again in coalition with the FDP, and promoted labour market flexibilisation and deregulation. Between 1998 and 2005, the SPD and the Greens formed the coalition government. Between 2005 and 2009, there was a grand coalition government between CDU/CSU and the SPD. Since 2009, a coalition government between the CDU/CSU and the FDP has been in power.

The legal infrastructure was put in place after 1945, although its institutional roots extend from the Weimar Republic (1919–33) (Jacobi et al. 1998). According to the Constitution, the Basic Law (*Grundgesetz*) of 1949, Germany is a federal system. The states (*Bundesländer*) have been granted autonomous rights in different fields of public policy (e.g. cultural affairs, education and science). In employment relations, however, the legal foundations are the same for all states, and in this regard Germany differs from other federal systems such as Canada or the United States. Germany is, like some other Western European countries, a developed welfare state with all-encompassing systems of social protection (including unemployment insurance, health insurance and pension schemes). This extensive social regulation, which has focused on occupational status and the insurance principle, has always been regulated by law and not by collective bargaining (Leibfried & Wagschal 2000; Manow & Seils 2000).

THE EMPLOYMENT RELATIONS PARTIES

Employers and their associations

As in Switzerland and Scandinavia, employers have various types of interest organisations in Germany. The three types are called general business or trade associations (*Wirtschafts- or Unternehmensverbände*), special employers' associations (*Arbeitgeberverbände*) and chambers of industry and commerce (*Industrie- und Handelskammern*) as well as chambers of trades (*Handwerkskammern*) (Grote et al. 2007; Schroeder & Weßels 2010). The business or trade associations represent general economic and product market interests *vis-à-vis* the state, whereas the employers' associations are concerned with social policy, labour market interests and employment relations, including collective bargaining. These two types of voluntary organisation cooperate closely. The chambers of industry and commerce or trades, on the other hand, are public entities that perform a variety of public and semi-governmental tasks, and membership is compulsory for all enterprises.

Individual employers' associations (*Arbeitgeberverbände*) represent firms according to industries (*Fachprinzip*) as well as regions (*Regionalprinzip*), and these industry and regional associations are affiliated to the Confederation of German Employers' Associations (*Bundesvereinigung Deutscher Arbeitgeberverbände*, or BDA). The industry associations are responsible for collective bargaining.

The exact membership densities of employers' associations are unknown, but their member organisations were estimated to employ around 75 to 80 per cent of all employees in the past (Visser & van Ruysseveldt 1996). Since the 1980s, however, employers' associations have experienced declining membership. For example, membership density in *Gesamtmetall*, the metal and electrical industry employers' association, has decreased from almost 80 per cent in West Germany in the early 1980s to about 52 per cent in unified Germany in the mid-2000s.

Legally, all member companies must adhere to the conditions of the collective agreements that their employer association negotiates with a union. However, employer associations are finding it increasingly difficult to balance the interests of various member groups. Many small and medium-sized enterprises (SMEs, or *Mittelstand*) are dissatisfied with their associations' collective bargaining policies, particularly their policies of decreasing working hours. As they consider their associations' policies to be dominated by the interests of large enterprises, many SMEs decide to cancel their membership (Voelkl

2002). These tensions between member groups have weakened employer associations' capacity to exercise discipline and authority over their member companies during the collective bargaining process and in the implementation of collective agreements.

In response to membership loss, some employer associations now allow companies to join and receive membership benefits such as information and legal advice without being bound to the collective agreements (membership *ohne Tarifbindung*, or OT). Other associations have established separate associations offering OT membership. This strategy is controversial among employers' associations and academics, and it is unclear whether it will solve the problems of declining membership, or lead to the rise of a new type of association and the further decline of the existing ones—and with that to a weakening of industry-level collective bargaining (Schroeder & Wessels 2010).

Unions

Unions were established after World War II according to the principles of industrial unionism (*Industriegewerkschaft*) and unitary unionism (*Einheitsgewerkschaft*). The principles mean that, first, all employees of an enterprise join the union that covers their industry (e.g. engineering, retail or chemicals), irrespective of their occupation or blue- or white-collar status, and second, that the unions are not closely affiliated with political parties. The industry unions engage in collective bargaining, while the relatively weak peak federation, the German Trade Union Federation (*Deutscher Gewerkschaftsbund*, or DGB), is responsible for political activities including lobbying (Schroeder & Wessels 2003).

More than 80 per cent of union members belong to unions affiliated to the DGB. The remaining 20 per cent of union members belong to unions affiliated with the Confederation of Christian Unions (*Christlicher Gewerkschaftsbund*, or CGB) or the German Civil Service Association (*Deutscher Beamtenbund*, or DBB). The CGB has about 300 000 members, and the DBB has about 1.2 million members. The DBB organises exclusively in the public sector and mainly looks after civil servants. It is the only association with membership growth since the 1990s (Keller 1999).

As Figure 8.1 shows, the organisational structure of around seventeen DGB-affiliated industry unions was remarkably stable until the mid-1990s. While union mergers are relatively common in many countries (Waddington 2005), they were unknown in Germany until shrinking membership, decreasing financial resources and structural

Figure 8.1 Union mergers

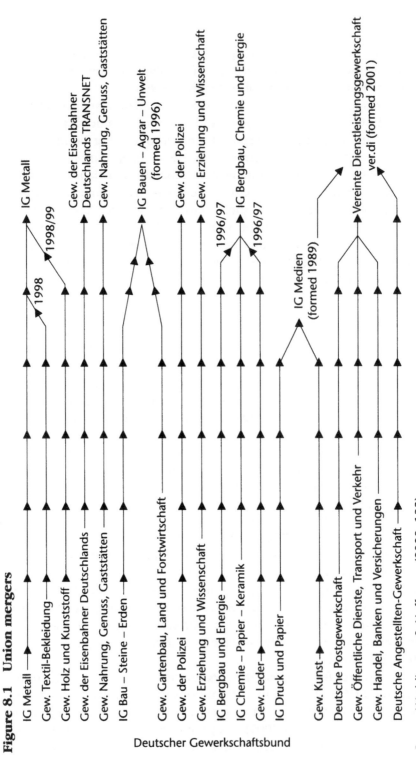

Source: Waddington & Hoffmann (2000: 133)

changes in the economy, including labour market flexibilisation and deregulation, led to a 'merger mania' that has gradually replaced the system of industrial unionism with eight unions. The two biggest unions, IG Metall and ver.di, make up 70 per cent of all members of DGB affiliates.

Membership density in the DGB unions fluctuated around 30 to 35 per cent from the 1950s to 1980s. Figure 8.2 shows that after a short-lived surge in membership following unification in 1990 (from eight to twelve million), all unions experienced significant losses. Density fell to a historical low of 20 per cent in the early 2000s (Ebbinghaus & Visser 2000; Ebbinghaus 2003a). These losses contributed to a decline in union bargaining power and the rise of a major non-union sector. German union density is presently lower than the Western European average, and German unions have suffered more than the majority of their counterparts with the only exception being the United Kingdom (Visser 2006).

Figure 8.2   Membership in DGB-affiliated unions

Source: DGB <www.dgb.de>

Union membership is concentrated among skilled, male, full-time workers in the manufacturing sector and among public sector employees. However, changes in the composition of the workforce mean that women, younger employees, highly educated and qualified employees, private service sector employees, foreign workers and workers in atypical employment are under-represented. To secure their long-term survival as powerful actors, unions need to organise the unorganised, especially women and white-collar employees (*Angestellte*) in the private services sector, and formulate new policies that appeal to both existing and new membership groups (Traxler et al. 2001).

The state

Unlike the more voluntaristic systems of Anglo-Saxon countries, German employment relations are characterised by a high degree of juridification (*Verrechtlichung*) (Weiss & Schmidt 2000). The most important laws governing employment relations are the *Works Constitution Act*, the *Co-Determination Acts*, the *Collective Agreement Act* and the *Social Security Act*. Collective labour disputes, however, are subject to case law (*Richterrecht*), a series of binding decisions from the independent Federal Labour Court as well as the Constitutional Court (Brox et al. 2007). In contrast to other countries, there is an independent and specialised system of labour courts at the local, regional and national levels.

The Constitution (*Grundgesetz*) guarantees all individuals the fundamental right of freedom of association. Hence membership of interest associations is voluntary, and union security arrangements such as closed shops and union shops are illegal. Furthermore, the 'social partners', as unions and employers and their associations are often called, have the right to free collective bargaining (*Tarifautonomie*) as specified in the *Collective Agreement Act* (*Tarifvertragsgesetz*) of 1949, amended in 1969 and 1974. This means that the social partners engage in collective bargaining without any active state interference. Informal and/or public recommendations are the only means of intervention. Collective agreements are binding for both signatory parties and their members. Employers frequently extend the terms of the agreements to all their employees in order not to provide incentives for joining unions. There is a strict peace obligation during the term of an agreement. This rule limits opportunities for industrial action and contributes to the comparatively low degree of industrial conflict.

There are mediation agreements (*Schlichtungsvereinbarungen*) in all major sectors of industry. These procedural arrangements are the results of voluntary negotiations between the social partners and are not determined by legal enactment or any other form of state interference. By contrast with many other countries, federal and/ or state mediation and conciliation services are of little importance.

Active state intervention in this crucial period would be incompatible with the fundamental principle of free collective bargaining.

Until the 1980s, the extensive legislation governing the German employment relations system was often criticised as being too restrictive. More recently, it has been recognised that it contributes to the stability of the employment relations system. Furthermore, within the legal framework, the social partners have more freedom to determine their own structures and their dealings with one another in the form of collective bargaining and mediation than is the case in countries that are generally characterised as voluntaristic, such as the United Kingdom.

Besides providing a legislative framework, the state may take an active role in employment relations through corporatist arrangements. The late 1960s and the 1970s were the heydays of neo-corporatism in several European countries, when governments included unions and employer associations in processes of socio-economic policy-making in exchange for wage restraint by the unions or even the implementation of a binding incomes policy. In Germany, the SPD-FDP coalition government of the 1970s used tripartite management of the economy by means of Keynesian instruments of macro-steering and demand-side economics to pursue macro-economic goals such as the relative stability of prices, full employment, steady economic growth and a foreign trade balance.

As the German central bank, the *Bundesbank*, was a completely independent institution, the 'Concerted Action', as this corporatist arrangement was called, was based on voluntary wage restraint (rather than a statutory incomes policy as in other countries), and has therefore been termed a 'weak form of macro-level coordination' (Iversen 1999: 159). On comparative scales of corporatism (Siaroff 1999; Molina & Rhodes 2002), Germany has always scored in the middle, between non-integrated pluralism (as in the Anglo-Saxon world) and integrated corporatism (as in Austria or the Scandinavian countries).

As in the majority of other European countries, the classical form of centralised, macro-corporatist arrangement gradually lost its importance with the decline of Keynesianism and its macro-steering capacities, shifting political preferences towards conservative majorities, and the rise of neo-liberal ideologies and supply-side economics. More recently, however, there has been a revival of neo-corporatism in some Western European countries (Fajertag & Pochet 1997, 2000; Katz 2005). This 'competitive corporatism' takes non-classical, network forms of macro-coordination and intends to increase national competitiveness and employment (Traxler 2004).

In Germany, attempts to introduce such new mechanisms by the conservative Christian Democratic-led government in the mid-1990s as well as by the Social Democratic-led government in the early 2000s failed. Their 'Alliance for Jobs' sought to achieve not only less overtime work, more part-time work, more opportunities for vocational training and more jobs for the long-term unemployed, but also a general reorientation of social and fiscal policies. Modest wage demands and increases below the level of productivity growth were supposed to stimulate investment and to generate more employment.

EMPLOYMENT RELATIONS PROCESSES

This section discusses the main processes in the German employment relations system: co-determination at the workplace and company levels, collective bargaining, and industrial disputes.

Co-determination

Co-determination is the distinguishing feature of employment relations in Germany. This form of employee participation in management is based on the idea of industrial democracy and originated in the Weimar Republic. Legislation institutionalises labour–management cooperation at both the workplace and the company levels.

Co-determination at the workplace level

The *Works Constitution Act* (*Betriebsverfassungsgesetz*) of 1952, amended in 1972, 1988 and 2001, is the legal basis for co-determination at the workplace level. It gives works councils (*Betriebsräte*) a set of rights relating to specific issues. As Table 8.1 shows, these rights range from information, through consultation to binding co-determination and veto rights, and relate to social policy issues such as payment methods and systems, work schedules and the regulation of overtime; personnel issues such as recruitment, transfers and dismissals; and economic or financial issues. Generally, these rights are stronger in social matters than they are in personnel, economic and financial matters. Through these rights, works councils are able to influence issues that remain 'managerial prerogatives' in other countries.

The *Works Constitution Act* does not apply to very small enterprises (with up to five permanent employees) or to public-sector employees, who are covered by separate *Staff Representation Acts*. Furthermore, enterprises that serve political, religious, charitable, educational and scientific aims are only partially covered.

Table 8.1   Works councils' rights

Rights (from weak to strong)	Examples
Right to information	The works council (WC) has the right to meet with management monthly. Management must supply the WC with information on the economic and financial situation of the company and on strategic decisions such as changes to the premises and working procedures and operations. It must also inform the WC on present and future human resources needs, vocational training measures and resulting staff movements.
Right to inspect documents	The WC must be given access at any time to documentation it may require to carry out its duties. It is entitled to inspect payrolls and personal files.
Right of supervision	The WC has the right to ensure that the employer observes and complies with laws, safety regulations, collective agreements and works agreements.
Right to make recommendations and give advice	The WC can make recommendations to the employer for action on social matters such as policies on smoking or parking. The WC may make recommendations regarding manpower planning.
Right to be consulted and right to object	The WC must be consulted before every dismissal and informed about who is to be dismissed, why it should take place and when. Dismissals carried out without consulting the WC are null and void. The WC may object to a dismissal if it believes that it is unfair, breaches selection guidelines, or if job transfer, re-training or changes to the job are possible.
Right to veto a decision	The employer must inform the WC about every recruitment, classification, re-classification and transfer, explain the consequences of such personnel measures and obtain the WC's consent. The WC can refuse to consent to such decisions for a number of reasons, e.g. if the measure is unlawful, breaches selection guidelines, or if the WC is concerned that the measure will lead to unfair and avoidable disadvantages for employees. The employer may apply to the Labour Court for a decision in lieu of WC consent.

Rights (from weak to strong)	Examples
Right to initiate and negotiate matters with genuine co-determination between the employer and the WC	The WC has the right to co-determine social matters at the workplace such as the distribution of working hours and breaks; leave schedules; the introduction and use of technical devices for monitoring employee behaviour and performance; when, where and how employees are paid; and how piece rates and other performance-related pay components are determined. The employer and WC may, after negotiation, sign a works agreement on these matters which has a direct and binding effect on all employees. If no agreement can be reached, a conciliation committee decides the matter. If the employer plans to make significant changes to operations such as merging, spinning off, offshoring or closing down parts of a business or changing production methods, the WC must be consulted. The employer and the WC negotiate a Social Compensation Plan that compensates employees for disadvantages that result from such changes. If no agreement can be reached, a conciliation committee decides the matter.

Source: Page (2006: 14–16)

These rights are legally guaranteed and enforceable, and on the basis of these rights, management and works councils negotiate works agreements (*Betriebsvereinbarungen*) that regulate issues such as rostering, redundancies, and so on. As works councils and management are obliged to cooperate 'in a spirit of mutual trust for the good of the employees and of the establishment', and as works councils are not allowed to strike, these negotiations are generally not conflictual (Weiss & Schmidt 2000). Works agreements are not allowed to contradict the provisions of industry-wide collective agreements.

In legal terms, works councils are independent and separate from the unions. Co-determination at the workplace and collective bargaining at the industry level are supposedly strictly separate, and works councils are meant to be detached from all 'quantitative' problems of wages and income distribution. In reality, however, many works councillors are active union members, and unions provide important services (e.g. information, training, legal expertise and advice) that facilitate works councils' everyday activities. Unions depend on works councils to recruit new members, to monitor the implementation of collective agreements and to assist in organising industrial action. In this regard, works councils show some functional similarities with company (or enterprise) unions in other countries. Thus, despite the legal separation of both institutions, a system of mutual dependence has developed over several decades. More recently, a certain gap between both institutions has evolved.

Although works councils are mandatory, the *Works Constitution Act* does not oblige employers to initiate their election, so they must be formed upon employee initiative. This means that in many enterprises there are no works councils. Recent data (see Figure 8.3) indicate that only about one-quarter of all eligible private enterprises have elected works councils. However, these cover about 50 per cent of the private sector workforce (Ellguth & Kohaut 2007).

These figures indicate that one half of all private sector employees are *not* covered by works councils. This percentage has been rising since the mid-1980s (Bertelsmann-Stiftung & Hans-Böckler-Stiftung 1998). Employees in eastern Germany, in the private services sector and in SMEs are least likely to be represented by works councils, and even some large companies have (more or less actively) prevented the establishment of works councils. In other words, in contrast to

Figure 8.3   Coverage rate of works councils (percentage of employees covered)

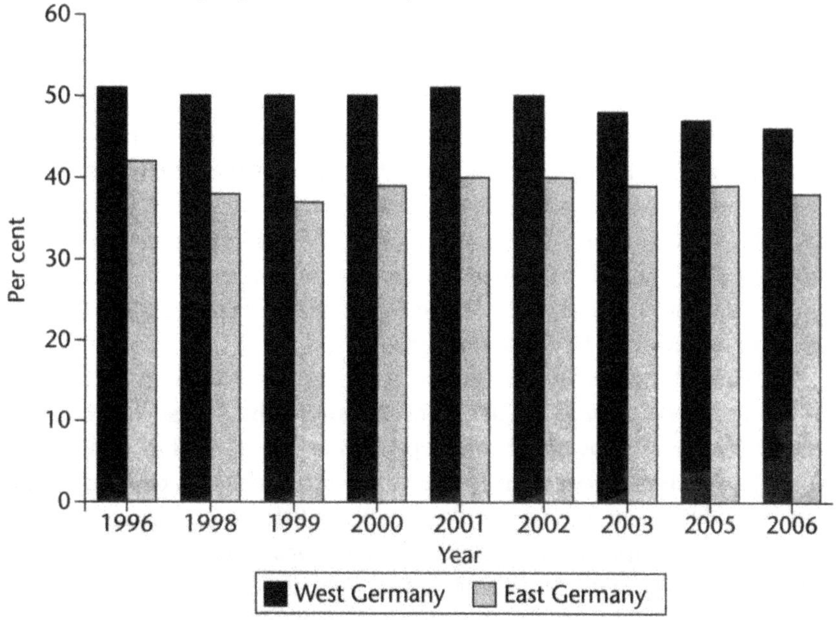

Source: Ellguth & Kohaut (2007)

widespread assumptions about the German system of corporate governance, the majority of all private-sector employees have no access to shop-floor interest representation. Thus there is a growing 'representation gap' despite the legal guarantees.

Traditionally, co-determination has been justified as a basic political right rather than on grounds of economic efficiency. However, since the mid-1990s there has been some controversial discussion in political and academic circles about the impact of co-determination on indicators such as productivity, fluctuation, innovation and earnings. Most recent econometric studies with large samples do not find any evidence of detrimental impacts that could be used to justify changes to the existing forms of co-determination (Dilger 2002; Frick et al. 1999; Frick 2003).

Co-determination at the company level

German companies have a two-tier board structure—in contrast to the one-tier boards in the Anglo-Saxon countries. Theoretically, all strategic decisions are made by the supervisory board (*Aufsichtsrat*), which represents the owners and stakeholders of the company. It appoints and controls the members of the smaller management board (*Vorstand*). The full-time managers on the management board implement strategic decisions, and monitor and control everyday affairs. In practice, however, their impact is more encompassing (Gerum 2007).

A specified percentage of members of the supervisory board (from one-third to almost one-half, depending on individual Acts) are employee representatives. Often they are works councillors or union officials. Furthermore, one member of the management board, the labour director (*Arbeitsdirektor*), is supposed to represent employees' interests. In the majority of companies, he or she is in charge of employment relations and human resource management.

For historical reasons, there are three Acts on co-determination at the company level (*Mitbestimmungsgesetze*).

The *Co-determination Act for the coal and steel industries* (*Montan-Mitbestimmungsgesetz*) of 1951 established the most far-reaching form of 'full parity' between the representatives of capital and labour on the supervisory board. In quantitative respects, it is only of minor importance because of the secular decline of these industries—today, less than 40 companies are covered by its provisions. However, it is still of enormous symbolic value to the unions.

The first version of the *Works Constitution Act* (1952) granted comparatively weaker rights to employees: one-third of the seats on the supervisory board. It covered joint stock and limited liability companies with 500 to 2000 employees. In 2004, it was superseded by the *One-Third Participation Act* (*Drittelbeteiligungsgesetz*) that applies to about 1500 enterprises.

The *Co-Determination Act* (*Mitbestimmungsgesetz*) of 1976 grants rights close to parity. It is the most important Act because it is valid for all limited liability companies with more than 2000 employees. Throughout the 1980s, it applied to about 500 companies. Since the early 1990s, this number has grown to more than 700 due to unification, the splitting of large companies into smaller ones and the privatisation of public enterprises (Ehrenstein 2007).

These two channels of co-determination through works councils and employee representatives on supervisory boards have contributed to the gradual development of sophisticated forms of cooperation at the company and shop-floor levels. Therefore, the relations between capital and labour in Germany are characterised more accurately by the notion of mutual recognition within a 'social partnership' than by concepts of class antagonism or 'adversarial' employment relations. However, nowadays only a minority of employees work in companies where their interests are represented both by works councils and by representatives on the supervisory board. The majority has no representation at all, and this will surely have an effect on the nature of employment relations in the future.

Collective bargaining

Unions and employer associations (or individual employers) engage in collective bargaining in order to regulate pay and working conditions. The basic procedures are stipulated in the *Collective Agreement Act* (*Tarifvertragsgesetz*). There are three kinds of collective agreement: first, wage agreements (*Lohn- und Gehaltstarifverträge*) fix the level of wages and their periodic increases; second, framework agreements (*Rahmentarifverträge*) specify wage-payment systems; third, umbrella agreements (*Manteltarifverträge*) regulate all other conditions of employment (e.g. working time, overtime, holidays). In total, there are about 69 000 agreements currently in place (Bispinck & WSI-Tarifarchiv 2008), indicating an enormous heterogeneity and flexibility.

In the majority of industries, collective bargaining takes place at the regional and industry levels—for example, between the regional branches of the employer association *Gesamtmetall* and the union *IG Metall* in the metal and electrical industry. These regional activities occur (with some recent exceptions) annually, and are centrally coordinated by the national unions and employer associations. In most cases, this structure has led to pattern bargaining, especially in engineering. Pilot agreements concluded in specific, carefully selected bargaining districts are transferred to other districts of the same industry, and they also predetermine the results in all other major industries.

The comparative employment relations literature has examined the impact of bargaining centralisation on macroeconomic performance (e.g. unemployment, inflation and economic growth). Early studies seemed to indicate that highly centralised as well as highly decentralised systems of collective bargaining would perform much better than intermediate ones (Calmfors & Driffill 1988). Germany seemed to belong to the least favourable group of intermediate countries that were supposedly unable to deliver moderate pay rises. More recently, this 'hump-shaped' relationship was called into question when studies showed that it was not so much bargaining centralisation but coordination that influenced macroeconomic performance (Soskice 1990; Traxler et al. 2001). Germany belongs to the group of countries with intermediate levels of centralisation but comparatively high degrees of bargaining coordination within, as well as between, industries.

In such moderately centralised and highly coordinated systems of collective bargaining, wage differentials between individuals and groups of employees, industries, regions and qualification levels are relatively narrow and working conditions, particularly working time, are more standardised than in decentralised systems. This means that changes in labour costs and nominal wages are similar for all companies in a particular industry, and wages are taken out of competition. However, in Germany wage differentials, and thus differences in living conditions, have been increasing in the most recent past (Schettkat 2006).

Instead of adhering to an industry-wide agreement, some companies—particularly SMEs—conclude their own enterprise agreements with unions. Although the number of enterprise (or company-level) agreements has increased from about 3000 in the early 1990s to about 9000 in the late 2000s, their macroeconomic impact remains small (Bispinck & WSI-Tarifarchiv 2008: 96). Only about 8 per cent of employees in western Germany and 13 per cent in eastern Germany are covered by company-level agreements (Schnabel 2000).

Although the significance of company-level agreements remains limited, the coverage rate of industry-level agreements has decreased to an extent that it is sometimes referred to as a 'crisis of sectoral collective bargaining'. As Figure 8.4 shows, since the mid-1990s coverage has declined from more than 70 per cent to about 55 per cent of all employees in western Germany (Ellguth & Kohaut 2007; Kohaut 2007). In eastern Germany, coverage has decreased even more, to about 40 per cent (Bellmann et al. 1999). There is significant variation between sectors—while the public sector and the social insurance, mining, energy, construction and finance industries maintain industry-wide agreements, the service sector, SMEs and new firms have much lower coverage rates. Some 35 per cent of employees in western Germany and 45 per cent in eastern Germany work in companies that are not legally bound to any collective agreement at all (WSI Tarifarchiv 2007). Compared with other OECD countries, Germany has only medium coverage rates (Traxler 2003).

Another problem that has been threatening the stability of the collective bargaining system since the 1990s is the so-called 'tacit escape from collective agreements' (*stille Tarifflucht*). This means that some companies maintain their membership of employers' associations but do not comply with the terms of the industry-wide collective agreement, despite the legal requirement to do so. Most frequently,

Figure 8.4   Industry bargaining coverage rates (percentage of employees covered)

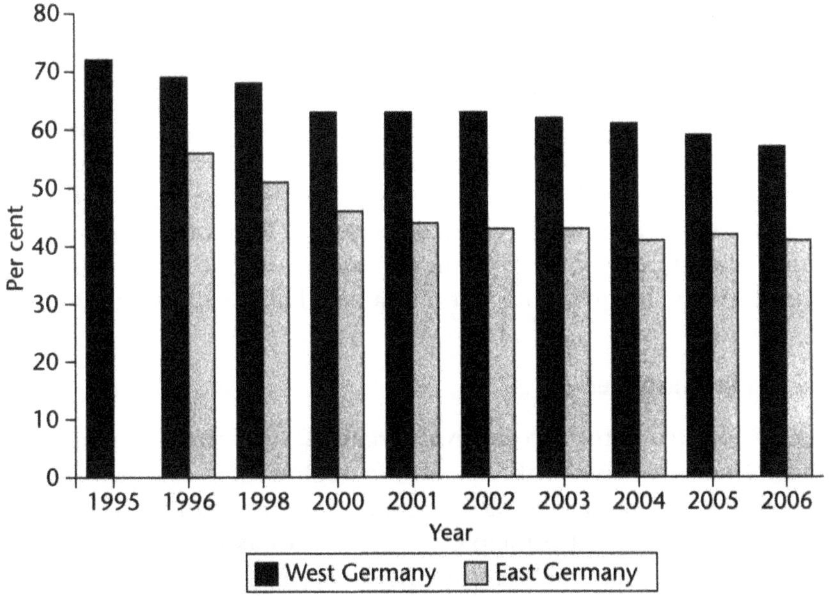

Source: Kohaut (2007); Ellguth & Kohaut (2007)

they deviate from the provisions on working hours, but also on fringe benefits and even wages. While works councils and unions generally ensure that individual employers actually implement the standards defined in collective agreements, they tolerate this non-compliance quietly in order to save scarce jobs in times of high unemployment, to prevent offshoring and outsourcing, or to increase the productivity of 'their' company. The phenomenon is, almost by definition, difficult to quantify but is more widespread in the east than in the west (Artus 2001).

A consequence of this 'tacit escape' is that the official statistical coverage rates of collective agreements over-estimate their real scope. Together, this creeping, internal erosion of sectoral bargaining and the membership loss of employers' associations indicate that the viability and legitimacy of collective bargaining and its key players have been undermined and challenged. Collective agreements are no longer able to fulfil their original function of taking wages out of competition. Informal and uncoordinated 'wildcat cooperation' between managers and works councils seems to be widespread, and has grown since the 1990s. Comparative studies have argued that 'the growing variation in employment systems that appears within countries has resulted from a shift in bargaining power in management's favour' (Katz 2005: 275). Germany is a prototypical example of this trend.

Overall, in the German model of employment relations employee interests are represented in a dual system: co-determination at the workplace and company levels as well as collective bargaining at the industry level. However, as we have seen, only a minority of employees actually enjoy these conditions. In fact, less than one-third of all employees in western Germany and about 20 per cent in eastern Germany are covered by an industry-wide collective agreement *and* are represented by a works council (Ellguth & Kohaut 2007). In other words, the 'duality' of the German system, one of its fundamental characteristics, has gradually been weakened and is disintegrating.

Industrial disputes

Due to the structure of collective bargaining, industrial disputes are usually industry wide within a certain region, and are coordinated centrally by unions and employer associations. According to the Basic Law and its enshrined principle of freedom of association, strikes as well as lockouts are legal instruments in an industrial conflict. When unions organise a strike, they conduct membership ballots to ensure the necessary support for collective action. However, these ballots are prescribed by unions' statutes and not by legislation, as in other countries such as Australia. Employers associations use lockouts to intensify and extend disputes to additional workplaces. Doing so exhausts the unions' resources because they have to provide strike pay to their members.

Although there is a pattern of occasional, major disputes every few years, Germany has a relatively low level of industrial disputes compared with other countries. Only small countries such as Switzerland, Austria and the Netherlands have lower rates (Eaton 2000; Ryan et al. 2004). The disputes have had only limited aggregate economic impact on a range of indicators (e.g. companies affected, employees involved or working days lost per 1000 employees). Lockouts mainly occurred between the 1950s and early 1980s and were concentrated in a few industries, primarily engineering. Since then, employer associations have found it increasingly difficult to organise lockouts due to the heterogeneity of their members' interests.

There are several reasons for the low degree of industrial conflict in Germany. First, relatively centralised systems of collective bargaining tend to result in less industrial conflict than more decentralised ones. Germany fits very well into this general pattern. Second, the 'dual' system of employment relations promotes long-term cooperation and mutual trust rather than industrial conflict. Third, there is a clear legal distinction between disputes regarding the interpretation of existing collective agreements—disputes of rights—and disputes about the terms and conditions of new collective agreements—disputes of interest—(*Rechts- und Regelungsstreitigkeiten*). For the former, either the existing conciliation committees at the company level operate as efficient grievance machinery, or these disputes are resolved in labour courts. Either way, they are settled by peaceful means. Only conflicts about the terms and conditions of new collective agreements can be the subject of legally sanctioned industrial action.

Current and future issues

This section explores changes to public sector employment relations, the discussions surrounding the introduction of a statutory minimum wage, various kinds of labour flexibility and the decentralisation of collective bargaining.

Public sector employment relations

The state is Germany's largest employer, and employment relations in the public sector are characterised by the legal distinction between

213

public employees (formerly blue- and white-collar employees or *Arbeiter* and *Angestellte*) on the one hand and civil servants (*Beamte*) on the other. While employees enjoy the same rights as their counterparts in private industry, civil servants and their interest organisations are not allowed to bargain collectively or to strike. Instead, civil servants' employment conditions are determined by law and their interest associations influence the determination of wages and conditions through lobbying (Keller 1993). For decades, collective bargaining by public sector unions and lobbying by civil servants' organisations led to similar or even identical wages and conditions for employees and civil servants. More recently, public employers have changed this long-term practice of equal treatment of status groups to the disadvantage of civil servants.

Collective bargaining used to be highly centralised and took place at the national level for all federal (*Bund*), state (*Bundesländer*) and municipal (*Gemeinden*) employers. For a long time, this structure contrasted with the growing decentralisation of public sectors in other European countries (Bach et al. 1999, Dell'Aringa et al. 2001). However, German public employers have recently decentralised bargaining; nowadays, the states bargain separately from the federal state and the municipalities. It is likely that this trend will continue or even increase (Keller 2007). Collective disputes are rare—major strikes took place only in 1974, 1992 and 2006. In the 2006 strike, unions tried to resist bargaining decentralisation. In general, differences in labour market strategies between private and public sector employers have been diminishing as both pursue greater flexibility and take advantage of the present labour market conditions (Keller & Henneberger 1999).

Public sector employment grew in the early 1990s when the overstaffed East German public sector was integrated into the West German system. Since then, employment has been decreasing. This is partly due to the strict stability criteria established for the countries participating in the European Monetary Union. The rules restricting new public debts to no more than 3 per cent of GDP encouraged privatisation and placed increased pressure on all public sector budgets. Therefore, the overall number of public sector employees (currently about 4.5 million) is much smaller than it used to be, and in comparison with other countries Germany has only a medium-sized public sector.

Privatisation has been on the political agenda for many years. During the 1990s, privatisation took place mainly at the local level (e.g. refuse collection and cleaning). Some former state monopolies, including the postal service and the railways, have also been privatised.

Privatisation has had an impact on employment practices, but it has been less significant than in other countries such as the United Kingdom.

Minimum wages

In contrast to the vast majority of EU countries there is no statutory national minimum wage in Germany (Schulten et al. 2006). In the past, a statutory minimum wage was unnecessary, as collective bargaining coverage was extensive. However, in recent years bargaining coverage has declined substantially and in many areas of expanding employment, especially in the service sector, there are no collective agreements in place. In addition, the mere existence of a collective agreement does not guarantee a sustainable wage level, as unions find themselves unable to secure adequate wages through collective bargaining in industries in which they have few members and little bargaining power. Most recently, the low-wage sector—that is, wages below two-thirds of the median wage—has been increasing to a remarkable degree even in comparison with other EU countries and the United States (Bosch & Weinkopf 2008). The phenomenon of the 'working poor', formerly unknown in Germany, is now an urgent problem not only among contingent and part-time workers but also among full-time employees.

Therefore, there is a heated political debate about the introduction of some form of binding minimum wage. One single national minimum wage could be established by legislative means, or several minimum wages that differentiate between industries, occupations or regions could be established through collective bargaining. As in other countries, those opposing minimum wages argue that they would put jobs at risk and limit employment opportunities, despite empirical evidence from comparable countries—especially the United Kingdom—showing that this is not necessarily the case. Actual effects of minimum wages on the economy would, of course, depend on their level.

Unions are strictly in favour of a minimum wage, while the majority of employers' associations vehemently oppose all suggestions to set a binding lower limit. The grand coalition government was divided on this issue and was not able to reach a clear decision. In mid-2008 it slightly amended two already existing Acts, the *Posted Workers Act* of 1996 (*Arbeitnehmer-Entsendegesetz*) and the *Act on Minimal Working Conditions* of 1952 (*Mindestarbeitsbedingungsgesetz*) in order to make it easier to declare collective wage agreements generally binding for all employers in a specific industry, especially in industries with low coverage rates and more than one existing collective agreement. In other words, the political compromise avoids general legislation but allows for industry-specific solutions. The present coalition government is opposed to general minimum wages and prefers industry-level arrangements. In the future, it is likely that the social partners, rather than the government, will agree on industry-specific minimum wages, especially in the service sector—for example, in mail delivery services, commercial cleaning and temporary agency work.

Increasing flexibility

Since the early 1980s, employers and their associations have voiced demands for more 'flexibility'. The reasons advanced have included the changing conditions of labour and product markets, as well as new patterns of work organisation following the demise of the Taylorist-Fordist age of standardised mass production. However, the concept of 'flexibility' has various meanings (OECD 1986; Esping-Andersen & Regini 2000). Here, we distinguish between temporal flexibility, flexibility of wages and salaries, functional flexibility and flexibility in forms of employment.

Temporal or working time flexibility was a key concern in collective bargaining in the 1980s. The unions, principally *IG Metall*, demanded shorter weekly working hours (i.e. the 35-hour week) in order to decrease the supply of labour and to create additional jobs. After a major industrial dispute in 1984, an agreement was struck that combined the union's goal of reduced working hours with the employers' goal of greater flexibility and differentiation in the allocation of working hours at the enterprise level (Seifert 2005).

Nowadays working hours can be quite flexibly arranged and can be unevenly distributed across days, weeks or even seasons, with long periods of equalisation of about one year or longer. Working hours have been decoupled from the operation time of the enterprise by means of new shift systems and variable working hours over longer periods of time. Thus enterprise-specific productivity and production hours have increased, despite shorter working hours for individuals. The management of working-time arrangements has become a new field of specialisation and has led to a diverse array of models, particularly in larger companies (Seifert 2006).

Further collective reductions of working time are no longer on the bargaining agenda. Employers have strongly opposed further reductions, and employees have had to find a balance between wage rises and shorter hours. Instead, the individualisation of working hours has become the main focus of attention. In all major sectors of the economy, individual working-time accounts have been introduced for the majority of employees. These arrangements can be used for various purposes, such as extended leave, further training or early retirement. Their negotiation and implementation are a major concern of works councils (Seifert 2008).

However, working time is still a contested terrain. Most recently, some companies and industries have successfully reversed the secular trend towards shorter working hours. They have managed to conclude collective agreements with extended working hours, at times with only partial compensation or even without additional pay. Today, the average collectively agreed weekly working time for full-time employees is 37.6 hours (38.8 in the east and 37.4 in the west) (Bispinck & WSI-Tarifarchiv 2008: 114). Effective working times are longer, at about 40.3 hours, and are increasing. At the same time, part-time work has significantly increased to more than 25 per cent of the labour force, so all in all there is a trend towards the polarisation of working time.

Flexibility of wages and salaries (including fringe benefits) became a major topic in collective bargaining only after the introduction of temporal flexibility. Employers argue that wages should correspond to a company's 'ability to pay'. However, since the 1990s, unions have hardly been able to increase real wages, and in some cases there have been reductions in real wages. Issues of wage redistribution have declined in importance, and labour's share of the national income has fallen to the level of the early 1970s. Since the mid-1990s, income inequality between the low-paid and high-paid, as well as between blue- and white-collar workers, has increased considerably (Schettkat 2006).

Functional flexibility is not a central concern in collective bargaining because the dual system of vocational training, a peculiarity of the German-speaking countries, provides many young people (about two-thirds of the age group) with a broad range of skills. Apprentices spend part of their time undertaking general training in highly special-ised vocational schools, and also acquire specific skills at their work-places in individual companies. This system of creating human capital is jointly run by employers, unions and the state, and provides Germany with a competitive advantage over countries with less integrated training structures. It creates large pools of qualified labour, fosters a multi-skilled workforce and leads to the continuous supply of employees with standardised theoretical as well as practical qualifications, which are necessary in 'high-skill/high-wage' economies.

Due to the functional flexibility of employees, the introduction of greater flexibility in work organisation, work rules and production processes has been less controversial in Germany than in many other countries, such as the US, where job demarcations and strict seniority rules are prominent. From an international perspective, this dual system of vocational training results in a comparatively low percentage of youth unemployment, because it eases the transition from school to the labour market. However, in recent years there has been a shortage of apprenticeships offered by employers.

The final type of flexibility discussed here is flexibility in forms of employment. Since the 1980s, there has been an encompassing trend away from the standard employment relationship (*Normalarbeitsverhältnis*) that comprises full-time, continuing employment and inclusion in the social insurance schemes (including health care and pensions). As in other countries (Houseman & Osawa 2003; Gleason 2006), atypical employment has increased and includes part-time work, petty employment, 'new' forms of self-employment, fixed-term contracts and temporary agency work (see Table 8.2). Currently, more than one-third of the workforce is engaged in such 'non-standard' employment, and this trend will most likely continue. With the only exception being agency work, women are over-represented in all these atypical forms.

The growth of non-standard employment has increased tendencies of segmentation of the labour market into a core unionised and protected segment and a peripheral unorganised and unprotected segment. Workers in non-standard employment have less employment security and are less likely to be union members or to be represented by works councils. It is likely that this trend will have serious negative consequences, not only for the composition of the labour force but also for social cohesion, the degree of inequality and the employment-related social insurance schemes, particularly pensions. All in all, the consequences of these changes for employment relations practices are far-reaching (Keller & Seifert 2007; Kronauer & Linne 2007).

Decentralisation of collective bargaining

There is a trend towards collective bargaining decentralisation in many countries, including Germany (Katz 1993; OECD 1997a; OECD 1997b; Traxler et al. 2001). However, the processes through which decentralisation is taking place in Germany differ from those in other countries, and have been categorised as 'organised' as opposed to 'disorganised' decentralisation (Traxler 1995). Since the 1980s,

Table 8.2 Development of forms of non-standard employment

Year	Overall employment in 1000	Part-time work		Petty employment[b]		Temporary agency work[b]		Overall employment (excluding vocational training)[d]	Fixed-term contracts (excluding vocational training)	
		in 1000	in per cent of overall employment[a]	in 1000[c]	in per cent of overall employment	in 1000	in per cent of overall employment		in 1000	in per cent of overall employment
1991	33 887	4736	14.0			134	0.4	32 323	2431	7.5
1992	33 320	4763	14.3			136	0.4	31 891	2495	7.8
1993	32 722	4901	15.0			121	0.4	31 151	2221	7.1
1994	32 300	5122	15.9			139	0.4	30 958	2322	7.5
1995	32 230	5261	16.3			176	0.5	30 797	2388	7.8
1996	32 188	5340	16.6			178	0.6	30 732	2356	7.7
1997	31 917	5659	17.7			213	0.7	30 436	2453	8.1
1998	31 878	5884	18.5			253	0.8	30 357	2536	8.4
1999	32 497	6323	19.5			286	0.9	30 907	2842	9.2
2000	32 638	6478	19.8			339	1.0	31 014	2744	8.8
2001	32 743	6798	20.8			357	1.1	31 176	2740	8.8
2002	32 469	6934	21.4	4 100	12.6	336	1.0	30 904	2543	8.2
2003	32 043	7168	22.4	5 533	17.3	327	1.0	30 513	2603	8.5
2004	31 405	7168	22.8	6 466	20.6	400	1.3	29 822	2478	8.3
2005	32 066	7851	24.5	6 492	20.2	453	1.4	30 470	3075	10.1
2006	32 830	8594	26.2	6 751	20.6	598	1.8	31 371	3389	10.8
2007	33 606	8841	26.3	6 918	20.6	731	2.2	31 906	3291	10.3
2008	34 241	9008	26.3	6 792	19.8	794	2.3	32 232	3106	9.6

a by end of April
b by end of June
c so-called mini-jobs up to 400 Euro on a monthly base
d in general contracts for vocational training are fixed-term and are, therefore, not included

Source: Federal Statistical Office, F 1, Reihe 4, 1, 1, several volumes and https://www.ec.destatis.de/csp/shop/sfg/bpm.html.cms.cBroker.ds?cmspath=struktur.sfgsuchergebnis.csp; Federal Employment Office (http://pub.arbeitsamt.de/hst/services/statistik/detail/b.html)

so-called 'opening clauses' (*Öffnungsklauseln*) have become the major instrument of reform. Opening clauses are increasingly included in industry-wide collective agreements (e.g. in engineering, chemicals, retail, textiles and printing) to secure, innovate and reform the system of industry-wide collective bargaining. Such clauses allow individual companies to vary or deviate from certain provisions in the industry-wide collective agreement in order to adapt the agreement to their own circumstances. Such variations must be negotiated between employers and works councils at the company level and laid down in a works agreement. Depending on the type of opening clause, the unions and employer associations party to the industry-wide collective agreement may also have to give their approval for the variation (Kohaut & Schnabel 2007; Schnabel 1998).

A consequence of this decentralisation is that works agreements are of growing importance (Nienhüser & Hoßfeld 2004). Their number and the issues they regulate have increased since the mid-1980s, when flexibility of working time became a major concern to employers. Many collective agreements now define a number of options for regulating issues such as the distribution of working time, work organisation, payment systems and wages at the enterprise level. As a result, the power of managers and works councils has gradually intensified, while that of unions and employers' associations has been constrained and weakened. In other words, the formal structures of industry-wide collective bargaining have remained intact, but its outcomes and functions have changed significantly as final decisions about substantive issues (particularly working time and wages) have gradually been shifted to the enterprise level.

It must be noted that the use of opening clauses assumes the existence of works councils. However, as we explained earlier, many enterprises do not have works councils. Furthermore, the tasks of works councils are changing. The introduction of individual working-time accounts and the plant-level implementation of agreements on job security for temporary employees, for example, add to their workload (WSI-Projektgruppe 1998). The devolution of bargaining authority regarding substantive, distributive issues to the enterprise level also calls into question the peace obligation that prevents works councils from taking industrial action. If works councils are negotiating such issues, they need to be able to take industrial action. However, this would most likely lead to less cooperation and more conflict in the workplace.

Overall, the established employment relations regime has lost its original power to determine wages and working conditions. The balance of power and the division of labour between unions and employer associations at the industry level on the one hand, and employers and works councils at the enterprise level on the other, has shifted as the scope of negotiations at the enterprise level has broadened. The distinction between collective bargaining at the industry level and co-determination at the enterprise level has become blurred.

CONCLUSIONS

The traditional 'dual system' of German employment relations, which has been called 'the paradigm of the highly regulated industrial relations system' (Ferner & Hyman 1998: xiv), is in deeper and more serious difficulties than ever before. Since the early 1990s, fundamental processes of gradual disintegration have taken place and partially replaced the former highly integrated system. This development towards more variation was caused by internal factors, especially German unification, changing modes of production and new forms of employment, as well as external factors, particularly Europeanisation and globalisation. We are witnessing the decline of what has been called the 'German model of negotiated adjustment' (Thelen 1991) and the 'negotiated approach to industrial adjustment' (Wever 1995), with its emphasis on long-term cooperation.

The traditional German model is in the midst of an encompassing transformation of its key institutions and procedural rules, and in some ways is developing some rather striking similarities to the Anglo-American model. Germany is no longer the prototypical example of highly regulated, well-integrated, consensus-driven employment relations. Furthermore, the German approach to corporate governance, with its emphasis on the long-term interests of multiple stakeholders, is gradually being replaced by a more neo-liberal, market-driven orientation towards the short-term maximisation of shareholder interests. Nevertheless, increasing heterogeneity between industries and between enterprises of different sizes or even the dualisation between core and peripheral segments of employment is more likely than a wholesale convergence towards the Anglo-American model.

A CHRONOLOGY OF GERMAN EMPLOYMENT RELATIONS

1844	Silesian weavers' revolt.
1848	Year of revolutions.
1848–54	General German Workers' Fraternity.
1848–53	Association of cigar-producing workers.
1849–53	Printers' association is formed.
1863	Foundation of the General German Workers' Association.
1865–67	First national associations of cigar workers, printers and tailors.
1869	Foundation of Social Democratic Workers' Party.
1869	Prussian Trades Law grants freedom of coalition.
1873	First collective agreement (in the printing trade).
1878–90	Anti-socialist legislation.
1891	First industrial union—German Metalworkers' Association.
1892	First trades union congress.
1894	Foundation of first large Christian trade union (coal miners).
1899	Congress of Free Trade Unions recommends collective agreements.
1904	Main employers' association founded.
1905	First long strike by the German miners' union.
1913	Association of German Employers' Federations is established.
1914–18	World War I.
1916	Law to enforce works committees in all production establishments with more than 50 workers.
1918	Law on collective agreements.
1918–24	Central Working Commission of employers and workers in manufacturing industries and trades.
1919	Foundation of General German Trades Union Federation (ADGB).
1920	General strike against rightist riot (Kapp-Putsch).
1920	*Works Councils Act*.
1927	Law on labour courts.
1928	Law on collective agreements.
1928	Thirteenth ADGB Congress discusses co-determination.
1933	Unions abolished by National Socialist government.
1939–45	World War II.

1949	Founding Congress of DGB.
1951	Co-determination Act for coal and steel industries.
1952	*Works Constitution Act*.
1955	Staff Representation Act (for employees in the public sector).
1963	Foundation of Christian Trade Union Movement. Lockout of metal workers.
1967	'Concerted action' begins.
1972	Revision of the *Works Constitution Act*.
1974	Strike in the public sector.
1974	Revision of the *Staff Representation Act*.
1976	Co-determination Act for firms with more than 2000 employees.
1978–79	Steel strike: dispute about a shorter working week.
1984	Metalworkers' strike and lockout about shorter working week.
1989	Amendment of the *Workers Constitution Act*.
1990	Reunification of West and East Germany. Dissolution of the FDGB
1992	Public services strike.
1995	Failure of attempts to establish a joint platform between government, employers and unions to confront increasing unemployment.
1998	Alliance for work, education and competitiveness.
2001	Revision of the *Works Constitution Act*. Merger of five service sector unions, foundation of ver.di.
2003	Failure of the alliance for work, education and competitiveness.
2003–04	Major reform of labour market and employment policies as well as parts of the social security systems ('Hartz reforms').
2006	Extended public sector strike.
2008-10	Most severe economic downturn since the late 1920s.

CHAPTER 9

Employment relations in Denmark

Jørgen Steen Madsen, Jesper Due
and Søren Kaj Andersen

From a European perspective, Danish labour market regulation has been held up as a good example. This has primarily been in relation to Denmark's so-called 'flexicurity' policy, which has come to influence large parts of the European political debate on labour market regulation. It is well known that the social security of wage-earners in the event of unemployment is relatively high in Denmark—as it is in the other Nordic countries. However, the regulation of terms of employment and dismissal is relatively flexible. Hiring and firing staff is associated with low financial and administrative costs for employers. Denmark's degree of flexibility in this area is on a par with that of the United Kingdom, and consequently different from that of the other Nordic countries.

The explanation for this flexibility is to be found in characteristics of Danish labour market regulation, which has deep historical roots. The unification of the labour market parties into confederations at a national level and the establishment of both the system of collective bargaining and labour law were all elements which came into being around 1900. Collective bargaining subsequently became the preferred method of regulation for pay and working conditions.

The state has played the role of the third actor in the industrial relations system (Dunlop 1958). This has occurred in relation to labour market policy, which to a large extent has been formulated within the framework of tripartite agreements. Welfare issues, such as questions of pensions and further training, have also been the subject of tripartite negotiations and agreements, particularly over the last couple of decades. From this perspective, the Danish political

224

economy is a typical coordinated market economy (Hall & Soskice 2001), with policy development and coordination taking place in a network of key actors, namely trade unions, employers' associations and the political-administrative system.

However, Danish labour market regulation also encompasses clear liberal elements, based on the fundamental political acceptance of self-regulation by the labour market parties. Apart from legislation on freedom of association, there are no specific laws governing the trade unions and employers' associations. Only the Labour Court and the State Conciliation Board on Labour Disputes have a legislative basis. Hence, in relation to the actual regulation, there is only limited legislation.

The importance of collective agreements as the preferred form of regulation in the Danish labour market may be gauged from a benchmarking survey of national legislation on employment conditions undertaken by the World Bank. On this ranking, the Danish labour market was found to be the most flexible in Europe, and the third most flexible among 130 countries around the world (World Bank 2004: 36). The explanation is not that the Danish labour market is one of the most deregulated in the world, but rather that the greater part of its regulation takes place within the framework of collective bargaining and not via legislation.

Denmark has been described as a 'negotiated economy' (Pedersen 2006), which is also known as 'the Danish model' (Due et al. 1993, 1994; Andersen 2001). The special characteristics and social significance of the IR system must be seen in the light of the fact that Denmark is a small country with a population of just under five and a half million which, in economic terms, is greatly dependent on other countries. It is often characteristic of such countries that, lacking the ability to protect themselves through protectionist strategies, they develop internal coordination between the state, trade unions and employers in order to be able to adapt to external challenges (Katzenstein 1985).

The industrialisation of Denmark at the end of the nineteenth century was mainly based on agricultural exports. The situation is different today, in that manufacturing industry accounts for more than half of Danish export revenues. These principally involve the export of machinery and instruments, but also encompass a large number of other products. Denmark's sizeable exports of oil and natural gas from deposits in the North Sea are also of considerable importance. The value of the import and export of goods and services has risen from just under 30 per cent of GDP in the 1970s to more than 40 per cent of GDP in recent years. The balance of goods and services has thereby gone from a deficit in the 1970s to a surplus—as has the balance of payments.

The three largest areas of employment in the Danish private sector are manufacturing industry, financing/business services and retail trade/hotels/restaurants. Each of these three areas represents around one-quarter of total private sector employment. The other significant areas of employment are construction and transport/post/ telecommunications, each of which represents around 10 per cent of private sector employment. The public sector comprises the largest overall area of employment, accounting for just over 37 per cent of total employment.

Unemployment in the Danish labour market fell to a historically low level in the autumn of 2008, when only 1.6 per cent of the total labour force was unemployed. This was the culmination of a fall in unemployment from the first half of the 1990s, when unemployment peaked at more than 12 per cent. The explanations for the positive employment trend of recent years include labour market reforms, which emphasised active labour market training, rather than the provision of passive support. Similarly, the development of the collective bargaining system helped to create a more flexible labour market. Moreover, the favourable international economic climate during the period has clearly also contributed to the positive trend.

The labour force participation rate in Denmark is high, and at more than 80 per cent of 15- to 64-year-olds, it is among the highest in the OECD countries. The high level of labour force participation among women in particular tends to boost the figures, with more than 76 per cent of Danish women active in the labour market (OECD 2008). Various forms of atypical employment do not generally apply to the Danish labour market. The economic boom has, however, created new markets for temporary workers, though they make up only just over 1 per cent of the total labour force, which is a typical European level.

LEGAL, ECONOMIC AND POLITICAL BACKGROUND

The fundamentally liberal characteristics of the Danish model have been prevalent since the establishment of the collective bargaining system, with the signing in 1899 of the 'September Compromise' between the two newly founded confederations for wage-earners and employers, namely the Confederation of Danish Trades Unions (LO), and the Danish Employers' Confederation, Dansk Arbejdsgiverforening (DA).

The nature of the Danish employment economy at the time, composed of many relatively small handcraft-dominated companies and few large enterprises, meant that employers had difficulty in countering the decentralised wages strategy of the blossoming trade unions—the so-called 'leap-frogging' strategy. As the unions could not be eliminated directly, the employers sought instead to establish a centralised collective bargaining system. The employers also counter-attacked through lockouts, which in 1899 resulted in a nationwide dispute that lasted from spring until September. At the time, this was considered to be the most extensive labour conflict yet encountered, both in Denmark and by international comparisons (Crouch 1993).

Although the new 'basic agreement'—from the September Compromise—created the foundation for an institutionalised collective bargaining system, conflicts between the labour market parties continued in the years after the turn of the century. There was no formal system to handle conflicts. This led to the establishment of the August Committee of 1908 with representatives from the two confederations, LO and DA.

The August Committee of 1908 established a comprehensive labour law system in 1910. Hereafter, rights disputes concerning the interpretation of current collective agreements were to be settled by industrial arbitration, while rights disputes on breaches of the agreements would be handled by a new labour court with advocates for the parties, and presided over by professional judges. The rules for industrial arbitration were left to the parties themselves to determine. The guidelines for the Labour Court, on the other hand, were laid down by a special *Labour Court Act*. The same principle applied to another achievement of the August Committee, the establishment of a state conciliation board. The new labour court system kept the industrial peace during the agreement periods, and ensured that conflicts could only be initiated in connection with the renewal of the collective agreements, after an appropriate period of notice. The task of the conciliation board was to mediate between the parties during collective agreement negotiations, and thereby further reduce the threat of conflict.

Even prior to the introduction of state support for the labour law system in 1910, legislation had been enacted which was of vital importance for the parties in the labour market. The Act on state-recognised unemployment insurance funds set out the rules for unemployment benefits in accordance with the so-called 'Ghent system', under which unemployment benefits from 1907 were administered via the unemployment insurance funds of the trade unions. A welfare service, which in many countries is administered by the public authorities, thus came to be placed under the control of the

227

trade unions. In practice, this made membership of an unemployment insurance fund synonymous with membership of a trade union, thereby contributing to strengthening the unions and securing high levels of union density, and consequent high levels of collective agreement coverage. These were necessary ingredients in the development and retention of a form of labour market regulation that was primarily based on collective bargaining.[1]

From the time of the enactment of the supportive labour law legislation, the decisive characteristics of the relations between the parties and the political system were becoming clear. The essential condition for self-regulation, and the ability of the parties to continue to wield decisive influence over subsequent alterations in the supportive procedural legislation, was that the employees' and employers' organisations would be able to arrive at compromises between their different interests, and present joint solutions to the political system. This principle, which has been designated the 'consensus principle', has almost always been adhered to in the history of the collective bargaining system in relation to the legislation that underpins the tripartite system (Due & Madsen 2006).

However, the principle of consensus has been less apparent in legislation that, despite self-regulation, has been enacted to govern the contents of the regulation, such as the *Holiday Act* and the *White-Collar Workers Act*, and with regard to the consultation of the parties in political regulation—not only in relation to labour market policy, but also on broader social issues.[2] There has occasionally been competition between the labour market parties to secure the greatest possible influence, but experience seems to show that the parties are able to secure the most effective and lasting level of influence when they adhere to the consensus principle in this area as well.

The new labour law system did not lead to the immediate realisation of the employers' wish to see a system of coordinated collective bargaining under the control of the confederations, because the individual unions still held on to their right to directly negotiate agreements. The power struggle continued over the degree of centralisation of the collective bargaining system. The differing strategies of the parties were reflected in their internal power structures, with DA becoming characterised by a strong centralisation of power, while the leadership of LO never managed to establish central control over the collective bargaining rights of its member unions.

DA had to continue efforts to develop the centralisation project, and this centralisation phase spanned the first half-century of the history of the Danish collective bargaining system. DA used the threat of sympathy lockouts by employers as a means of securing a unified process. An important change occurred, however, with the amendments to the negotiation rules and the *Conciliation Act* in 1934 and 1936. This established de facto centralisation by extending the powers of the conciliator to put forward settlement proposals and introduce linked coordination through a common ballot for all the involved unions and employers' associations. The principle was that either all of the parties entered into an agreement, or else all participated in a conflict. The conciliator's proposals in mediation attempts thereby became 'the crucial stage in collective bargaining' in Denmark (Galenson, 1952: 112).

The 1930s, the first decade of Social Democrat-led governments, also saw the development of the practice of political intervention in conflicts. When the State Conciliation Board was unable to achieve an agreed solution, several times the government chose to intervene to stop industrial conflicts that, in the light of the economic depression of that decade, were regarded as a socio-economic threat. Since then, interventions by the political system in labour market conflicts have proved to be more the norm than an exception. Industrial conflicts are certainly recognised as being an important element in the Danish model, as a means of forcing the labour market parties to compromise, but if a conflict breaks out with no prospect of an early solution, and there is considered to be a risk of negative economic and/or political consequences, the political parties in the Danish Parliament are generally inclined to intervene.

It should be added that the development of the Danish model in the decades prior to World War II was not solely characterised by a tendency towards centralisation. The collective bargaining model also developed from the beginning into a coherent regulatory system with several levels. There were strong relations between unions and employers, not just at the central level but also at the enterprise level, where there was a dense network of shop stewards, union branches and cooperation committees; this helped to secure the effective implementation of the agreements.

The possibility of holding local negotiations on pay was also introduced. The Danish model thereby became a system of consider-able depth. From the establishment of the system at the beginning of the twentieth century, a ground-breaking agreement in the iron and steel industry created a system where the actual pay rise was negotiated by the involved parties in the individual companies. The clear risk that centralised collective bargaining might lead to a lack of flexibility was thereby countered in the most export-dominated sector.

A new phase in the history of the collective bargaining system became a reality at the beginning of the 1950s, when the regular collective bargaining rounds began to take place under the control of LO and DA. The phase of central negotiations lasted from the start of the 1950s to the end of the 1970s. From a formal perspective, the individual trade unions and their respective employer counterparts retained their negotiating powers, but due to a division between special and general issues, the result in practice was that the crucial issues were directly negotiated between the confederations—usually with the participation of the State Conciliation Board.

A culture of consensus developed, characterised by the ability to make distributive bargaining integrative (Walton & McKersie, 1965; Walton et al. 1994), which implies that negotiations must lead to results that balance the interests of the parties, while remaining socio-economically justifiable. Walter Galenson, termed this 'the Danish genius for compromise' (Galenson, 1952).

The decades after World War II can justifiably be termed the golden age of the collective bargaining model. It was during this period that the principles introduced at the time of the foundation of the bargaining system came to full fruition. At the same time, however, the high level of centralisation also began to produce problems. The regulation had become too inflexible, and it was difficult for companies to adjust to the increasing level of international competition.

It was also during this period that the public sector labour market began to be expanded greatly, particularly with the development of the welfare state in the 1960s and onwards. The civil service reform of 1969 initiated a development that gradually led to a shift from civil servant status to contractual employment as the dominant form of employment in the public sector. At the same time, a new collective bargaining system was developed on the basis of the old civil servant system, under which collective agreements became the new, norm-setting form of regulation. Negotiations on the renewal of these collective agreements were handled via a strongly centralised collective bargaining system, in which the trade unions negotiated collectively from top to bottom via large cartels in the two main areas, respectively the state and the municipal and county area.

From the mid-1970s, Denmark saw the establishment of its most coordinated rounds of collective bargaining. The two-year agreements were renewed in a coherent process every second year on the basis of the negotiations in the LO/DA area in the private sector. Once negotiations were concluded, the result could be transferred to the public sector. This created a clear hierarchy in the coordinated agreement model, with the competitive industries setting the pattern and the government ensuring that all parts of the public sector adhered to the central principle that, while public employees should not lead the way in pay rises, they should be secured pay rises which more or less corresponded to those of private employees. The other main employer areas in the private sector, agriculture and finance, also renewed their collective agreements at the same rate as the LO/ DA area.

THE MAJOR PARTIES

The employers' associations

The Danish Employers' Confederation, Dansk Arbejdsgiverforening (DA), was established in 1896, and quickly gained a strongly centralised power structure.

Since the end of the 1980s, many of the formerly numerous small employers' associations have amalgamated to form fewer, larger units under DA. Currently, of the more than 150 member organisations that existed at the end of the 1980s, just thirteen remain. Of these, three large conglomerates—the Confederation of Danish Industry, Erhvervenes organisation (DI), the Danish Chamber of Commerce, Dansk Erhverv, and the Danish Construction Association, Dansk Byggeri, account for almost 90 per cent of the total payroll of enterprises covered by DA. DI alone accounts for 62 per cent of the total. Overall, it thus appeared as though the end result would be a single organisation for each of the three main sectors: manufacturing industry, service and construction. However, the competition for members has now crossed sectoral boundaries.

The amalgamation into a few large member associations has also altered the power structure in DA. From being a confederation in which the daily management held decisive power, DA has developed to become more of a coordinating body for the large organisations— much the same role that has always been played by the Danish Confederation of Trade Unions, Landsorganisationen i Danmark (LO), with respect to the member unions.

DA is by far the largest employers' confederation in the private labour market, but there are two smaller associations, the Danish Confederation of Employers' Associations in Agriculture, Sammens- lutningen af Landbrugets Arbejdsgiverforeninger (SALA), and the Danish Employers' Association for the Financial Sector, Finansektorens Arbejdsgiverforening (FA).

As can been seen from Table 9.1, DA, SALA and FA together cover 58 per cent of the private sector labour market. To this can be added a few small employers' organisations outside the main confederations. However, companies accounting for more than 40 per cent of the private sector labour market are not members of any employers' association. The proportion of membership density among employers has been rising slowly in recent years, with the member associations of DA in particular managing to attract an increasing number of enterprises. This has been due less to their function as employers' organisations than to the development of their simultaneous role as special-interest business organisations.

Table 9.1   Collective agreement areas in the Danish labour market

	Number of wage-earners (in thousands) converted to full-time equivalents		
	Share of main sector	%	Share of overall labour market (%)
Private sector	1 464		64
DA	740	51	32
FA	65	4	3
SALA	38	3	2
Other/not organised	621	42	27
Public sector	838		36
Total	2 302	100	

Source: DA, on the basis of special analyses by Statistics Denmark and information from FA and SALA (DA: Labour Market Report 2008: 165)

With the expansion of the welfare state since the 1960s, the number of public sector employees has grown enormously, while at the same time there has been a shift from civil servant status to contractual employment as the dominant form of employment in the public sector. The *public sector* has thereby acquired increasing importance as an element in the overall system. From the beginning of the 1970s, two main areas underwent development. Local authorities became dominant, as the welfare services are administered by local political units, while the state diminished in size. However, it has always been the minister in charge of public sector pay (usually the Minister of

Finance) who, together with the agency acting as the employer, plays the most decisive role in public sector collective bargaining. The fourteen counties and 373 municipalities negotiated via their two associations, the Association of County Councils in Denmark (Amtrådsforeningen i Danmark) and Local Government Denmark (KL), with the larger KL taking the leading role.

The local government reform of 1 January 2007 reduced the fourteen counties to five regions, and the number of municipalities to 98. Hereafter, the municipalities and regions covered three-quarters and the state sector one-quarter of public employees.

The municipalities have, by and large, retained their position, and still negotiate their collective agreements via KL. The regions—almost the only remaining function of which is the administration of the public hospitals—have a less independent function than the former counties. The regions cannot, for example, levy their own taxes. With respect to collective bargaining, the state has also been given a direct right of veto over the regional area, and consequently the municipalities have not wished to maintain the joint regional/municipal negotiations that formerly characterised negotiations by the counties and municipalities. The regions thus now hold separate negotiations.

Trade unions

The Danish Confederation of Trade Unions, Landsorganisationen i Danmark (LO), was founded in 1898. LO was, and remains, by far the largest confederation of trade unions in Denmark. Its member organisations mainly represent skilled and unskilled manual workers, but also include a number of groups of salaried employees. LO is the dominating confederation on the employee side in the private sector, and is also the largest confederation in the public sector labour market.

Most of LO's member unions began as craft unions, but from the start there have also been a limited number of industrial unions and general workers' unions. Recent decades have seen a tendency towards concentration in fewer and larger units. In 2008, LO was made up of seventeen member unions, of which the four largest represented 80 per cent of the total membership (Due & Madsen 2005).

LO's power structure has to a large extent been determined by the wish of the large member unions to retain their right to independently negotiate agreements. LO has therefore always functioned more as a coordinating organ for the major unions than as an independent power in itself. However, as the unions have often had divergent

233

interests, LO has been able to acquire independent influence by acting as a mediator between the large member organisations. The LO unions quickly achieved a high level of union density in the urban industries, and thereby the strength to be able to establish collective agreements as the dominating form of regulation in the private sector labour market.

The Confederation of Professionals in Denmark, FTF, mainly represents professional groups such as nurses, teachers and kindergarten teachers in the public sector, but it also plays a decisive role in the financial sector. These organisations are based around the common educational background of their members, and are thereby characterised by profession-based strategies. In collective bargaining, FTF has had only limited influence, as the right to negotiate lies with the individual member unions. FTF plays a larger political role as the representative of the common interests of its member organisations in tripartite negotiations.

The Danish Confederation of Professional Associations, Akademikernes Centralorganisation (AC), is a confederation of unions representing employees with an academic education. AC covers both the public and private sector, but its principal weight is in the public sector. In contrast to LO, AC also directly negotiates collective agreements in the public sector labour market, and moreover enjoys the same political role as the other confederations in relation to tripartite negotiations, and so on.

The organisational structure in Denmark is influenced by the existence of independent associations in the private sector labour market for the various managerial groups. This trend can be traced back to the September Compromise of 1899, in which the employers had a provision inserted stating that employees who acted as representatives of the employers in the workplaces should not be obliged to join the same unions as the other wage-earners.

The majority of managers are represented by the Organisation of Managerial and Executive Staff in Denmark, Ledernes Hovedorganisation (LH). LH has only limited collective bargaining powers. The majority of managers in the private sector labour market are employed solely on the basis of individual employment contracts. LH and DA have negotiated an overall framework agreement, which lays down guidelines for regulation, but this is entirely without provisions regarding pay.

There has been, in general, intense competition between the confederations, with LO regarding the others as 'yellow'—in particular FTF, which recruited clerical workers and others from the private sector in competition with LO's clerical workers' unions. The conflicts gradually diminished, however, to be replaced by increasing cooperation. The current situation resembles more a division of the market, and consequently the four confederations represent the established trade union movement in Denmark. One major difference has been that LO and its member unions have always enjoyed a close relationship with the Social Democrats, while the other confederations have been politically neutral—albeit increasingly active on the political front. Over the past decade, LO has severed its formal political and economic ties with the Social Democrats, and although informal ties remain, this has helped to reduce the gap between the confederations. Another sign of closer cooperation between the confederations has been the joint participation by LO, FTF and AC in the European Trade Union Confederation, the ETUC.

In recent decades, LO has seen a relative decrease in membership. Although it represented 65 per cent of all organised wage-earners in 1996, LO's proportion had fallen to 56 per cent by 2008. As current alterations in the structure of education and industry encourage a continuation of this trend, the time will come when LO represents only every second trade union member. For the time being, however, LO remains the largest confederation, and possesses decisive influence, as it is the LO unions that play the leading role in collective bargaining with the DA organisations in the private sector. This also means that LO enjoys special status in the tripartite negotiations.

While the large confederations have more or less declared peace among themselves, they are still in sharp competition with the individual alternative, or so-called 'yellow' organisations. This competition can be traced back to the breakthrough years of the unions, when alternative organisations, often established by the employers, acted as strike-breakers.[3] In Denmark, the Christian Trade Union Movement was established in 1898, at the same time as LO. The Christian Trade Union Movement rejected from the start the principle of the right to strike, and was also an integrated part of the Christian employers' association.

The Christian Trade Union Movement remained a marginal phenomenon right up to the 1990s; it never succeeded in breaking the collective bargaining monopoly of the established unions, and its membership remained at a low level.

In an attempt to alter the situation, the Christian Trade Union Movement cut its ties with the Christian employers. At the same time, several other alternative trade unions began to arise. It was not until the mid-1990s, however, that major growth began to occur in the membership numbers of the alternative organisations, and this trend has continued in recent years. As can be seen from Table 9.2, membership of the alternative or 'yellow' organisations almost tripled between 1996 and 2008. These unions had a total membership in 1995 of 53 000. By 2008, this figure has grown to 145 000, representing a growth rate of 174 per cent in a period when the total membership of trade unions had otherwise been stagnating.

Whereas the 'yellow' organisations were a marginal phenomenon in 1996, with a membership share of 3 per cent, their 8 per cent share in 2008 has made them more of a real alternative, and thereby a potential threat to the established trade union movement.

Table 9.2   Confederations of trade unions membership

	(Figures in thousands)				
	1995	2000	2005	2007	2008
LO	1208	1176	1142	1052	1017
FTF	332	350	361	356	359
AC	132	150	163	169	174
LH	75	80	76	74	76
Alternative unions*	53	68	94	125	145
Other unions outside the confederations	62	55	57	54	57
Total	1862	1879	1893	1830	1828
Wage-earners and unemployed**	2547	2614	2640	2657	2649
Union membership %	73%	72%	72%	69%	69%
Excluding alternatives %	71%	69%	68%	64%	64%

*   Unions outside the confederations, which also regard themselves as alternatives to the established unions, the so-called 'yellow' unions

**   Labour force, minus self-employed

Sources: *Statistical Yearbook*, AKU (Labour Force Survey) and LO statistics

Government

The Danish model, with extensive self-regulation by the parties in the labour market, does not mean that the role of the state as an actor in the IR system is insignificant. The role of the state is merely more limited than is the case in some other countries.

Apart from supportive procedural legislation mentioned above, the collective bargaining system is self-regulating. The relations between the organisations, and the rules for industrial conflicts, are thereby fixed in the basic agreements between the parties in the various bargaining areas. There are, for example, no legislative rules governing the conditions for the formal registration of trade unions. It is, in principle, a free market. However, by entering into sector agreements, which apply both to their own members and to non-union members within the specific bargaining area, the established unions have in practice established a monopoly on the right to collective bargaining.

In substance, the legislation is extremely limited. For example, there is no statutory minimum wage. As a legacy from the 1930s, the *Holiday Act* gives all wage-earners the right to annual holidays, and the *White-Collar Workers Act* grants white-collar workers special security in employment.

Over the past decade, there appears to have been a renewed tendency towards increased political intervention, reflecting the fact that more welfare issues are now being encompassed by the collective agreements. It can also be seen as an effect of Denmark's membership of the EU, as various EU directives have introduced regulation via legislation.

With regard to labour market policy, there has always been formal consultation of the labour market parties in the form of participation in the councils and boards that administer the policy, as well as in the work of the committees and commissions where reforms are prepared and implemented. Apart from this area, though, it should be noted that tripartite cooperation has always been of an ad hoc nature.

The significant role of the state in the labour market has been concentrated particularly on the growing and stabilising public sector, which has resulted from the development of the welfare state in the second half of the twentieth century.

THE PROCESSES OF EMPLOYMENT RELATIONS

Table 9.3 shows coverage of the Danish labour market by collective bargaining. The level of coverage of the collective agreements is very high, with more than 90 per cent of employees covered in the DA, FA and SALA areas. The remaining employees belong to some white-collar groups, including university-educated staff and managers employed on individual contracts.

In addition to the three confederations, there are also some smaller employers' associations. However, a very large group of enterprises,

Table 9.3 **Collective bargaining agreement coverage in the Danish labour market**

2007	(Number of wage-earners converted to full-time equivalents)		
	Covered by agreement	All	% covered
Private sector	1068	1464	73
DA	665	740	90
FA	59	65	91
SALA	32	38	84
Other/not organised	312	621	50
Public sector	838	838	100
Total	1906	2302	83

Source: Statistics Denmark, FA and SALA (DA: Labour Market Report 2008: 165)

encompassing more than 40 per cent of employees on the private labour market, are entirely outside the employers' associations. As a result, it is primarily the ability of the trade unions to enter into adoption agreements with the non-organised companies that has secured them such a high level of collective agreement coverage, which comprises 73 per cent of the private labour market.

Despite this high level, more than a quarter of wage-earners in the private labour market are not covered by a collective agreement. Their pay and conditions are regulated solely through individual contracts. However, as these contracts are entered into in collective bargaining environments, there is a considerable knock-on effect on the group of non-covered employees.

In the decades following World War II, collective bargaining negotiations in Denmark constituted a coherent system with simultaneous and coordinated negotiations in all major areas. However, the process of decentralisation that began in the 1980s brought about a breakdown in this system.

A new pattern has since developed, in which the large LO/DA area negotiates in one year, followed by the remaining areas of the private labour market, together with the public sector, in the following year. This has increased the scope for leverage effects. The public sector and the financial sector typically set the standard with regard to the development of social welfare elements in collective agreements.

The determination of wages

The collective bargaining model which has emerged during the past decades has its roots in the economic crisis of the 1970s, when it was becoming more difficult for the two main confederations, DA and LO, to continue the culture of consensus and create joint solutions while satisfying their divergent interests. The collective bargaining of the 1970s began with a major strike in the private labour market in 1973, followed by three consecutive political interventions in 1975, 1977 and 1979. By the end of the 1970s, the collective bargaining system was in crisis.

Centralised decentralisation

The answer to the crisis of the 1970s was not further centralisation in the form of an institutionalised tripartite system, as was desired by parts of LO, but rather a movement in the opposite direction, with the focus on the collective bargaining process being returned from the confederations to the sector organisations. However, overall coordination was retained, with a common ballot for the entire LO/DA area via the State Conciliation Board on Labour Disputes.

In addition, especially from the end of the 1980s, an organisational centralisation took place, with new, large sector-wide organisations being formed. Within the bounds of framework-governed collective agreements, these organisations retained overall coordination despite the transferral of negotiations to the parties at enterprise level. This new phase in the development of the Danish model, which took place from the 1980s to the 1990s, may be characterised as centralised decentralisation.

From the time of the establishment of the collective bargaining system, the parties in the iron and steel industry—which the sector must subject to competition—came to constitute the key bargaining area. After the start of the 1990s, this was expanded to include all of manufacturing industry, with the establishment of a new large confederation, the Confederation of Danish Industry (DI) on the employers' side, followed on the wage-earners' side by the Central Organisation of Industrial Employees in Denmark (CO-industri), which could match DI.

As well as the displacement in the collective agreement negotiations, this period also saw decentralisation taking place in two concurrent processes. First, more collective agreements changed from being standardised pay agreements, with wages centrally determined at the negotiating table, to various kinds of flexible pay systems, with wages determined by negotiations at enterprise level. Since the mid-1990s, approximately 85 per cent of the overall LO/DA area has encompassed flexible pay systems. At the same time, a development has occurred in recent years in the direction of more individual pay negotiations. While only around 4 per cent of the LO/DA area was covered by collective agreements without specified pay rates in 1993, this had risen to 23 per cent by 2007 (DA 1998, 2008).

Second, in addition to the negotiation of pay, a transfer of negotiating responsibility to the parties at enterprise level also occurred in connection with other areas, particularly over working hours. This has given enterprises greatly enhanced possibilities for introducing flexibility, such as wide-ranging powers to organise flexible working hours. This was achieved through a loosening-up of the collective agreement provisions during the 1990s, with the collective bargaining parties in manufacturing industry leading the way. This development provided an opportunity for local trade-offs between the parties, which can be viewed as a form of flexicurity agreements at enterprise level.

Katz (1993) has proposed three hypotheses to explain the decentralisation process. The most convincing of these is the emergence of new kinds of work organisations, which put a premium on flexibility and employee participation (Bamber et al. 2004: 12). This has also played a role in Denmark, although employers have generally justified their demands for more flexible, decentralised regulation on the basis of Danish companies needing to be competitive in international markets.

The employers have recognised the necessity of strong local union representation in the enterprises, as this is a prerequisite for companies being able to make use of the possibilities for flexibility, which are built into the agreements. The establishment of a well-developed network of shop stewards has become a common interest of both employers and wage-earners. Although the decline in union membership in recent years has made it more difficult to recruit and retain shop stewards, the parties have jointly begun to tackle this problem. By international comparisons, Danish companies continue to have very strong local union representation, with approximately 80 per cent of employees represented by shop stewards (Ilsøe et al. 2007; Ilsøe 2008).

Greater scope of the collective agreements

In recent times, there has been an expansion in the scope of collective agreements. While these had previously dealt almost exclusively with wages and working hours, from the start of the 1990s they also began to encompass a number of welfare-related issues. Following a breakthrough in the public sector in 1989, the LO/DA area, the manufacturing industry began to develop occupational pensions schemes (*Arbejdsmarkedspensionsordninger*).

This was the culmination of a lengthy process of tripartite negotiations, which led to the Common Declaration of 8 December 1987—a tripartite agreement between the government and the labour market parties that committed the trade unions to enforcing a competitiveness-enhancing wages policy. This was adhered to by the parties for the next 20 years. The price exacted for this responsible attitude towards the national economy was that the right-of-centre government would support LO's demand for the introduction of occupational pension superannuation. In 1991, the development of occupational pensions became a part of the collective agreements.

Besides occupational pensions, the scope of the collective agreements has also been expanded with new provisions dealing with the right to further training, social chapters, sick pay and paid parental leave. A kind of double regulation has developed, under which welfare-related issues such as the right to pay during parental leave are regulated via both collective agreements and legislation. This creates a large area of interplay between the labour market parties and the political players, and legitimises the direct influence of the politicians over the agenda of the various collective bargaining rounds. This in turn places the self-regulation of the parties under pressure.

The increased scope of the collective agreements is partly a result of the need of the political system for support to finance the growing welfare state. The interest of the unions lies in their ability to secure desirable benefits schemes for their members, while the employers acquire a certain degree of control over the structuring and extension of such schemes.

International regulation

Ever since Denmark became a member of the European community in 1973, Europe has in various ways questioned and placed pressure on the existing Danish labour market regulation. This became especially clear at the start of the 1990s, when a number of labour law directives, and thereby common legislation, became adopted at European level. These directives were aimed at regulating such matters as working hours, part-time employment, fixed-term work, European works councils and the posting of workers to other member states. A debate developed concerning how such directives should be implemented in the Danish labour market. The reason for this was that the implementation of these European directives touched upon a fundamental principle of Danish labour market regulation, namely the subtle balance between collective bargaining and legislation. It is this balance that secures the autonomy of the parties with respect to adjustments in pay and working conditions, while at the same time ensuring that the political system will accept these changes.

The problem was that European regulation demanded that all wage-earners should be covered by the same common directives. However, despite the relatively high degree of collective agreement coverage in Denmark, there were always some employees excluded. The Ministry of Labour and the labour market parties tried to convince the European Commission that 'adoption agreements' entered into with unorganised employers, together with the so-called 'knock-on' effect of the collective agreements, would mean that more or less all wage-earners would be covered by the directives. But this did not stop the European Commission threatening to bring Denmark before the European Court of Justice for insufficient implementation.

The outcome was that a tripartite Implementation Committee was established with representatives from the labour market confederations and the state, to assess how the directives should be implemented. In general, the labour market parties first implement the directive provisions via the collective agreements; this is then followed by secondary legislation in the Danish Parliament, which ensures that the remaining group of wage-earners is also covered by the directives. Technically, this adds a kind of extension mechanism to the provisions of the collective agreements dealing with the implementation of European labour law directives. Hence Denmark has become subject to legislation on working hours and part-time and fixed-term work, areas which previously were more or less exclusively regulated through the collective agreements (Andersen 2003).

Dispute settlement

The right to initiate conflict is in practice reserved solely for *conflicts of interest*—in connection with the renewal of existing collective agreements, or when entering into collective bargaining in new areas. The parties are in agreement that their potentially conflicting interests during the process of bargaining make it essential that both sides are able to use the weapon of conflict as a necessary threat to force the other side to make concessions. But if the threat of conflict is to be taken seriously, it must be used from time to time, and in the recent history there have been four major conflicts. Since the industrial conflict of 1961, a number of strikes have taken place in the labour market with their basis in the LO/DA area, at 12- to 13-year intervals: in 1973, 1985 and 1998.

In general, the mediation efforts of the State Conciliation Board have proved an efficient means of getting the parties to compromise. This institution functions to a great extent as the parties' own tool, with the conciliator putting forward proposals only if the parties accept this in advance—or at least do not actively oppose it. The Conciliation Board thus provides a buffer for the negotiators in situations where, due to pressure from their rank and file, it can be difficult for the parties to openly make the necessary concessions.

In those instances where the parties have been unable to reach agreement, despite the assistance of the Conciliation Board, conflict is the only possibility. But only rarely are widespread conflicts in the labour market allowed to go on for very long, due to the established tradition of political intervention.

There was a conflict in the Danish labour market in the public sector in the spring of 2008. In this instance, a joint settlement had been reached between the negotiating cartels, but a few areas rejected the offer. The result was that large parts of the health sector, together with the elderly care and kindergarten sectors, went on strike. This was the largest ever independent conflict in the public sector, with the participation of unions representing more than one-third of all public sector employees.

During previous minor strikes in the health sector in the 1990s, the Danish Parliament had intervened to stop the conflicts, with the justification that these were highly vulnerable areas. However, although the 2008 strike was much larger than the conflicts of the 1990s, the government chose not to intervene. This decision was justified on the basis of respect for the self-regulation of the Danish model, but was probably also due to the complicated parliamentary situation, in which the government could not be certain of achieving a broad majority for the kind of intervention that had been seen in the past. The conflict therefore became a trial of endurance, with the last unions, after more than eight weeks of conflict, finally accepting a settlement that fell well short of their demands.

Seen in relation to the preservation of the self-regulation principle in the Danish model, it may turn out to have been a good thing that the government chose not to intervene in the 2008 conflict. The fact that, until 2008, a conflict would practically automatically have been

243

stopped by political means did not encourage the parties to show responsibility, and international observers—with some justification— have pointed out that the Danish tradition of political intervention represents a threat to the autonomy of the labour market parties (Elvander 2002).

Although, according to the rules, it is only permitted to give notice of strikes and lockouts in connection with interest conflicts, this does not mean that the Danish labour market is entirely peaceful. Local disputes often lead to unofficial strikes. In recent years, however, the number of such conflicts has been diminishing. Strikes are thus a rarely utilised means of solving local disputes over the collective agreements. Most *conflicts of rights* are resolved through the labour law system. The vast majority of disputes are solved locally, solely with advice from the organisations, or at meetings with the participation of the parties to the collective agreement. Disputes rarely progress beyond this level. However, if agreement cannot be achieved, disputes on the interpretation of the collective agreements are handled by industrial arbitration, while breaches of the collective agreements are handled by the Labour Court.

The increasing degree of international regulation has also influenced the Danish system, inasmuch as it can be difficult to accept this form of collective regulation in other, more individually oriented IR systems, particularly in relation to the private arbitration system. This has resulted in amendments to the Danish industrial relations legislation in 2008, so that the *Labour Court Act* now also lays down guidelines for the treatment of cases through industrial arbitration. These amendments have been undertaken with the agreement of the labour market parties, who thereby hope to have secured the future of the Danish labour law system.

CURRENT AND FUTURE ISSUES AND TRENDS

In recent years, changes to collective bargaining and labour market regulation in Denmark have clearly revealed some of the challenges facing the Danish model. There has been considerable pessimism among the labour market parties with regard to the possibilities of avoiding increased political control of collective bargaining. However, the situation was considerably better in advance of the collective bargaining round in the private sector in 2007, which saw a tripartite agreement on further training that secured a coordinated strengthening of this area via both public and collective agreement funding.

Similar tripartite negotiations took place in advance of the collective bargaining round in the public sector in 2008. However, there was some concern among the parties at a tripartite agreement dealing with funding that, under normal circumstances, would be negotiated directly during the subsequent collective bargaining. This might herald the introduction of a new form of regulation, in which the tripartite arena takes over some areas of negotiation from the bipartite collective bargaining arena (Mailand 2008).

There was, however, a more pressing problem, as several political parties in the Danish Parliament extraordinarily promised to direct extra funding to the collective bargaining round, earmarked for particular groups. The political parties were thereby directly intervening in the core of the collective bargaining system, namely pay negotiations. The conclusion of the negotiation round, however, removed the threat to the self-regulation principle (Due & Madsen 2008b).

The collective bargaining rounds in 2007 and 2008, moreover, challenged the pay policy of improving competitiveness, which has applied since the Common Declaration of 1987. The protracted period of economic boom had raised expectations about pay increases. The public sector unions, which ended up on strike, were demanding wage increases that in fact exceeded the rate of increase in the private labour market. This represented a break with the principle that the level of wage increases should be set by the industries subject to competition.

Declining organisation membership

The special position of the labour market parties in the Danish model is legitimised by a high level of membership and collective agreement coverage. How far can membership continue to fall before this becomes a problem? Union density rose steadily from the mid-1920s until the mid-1990s, at which point approximately 73 per cent of all employees belonged to unions. Since then, however, overall trade union membership has fallen, reaching just under 69 per cent in 2007. The fall has not been dramatic, but the trend looks likely to continue, and seems especially serious when we consider the sizeable growth in membership enjoyed by the alternative 'yellow' unions during the same period.

Part of the explanation for the decline in levels of unionisation lies in the alterations in the former close ties between the trade unions and the unemployment insurance funds by an Act of Parliament which from 2002 permitted non-trade-specific unemployment insurance funds to be established. Joining the unemployment insurance funds of the alternative 'yellow' unions thereby became a genuine possibility—a factor that has contributed to the growth of these associations.

In general, the trend raises the question of whether the trade union movement can manage to maintain its legitimacy among wage-earners and employers, as well as a political system that can be expected to try to exert pressure on the overall bargaining system.

International pressure

In Denmark, the combination of economic prosperity and the expansion of the EU with the admission of the Central and Eastern European states created a rather large influx of foreign workers, mainly from Poland. At the same time, there was a marked rise in the number of foreign companies sending workers to Denmark, mainly Polish and German building and construction companies, which operated as subcontractors.

It is difficult to obtain an overall picture of the number of East Europeans and other foreigners working in Denmark, but in relation to the building and construction industry, it is estimated that in 2007 foreign workers represented more than 20 per cent of the total workforce (Hansen & Andersen 2008).

Particular debate has centred on the so-called *Laval Case* brought before the European Court of Justice in 2007. The case dealt with the degree to which a trade union can place demands on a foreign company with regard to the pay and conditions of workers sent from the home country. The company in question was a Latvian enterprise working in a Stockholm suburb. The Swedish trade union demanded that the company should pay wages corresponding to those specified by the relevant collective agreement in the area—that is, a sector agreement which encompassed local supplementary pay negotiations. The European Court of Justice found this demand to be discriminatory, since it was not made clear to the foreign company that it could face pay demands for its Latvian workers based on Swedish labour market standards.

The Danish trade unions, particularly in the construction sector, feared that the ruling might lead to a cementing of the differences in pay levels between Danes and foreigners. This would occur if foreign workers were to receive a kind of minimum wage, while Danish workers, via local negotiations, were able to secure a considerably higher rate of pay.

International legal regulation has also influenced Danish labour market regulation in other respects. In 2006, the European Court of Human Rights handed down a ruling stating that the closed-shop agreements established by Danish trade unions were in violation of negative freedom of association—that is, the freedom to choose not to belong to a trade union. The decline in membership of the past few years can thereby also partly be explained by the abolition of the closed shop under Danish labour laws.

Just as was the case in the implementation of the EU labour law directives, the ruling by the European Court of Human Rights may be seen as an expression of the pressure being exerted on the Danish collective bargaining system by the more individual rights-oriented European regulation. In other words, there is a conflict between two regulation systems based on different principles.

Labour shortages

The numbers of persons of working age is predicted to decline, not just in Denmark but in Europe generally. The employers in the Confederation of Danish Industries (DI) have estimated that by 2015 there will be a shortage of 200 000 employees in the Danish labour market. On the trade union side, the Economic Council of the Labour Movement has arrived at slightly different figures: it has calculated that by 2015 there will be a shortage of around 136 000 skilled workers and around 66 000 tertiary graduates. At the same time, it is estimated that there will be a surplus of almost 170 000 unskilled workers, including persons with only upper-secondary or vocational education, who will be unable to find work. Consequently, the challenge will be to improve educational levels and thereby ensure that a situation can be avoided in which there is both a shortage of qualified labour and large groups of unemployed.

This has raised the question of whether access should be made easier for migrant workers from countries outside the EU, as well as whether it is possible to get the Danes to work longer. The debate has primarily centred on the early retirement scheme, under which approximately half of all members of unemployment insurance funds aged 60 to 66 currently choose to take early retirement (Statistics Denmark 2006). The proportion has been declining in recent years, but the employers' associations, among others, have argued that the scheme should be completely abolished. So far, however, there has not been a parliamentary majority in favour of this change in policy.

The post-2008 financial crisis and the economic recession have also led to a decline in employment in the Danish labour market. Accordingly, the problem of labour shortages has diminished and more or less disappeared from the political agenda. Growing levels of unemployment will again be a question of major political concern. But as the economy recovers, the problem of labour shortage can be expected to reappear on the political agenda. Extraordinary efforts will then be required in education and training to address these problems, and consultation of the labour market parties will be an essential element in achieving lasting solutions.

CONCLUSIONS

The past decade has shown a tendency towards the development of three key pressures that threaten the self-regulation of the labour market parties, and thereby one of the central characteristics of the Danish model. The pressure comes first from the players in the political system, second from the labour market parties at local level, and third from the players at EU level. Instead of 'centralised decentralisation' with controlled coordination, labour market regulation in the future appears to be in the direction of a form of multi-level regulation, which is challenging the national collective bargaining actors and the position of the confederations.

Despite the current problems, the Danish agreement model for the regulation of pay and conditions appears to be in remarkably robust condition. The trade unions and the employers' associations both remain strong, and a high level of collective agreement coverage has been retained. If the unions, particularly those in LO, can stem their loss of members in the coming years, there will also be a future for the Danish model.

A CHRONOLOGY OF DANISH EMPLOYMENT RELATIONS

1898	Establishment of the two major confederations, LO (the Danish Confederation of Trade Unions, and DA (the Danish Employers' Confederation). The September Compromise—the first basic agreement between the major confederations.
1900	Wage bargaining at enterprise level became a part of the collective agreement in the iron and steel industry. At the same time, the parties reached an agreement regarding shop stewards.
1907	The Act on state-recognised unemployment insurance funds set out the rules for unemployment benefits in accordance with the so-called Ghent system, thereby contributing to strengthen the unions.
1908–10	Representatives from the two major confederations agree in the August Committee of 1908 on a new system of labour law established by an agreement between the parties on arbitration and Acts on a new labour court and a board of conciliation in 1910. The main pillars of the Danish model are in place: self-government of the parties of the labour market with limited legislation on wage and labour conditions and involvement of the confederations in the political processes concerning the labour market in the broadest sense.
1933	Starting point of a praxis of political intervention in industrial conflicts.
1934–36	De facto centralisation of collective bargaining between the member organisations of LO and DA by extending the powers of the conciliator to put forward settlement proposals and order a common ballot for all the involved unions and employers' associations.
1947	The first agreement between LO and DA on work councils in private sector companies.
1969	The starting point of a renewed public sector industrial relations system based on collective bargaining and the right to take industrial action. Employees covered by collective agreements replace public servants as the major group of public employees.

1950–80	Centralised collective bargaining under the control of the confederations usual through the board of conciliation.
1970s	The centralised bargaining system is marked by a period of crises leading to three subsequent political interventions.
1981	The parties began a renewal of the collective bargaining system.
1987	In a joint declaration between the confederations of the labour market and the government, the trade unions commit themselves to wage restraint in order to secure the competitiveness of Danish enterprises as well as to safeguard jobs and job creation.
1989	Structural reform of the DA from a confederation with many small member associations to a confederation dominated by a few large associations.
1991–92	The breakthrough of a new sector-based collective bargaining system transferring the bargaining responsibility from the confederations' member organisations at sector level. The role as the key bargaining area is expanded to include all of manufacturing industry, with the establishment of a new large employer confederation, DI, followed on the wage-earners' side by CO-industri. At the same time, the sector organisations agree on a transferral of negotiating responsibility to the parties at enterprise level on wage and working time. These structural changes to the Danish model contain both elements of centralisation and decentralisation, so this new phase in the collective bargaining system can be designated centralised decentralisation.
1989–91	Establishment of occupational pension funds through the system of collective bargaining. Other welfare issues become part of the collective agreements in the following rounds, expanding the scope of the collective agreements and creating a kind of double regulation of welfare issues through both legislation and collective agreements. An unintended consequence is a growing political pressure on the principle of self-regulation in the Danish model.

1998	A major conflict on the LO/DA area of the private labour market is halted by political intervention after two weeks.
2000	Implementation of EU directives challenges the collective bargaining model, which cannot guarantee that all wage-earners are covered. The problem is solved by a two-phase model: first, the directive is implemented via collective agreements; second, supplementary legislation is introduced which ensures that wage-earners not covered by collective agreements will be embraced by the requirements of the directive. This supplementary legislation is implemented via a new tripartite Implementation Committee.
2008	The hitherto largest and longest conflict takes place solely on the public labour market covering health care, elderly care and child care—that is, more than one-third of all public employees. The conflict is not halted by political intervention, but through a new compromise after more than eight weeks of strike action.

Chapter 10

Employment relations
in Japan

Hiromasa Suzuki and Katsuyuki Kubo

This chapter starts by putting Japanese employment relations into context, sketches some historical background, then discusses the changing roles of unions and employers and the Japanese approach to collective bargaining and labour-management consultation. The issues discussed include regulation and deregulation of the labour market, growth of atypical employment and changes in corporate governance.

With its population of 127 million people and GDP of more than $4 billion, Japan is the second-largest economy among the countries discussed in this book (the United States is the largest). Since the early 1990s, the Japanese economy has had two distinct periods. From the burst of the 'bubble' economy around 1991 up to 2002, there was a period of economic downturn and low economic growth. This was followed by a slow growth period up to 2008. The poor economic performance of the 1990s is often referred to as the lost decade. After the bubble burst in 1991, financial institutions accumulated immense bad loans due to a huge drop in asset values (real estate, stocks). In 1998, the financial collapse and other adverse factors caused economic growth in Japan to fall to negative 0.7 per cent over the previous year for the second time in the post-war period. After the start of the twenty-first century, the Japanese economy recovered—albeit at a slow pace—thanks to the export drive toward the United States and emerging economies, in particular China. Many Japanese manufacturing firms, faced with increasing global competition, accelerated their overseas production in an attempt to retain their competitive edge.

Japan has a labour force of 66 million; the labour force participation rate was 73 per cent in 2007. Some 85 per cent of the labour force consists of employees. Japan's labour force peaked in 2000 but a considerable decline is forecast if the present participation rate remains constant. The decline of the fertility rate (the fertility rate was only 1.3 in 2007) has recently attracted much attention in public debate. In 2007, about 4 per cent of the labour force worked in primary industries, including agriculture and fisheries. Manufacturing, mining and construction industries employed 28 per cent, while 68 per cent worked in the tertiary industries, including services, wholesale and retail, finance, utilities and government.

In many respects, Japan appears to be different from most other countries. On average, the Japanese enjoy the longest life span (86 years for women and 79 years for men). It is estimated that the Japanese ageing ratio (the total of people 65 years old and over divided by the total population) will be the highest among the major developed market economies by the year 2025. The structure of Japan's population will change substantially from the pyramid shape of the 1950s to a top-heavy shape by 2025. Population ageing is a serious issue, one that has an impact on both the supply and demand sides of the Japanese economy.

There has been a remarkable change in the labour market. Unemployment was about 1.1 per cent at the end of the 1960s, when the economy enjoyed high growth. The unemployment rate was one of the lowest in the world until the mid-1990s. It rose to 3.4 per cent in 1997 and 5.4 per cent in 2002 before going down to 4 per cent in 2008. The contemporary employment situation has many contrasting features. Many elderly workers have difficulty finding jobs and an increasing number of young workers are unable to find career positions that match their expectations (they do precarious jobs or they are in atypical employment in the secondary labour market). On the other hand, several firms in the IT sector and low-wage firms in manufacturing and services find it difficult to hire workers.

Another labour-market indicator, the ratio of job openings to job-seekers (for regular workers), fell from 1.51 in 1990 to 0.64 in 2000, aggravating the disparity between jobs and job-seeker profiles. After the start of the present century, the ratio recovered slowly to attain 1 in 2007. The ratio of 1 could be seen as a form of labour market equilibrium. Regional differences are considerable: Tokyo and some industrial centres (Nagoya, Hiroshima) have a ratio above 1, but rural areas have much worse ratios.

A significant feature of the post-1945 period has been a reduction in the number of working hours. In the pre-war period, twelve-hour workdays were common. Since then, the number of hours per day had been cut substantially. However, when the slow growth period started, the number of working hours declined further to around 2100 hours per year. In 1987, the legal limit of weekly hours was set at 40 hours. Since the 1990s, average annual working hours have stayed between 1950 and 2000 hours per year. The increase of part-time workers tended to lower the average working time. If we consider only full-time workers, the length of working time does not show any decline. A quarter of full-time male workers in the 30–49 years age-bracket worked more than 60 hours a week. Long and excessive working time is still a major public concern.

The post-1945 period has seen Japanese politics dominated by the conservative Liberal Democratic Party (LDP). Opposition parties have exerted influence from time to time; however, apart from a brief period after the war, none obtained enough power to hold office in national politics. Opposition parties traditionally have been ideologically divided. The Japan Socialist Party (JSP) was formed in the main by the radical left and some moderates with a close relationship with the main union federation, Sohyo. The moderate small Social Democratic Party (SDP) had a link with the moderate union movement, Domei, which primarily recruited in the private sector. There was a major political change after the dissolution of the Soviet block; socialist ideals lost political credibility in Japan as they did in many other developed countries.

In the 1990s, there were frequent changes of government, as successive elections resulted in fluctuating losses and gains of LDP seats in the lower house (*shu-giin*) and the upper house (*sangiin*). In 1993, for the first time since 1955, a coalition of parties succeeded in forming a non-LDP government for a short period (less than a year), and then a coalition government including the LDP was headed by a leader of the JSP (Tomiichi Murayama). Between 1996 and 2001, the LDP retained power, allying with the small but well-organised Buddhist Party (Koumeitou). In 1997, a new Democratic Party was created, regrouping factions from the LDP, JSP and SDP. Between 1993 and 2001, there were seven different governments in only eight years. The electoral basis of the LDP (rural population, business circles and small commerce) was gradually eroded in this period, but there was no major united opposition party. Unable to get a stable political basis, successive governments could not implement the decisive political and economic reforms necessary to solve the financial and economic problems of the 1990s.

With the election of Junichiro Koizumi as prime minister (2001–06), a new era of relative political stability emerged. The Koizumi government shifted its emphasis toward a market-oriented approach. He won several elections with policies such as privatisation of the postal office and deregulation. Thanks to his personal popularity, Koizumi and his government could centralise decision-making processes, circumscribing LDP factions and ministerial bureaucracy. His government put a brake on the increasing public expenditures by privatising public corporations and reducing welfare costs. He is credited with overcoming the lingering financial crisis of the 1990s. But this experience of strong premiership appeared to be short-lived after the resignation of Koizumi in 2006.

Unions are associated with various parties, including the SDP (formally JSP), the Democratic Socialist Party (DSP) and the Japan Communist Party (JCP), depending on their dominant ideology. Successful candidates from these parties may be recommended or supported by a union, or may have been associated with a union in the past. Despite these relations between parties and unions, rank-and-file union members tend to make up their own minds about who to vote for. There has been an increase in the number of voters who do not adhere to particular parties on a long-term basis. As a result, the influence of unions on voters has declined.

THE 'JAPANESE' MODEL

Since the mid-1970s, Japan has attracted much attention for its favourable economic performance and its 'cooperative' approaches to employment relations, which have allegedly supported this economic performance. The initial international interest in Japanese management and industrial relations after the 1960s was perplexing to Japanese people, as earlier in the twentieth century Japan had tried to follow models from the West (e.g. Britain, the United States and Germany). Before the 1973 oil crisis, the Japanese tended to see such countries as much more advanced, so that various management techniques and technologies were imported from them.

Because some of the Western countries that had once led Japan in economic prosperity had sluggish economies, especially after the 1973 oil crisis, some of these Western countries were no longer seen as models. Moreover, when these Western countries were looking for a new model themselves, ironically Japan was often the source of inspiration, as the Japanese economy seemed to be a success story. Although the interest in Japan waned after the failure of its economy in the post-bubble period of the early 1990s, some countries in Asia are still eager to 'import' the 'Japanese' model. In the tough economic circumstances of the 1990s, the management systems of some Japanese companies (e.g. Toyota, Honda and Sony) were refined to foster success in competitive world markets. Not only these large companies, but also many other smaller companies are shifting their production bases to other Asian countries, including China. To what extent are Japanese production and employment relations systems transferable to other countries?

To begin to answer such questions, some historical background is required. Japan's feudal era ended with the Meiji Restoration of 1868. Hitherto, Japan had experienced little contact with Western countries. Industrialisation began in the following decade, a century later than in Britain. Japan's early factories in major industries were begun by the state, but in the 1880s it had sold most of them to a few selected families. These were the origin of what later became the powerful *zaibatsu* groups of holding companies, which were based on these groups' commercial banks.

Although some unions, such as those covering printers and iron-workers, began during this period, the familial basis of industrialisation continued well into the twentieth century. Many factories had their own dormitories, especially in the textile industry. In many industries, they had master workers (*oyakata*), who were subcontractors like the early British foremen. After World War I, there was an acute shortage of skilled workers. Firms wanted to recruit workers directly. Hence many large enterprises intervened in the *oyakata*'s prerogative to recruit. With the rapid development of industries, the system of learning skills through apprenticeship was absorbed into internal training within enterprises.

As the paternalistic tradition developed in the 1920s and 1930s, the unions exerted little sustained influence. Faced with pressure from the militaristic regime, unions were dissolved between 1938 and 1943 and the employers' associations were absorbed into the mobilisation for war production.

After Japan's unconditional surrender in 1945, the Allied powers' General Headquarters (GHQ) sought to rebuild the organisation of work and employment relations as part of the post-war reconstruction. Many elements of the present model were shaped after the war under American influence.

EMPLOYEES AND UNIONS

The Japanese labour movement developed rapidly under the GHQ's democratisation program. Although much of Japan's industrial base was destroyed during the war, only four months after its end, union membership had returned to pre-war levels, and by 1949 there were 6.6 million union members, a peak density level of 56 per cent. There were, nevertheless, also setbacks for the unions. For instance, their plans to hold a general strike in 1947 were suspended by order of the GHQ. But the unions continued to grow, and reached a peak membership of 12.6 million members in 1975 with a density of 34 per cent.

After this peak, membership and density of union organisations stagnated for a while, before gradually declining year after year. In 2007, membership had fallen to about 10 million; unions had lost more than two million members from the beginning of the 1990s. One of the main causes of this decline was a change in the industrial structure, especially the shift towards the service sector. Union density varies by industry. Although the average density was 18 per cent in 2007, it was 44 per cent in the public services and 59 per cent in public utilities such as electricity, gas and water. By contrast, union density in wholesale, retail and restaurants was only 11 per cent. There are very few unions in SMEs that have fewer than 30 employees. Union density in these SMEs is below 10 per cent.

During the decade after the 1973 oil crisis, there was a substantial rationalisation in the highly unionised manufacturing sector. As most larger establishments adopt union-shop clauses, union membership tends to vary with the growth and decline of unionised firms or industries. When the firm is expanding, union membership generally rises and vice versa. Although there has been a rise in the number of employees, membership in the service sector tends to be relatively small; it is generally more difficult and costly for unions to organise SMEs than large enterprises.

Another cause of union decline has been the general improvement in living standards, which has tended to make employees less enthusiastic about union activities. Pay rises vary according to pre-vailing macro-economic conditions. Since the peak in 1990, when the pay rise in centralised annual wage negotiations was 5.9 per cent, such pay rises have been minimal in recent years. For instance, the average monthly pay in unionised firms did not increase in the decade after 1998. (Workers in firms with more than 1000 employees received almost the same wages between 1998 and 2007, although in real terms they received a minor gain due to declining prices). These unfavourable outcomes might have discouraged workers' interest in unions. Thus it is widely assumed that unions have outlived their usefulness, and that the centralised mode of wage negotiations is outdated.

There has been a steady increase of atypical employment—part-time workers, seasonal workers, temporary agency workers and fixed-term workers. Currently, about two in three workers ars considered to be non-regular workers. As most Japanese unions organise regular employees, but do not organise the enterprise's non-regular workers, this increase of atypical employment implies a decline of union members. Some industrial unions such as UI Zensen (textiles, supermarkets) have tried to organise part-time workers, but with only limited success. As a whole, the union density of part-time workers is less than 5 per cent.

Although the level of unemployment in Japan has remained lower than in most Western countries, it gradually increased in the 1990s to reach 5.4 per cent in 2002, before falling to 3.9 per cent in 2007. In recent years, management and employees in large firms have placed a high priority on the employment protection of regular employees to the detriment of non-regular employees. Regular employees have become more concerned about the competitive position of the companies for which they work, and most seem to have a high degree of commitment to the enterprise.

This reflects the Japanese expectation of 'lifetime employment' and seniority-based wages; such practices were consolidated after World War II, in particular during the high growth period (1955–73). Permanent manual and non-manual staff are employed not for specific jobs or occupations, but as company employees. Companies prefer to employ new school leavers or university graduates rather than experienced workers who have been trained in other firms. Their induction program is designed to encourage them to conform to the company's norms.

Young recruits start at a comparatively low level of pay, which is based on their educational qualifications. Their pay rises in proportion to their length of service up to a certain age limit in the enterprise. Promotion is generally based on length of service, which is assumed to correlate with the employee's level of skill developed within the enterprise. Therefore, it is disadvantageous for workers to change employers and for employers to lay off employees who have accumulated specific skills required in that particular enterprise. Typically, in the so-called primary labour market comprising permanent or regular employees working for large enterprises, there is a tacit understanding about the long-term commitment between employer and employees. However, this is not confirmed in a written contract. Although the length of service among female workers has increased, 'lifetime employment' generally applies to male rather than female workers.

Most unions in Japan are organised not by occupation or by job but by enterprise or establishment. An enterprise union consists solely of regular employees of a single company, regardless of their occupational status, up to lower management levels. As enterprise unions usually include non-manual and manual workers as members, the union density in unionised firms is high among non-manual as well as manual regular workers; only managerial positions are excluded from membership. These employees are expected to stay in the same company until their mandatory retirement age, unless they are made redundant or leave voluntarily (both being less usual than in most Western countries). The mandatory retirement age in most enterprises is fixed at 60 years.

However, in view of the ageing population and the financing of public pension schemes, which put the full pensionable age at 65 years, legislation in 2005 stipulated that enterprises should offer employment up to 65 years by 2013 (this provision is being implemented in stages). It does not specify that mandatory retirement age should be raised to 65 years, but leaves the possibility to offer fixed-term contracts to workers. So far, most firms have maintained the retirement age of 60 years, after which they offer a fixed-term contract. This is preferred by enterprises, because upon retirement the open-ended employment contract is terminated (the workers concerned are no longer on the general wage scales) so that the enterprises could offer a new contract of fixed duration with substantially lower wages. Even beyond this prolongation of employment terms, many Japanese workers find other jobs in subsidiaries or similar enterprises by recommendation of the parent companies, or they start small businesses. In 2007, 48 per cent of male workers in the 65–69 years age group were still active in the labour force.

The primary core of regular employees constitutes only about one-third of all employees. This is an estimate of the proportion of employees working in the public sector (civil servants) and in large enterprises, compared with the total number of employees, including those who work for SMEs. Regular employees with longer job tenure are typically found in the primary labour markets, where there are large enterprises. Many of the remaining two-thirds of the labour force work for SMEs, or on a temporary or part-time basis, and are often not union members. Therefore, union density among women, who constitute the majority of part-time workers, is much lower than among male employees.

In SMEs that are stable or expanding, there are many regular employees who stay in the same company for most of their working lives. The prevalence of SMEs is a notable factor in maintaining flexibility in the Japanese labour market. In practice, therefore, it is difficult to make a precise distinction between the primary and secondary labour markets according to the size of firms or sectors in Japan. The demarcation line has shifted rather to the difference in status between regular employees and non-regular employees.

As enterprise unions include non-manual staff and manual workers in an enterprise, a worker leaving the enterprise automatically loses union membership. The same is true for employees promoted to managerial positions. In spite of its name, an enterprise union functions not only for the benefit of the enterprise; it has legal protection against employer interference into its affairs and from other unfair labour practices.

Many enterprise unions grew sporadically in the period of turmoil after 1945. Some of them developed from the factory- and company-based wartime production committees. As most Japanese unions are organised for whole enterprises or individual plants, there are more than 58 000 unions, according to an official estimate in 2007. About 97 per cent of enterprise union members work in firms employing more than 100 employees (in the private sector). Although there are other types of union organisations, such as industrial, craft and general unions, these are exceptions. Kaiin, the Seamen's union, is a rare example of an industrial union.

Most enterprise unions within the same industry join an industrial federation of unions. There are more than 100 such federations. The major functions of the industrial federations include coordinating the activities of the member enterprise unions with the aim of improving wages and working conditions; dealing with problems common to a whole industry; guiding and assisting member unions in specific disputes; and political lobbying in the interest of workers. These industrial federations themselves belong to national centres, of which Rengo (JTUC, Japan Trade Union Confederation) is the largest.

After the two oil crises of the 1970s, unions at the industrial and national levels led what they called a 'policy-oriented struggle', with the aim of ensuring stable employment and maintaining their members' standards of living. Another movement 'to unite the labour front under the initiative of private-sector unions' emerged in 1982 under the name of Zenminrokyo, the Japanese Private Sector Union Council. It was formed by the labour federations in the private sector and reflected their quest for further unification to increase their strength. This organisation developed into a larger union centre, Rengo, which also integrated the public-sector unions. The new

Rengo was established in 1989, when it had 78 industrial federations with nearly eight million members. Public-sector unions used to be more political and have more power than those in the private sector. However, their membership and power have diminished since 1978 due to the privatisation of public corporations and cuts in public services. In the early twenty-first century, private sector unions tend to be more powerful than those in the public sector.

Rengo has pursued cooperative labour–management relations. At the beginning, Rengo tried in vain to play a political role, to form an expanded liberal democratic league. During recessions, its role was restricted to participation in policy-making consultation at the national level. An association of enterprise unions and their federations, Rengo has found it difficult to represent the interests of union members at the grass-roots level. The structure and policy orientation of Rengo have seriously been challenged by the unfavourable economic climate, high unemployment rates, university graduates' difficulties in finding employment, and the restructuring of industries and enterprises.

Although the national confederations (Rengo and the smaller Zenroukyou) play important roles, the enterprise unions have more resources and are more powerful. The latter are autonomous in running their organisations and in promoting their members' interests. Furthermore, they are financially independent and self supporting. Most union activities occur at the enterprise level rather than the federation level. As the company's success greatly influences members' working conditions and employment opportunities, enterprise unions generally have a cooperative attitude towards management. Employees usually identify with their employer in making decisions that would enhance the competitiveness of the enterprise. Thus a key aspect of the work environment in Japanese companies is this interdependence and the belief that the company is a 'community of shared fate', where 'everyone is in the same big family'. In addition, the relatively modest wage differentials between managers, non-manual staff and operatives tend to reinforce the workers' sense of identification with the enterprise. Furthermore, most senior managers, directors and executives, including the CEO, are promoted internally from the ranks after long years of service and internal competition. Some of those people were leaders of enterprise unions when they were rank-and-file employees. This contrasts with some Western countries, where there is more class differentiation and far greater pay differentials.

Are enterprise unions really independent of the control of the employer? If a company is unionised, the enterprise union is usually the only organisation that is recognised as representing the employees at the enterprise. Financially, such unions are independent from the employer, since by regulation full-time union officials are paid out of union fees. Employers usually offer various facilities to the union, including an office, but such facilities are offered on a voluntary basis after negotiations between the parties. To an extent, the availability of these facilities helps establish a basis for cooperative labour–management relations in enterprises.

It is generally believed that an advantage of enterprise unionism is that its policies are adapted to each enterprise, rather than reflecting more sectional craft, ideological or political issues. Employment relations based on enterprise unionism tend to be more flexible than those based on, for example, craft unionism. On the other hand, there are disadvantages from a union's point of view. Newly employed workers automatically acquire union membership and their union dues are 'checked off' from their pay automatically, thus their 'union consciousness' is generally less than their 'enterprise consciousness'. Union membership usually ceases on retirement, which also reduces the workers' commitment to the union.

The reason why enterprise unions do not organise non-regular employees working in the same workplace is to do with the special status enjoyed by regular employees. In Japanese companies, the word *sei-shain* is often used (it really means regular 'member of the company'). The word contains nuances that do not have an equivalent in Western terminology. It means more than a mere hired worker and implies belonging to a community formed by people with the same interests. Therefore, entry to an enterprise union is generally restricted to the members of the community.

Non-regular employees such as part-time workers, seasonal workers, temporary workers and immigrant workers are usually not allowed to join enterprise unions. This situation is undermining the basis of unionism at the establishment or plant level, because large firms use temporary workers and those from subcontracted firms. Since 2004, temporary workers have been allowed to work in the manufacturing sector, with a maximum duration of three years. Although some new types of unions for certain categories of workers are emerging, they are still exceptions.

During the long recession, in an effort to reduce surplus workers, companies specifically designated middle-aged and older employees for redundancy. Such employees had already retired from unions after becoming managers, so they could not gain support from the unions in their efforts to keep their jobs. Critics of enterprise unionism point out that enterprise unions are defending the interests only of core workers of large firms (the relatively well-off workers), while neglecting to help more vulnerable groups of workers.

EMPLOYERS AND THEIR ORGANISATIONS

During the period immediately after 1945, there were many violent labour disputes in Japan. These tended to reflect the economic disorder and the shortage of food and daily necessities. Neither employers nor workers then had much industrial relations experience. To cope with this labour offensive and to establish industrial peace and order, employers organised regional and industrial associations. However, partly because of the so-called 'democratisation' policy of GHQ, employers were often obliged to yield to union pressure, thus facing an erosion of their managerial prerogatives.

To help to restore managerial authority, Nikkeiren, the Japan Federation of Employers' Associations, was founded in 1948. It was the most important employers' organisation from an industrial relations point of view, and had many functions. It played a considerable role until the 1970s, when annual wage negotiations had a strong impact on national economy. But the importance of these negotiations waned in the 1980s and 1990s. Business groups thought that an employers' federation that specialised in labour matters was no longer necessary; therefore, Nikkeiren merged with the powerful Keidanren in 2002 to form Nihon Keidanren (Japan Business Organisation). Most of the functions the former Nikkeiren had previously carried out were then entrusted to Nihon Keidanren, which especially represents large firms.

Like Nikkeiren, Nihon Keidanren coordinates and publicises employers' opinions on labour problems, selects employer representatives to various government commissions, councils and International Labour Organization (ILO) delegations, and provides its member organisations with advice and service on labour conditions and employment practices. Nihon Keidanren's members include employers' associations organised at the regional and industry level. Every year at the time of *Shunto*, the Spring Labour Offensive, Nihon Keidanren releases guidelines for employers to follow when dealing with demands from unions during collective bargaining. Although many of them do not have a direct role in bargaining, the employers' associations have an important role to play behind the scenes (Levine 1984: 318ff).

Three factors strongly influence the magnitude of *Shunto*: demand and supply conditions in labour markets; consumer price levels;

and business conditions (a company's performance) (Ministry of Labour 1975). In recent years, the main determinant of the outcome of collective bargaining has been business conditions. Compared with the declining power of unions, employers have increased their influence over employees. Many large enterprises—for example, in the automobile, electrical appliances, construction and banking sectors—resorted to downsizing, but most enterprise unions were relatively restrained in their response.

COLLECTIVE BARGAINING

Collective bargaining has some peculiar features. First, collective bargaining takes place exclusively at the level of enterprise. There is no collective bargaining at industry or national levels. Union federations may coordinate the process of negotiations, but ultimately individual enterprises and enterprise unions have the autonomy to make final decisions.

Second, in most unionised enterprises there are elaborate joint consultation mechanisms, in which union representatives participate. Historically, joint consultation machinery was developed in the 1950s, on the initiative of the Japan Productivity Centre, which advocated industrial peace in enterprises through dialogue. Joint consultation is often seen as a means of information-sharing, but most labour issues are discussed at consultation meetings. The line between collective bargaining and joint consultation is blurred, since the same people (top managers and union officials) attend the consultation and negotiation meetings. Third, collective bargaining focuses on pay issues, particularly during the Spring wage round.

Pay agreements may be concluded separately from agreements on other matters. Most unions conduct pay negotiations during *Shunto* in March, April and May each year, while negotiations on more comprehensive labour agreements may be conducted at other times. However, an increasing number of unions also make other claims during *Shunto*—for example, for increases in overtime rates, revisions of allowances, shorter working hours, raising the retirement age and pensions. A decline in union density and a sluggish economic climate have helped change the characteristics of *Shunto*. Its relative importance in national wage bargaining has declined since the focus of wage bargaining shifted towards the enterprise level. Increasing differences in the profitability of enterprises, reflecting increased global competition, have been a major cause of this change.

The structure of enterprise unions usually corresponds with the organisation of the enterprise and its establishment, department or divisional groupings. Grievances are often settled informally, with formal procedures rarely used. Managers often attempt to settle tensions and conflict, and to reinforce feelings of shared community. These informal procedures to avoid formal conflicts were set up by managers and unions in the past. In the 1940s and 1950s, there were many large-scale and long disputes in mining and major manufacturing enterprises. Some strikes were led by radical union leaders, and many of these disputes left wounds in employment relationships that were not easily healed.

Such disputes taught the unions and employers some important lessons. Although there were many stoppages in 1974, subsequently the number of stoppages fell substantially. Disputes are usually settled directly between the parties concerned, but sometimes a third party conciliates. Conciliation machinery for the private and public sectors is provided by the central and local labour relations commissions. Special commissions act for public sector employees and for seamen. Nearly all the disputes submitted to these commissions are settled either by conciliation or mediation; few disputes go as far as arbitration.

Most disputes presented to the labour relations commissions are those that go beyond the limits of labour–management relations at the enterprise level. The relative importance of the commissions has declined, as there has been an improvement in cooperation between labour and management at the enterprise level.

Contemporary Japanese employment relations are relatively stable, and relations between the parties can generally be characterised as cooperative. Some see this in a positive light. Others have a more negative view, arguing that enterprise unions are too dependent on employers, and that the relationship is one of collaboration and incorporation. Beyond individual opinions, there are differences between sectors and firms: some enterprise unions are well organised and effectively check most of the important managerial decisions, while in others union shop stewards do not play any checking role. Enterprise unions have diverse characteristics. However, for most Japanese workers, including union officials, the pursuit of company profits tends to have a higher prority than consideration of individual employees' interests.

Unions represent sectional interests, and enterprise unions are no exception. Many employees expect to work for many years for the same enterprise; they tend to emphasise the improvement of their working conditions. They pay less attention to the interests of non-regular workers at the same establishment. This may be an unfortunate characteristic of Japanese firms, where regular employees want to maintain their position, even at the expense of non-regular employees such as part-time workers and temporary workers, who are disproportionately likely to be women.

Why has the relationship between unions and employers changed so fundamentally since the 1950s? There has been increased global competition, improved standards of living and a shift towards a service-oriented economy. Public opinion is also more conservative than it was in the 1950s. The 1970s oil crises further accelerated the change. Despite the long recession after the early 1990s, the number of industrial disputes has shown little sign of increasing. In 1975, the total number of industrial disputes reached a peak of 8435. However, there were only 662 in 2006. Where has all the discontent gone about redundancies during the recession? One of the remarkable changes is that the weight of disputes has shifted from the collective to the individual. There have also been higher levels of labour turnover. These developments represent challenges to unions as well as to the employment relations system.

CURRENT ISSUES

After the long recession of the 1990s, a slow economic recovery has been driven mainly by exports in the manufacturing sector, because of the low level of domestic consumption. Exports were also facilitated by the exchange rate (there was a relatively cheap yen) caused by zero interest rate set by the Bank of Japan. Most large Japanese firms had invested in overseas subsidiaries so that many of them became multinational enterprises with their headquarters in Japan. Toyota exemplifies such a transformation; this Nagoya-based auto maker, which perfected the famous 'just-in-time' system, was very cautious about becoming a multinational until the 1980s. It opened its first large factory in the United States only in 1987. This was prompted by current United States–Japan trade friction. Two decades later, Toyota had a global network of production, in particular, in the United States, the EU and Asia, including Australia. In most cases, Toyota's parts makers (e.g. Denso and Aishin) became as globalised as Toyota itself. In 2006, most of the Toyota's profit came from overseas subsidiaries, especially from the United States and emerging economies. Thus the overseas production activities of Japanese firms have substantially expanded since the 1980s. Such Japanese firms employed about 2.9 million workers abroad, which amounted to a quarter of domestic employment in the manufacturing sector (Fukao 2002).

The international context surrounding Japan has changed considerably since the 1980s. Korea and Taiwan have become strong competitors in many hi-tech industries. Thailand has become a regional centre for certain types of cars (pick-up trucks). Once Japan had a huge technological and economic advance, but these neighbouring countries have become competitors and also partners. Of course, Japanese firms also benefit from the proximity of such dynamic markets, including China and India.

Inside Japan, the social and economic context is changing, revealing some long-term problems. There is an ageing population and a decline in the fertility rate, which heralds a decline of the labour force and, in the long run, of the total population. There are sporadic debates about immigration, but the fundamental questions about immigration policies have not been settled. Female participation in the labour market has been growing, but many women take up part-time jobs without career prospects. The cleavage between regular and non-regular workers (typical versus atypical employment) is generating social concern and considerable public debate.

REGULATION AND DEREGULATION OF THE LABOUR MARKET

Successive conservative governments have subscribed to the ideologies of free markets and deregulation. Therefore, there has been some relaxation of labour market regulation. In terms of deregulation of labour law, the most far-reaching aspect concerns temporary work. The initial law on temporary agency workers in 1986 was aimed at restricting agency workers to deployment only in certain technical jobs or specified occupations. In 1999, the law was amended so that most occupations, except manufacturing and construction, were open to agency workers. Since 2004, the use of temps has become legalised, even in the manufacturing sector. Many manufacturing firms have made use of temporary workers at times of high demand. The official estimate put the number of agency workers in the manufacturing sector at around half a million in 2008. The regulation of temporary agency work is loose; there is no limitation on the renewal of contracts except for a maximum duration of three years, nor a reason for its utilisation. According to an official 2006 survey by the Ministry of Health, Labour and Welfare (MHLW), there were 1.3 million agency workers, of whom a majority (60 per cent) were female. These agency workers on average are paid much less than regular workers. Many South Americans of Japanese descent work as agency workers in such regional industrial cities as Hamamatsu and Nagoya.

Another relaxation of the regulations relates to the maximum duration of employment contracts. For a long time, the maximum duration of fixed-term contracts was one year with the possibility of renewal, but in 2006 this was been extended to three years. Furthermore, overtime regulation was deregulated for certain core employees. These are the main changes that have occurred in labour law since the 1980s. They are modest in scope, except with regard to temporary agency workers.

Why are the changes so modest? The answer does not reflect the opposition of unions (they are weak), but rather points to the flexibility that is already inherent in the Japanese employment system. For instance, employment protection is not enshrined in law, but custom and judicial interpretations have made dismissal difficult. In case law, abuses in terms of dismissals are clearly defined. If they are to avoid infringing their right to terminate an (open-ended) employment contract, employers should have a valid reason to terminate a contract (economic conditions) and make sufficient efforts to avoid dismissals (restrictions on overtime, temporary freeze of recruitment, internal transfers and voluntary redundancies). There is also a defined procedure to follow (consultation with unions, where they are present, and the selection of workers for dismissal should not be discriminatory. But this case law can be interpreted in different ways. Furthermore, lengthy and costly court cases (one case going to the supreme court might take ten years) discourage most individual workers who feel unfavourably treated to go to court. Many labour specialists think the cases that have gone to court are only the tip of a large iceberg, and that in practice workers have little protection in individual disputes (for instance, concerning dismissal or pay and bonus). In 2006, to expedite judicial procedures about individual disputes, a labour tribunal was established. This includes a judge and two experts recommended by employers and unions respectively. In principle, cases should be resolved within three sittings. If one of the parties does not agree with the decision of the labour tribunal, then it can raise the case through the formal judicial procedures. It is too soon to evaluate the labour tribunal's impact, though the number of cases brought to the labour court has been rising.

Another instance of flexibility concerns workers in subcontracting firms. Most large firms (e.g. in the steel and shipbuilding industries) use many workers from subcontracting firms, mainly because wages are much lower in such small firms. These workers do the job alongside regular workers within large firms. Since they do not have a formal employment relationship with those workers, the large firms are not constrained by employment protection laws. Before the deregulation of temporary agency workers in manufacturing, such utilisation of outside workers could give firms flexibility in employment adjustment. In addition, there is no limitation concerning the renewal of seasonal or fixed-term workers' contracts. Therefore, the modest deregulation of the labour law exemplifies the flexibility in the Japanese labour market. Perhaps the question is how to protect the employment and working conditions of non-regular employees, who are outside the scope of collective bargaining. This was highlighted by the post-2007 global financial and crisis and its impact on temps.

LONG-TERM EMPLOYMENT OF REGULAR WORKERS

Long-term employment is the cornerstone of human resource management in large Japanese firms. These firms annually recruit (in April) new high school leavers and new university graduates with open-ended contracts. Young employees with several years' experience or graduate studies may join the cohort of regular employees, but preference is still given to new graduates without occupational experience. Once recruited, young employees receive a lengthy development (mostly on-the-job training) and periodical transfers of assignment (every three to five years). A cultural acclimatising of young employees to the firm's customs is part of this training, since the notion of a firm as a community is deeply rooted in Japan. Pay is linked to this long-term employment practice, even though the performance-related element increases from mid-career. Many employees are reluctant to change employers, because their pay could be lower after moving to another employer.

Vacancies in managerial positions are filled by internal promotions. Directors are usually promoted from among the senior managers, who may have worked for the company for 25 to 30 years, after graduating from university or high school. Some of these people may have been leaders of enterprise unions when they were rank-and-file employees. Many employees that have been promoted to senior management positions were previously union members. When promoted from senior managerial positions to be directors, individuals are asked to change their employment status as they become directors, but this is a gradual change from being an employee to being a top manager. Directors that have been promoted internally after a long career might be expected to place the interests of the enterprise community (of executive members and employees) above the interests of shareholders. Pay levels of executives in these firms are generally linked to employees' pay, which explains the enormous differences of pay between US and Japanese top executives.

These long-term employment practices have been under pressure since the 1990s downturn of the Japanese economy. Large firms resorted to employment adjustments through the reduction of intake of new recruits and transfer of employees to related companies, but compulsory collective redundancies of regular (core) employees were extremely rare. Nevertheless, such firms have reduced the proportion of regular employees to a minimum. More routine or less essential jobs are allocated to non-regular workers or outsourced. As far as regular workers are concerned, there is little change in long-term employment practices. The average length of service of male graduate regular workers in firms with more than 1000 employees is relatively stable (Ministry of Health, Labour and Welfare, 2010). The average length of service for all workers actually increased from twelve years in 1985 to about fourteen years in 2004. In terms of workers who are in the 55–59 years age group, the length of service has been getting longer, from 25.5 years in 1985 to 28.6 years in 2004. The average length of service was stable for male university graduate (regular workers) in large firms. However, for those who are excluded from the long-term employment track, their future prospects are bleak. There has probably been a decline in the number of people with long-term employment status in recent years.

GROWTH OF ATYPICAL EMPLOYMENT

A related change in the Japanese labour market in recent years has been an increase in atypical employment. Atypical employment covers a wide range of jobs and workers: it includes part-time workers, fixed-term workers and temporary workers. One of the most important differences between regular and non-regular employees is job security. While most regular workers are working with an open-ended contract, which makes it difficult to terminate the contract, similar guarantees are not given to people in atypical employment.

Figure 10.1 shows the change in non-regular workers (male and female) according to the labour force survey data. In this survey, employees were classified into five categories of 'regular staff', 'part-time workers', '*arubaito*' (*arbeit* means temporary worker), 'dispatched workers from temporary labour agency' and 'contracted or entrusted worker, and other'.[1]

Figure 10.1 shows that the number of all types of non-regular workers has been increasing during this period for both men and

Figure 10.1 Changes in the number of regular and non-regular workers

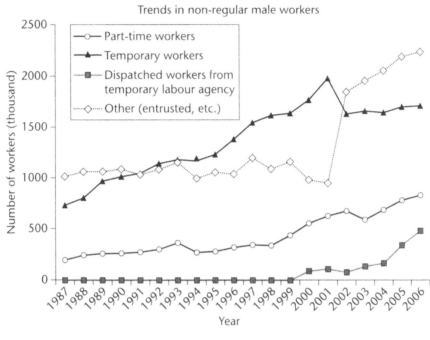

Source: The Labour Force Survey (Ministry of Internal Affairs and Communications, 2010)

271

women For example, the number of non-regular male workers was less than two million in 1987, but had risen to more than five million by 2006. The number of regular workers declined only slightly from 23.5 million in 1987 compared with 23.3 million in 2006; the proportion of non-regular workers among employees increased from 7.6 per cent to 18.5 per cent. In particular, the number of dispatched workers from temporary agencies increased dramatically. It rose from 250 000 in 2000 to 720 000 in 2006. The increase was even more dramatic for female workers. The number of non-regular female workers was 5.2 million in 1987 compared with 11.3 million in 2006. The number of regular women workers rose from 9.9 million in 1987 to 10.1 million in 2006; the proportion of non-regular workers among female employees increased from 34.3 per cent to 52.9 per cent. Since the long-term employment system usually does not apply to these workers, more and more workers have been working without job security.

A survey on HRM strategy and workers' sentiment (based on 1602 firms and 7566 employees) revealed that among 1602 firms, 1460 firms non-regular workers (Japan Institute of Labour Policy and Training 2003). The survey asked those firms why they hired non-regular workers.

The most common reason, chosen by almost 77 per cent of firms, was to reduce labour costs. Firms have been able to reduce labour costs by hiring non-regular workers because non-regular workers' salaries have generally been less than those of regular workers. In addition, about 47 per cent of respondents said that the reason was to adjust employment according to fluctuations in the business cycle.

The distinction between regular employees and non-regular workers is all the more serious because there is almost no bridge or access to the regular workers' track. Hence people can be trapped into atypical employment. This is the case with mobile young people (called 'freeter') and women rearing children—even with higher education.

ECONOMIC INEQUALITY

Economic inequality is widening. According to the National Survey of Family Income and Expenditure by the Ministry of Internal Affairs and Communications, the Gini coefficient, which shows the degree of inequality among families, has become larger. Ohtake (2005) found that the coefficients did not increase within age groups except for those under 30 years of age. He suggests that one important factor causing more economic inequality is the ageing society. Since inequality among older people is greater than that among younger people, the economic inequality of Japan's society is likely to increase as the proportion of older people increases. This may imply that the introduction of performance pay and an increase in non-regular workers were not the main factors for the widening economic gap. However, economic inequality has become larger within younger age groups. This trend arguably reflects the growing proportion of non-regular workers among younger people.

Some scholars, such as Tachibanaki (2005), have underlined the relationship between the changes in employment relations and the increase in economic inequality. These researchers have focused on other indicators, rather than the Gini coefficient. For example, the poverty rate has increased. Förster and d'Ercole (2005) examined the change in the relative poverty ratio of OECD countries from the mid-1980s to 2000. The relative poverty ratio was defined as the proportion of individuals whose income was less than half of the median for the population. Their study showed that the relative poverty rate has been increasing in Japan since the mid-1980s. While the poverty rate has been less than 5 per cent in countries such as the Czech Republic and Denmark, it has exceeded 15 per cent in Japan, along with the United States, Ireland, Turkey and Mexico.[2]

The inequality of assets has been widening too. According to the Public Opinion Survey on Household Financial Assets and Liabilities by the Central Council for Financial Services Information, the proportion of households without savings has been increasing dramatically. In 1988, some 8.7 per cent of the household respondents said that they did not make any deposits. The figure increased to 21.8 per cent in 2003. This trend also suggests that economic inequality in terms of assets has increased.

RESTRUCTURING OF FIRMS

In the late 1990s, many firms restructured themselves through mergers and acquisitions. In addition, changes in Japan's legal system have contributed to the increase in corporate reorganisations. These changes make it easier for firms to reorganise themselves. In addition to mergers and acquisitions, many large firms have been reorganising themselves in other ways.

One big change is that some firms have moved to a pure holding company system. Such a holding company does not conduct business operations, but holds stock in other companies. By shifting to a pure holding company, firms can more easily reorganise themselves in the future through a merger, acquisition or divesture. Also, companies can use different employment conditions for their subsidiaries. It is difficult for a single firm to practise various employment conditions, but it is much easier for a holding company to use different employment relations systems for its various subsidiaries. For example, management may set lower wages for subsidiaries with lower profitability or for those located in areas where the unemployment rate is high.

In addition, many companies have changed their boards. A board of directors has several characteristics. There is a strict hierarchy within company boards. The directors are classified as chairperson, president, vice-president, senior executives, executives and non-titled directors. All of these directors are full-time members of the board. Because of these features, it is argued that boards of directors fail to monitor the firm's president, since presidents face little challenge from outside directors.

A 2003 amendment to company law enabled large companies to choose a US-type corporate-governance system with nomination committee, compensation (remuneration) committee and audit committees. If a company chooses this type of committee system, the board of directors can delegate substantial management authority to executive officers. However, only a few companies adopted this system. Instead, most introduced an executive officer system. When firms adopt an executive officer system, they distinguish the monitoring role, which is undertaken by the board of directors, and the managing role, which is conducted by executive officers. Although day-to-day important decisions are delegated to executive officers, major decisions are made by the board. There is only a low proportion of non-executive directors in these firms. Firms also reduce the number of directors. More than half of the listed firms on the Tokyo Stock Exchange have introduced this executive officer system. It is not yet clear what the consequences of these changes will be on employment relations at the enterprise level. However, as Japanese firms have become sensitive to the risk of a hostile takeover by foreign investors, they have clearly given precedence to the payment of dividends over wage increases.

PERFORMANCE-RELATED PAY

One of the biggest HRM issues has been the introduction of performance-related pay systems. Although the definition of performance-related pay has varied, evidence suggests that more and more employers have been trying to introduce some kind of new system to strengthen the link between pay and performance.[3]

A survey of wage determination shows that more and more firms put an emphasis on performance, with 219 (86.2 per cent) out of 254 respondents having introduced performance-related pay (Japan Institute for Labour Policy and Training 2006). About 62 per cent of firms in the survey reported that performance had become more important in determining wages and almost 60 per cent said an employee's ability had become a more important criterion. In contrast, more than 30 per cent of firms said the importance of age, education and length of service was decreasing. Less than 10 per cent of firms said they put more emphasis on age, education or length of service than before.

Several surveys have examined employees' responses to performance pay. The 2004 General Survey on Working Conditions asked how firms evaluated the introduction of performance-related pay. Of those surveyed, 15.9 per cent said 'good', 45.3 per cent said 'good but needs to be modified' and 30.4 per cent said 'needs major revision'. The survey also showed that the main problem with performance pay was the performance appraisal; approximately half of the firms' respondents reported that managers did not have enough skills to evaluate their subordinates. In addition, 54.5 per cent said it was difficult to compare the appraisals of employees who worked in different divisions of the firm.

One survey asked employees whether they agreed with the general principle that wages should be determined by individual performance (Japan Institute of Labour Policy and Training 2003). Almost 28 per cent of employees agreed, while 60 per cent said that they agreed, but were also anxious about it, while only about 7 per cent of employees said that they did not agree. Among those who felt anxious or who were opposed to the principle, 79 per cent said that they were not confident that their performance or skills were fairly evaluated. In addition, 51 per cent said that performance might depend on the job assigned, rather than on their effort. Nearly 38 per cent were anxious that their income might fluctuate.

CONCLUSIONS

Since the 1970s, employment relations have undergone a series of considerable changes. These reflect macro-economic changes in the Japanese economy as well as in employment relations. In terms of macro-economic changes, we highlight in particular the relative decline of predominance of Japanese economy in the world, increasing global-isation of Japanese firms, the shift towards a service economy and the ageing population. As noted, the Japanese economy experienced difficulties during and since the 1990s. In contrast with Japan in this period, China has experienced high growth. The relative position of Japan compared with China has changed considerably, though Japan is still the second largest economy in the world (after the United States), and there is still a big gap between Japan and China in terms of per capita income. Nonetheless, Japanese firms can no longer sustain global competition without their Chinese plants and the Chinese market. This is in stark contrast to the 1980s or earlier, when Japanese firms had a dominant technological and financial position in Asia and beyond.

The transformation of the Japanese economy is continuing so that the tertiary sector accounts for two-thirds of all employment. This sector is heterogeneous, but in terms of employment it is very important. The wholesale and retail segment alone employs as many workers as the whole of the manufacturing sector. Other segments like health and welfare, transportation and educational activities are also important. The growth of atypical employment can be ascribed to this trend towards a service economy. Part-time workers, mainly comprising women and students, are numerous in these services. What is the quality of employment in particular in the service sector? Most part-time female workers annually earn less than 1.3 million yen (around US$13 000, if US$1 = 100 yen). This is the threshold to be considered as a dependent family member in terms of taxation and social security contributions.

Japan has one of the most rapid ageing rates among developed countries. In 2005, already one in five people were above 65 years old and this proportion is projected to increase to around 40 per cent by 2050. The usual retirement age up to 65 years (by 2013) was legislated, but we wonder if this measure is enough. Probably, in the near future, the retirement age will be raised again in view of the demographic structure and difficulty of maintaining the public pension scheme. For the moment, aged workers generally tend to show a strong desire to stay in employment after the mandatory retirement age, but there are still few employment opportunities offered to older workers and these tend to be poor-quality jobs. For an ageing society, there is still much to be done.

Several marked changes have occurred in the Japanese employment system since the 1990s. First, firms having experienced surplus labour (labour hoarding) during the long recession restricted the recruitment of career employment to the strict minimum. As a result, young regular employees (25 to 35 years of age) are often overworked, with excessive working hours and little paid leave. On the other hand, there is a growth of atypical employment. In many service sector companies, it is not unusual that the bulk of employees are part-time or fixed term. Combined with the reduction of employment in former public corporations (e.g. telecommunications, national railways) and large manufacturing firms (steel, electric appliances), which were strongholds of long-term employment, the erosion of long-term career employment is evident. In the past, although lifetime employment used to be applied to a minority of workers, it was accepted as a social norm by management as well as employees. However, this social norm of lifetime employment has become much diluted and more fragile.

The issue of atypical employment not only raises questions about quality of work, but also the distinction between the two categories of regular employees and non-regular workers. There is almost no bridge or possibility of access to the pool of regular employees once workers are trapped into the atypical pool—whatever their reasons (family responsibilities or simply difficulty finding first jobs after education). This adds up to a huge loss of human resources.

Another disquieting aspect of Japanese employment relations is the absence of a collective dimension. The persistent decline of unionisation and also the lack of solidarity among enterprise unions imply that the employee voice is hardly audible. Growing numbers of individual labour disputes indicate that at least certain employees are dissatisfied with their jobs.

The Japanese employment relations system has been shaped by the employment practices of large established employers. Nevertheless, the growth of the service sector raises issues that seek to combine long-term security of workers, including atypical workers, with flexibilities that employers may need—especially at a time of continuing economic change.

A CHRONOLOGY OF JAPANESE EMPLOYMENT RELATIONS

1868	*Meiji* Restoration ends the feudal era.
1880	Early government factories are sold to family groups, the genesis of *zaibatsu*, or holding companies.
1894–95	Sino-Japanese War.
1904–05	Russo-Japanese War.
1911	Factory Law promulgated.
1912	Founding of Yuaikai (Friendly Society).
1921	Founding of Nippon Rodo Sodoumei (Japan Labour Foundation).
1931	Pre-war record for the number of labour disputes. The Manchurian Incident starts.
1937	Sino-Japanese War starts.
1938	The National General Mobilization Law (*Sodoin ho*) enacted, which gives the government powers to control vast areas of life and business.
1940	Organisations of workers and farmers dismissed. Dainihon Sangyo Hokokukai (Great Japan Federation of Patriotic Industries) inaugurated. .
1945	The end of World War II. Trade Union Law promulgated (implemented in 1946).
1946	Japanese Confederation of Labour (Sodomei) organised. Labour Relations Adjustment Law promulgated. Constitution of Japan promulgated (effective on 3 May 1947). Nichirokaigi (Congress of Labour Unions of Japan) organised.
1947	General Headquarters (GHQ) orders the suspension of 1 February general strike. The Labour Standard Law promulgated.
1948	Japan Federation of Employers' Association (Nikkeiren) organised. Trade Union Law and Labour Relations Adjustment Law revised.
1950	Korean War breaks out. Conference for organising the General Council of Trade Unions of Japan (Sohyo).
1954	All Japan Federation of Labour Unions (Zenro) organised. Sohyo consolidates five industry-level offensives into a united wage rise in spring.
1959	Minimum Wages Law passed by the Diet. Labour disputes at Miike Coal Mines.

1965	Japan ratifies ILO's Convention 87.
1974	The biggest strike in the history of the Spring Offensive—about six million participants.
1982	Japanese Private Sector Trade Union Council (Zenminrokyo) formed.
1986	Equal Employment Opportunity Law (amended) is introduced.
1987	Japanese Private Sector Trade Union Confederation (Rengo) formed. Revision of Labour Standard Law (promotion of shorter working hours). Privatisation of the National Railways.
1988	Start of new Rengo (Japan Trade Union Confederation), which merges the public-sector unions.
1990	Revision of the *Immigration and Refugee Recognition Act*. Fall of the Nikkei index, a sign of the end of the 'bubble' period.
1997	Financial crisis peaks with the bankruptcy of some large financial institutions (Yamaichi Securities, Hokkaido Takushoku Bank).
1999	Amendment of the Temporary (Dispatching) Agency Law, which relaxes restrictive provisions.
2001	Junichiro Koizumi becomes Prime Minister. Law on settlement of individual labour disputes. In December, the unemployment ratio records a high level: 5.5 per cent. The Ministry of Health merges with the Ministry of Labour (Ministry of Health, Labour and Welfare).
2002	Merger of two employers' federations, Keidanren and Nikkeiren, into Nippon Keidanren (Japan Business Federation).
2005	LDP sweeps the election of the lower house. Privatisation of postal services.
2006	Resignation of Koizumi. Shinzo Abe becomes prime minister.
2007	DP and other opposition parties win the majority in the upper house.
2008	Resignation of Takeo Fukuda (LDP). Taro Aso (LDP) becomes Prime Minister. Manufacturing firms suffer from a huge drop in export markets following the

| | global financial crisis. Protests about dismissed temporary workers (*haken giri*), with large media coverage. |
| 2009 | Large manufacturing firms (e.g. Toyota, Hitachi, Sony and Panasonic) announce big losses for the fiscal year ending March. |

CHAPTER 11

Employment relations in South Korea

Byoung-Hoon Lee

South Korea (the Republic of Korea, hereafter Korea) is an exemplary case of successful late industrialisation. Its late development has been attributed to Japanese colonial occupation (1910–45), division of the nation (1945–48) and the Korean War (1950–53). Despite its late industrialisation, the country has achieved remarkable 'compressed development' since the early 1960s, by recording export growth at an annual rate of 30 per cent, as well as averaged economic growth of GNP at an annual rate of over 8 per cent for 30 years. Until 1987, the 'compressed economic growth' was led by the authoritarian state, pursuing a policy of export-oriented industrialisation. As of 2007, Korea has a population of 48.5 million and is globally ranked thirteenth (US$969.9 billion) in terms of gross domestic product. Korea's per capita GNP has notably risen from $87 in 1962 to $20240 in 2007. Korea has been a member country of the OECD since 1996.

Korea has also demonstrated a tumultuous, but impressive trajectory toward democratisation over the past 60 years. Right after national liberation in 1945, the country was governed by the American Military Government until 1948, and the republic system was founded by the first President, Syngman Rhee, who was ousted by student demonstrations in 1960. President Chung-hee Park, who took power through military coup in 1962, built an authoritarian regime to lead the export-oriented industrialisation over his eighteen-year rule (1962–79), which ended with his assassination. President Doo-hwan Chun, who gained power by military coup in 1980, succeeded to the authoritarian leadership. In June 1987, the growing power of the

281

civil society pressured the ex-military ruling group to proclaim the Declaration of Democratisation, which provided critical momentum for political democratisation. After the two terms of Presidents Tae-woo Roh and Young-sam Kim, Dae-jung Kim won the presidential election against the backdrop of the economic crisis at the end of 1997, which symbolised the first peaceful power shift to the opposition party in the political history of Korea. After the ten years (1998–2007) of the liberal governments led by Presidents Dae-jung Kim and Moo-hyun Roh, Myung-bak Lee, the presidential candidate of the conservative party, regained power in the election of 2007 and is now pursuing 'business-friendly' economic reforms.

This chapter delineates the historical evolution of employment relations in Korea, mainly focusing on the post-1960s period of industrialisation, and discusses principal characteristics of key actors and processes in the Korean employment relations system. In addition, it addresses recent key issues of employment relations in the country.

HISTORICAL EVOLUTION OF EMPLOYMENT RELATIONS

Until the early 1960s, Korea was an agricultural economy, demonstrated by the fact that 63 per cent of the national labour force worked in the primary sector in 1963. As the government, led by President Park, launched successive economic development plans after 1962, the country's economy was drastically transformed by export-oriented industrialisation in the next three decades. The period of industrialisation was mainly shaped by the 'Korean model' for the government-led economic development (Lee 2003). During this period, it was the government that set the goals and policy of economic development and dominated the fostering and allocation of financial capital and industrial technologies in an authoritarian manner. The government assisted in promoting the growth of business conglomerates, called *chaebols*, as partners of its export-driven policy, which results in the *chaebols'* dominant presence in Korea's economic structure today.

From 1962 to 1987, employment relations in Korea were controlled primarily by the government's interventionist labour policy, geared to guarantee the supply of cheap and strike-free labour as a necessary condition of economic growth. The so-called 'developmental state' prevented workers from taking collective action to organise labour unions or go on strike. At the corporate level, while union activities were restricted by the government's labour-exclusive policies, employers were free to exercise their managerial prerogatives in setting wages and working rules. Since labour unions were too weak to voice workers' discontent and demands, employment relations were dominated by state authority and employers' interest until 1987. The Federation of Korean Trade Unions (FKTU)[1] and its affiliates were under strict state control and colluded with management instead of actively representing the rank and file's interest. As a result, industrial relations were largely stable in the period of state-led industrialisation, and unemployment declined from 8.1 per cent in 1963 to 3.8 per cent in 1986, owing to successful industrialisation (Kim & Sung 2005).

In this context, the number of union members gradually increased as Korea industrialised in the 1960s and 1970s. However, as illustrated in Table 11.1, union membership plunged in the early 1980s and continued to decline into the mid-1980s, since President Chun adopted a hard-line stance against union activities. Democratic union activism, which was closely associated with the student movement, gained a foothold to challenge both the authoritarian government and the impotent FKTU leadership from the late 1970s.

In late 1987, the Great Labour Struggle that broke out following the political democratisation led to the dismantling of the state-controlled industrial relations system. Faced with a labour union movement that had taken the offensive, the government abandoned its interventionist labour policy and officially recognised the autonomy of labour unions and management in dealing with workplace labour issues. As a consequence, the number of trade unions nearly tripled (from 2742 to 7883) between 1986 and 1989. Union membership nearly doubled from 1.05 million to 1.93 million, and union density also soared from 11.7 to 18.6 per cent. The explosive growth of the labour movement created an unprecedented balance of power between workers and management. In the process, management's grip over workers was substantially loosened, and labour unions in many large firms took control of the shop floor. Management was forced to accept wage increases, improve working conditions and establish corporate welfare programs. Between 1987 and 1989, average nominal wage increases per year exceeded 12 per cent in all industries. In the manufacturing sector, average nominal wages increased by 18 per cent annually during the same period.

However, union membership and density both began dropping in the early 1990s because of the economic slump, the government's neo-interventionist labour policies, significant improvements in working conditions, including wages, and waning public sympathy towards militant unionism after the collapse of the communist bloc in the late 1980s and early 1990s (Lee & Lee 2003). The downward trend in union membership continued until 1998.

Table 11.1 Indexes of employment relations in South Korea

| Year | Unions | | Labour disputes | | | |
	Union members (000s)	Union density (%)	Number of labour unions	Number of strikes	Strike participants (000s)	Unemployment (%)
1970	473	12.6	3 500	4	1	4.4
1975	750	15.8	4 091	52	10	4.1
1980	948	14.7	2 635	206	49	5.2
1985	1 004	12.4	2 551	265	29	4.0
1986	1 036	12.3	2 675	276	47	3.8
1987	1 267	13.8	4 103	3 749	1 262	3.1
1988	1 707	17.8	6 164	1 873	293	2.5
1989	1 932	18.6	7 883	1 616	409	2.6
1990	1 887	17.2	7 698	322	134	2.4
1991	1 803	15.4	7 656	234	175	2.4
1992	1 735	14.6	7 527	235	105	2.5
1993	1 667	14.0	7 147	144	109	2.9
1994	1 659	13.3	7 025	121	104	2.5
1995	1 615	12.5	6 606	88	50	2.1
1996	1 599	12.1	6 424	85	79	2.0
1997	1 484	11.1	5 733	78	44	2.6
1998	1 402	11.4	5 560	129	146	7.0
1999	1 481	11.7	5 637	198	92	6.3
2000	1 527	11.4	5 698	250	178	4.1
2001	1 569	11.5	6 148	235	89	3.8
2002	1 538	10.8	6 506	322	94	3.1
2003	1 550	10.8	6 257	320	137	3.4
2004	1 537	10.3	6 107	462	185	3.5
2005	1 506	9.9	5 971	287	118	3.5
2006	1 559	10.0	5 889	138	131	3.3
2007	1 688	10.6	5 099	115	93	3.0

Note: Union density = union members ÷ total number in the labour force x 100

Source: Korean Labor Institute (2008), *2008 KLI Labor Statistics*, Seoul: KLI (in Korean)

By the early 1990s, the forces of globalisation had reached Korea, increasing national concern for the improvement of the country's economic competitiveness internationally. The government took a new approach in its attempt to settle labour–management disputes. Integral to the new government policy was the introduction of a 'social dialogue' model involving tripartite consultation among the unions, employers and government. With the assistance of the government, the FKTU and the Korea Employers Federation (KEF) reached nationwide agreements on wage increases and employment policy in 1993 and 1994. The FKTU–KEF agreements were used as a guideline for wage negotiations at the enterprise level. However, in 1995 these nationwide consultations were halted as the FKTU was discredited for supporting the government's wage-control policy.

Another tripartite attempt made by the government came in the form of the Presidential Commission on Industrial Relations Reform (PCIRR), established in May 1996. The Commission was formed as an advisory body to the President and consisted of representatives from trade unions, employers' associations, public-interest and academic groups. The PCIRR provided an open forum for social dialogue among those various stakeholders with regard to labour law reform. The PCIRR included representatives of the Korean Confederation of Trade Unions (KCTU), the second national centre of democratic labour unions. The KCTU, founded in November 1995, had yet to gain legal recognition.

Following a series of public hearings, sub-committee workshops and plenary sessions, the PCIRR submitted to President Kim Young-Sam a set of proposed changes to labour legislation. However, on 26 December 1996 the government and the ruling party passed their own Bill revising the existing labour laws, while opposition lawmakers were absent from the Parliament. The government's unilateral revision of labour legislation, which placed more emphasis on labour-market flexibility than on labour rights and unionisation, triggered nation-wide strikes and anti-government protests in late 1996 and early 1997. Under greater pressure from unions and the international community, the government abandoned its controversial revision of labour laws and eventually revised them through consultations with opposition parties in March 1997.

The foreign exchange crisis of November 1997 severely affected employment relations. The economic crisis at the end of 1997 had a great impact on the Korean labour regime and its transformation, as was the case with democratisation in 1987, dismantling the old employment relations system based on the labour-control policies of the developmental state. The economic crisis of 1997 caused tremendous changes in the employment regime that was forged in 1987, insofar as it triggered extensive restructuring and massive downsizing by the government and businesses. Following the 1997 economic crisis, the focus of employment relations between labour unions and management shifted from economic issues, such as wages and fringe benefits, to jobs and employment; this was accompanied by a sharp increase in the intensity of industrial conflicts. Trade unions made unprecedented concessions during the recession of 1998–99, by agreeing to wage freezes and reduced bonuses and welfare programs. For instance, the overall wage decrease in 1998 was 2.7 per cent. Widespread downsizing at unionised firms caused union membership to decline sharply by 197 thousand between 1997 and 1998. However, the union membership and density rose slightly in 1999, when the new labour law allowed teachers to form labour unions for the first time. Since then, union membership has rebounded to over 1.5 million, yet union density has dropped to 10.0 per cent in 2006 (see Table 11.1).

Confronted with the economic crisis, the Korean government resumed social dialogue. President-elect Dae-jung Kim established the Tripartite Commission in January 1998 to promote cooperation among government, labour unions and employers in overcoming the economic crisis. On 9 February 1998, the Commission concluded a historic social pact covering an extensive agenda of 90 articles, including the extension of employment insurance coverage, permission of layoffs and dispatched labour, and guarantee of labour rights for teachers and public servants (Lee 2003). The social pact made an important contribution to ending the economic crisis by improving the country's credibility among by foreign financial institutions. Immediately after signing the social pact, however, the KCTU leadership faced strong criticism from its members for agreeing to the passage of legislation authorising the dismissal of redundant workers. As a result, the KCTU withdrew its participation from the Commission, bringing to a halt the Commission's first round of policy consultations.

The second round of Tripartite Commission consultations began in June 1998. The main objectives in this round were to monitor the implementation of agreements made by the first Commission and to promote tripartite consultations on economic restructuring, particularly with regard to the banking, finance and public sectors. The second round reached tripartite agreements on detailed policy proposals, including legalisation of teachers' unions and integration of the two-tier health insurance system. The Commission eventually reached a dead end when the KCTU withdrew from the Commission for the second time in early 1999. Although the third round of the Commission started in September 1999, its role in promoting tripartite dialogue has seriously been weakened by sustained confrontations between the KCTU and the government. As a result, from 2000 up to now, the paralysed Tripartite Commission has been unable to contend with many exigent labour issues, such as intensified labour market segmentation, the proliferation of irregular labour and jobless economic growth, which largely have been attributed to neo-liberal reforms taken by the government after the economic crisis (Lee 2005).

In the post-1997 period, the quality of working life has been aggravated profoundly. In fact, the rapid increase in the size of the non-standard labour force, and the persistent discrimination against non-standard workers, combined with a decrease in decent jobs to polarise the labour market. More specifically, fractures involving employment status, firm size and gender have become more serious, exacerbating the segmentation of labour markets and industrial relations. Since the early 1990s, particularly in the aftermath of the financial crisis, there have been increasing disparities between regular employees of large firms and the remainder of the workforce, in terms of wages, welfare benefits, job training, employment conditions, and legal and union protection. Meanwhile, the industrial relations system has undergone some transformations in its formal shape—for example, the spread of industrial unionism and the revision of labour laws to meet global standards.

To sum, over the past four decades, employment relations in Korea have undergone a dynamic transformation in the context of industrialisation, democratisation, globalisation and the global financial crisis. Since 1987, Korea's industrial relations, controlled by the authoritarian state until 1987, have made some advances toward the democratic model, including social dialogue and enhanced labour regulations—albeit in the face of a steady decline of union density. During the post-1997 period, however, employment relations have posed crucial problems of labour market polarisation and intensified labour–management confrontation.

MAJOR PARTIES OF EMPLOYMENT RELATIONS

Labour unions

The late 1980s witnessed remarkable changes in the composition of labour unions as well as an explosive growth in labour movement. First, the most heavily unionised industrial sector shifted from the textile sector, whose workforce was predominantly female, to metal and chemical industries mainly composed of male workers.[2] This reflects the change in Korea's economic structure around 1980s. Since 1987, male-dominated labour unions organised in heavy industries have led labour union movement in Korea. Membership of white-collar labour unions in service industries such as banking, mass media, and health care also rose sharply in this period. Secondly, many of the newly organised trade unions were critical of the FKTU's submission to the government's labour control policies until the democratisation of 1987, so that they rejected affiliation with the FKTU. Those independent unions espoused the so-called 'democratic unionism' and actively formed their own federations in late 1980s. The independent union federations were merged into the KCTU in 1995.

Today, the labour union movement in Korea is divided between two national centers, the FKTU and the KCTU, as illustrated in Table 11.2. The KCTU, which gained legal recognition in 1999 and now has seventeen affiliated federations or industrial unions, tends toward militant activism, whereas the FKTU, having 26 affiliates, shows a more conciliatory stance toward the government and employers. As of 2006, KCTU-affiliated unions having an averaged size of 548.8 members are much larger than FKTU-affiliated unions with an average of 220.2 members. This reflects the fact that many labour unions, organised at large firms after 1987, are affiliated with the KCTU. The KCTU grew from 420 000 in 1995 (at the time of its establishment) to 668 000 in 2004 and then declined to 627 000 in 2006. The FKTU has lost the exclusive position in official union recognition and experienced a substantial loss of its membership in the same period. It is noteworthy that the number of independent labour unions withdrawing their affiliation from the FKTU and KCTU, has increased during recent years.

Table 11.2 Composition of unions by national centre affiliation

	No. unit unions		No. union members (000)	
FKTU	3429	(58.2)	755.2	(48.4)
KCTU	1143	(19.4)	627.3	(40.2)
Independent unions	1317	(22.4)	176.7	(11.4)
Total	5889	(100.0)	1559.2	(100.0)

Note: The figures in the parentheses represent the percentage of unit unions and union members

Source: Korean Labor Institute (2008), *2008 KLI Labor Statistics*, Seoul: KLI. (in Korean)

The majority of labour unions in Korea are enterprise based. Enterprise unions exercise substantial autonomy in union adminis-tration and collective bargaining at the firm level. In the early 1960s, President Park forced labour unions to transform their organisational structure towards an industrial model, in order that the government could control them in an effective manner. In the early 1980s, however, President Chun, who noticed that those industrial unions challenged the state control in late 1970s, forcefully reshaped the union structure into the enterprise model by law. Since the late 1990s, labour unions have made conscious efforts to transform their organisational structure from enterprise unionism to industrial unionism, as a way to establish a centralised bargaining system and strengthen their socio-political leverage.

In February 1998, the Korea Health and Medical Workers Union (KHMWU) was the first case of an enterprise union being transformed toward an industrial union, and many labour unions, such as the Korea Finance Industry Union (KFIU) and the Korea Metal Workers Union (KMWU), followed suit. As a consequence, membership in industrial unions grew from 10 per cent of total union membership in 1996 to about 45 per cent in 2007 (Lee & Kwon 2008). In particular, the KCTU adopted an official resolution to complete its organisational transformation towards industrial unionism by the end of 2007; nearly 80 per cent of its members were affiliated with industrial unions in early 2007. In contrast to the KCTU's determined efforts, the FKTU has been relatively inactive in terms of organisational restructuring, with only 20 per cent of its members being affiliated with industrial unions at present. Moreover, over recent years non-standard workers have made a new attempt to organise community-based general unions, in order to cope with the growing flexibility and mobility of labour markets. It is also noteworthy that 62.9 per cent of large firms with over 300 employees are unionised, even though union density remains very low at 10 per cent.

Employers

Until 1987, employers—who relied on the government's interventionist labour policies to restrain workers' collective activities—imposed authoritarian supervision over workers. In the pre-1987 shop-floor governance, employers treated employees by militaristic control, which imitated direct supervision of the rank and file by force in the military's hierarchical stratum (Park 1992). However, the explosive growth of the labour union movement in 1987 transformed corporate-level industrial relations from domination by management towards a balanced power relationship between labour and management. As a result, authoritarian control by management was eroded substantially, and shop-floor control was taken over by labour unions in many firms. In addition, management was forced to

289

allow high wage increases and improvements to working conditions and welfare programs following pressure by labour unions. Even job evaluation schemes, which had been used for determining individual workers' wages in a discriminatory manner and were therefore viewed as a core source of discontent among workers, were abolished by demand of the labour unions.

From the early 1990s, employers began to take a hard-line stance in their employment relations policies. Against the economic downturn that hit the Korean economy around the end of the 1980s and the early 1990s, employers began launching their so-called 'new management strategies' extensively during the early 1990s. The new management strategies consisted of three pillars: new personnel policies, flexible working systems and union-suppression strategies. Employers tried to implement a set of new personnel policies, including the introduction of flexible wage systems (e.g. pay for performance and job capabilities) and the restoration of the job evaluation scheme. At the workplace level, employers extended the use of automation technologies to promote flexibility of labour processes and increase labour productivity. The increasing implementation of advanced production technologies was also intended to reduce management's reliance on a recalcitrant workforce. At the same time, considerable management efforts were put into restricting the militant activism of labour unions by imposing strict penalties on union officials and activists for organising illegal dispute action. As a core part of the union-suppression strategies, the 'no-work, no-pay' policy was reinforced to prevent labour unions from taking strike action. Therefore, new management strategies were primarily pursued in order to weaken the strong shop-floor power of labour unions and make production systems more flexible.

Against the backdrop of the economic crisis of 1997, massive restructuring took place, particularly in the finance and public sectors and among large private firms. Management at those large firms commonly took action to downsize regular employees by permanent layoffs and/or early retirement in the context of economic crisis, while extending the use of the non-standard labour force and outsourcing business operations in the later period of business recovery. As a consequence, the employment practices of internal labour markets developed by those large firms in the period of economic prosperity, which had followed the Japanese model, were crucially weakened during the economic crisis. In the post-1997 period, it has been common for large firms to resort to external labour markets by increasingly the use of the non-standard workforce and undertaking organisational reengineering on a regular basis, following the American business model. It is noteworthy that wide variations of employment relations exist among *chaebols*, which have exerted dominant influence over the Korean economy and national industrial relations. For instance, Samsung, the first business conglomerate, has strictly pursued a HRM model that avoids unionisation; Hyundai Motor Group, the second conglomerate, has taken a confrontational stance toward labour unions; LG (the third conglomerate) and SK (the fourth) have maintained a relatively cooperative relationship with their labour unions. By contrast, small- to medium-sized firms, by and large, have poor employment relations practices, sometime below statutory labour standards, due to their inferior financial capabilities and outdated management style.

There are three significant bodies among contemporary employers' organisations that have substantial influence over national-level industrial relations: the Korea Employers Federation (KEF), the Korean Chamber of Commerce and Industry (KCCI), and the Federation of Korean Industries (FKI). The KEF, which was established in 1970 and is now representing about 3300 firms in the manufacturing and service sectors, has been the official voice of Korean employers at national-level negotiations and consultations regarding industrial relations issues. This association was invited as its employer representative to the PCIRR and the Tripartite Commission. The rapid growth in the labour movement in the late 1980s and the government-initiated tripartite efforts since the 1990s have made the KEF a body of growing significicance. The KCCI, which is the oldest employer association, founded in 1884, is now representing 45 000 firms in all business sectors, based upon the *Chambers of Commerce and Industry Act*, legislated in 1952. The KCCI has been treated as an employer representative for social dialogue concerning labour law reforms during recent years. The FKI, which was formed in 1961 and is mainly comprised of 380 large firms (including *chaebols*), also has exercised substantial influence on labour policy by the government and legislation of labour laws in the congress on behalf of *chaebol* interests.

Government

The government in Korea was an authoritarian regulator on industrial relations and employment practices until 1987 (as noted above). In the pre-1987 period, the government played an active role as a developmental state in promoting economic growth and suppressing workers' collective action. In this period, the government focused its policy efforts on job creation and educated the labour supply in a paternalistic manner. Confronted with democratisation and the explosive growth of the labour union movement after 1987, however, the government shifted its labour policy from an authoritarian control paradigm to a social dialogue one. Particularly since the early 1990s, the government—which was concerned about the worsening of national economic competitiveness and recurrent labour–management confrontations—adopted a tripartite model for promoting the peaceful and cooperative relations between labour unions and employers.[3] As a result, a journey toward tripartism, led by the government, started with the National Economic and Social Council, formed in 1990. It went through the stages of the national-level FKTU-KEF wage negotiations in 1993 and 1994, and the PCIRR's policy consultation for labour law reforms in 1996, to the Tripartite Commission since early 1998. The Tripartite Commission was renamed the Economic and Social Development Commission (ESDC), and its agenda of policy consultation was expanded with the revision of the law in April 2007. This Commission is now operating as a presidential advisory board for policy consultations concerning labour and social issues. Despite the eighteen-year journey of tripartism and its notable achievements— particularly in overcoming the economic crisis in 1997—the social dialogue has gained little credit from labour unions, which claim that it has been used as a cosmetic procedure for the government-initiated policy-making and is hampered by the recalcitrance of employer representatives. In addition, union members have stigmatised the commission as being responsible for the adoption of neo-liberal labour market flexibility and for doing little to resolve the social problems resulting from labour market polarisation.

The governmental office administering labour policies was established in 1963 and promoted to the Ministry of Labour in 1981. The Ministry of Labour is covering all work-related areas, such as labour standards, industrial relations, employment insurance and equality, vocational training and occupational safety. This ministry now consists of two offices (policy planning and employment policy) and three divisions (labour–management cooperation, labour standards, and industrial health and safety). The Ministry of Labour also has 46 local organs, which consist of six regional administration offices located in major cities—Seoul, Pusan, Incheon, Daegu, Incheon and Kwangju— and 40 regional offices. In the regional office, labour inspectors—totalling approximately 1350 at present—are charged not only to police and supervise working conditions in accordance with the *Labour Standards Act*, but also to take action to prevent and deal with labour disputes at firms in their regional area. Two commissions, affiliated with the Ministry of Labour, play a crucial role in shaping nationwide employment relations. The Labour Commission, which consists of three parties—unions, employers, and public interest groups—adjudicates such labour cases as unfair labour practices, unfair dismissal and work discrimination, and mediates labour disputes. The Minimum Wage Commission (MWC), which consists of 27 members evenly representing unions, employers and the public interest, manages the negotiations among three parties and the determination of the yearly minimum wages.

Note that labour unions have been critical of the submissive role and position taken by the Ministry of Labour for giving priority to the policy of economic growth from the era of the development state up to the present. At the same time, since President Dae-jung Kim's administration (1997–2002), the government has made policy to promote new labour–management culture and workplace innovations, as it regards confrontational labour–management relations as a crucial constraint to national competitiveness. It is also noteworthy that the government is the largest employer in Korea, employing 1.34 million people, including civil servants (656 000), public school teachers (415 000), and employees of public firms and institutes (272 000), as of the end of 2006. Teachers and civil servants were respectively given legal labour rights to organise and bargain (excluding strike action) in 1999 and 2004 respectively. Given the statutory constraints on union activities, the public sector is highly organised, with union density of 26.9 per cent for civil servants, approximately 25 per cent for teachers and 44.5 per cent for public firms. Therefore, the government has substantial influence over the employment relations of the private sector through the results of its collective bargaining with labour unions in the public sector.

PROCESSES OF EMPLOYMENT RELATIONS

Collective bargaining and labour dispute resolution

Collective bargaining is regulated by the *Trade Union and Labour Adjustment Act* (TULAA). Collective bargaining in most unionised firms is primarily conducted at the enterprise level in accordance with the enterprise-based union structure. The transportation sector (e.g. taxi and bus) and the textile sector are exceptions, in that those sectors traditionally have maintained regional or sectoral bargaining practices. As the TULAA, amended in 1997, stipulates that no collective agreement shall have a valid term exceeding two years, collective bargaining is held every year in most unionised firms. In practice, collective bargaining for a wage contract is conducted every year, while bargaining to determine collective contracts concerning working conditions and other contractual terms is conducted every two years.

Even though the collective bargaining structure is basically decentralised, two national centres and the employer association have had substantial influence on enterprise-level bargaining through their bargaining proposals. As demonstrated in Table 11.3, the FKTU and the KCTU have proposed bargaining guidelines for wage increases and other contractual changes (e.g. the reduction of working hours, employment security, regular employment of non-standard workers in recent years) at the beginning of every year; these serve as an influential reference to enterprise-level collective bargaining. In response to the national union centres' bargaining proposal, the KEF offers its own bargaining guidelines to member companies. Moreover, the national union centres and the KEF are involved in bargaining processes to set the minimum wage through the MWC every year.[4]

Industrial unions, reorganised by the organisational integration of enterprise unions over the past ten years, have demanded centralised bargaining, which is distinct from the decentralising trends of bargaining structure in Western countries. In particular, three major industrial unions, such as the KMWU, the KHMWU and the KFIU, have made notable progress in contracting national agreement with their employer associations. Now the KMWU has a three-level bargaining structure, comprising the national, regional and firm-levels, while the KHMWU and the KFIU have two tiers—national and firm levels. However, centralised industrial bargaining has not yet been well established, due to indifference and even opposition among employers, particularly *chaebols*.

The labour dispute procedure is stipulated in the TULAA. According to this law, the parties are obliged to enter into mediation with the Labour Commission. Prior to the revision of the TULAA in 2007, the government was able to award compulsory arbitration for resolving labour disputes at public firms providing essential service (i.e. water, electricity, gas, oil, telecommunications, railroads, hospitals, inner-city bus services and banking services). The revised TULAA abolishes compulsory arbitration, and instead prohibits labour unions from engaging into strike action in the units of essential service at public firms.

Table 11.3 **Trends in labour–management wage proposals and contractual wage increases (%)**

	Average increases of wage contracts	Wage bargaining proposals		
		KEF	FKTU	KCTU
1988	13.5	7.5–8.5	29.3	–
1989	17.5	10.9 (8.9–12.9)	26.8	37.3
1990	9.0	7.0	17.3–20.5	23.3
1991	10.5	7.0	17.5	22.2
1992	6.5	5.7(4.7–6.7)	15.0	25.4
1993	5.2	4.7–8.9	National level agreement by KEF and FKTU	18.0
1994	7.2	5.0–8.7		16.4
1995	7.7	4.4–6.4	12.4	14.8
1996	7.8	4.8	12.2	14.8
1997	4.2	Wage freeze	11.2	10.6±3
1998	0.0	Labour cost reduction by 20%	4.7	5.1–9.2
1999	2.1	Wage freeze	5.5	7.7±1.5
2000	7.2	5.4	13.2	15.2
2001	6.0	3.5	12.0	12.7
2002	6.7	4.1	12.3	12.5
2003	6.4	4.3	11.4	11.1
2004	5.2	3.8	10.7	10.5
2005	4.7	3.9	9.4	9.3
2006	4.8	2.6	9.6	8.0–12.6
2007	4.8	2.4	9.3	9.0

Source: Korean Labor Institute (2008), *2008 KLI Labor Statistics*, Seoul: KLI. (in Korean)

Labour–Management Council

The Labour-Management Council (LMC) is an institutionalised channel for promoting communication and cooperation between employees and management. The government enacted the *Labour–Management Council Act* in 1980, making it mandatory for all establishments with more than 50 workers to establish a council. Despite this statutory obligation, a limited number of firms formed LMCs until 1987. However, confronted with increasing labour disputes following democratisation in 1987, management tried to promote cooperation with workers by implementing the LMC. As a result, the number of firms with LMCs rapidly increased up to over 14 000 in the early 1990s.

In 1997, the *Labour–Management Council Act* was replaced with the *Act Concerning the Promotion of Worker Participation and Cooperation* (APWPC). The new Act stipulates that all firms with more than 30 workers must form a council and hold meetings every quarter. In accordance with the new law, the number of firms that formed the LMC almost doubled between 1996 (15 234) and 2001 (29 348). The number of LMCs continued to grow, reaching 40 018 in 2006.

The LMC is composed of equal numbers of representatives from employees and management, usually between three and ten persons from each side. When a company has a labour union that represents majority of workers, the union's leaders are entitled to participate to the LMC as employees' representatives. According to the APWPC, workplace issues to be dealt with by the LMC are classified into three categories: (1) issues requiring prior consent by employee representatives (i.e. training and development plans, fringe benefit programs, in-house welfare funds, grievance handling, and joint labour–management committees); (2) issues of consultation with employee representatives (i.e. human resource planning, workplace renovation and new technologies, prevention of industrial accidents, redundancy adjustment, working time rescheduling, wage system changes, and revision in work rules); and (3) issues to be reported (i.e. corporate strategies and performance, quarterly production plan, personnel issues, and the company's financial situation). It is noteworthy that many labour unions use LMC meetings as an extension of their collective bargaining, while top management at many firms is indifferent to the feasibility of cooperation and communication promoted by the LMC.

KEY ISSUES TODAY

Polarisation of labour markets

The economic crisis of 1997 came as a complete shock to labour markets. Most companies, which had achieved sustained growth and maintained the conventional human-resource policy of 'lifetime employment' in the pre-1997 era, undertook extensive restructuring of their businesses and employment practices. This resulted in a fundamental change of employment relations in Korean labour markets. According to a Korea Labour Institute survey conducted in 2000 regarding listed corporations, the share of companies that took action to downsize since the economic crisis reached 66 per cent, illustrating the massive extent of corporate restructuring at the time (Park & Roh 2001). The same survey showed that 74 per cent of responding companies carried out spin-offs, and that 57.6 per cent outsourced part of their business. Those companies recruited non-standard labour to fill what had previously been regular jobs after the economy recovered in 1999.

Korean labour markets, which experienced a sharp rise in unemployment during the economic crisis, witnessed a reduction in unemployment during the recovery phase of the early to mid-2000s. The unemployment rate remained at the level of 3 per cent from 2001 until 2008, and was the lowest among the OECD countries. Throughout the GFC, the official unemployment rate in Korea was close to 3 per cent, expect in March 2009 (4 per cent) and January 2010 (5 per cent). The short term increase in unemployment in March 2009 is related to the entry of college graduates into the labour market. The figure for March 2010 may be associated with the expiry of a number of job creation subsidies offered by the government in late 2009. However, the problem with Korean labour markets is the worsening employment structure, mainly derived from the sustained decline of good jobs and the widening disparity between good and bad jobs.

The loss of good jobs at large firms has mainly been due to management's determined policy to carry out downsizing and outsourcing. Employment at large firms with over 500 employees decreased from 2.1 million in 1993 to 1.3 million in 2005. As a result, the large-firm workforce's share of the total wage-labour population declined from 17.2 per cent to 8.7 per cent during the same period (Kim 2005). Instead, the number of non-standard workers has grown sharply since the economic crisis. Thus, the excessive use of and discrimination against those disposable employees has become a major issue in

Korean society. The share of non-standard employment has increased from 26.9 per cent in 2001 to 36.7 per cent in 2007.[5] Nearly 90 per cent of non-standard workers are employed at small firms with fewer than 300 employees. Moreover, the process of deindustrialisation has accelerated over the past decade, resulting in a reduction in the number of manufacturing jobs. This change in the composition of sectoral employment is associated with a lowering in the quality of jobs. Between 1997 and 2006, the percentage of employment accounted for by the manufacturing sector declined from 21.4 per cent to 18 per cent, while the sector's share of GDP increased from 26.3 to 27.8 per cent.

The increasing polarisation of labour markets is exemplified by the growing gap in overall employment conditions, including wages and fringe benefits, between the primary sector for regular workers at large firms and the secondary sector for workers in small firms and non-standard employees.

Figure 11.1 demonstrates the growing wage discrepancy between large and small firms between 1993 and 2006. For instance, the monthly wage at small firms with between ten and 29 employees declined from 72.4 per cent of large firms with over 500 employees in 1994 to 59.8 per cent in 2006. The wage gap between regular and non-standard workers has increased in recent years, in that the monthly wage of non-standard workers has dropped from 53.7 per cent of regular workers in 2000 to 51.3 per cent in 2006.

Moreover, labour market polarisation is evident in workers' fringe benefits and human resources development. The discrepancy in firm-level expenditures on fringe benefits and training between large and small firms has been constant over the past decade. Large firms with over 1000 employees expend twice as much on fringe benefits, and eight times more on training, than small firms with between 30 and 99 employees. Most non-standard workers have been excluded from statutory welfare and labour standards. Only about 30 per cent of these workers benefit from statutory welfare programs, such as national pensions, medical insurance and employment insurance. Only 15–20 per cent of those non-standard workers are protected by legal labour standards, including extra work premiums and severance pay.

An additional problem with polarised labour markets is the lack of job mobility between the primary and secondary sectors. Many studies have shown that non-standard jobs are trapped in the peripheral sector, rather than functioning as a 'stepping stone' to regular jobs (Nam & Kim 2000; Han & Jang 2000). At the same time, workers in large firms have experienced job insecurity, just as small-firm and non-standard

Figure 11.1 **Trends of monthly wage discrepancy by firm size (firms with over 500 employees = 100)**

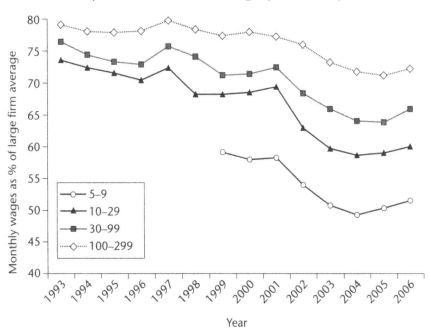

Source: Korea Labour Institute 2008

workers have. Employees at large firms in Korea have much shorter tenures than their counterparts in the United States and Japan (Jung 2006) Even workers at unionised large firms have been threatened by management-led restructuring initiatives, including outsourcing, spin-offs, business re-engineering, the reallocation of production facilities and the use of non-standard labour.

It is noteworthy that labour market polarisation results not only from the external shocks of the economic crisis, but also from the strategic choices of industrial actors and their political interactions. Intensified labour market segmentation in Korea can be attributed to (1) neo-liberal economic reforms, led by the government in the post-1997 period; (2) large firms' exploitative profit maximisation, making small subcontracting firms more inferior and resulting in a sharp increase of non-standard labour; and (3) business unionism focusing on the protection of union members' egoistic interest, excluding a majority of unorganised labour. As a consequence, the polarisation of the labour market has tended to worsen. There has been growing concern over the fact that labour market polarisation

299

results in social disintegration, as exemplified by the sharp rise in the number of crimes and suicides, and the erosion of the foundations for sustained economic growth. Note that although the weekly 40-hour working system was introduced by law in 2003, Korea has the longest working hours (2261 hours in 2008) among the OECD member countries.

The transformation of the industrial relations system

Confrontational industrial relations has been intensified in the post-1997 period. As illustrated in Table 11.1 above, the number of labour disputes declined to below 100 in the mid-1990s, but surged sharply after 1997 and peaked at 462 in 2004. Although the number of labour disputes has since dropped to 115 in 2007, industrial relations is still unstable due to deeply rooted mistrust among industrial parties. The instability of industrial relations has been seen as a crucial constraint in enhancing national economic competitiveness, with the IMD's World Competitiveness Report indicating that Korea is falling considerably in relation to competing countries such as Japan, Taiwan and Singapore.

While the labour disputes in the post-1997 period took place largely due to government-led and employer-driven restructuring, many labour disputes in recent years have been associated with non-standard employment and industrial bargaining. Over the past decade, the growing presence of non-standard labour has been a contentious issue in industrial relations. While the national labour centres—the FKTU and the KCTU—have launched campaigns organising non-standard workers, those workers at some firms have organised their own unions and engaged in collective action, demanding improvements to their working conditions and the change of their employment status to regular positions. The unionisation of non-standard workers tends to result in employers' adamant suppression, and sometimes conflicts with regular workers' unions. After the end of 2006, when the laws to protect non-standard labour was enacted, many firms terminated the labour contract with non-standard workers and decided to replace them with subcontracting labour, which incurred very intense confrontations with those non-standard workers. Even though the union density of non-standard workers was only 2.8 per cent in 2006, the excessive use of and discrimination against non-standard labour is likely to create acute tensions in industrial relations at both the national and firm levels.

Industrial unionisation—largely initiated by KCTU affiliates—has been successful, as noted above. Those industrial unions are confronted by such difficulties as very low organisational representation in each industrial sector, limited concentration of organisational resources (i.e. financial funds and union staff), employers' opposition to industry-level bargaining and little extension of industrial contracts to the unorganised or non-standard workforce (Lee 2002). In particular, since the response of employers to the industrial unions' demand for centralised collective bargaining has been firmly negative, the contest over bargaining structure is likely to persist as a contentious issue in Korean industrial relations.

In addition, there are several issues concerning the institutional framework governing union activities. The prohibition of wage payments to union officials and the permission of multiple unionisation at the establishment level[6] were legislated in 2001. However, these clauses of the TULAA are not currently in effect, because the FKTU and the KEF reached an agreement with the Tripartite Commission in 2006 that they were to be suspended until the end of 2009. The FKTU is concerned that the prohibition of wage payments to union officials results in a serious weakening of unions' organisational capacity, while the KEF is worried that the second clause leads to the intense competition of multiple unions at the firm level, which incurs big burdens to employers' industrial relations policy. At the same time, the FKTU-KEF agreement has been criticised by the KCTU and NGOs, which insist that the suspension of multiple unionisation at the establishment level deprives non-standard workers and other unorganised employees of their own labour right to organise. The process of labour law revision to put the two clauses into effect is likely to involve intense debate among the FKTU, the KCTU and employers. If these clauses do take effect, the traditional framework of enterprise-based industrial relations could be fundamentally reshaped, boosting the transition toward the industrial unionisation and intensifying inter-union rivalry at the firm level. Another issue has been raised by the unions of the public sectors: civil servants and teachers have complained about the restriction of collective bargaining and dispute action by the current laws and demanded a guarantee of their free rights of bargaining and strike action. Labour unions of the public firms and institutes are also critical of the statutory extension of the 'strike-free' essential service units, a policy introduced in 2007. Therefore, public sector industrial relations remain an area of considerable contention in Korea.

CONCLUSION

As delineated above, employment relations in Korea have shown remarkable changes since the late 1980s, along with the 'compressed development' of the country's political economy, such as industrial restructuring, democratization, and economic crisis. Under the developmental regime (1961–1987), employment relations was chiefly shaped and ruled by the government-led economic growth policy. The period of post-democratisation witnessed the institutionalisation of employment relations. After the 1997 economic crisis, employment relations in Korea has experienced substantial transformation toward a market-driven pattern, producing crucial problems, exemplified by the proliferation of the non-regular workforce. At present, however, it is not clear whether the market-driven pattern of employment relations in Korea will be further entrenched, or to be challenged by the current global economic crisis.

A CHRONOLOGY OF KOREAN EMPLOYMENT RELATIONS

1876	Japan forcefully opens up feudal Chosun.
1888	First unionised strike, by gold miners.
1898	Korea's first union, the Seongjin Stevedores' Union, formed. Chosun mining strike.
1910	Japan occupies Korea.
1919	March 1st National Independence Movement.
1920	The first national organisation, *Chosun Nodongkongjeahoe* (The Chosun Labour Fraternal Association), is initiated by the liberal intelligentsia.
1922	The socialist-oriented Chosun Nodongyeonmaenghoe (Chosun Labour Confederation) is formed.
1924	Chosun Nonong Chongyeonmaeng (Chosun Labour and Farmer Confederation) is formed. *Law and Order Maintenance Act* represses national unionism.
1929	First general strike, in Wonsan.
1938	Unions prohibited with onset of China–Japan War.
1945	Korea is liberated from the Japanese and the US Army Military Government in Korea (USAMGIK), known as the AMG, is established in Korea. National and Provincial Mediation Boards are set up. Chun Pyung (General Council of Korean Trade Unions) is formed.
1946	The Child Labour Law and the Basic Labour Law are enacted. The Labour Department is established. The September National Strikes are called. Daehan Dogrib Chockseong Nodong Chongyeonmyeng (General Federation of Korean Trade Unions, or GFKTU) is formed.
1947	Chun Pyung is banned by the AMG.
1948	Syngman Rhee is elected President of the First Republic of Korea. The Five-Year of Economic Rehabilitation Plan aims at economic independence from consumption aid.
1950–53	Korean War.
1953	The *Trade Union Act*, the *Labour Standards Act*, the *Labour Dispute Adjustment Act* and the *Labour Relations Commission Act* are enacted.

1957	The Chosun Textile Company dispute in Pusan in December splits the FKTU.
1959	Cheonkuk Nodongjohab Hyeobuiehyo (National Council of Trade Unions, or NCTU) is formed.
1960	The 'April 19 Student Revolution' deposes Syngman Rhee. The Chang Myeon government is elected. The FKTU and the NCTU merge to form a new national centre known as Cheonnohyeob.
1961	General Park Chung-hee takes power in a military coup in May. The FKTU is restructured into twelve industrial union associations.
1963	Park Chung-hee is elected President of the Third Republic of Korea. Labour laws revised.
1970	Restrictions on unionism in foreign-owned firms.
1971	Law Concerning the Special Measures for Safeguarding National Security (LCSMSNS) gives Park Chung-hee a lifetime presidency. Compulsory arbitration is extended to all industries. The Korea Employers' Federation (KEF) is established.
1975	*Labour Standards Act* extended to companies with between five and fifteen employees.
1979	Park Chung-hee assassinated.
1980	Military coup by General Chun Doo-hwan.
1981	The *Labour–Management Council Act*, the *Industrial Safety and Health Act* and the *Minimum Wage Act* passed, and the scope of the Industrial Accident Insurance and Compensation Act extended.
1987	Democratisation Declaration, 29 June.
1991	Cheonnohyup, the Korea Trade Union Congress (KTUC) formed. Korea joins the ILO.
1995	Minjunochong, the Korean Confederation of Trade Unions (KCTU) formed.
1996	The Presidential Industrial Relations Reform Commission (PIRRC) formed. Korea joins the OECD. December amendments to the labour laws provoke a public outcry.
1997	Wave of general strikes organised by the KCTU and FKTU, followed by the revision of the amended labour legislation. The financial exchange crisis occurs.

1998	Kim Dae-jung government begins. Presidential Tripartite Commission agrees to introduce more labour market flexibility measures, including layoffs for managerial reasons and the use of dispatched labour. The Korean Health and Medical Workers' Union is established as the first industrial union.
1999	The unemployment rate jumps to 8.5 per cent by February, a record high. The KCTU withdraws from participation in the Tripartite Commission. A general strike is called by the KCTU to protest the IMF's restructuring programs, but fails to gain widespread support.
1999	Teachers are granted the legal right to form a union. The KCTU is officially recognised by the government.
2001	The Tripartite Commission agrees to postpone the enforcement of the labour law clauses concerning multiple unions at the enterprise level and the prohibition of payment of full-time union officials by the end of 2006. The Tripartite Commission agrees to reduce standard working hours to 40 hours per week.
2003	Roh Moo-hyun government begins. The transport workers (truck drivers) union calls a general strike to demand labour rights for dependent self-employed workers.
2004	The Tripartite Commission reaches the Social Pact for Job Creation.
2005	The FKTU and the KCTU call a joint general strike to demand the enactment of non-regular labour protection laws.
2006	Public servants are granted the legal right to organise unions and engage in collective bargaining. The Tripartite Commission agrees to once again postpone the enforcement of the labour law clauses concerning the operation of multiple unions at the enterprise level and the prohibition of payment of full-time union officials until the end of 2009. Non-regular labour protection laws are passed.
2007	The Tripartite Commission is renamed the Economic and Social Development Commission of Korea.

2008	Lee Myung-bak government begins. President Lee announces the so-called 'MBnomics', which includes 'business-friendly' labour market deregulation to promote greater labour market flexibility.
2009	The government campaigns for a work-sharing program and adopts an active labour market policy to create jobs through youth internships and public works projects. A social pact is agreed between unions, employers, civic groups and the government to overcome the impact of the global financial crisis on South Korea.

CHAPTER 12

Employment relations
in China

Fang Lee Cooke

The People's Republic of China (hereafter China) was founded on
1 October 1949 and has been ruled by the Chinese Communist Party
for the last six decades. With a population of over 1.3 billion, it is
currently the most populated country in the world. The labour market
participation rate is high, as the social security system is rudimentary
and provides only partial coverage for a relatively small proportion
of the population, mainly those with urban resident status. In 2006,
58.1 per cent of the population was in employment (764 million), with
37 per cent of those employed based in the urban area (see Table 12.1).
Compared with their counterparts in other countries, Chinese women
have a relatively high employment participation rate, making up
38 per cent of the total workforce in full-time employment in the urban
area (*China Statistical Yearbook 2007*). It is worth noting that part-
time employment is uncommon in China, in part as a result of the
low-wage full-employment policy adopted by the government during
the state planned economy period (Cooke, 2005). In addition, driven
by the Marxist emancipation thesis, the state encouraged women to
participate in employment to gain financial independence and enhance
their political and social status.

The development of the labour market of socialist China can be
divided into three periods. The first period was a highly regulated—or,
more precisely, controlled—labour market governed through
administrative policy during the state planned economy period. Labour
mobility was highly restricted, monitored by the *hukou* system—a
residential registration system where individuals were registered with

Table 12.1 Employment statistics by ownership in urban and rural areas in China (millions of persons)

Ownership	1978	1980	1985	1990	1995	1998	2000	2003	2006
Number of urban employed persons	95.14	105.25	128.08	166.16	190.93	206.78	231.51	256.39	283.10
State-owned units	74.51	80.19	89.90	103.46	112.61	90.58	81.02	68.76	64.30
Collectively owned units	20.48	24.25	33.24	35.49	31.47	19.63	14.99	10.00	7.64
Cooperative units	–	–	–	–	–	1.36	1.55	1.73	1.78
Joint ownership units	–	–	0.38	0.96	0.53	0.48	0.42	0.44	0.45
Limited liability corporations	–	–	–	–	–	4.84	6.87	12.61	19.20
Shareholding corporations	–	–	–	–	3.17	4.10	4.57	5.92	7.41
Private enterprises	–	–	–	0.57	4.85	9.73	12.68	25.45	39.54
Units with funds from Hong Kong, Macao and Taiwan	–	–	–	0.04	2.72	2.94	3.10	4.09	6.11
Foreign-funded units	–	–	0.06	0.62	2.41	2.93	3.32	4.54	7.96
Self-employed individuals	0.15	0.81	4.50	6.14	15.60	22.59	21.36	23.77	30.12
Number of rural employed persons	306.38	318.36	370.65	472.93	488.54	492.79	489.34	487.93	480.93
Township and village enterprises	28.27	30.00	69.79	92.65	128.62	125.37	128.20	135.73	146.80
Private enterprises	–	–	–	1.13	4.71	7.37	11.39	17.54	26.32
Self-employed individuals	–	–	–	14.91	30.54	38.55	29.34	22.60	21.47
Total	401.52	423.61	498.73	647.49	680.65	706.37	720.85	744.32	764.00

Source: Adapted from *China Statistical Yearbook 2003*, pp. 126–7; *China Statistical Yearbook 2007*, p. 127

the local authority where they were born and lived. The population was divided into urban and rural residents. Rural residents were not allowed to enter urban areas for employment. This restriction was gradually removed during the period of deregulation that followed, between the 1980s and the early 2000s, when millions of farmers migrated to urban areas for employment and millions of state-owned enterprise (SOE) employees were laid off and forced to seek re-employment in the labour market for the first time. The promulgation of three major employment-related laws in 2007 (see below) marked the beginning of the third period, in which the government sought to re-regulate the labour market through legislative intervention in order to provide greater employment protection to workers, particularly those outside the state sector. Dealing with labour market transformation has been one of the most challenging tasks facing the Chinese government (Fleisher & Yang 2003). Employment relations at the workplace level have been developed within this broader context of labour market transformation.

THE MAJOR PARTIES

The role of the state

As a socialist country with the legacy of a state planned economy embedded in the country's political and economic system, the role of the Chinese government—or, more broadly, the state—as an employer, a legislator and an economic manager remains dominant. This is despite the fact that state sector employment has constituted a shrinking proportion of total employment over the last three decades. For example, in 1978—the year China adopted its 'open door' policy—over 78 per cent of the urban workforce was employed in the state sector. This had been reduced to less than 23 per cent by 2006 (see Table 12.1 above). The sharp decline of employment in the state sector, particularly from the late 1990s, was achieved mainly through downsizing, plant closure and the privatisation of SOEs as part of the state-driven reform. Begun in the early 1990s to revitalise the outmoded and largely loss-making SOEs, the momentum of SOE reform reached its peak in the late 1990s after then Premier Zhu Rongji announced his SOE reform plan in 1997. Poorly performing SOEs were given three years to 'sort themselves out'. In the ensuing five-year period between 1998 and 2002, over 27 million workers were laid off (*China Statistical Yearbook 2003*).

In the meantime, the private sector has been encouraged to grow (Garnaut & Huang 2001) through the removal of policy restrictions and operational barriers, together with the provision of financial incentives. The sector provides employment opportunities for those displaced by their state employers, new workers from the urban area and rural migrant workers. Once marginal and marginalised in the state planned economy due to the ideological clash between capitalism and socialism, the private sector now holds a major stake in the economy. This is despite the fact that the majority of the firms in this sector are relatively small, low technology based and compete mainly on price (Cooke 2005). Similarly, foreign investment enterprises (FIEs), and those funded by Hong Kong, Taiwan and Macao, have been given more autonomy to operate in China since the mid-1990s, including permission to set up wholly foreign-owned enterprise (FOE). FIEs are no longer required to establish joint ventures as the entry mode. They are also given more autonomy in determining their employment policies.

A number of labour laws and regulations have been promulgated by the government since the 1980s, landmarked by the launch of the Labour Law of China in 1995.[1] In 2007, the government stepped up its activities and passed three major pieces of employment-related legislation to take effect from 2008. They are the extensively debated Labour Contract Law, the Employment Promotion Law and the Labour Disputes Mediation and Arbitration Law. The promulgation of these laws signals the government's renewed and stronger determination to raise the level of protection for its workforce against the current labour market situation. Employees are afforded greater power to seek justice through legal channels when these laws are violated by employers. In addition, the government has issued a number of regulations in recent years—for example, the Labour Market Wage Rate Guideline (1999), the Regulation on Labour Market Management (2000, now superseded by the Employment Promotion Law), the Special Regulation on Minimum Wage (2004) and the Regulations on Employment Services and Management (2008).

These labour laws and regulations provide a legal framework within which the employment relationship is governed and the labour market regulated in principle. The primary objective of their implementation is to achieve a more efficient and equitable labour market. In parallel, a system for labour dispute resolution was formed—though it is far from being robust (see next section). It has been argued that, with 'the major exception of freedom of association', the labour standards established by the series of labour laws and regulations in China 'are not markedly inferior to those of comparable countries and indeed many developed nations' (Cooney 2007: 674). What remains most problematic is the lack of effective enforcement (Cooney 2007; Taylor et al. 2003). While implementation failures are a characteristic of all regulatory systems (Cooney 2007), the Chinese system is frustrated by the multiplicity of employment-related laws, directive regulations and administrative policies issued at the central, provincial and municipal government levels, the ambiguous status of some of these regulative instruments, and the confusing channels through which workers can seek to secure compliance of laws (Potter 1999; Cooney 2007).

In addition, it has been argued that the existing body of employment-related regulations primarily targets those in the formal employment sector with formal employment relationships (Hu 2004). There is considerable ambiguity about whether certain laws and regulations should apply to the informal sector and workers in informal employment (see further discussion below). Employers also tend to take advantage of these regulatory loopholes and argue for exemption (Cooke 2008b). While the labour laws carry more legal power, they provide limited regulations on the labour market. Although the labour market-related regulations are said to have some effect, these regulations, together with a series of other employment-related regulations, are essentially administrative policy regulations that have limited authority and enforceability (Hu 2004).

A unique feature of the Chinese laws and regulations is that central government provides the broad framework. It is up to local governments to devise their localised regulations to suit local characteristics, based on these national master prints. This flexibility is needed in a vast country like China, which has significant economic disparity across its regions. However, the decentralisation of interpretation and enforcement also opens up opportunities for implementation slippage, as the power and determination of local government officials and labour authorities may be circumvented by the priority of economic development; some of them may even be co-opted by employers.

The employers, workers and characteristics of employment relations

Unlike developed economies, where employers' associations are developed, provide a range of services to their member employers and form pressure groups to influence government policy and legislation, employers' associations in China are much less well established, with the exception of the China Enterprise Confederation (CEC), which plays a limited role in employment relations. As in the relationship with the All-China Federation of Trade Unions (ACFTU) (see below), the state recognises only one official employer organisation at the national level as the sole representative of the sectoral interests. The state forms some kind of unequal partnerships with these organisations, which often act on behalf of the state and help implement government policy (see Unger & Chan 1995). Nevertheless, it is important to note that the lobbying power of Chinese employers is rising. They are able to form pressure groups very quickly in order to exert pressure on the government if forthcoming regulations and policies are likely to have a significant negative impact on their business environment. The newly launched Labour Contract Law (2008) is a good example— the final version was watered down from the draft version as a result of employers' lobbying.

As we can see from Table 12.1, the state is no longer the dominant employer in the urban sector—though it is still a major one. Private firms and FIEs are becoming significant employers too. Employers of varying ownership forms operate under different historical, legislative, economic and labour market environment. Their business strategies and employment policies are heavily influenced by these external factors. Outside the state sector, employment relations are mainly shaped at the enterprise level and display different characteristics across ownership forms, as will be demonstrated below.

Not only has the Chinese government's economic policy triggered radical changes to its economic structure, it has also brought fundamental changes in the ideological identity and demographic profile of its workers. These changes bear different implications for their labour market positions and bargaining power. During the state-planned economy period, Chinese workers were, comparatively speaking, a homogeneous group, comprising employees in the urban areas who were primarily employed by the state. The status of 'workers' under the Socialist China was political as much as economic. Workers were regarded by the state as the 'masters' of the country (see Sheehan 1999 for a more detailed discussion). The term 'working class' differentiated urban workers from those who worked in the rural area (peasants). The former enjoyed a high level of social welfare and benefits, of which the latter have largely been deprived. Employment relations in the state sector were once portrayed as harmonious, with workers participating in the democratic management of the workplace and production activities through their trade union organisations and workers' representatives. The ongoing reforms in SOEs over the last two decades have led to profound changes in the employment relationships between the workers and their state employers. A notable change is the end of employment security and the reduction of workplace welfare provision. These changes have undermined, and in some cases practically ended, the paternalistic bond between the state employer and its workers. A significant proportion of the labour discontent and disputes come from those who are negatively affected by these changes. It must be noted, however, that a number of SOEs have managed to transform themselves successfully and continue to perform very well (e.g. see Nolan 2001). This is particularly the case for the super-large SOEs that are directly controlled by the central government (*yiangqi*). Well-performing SOEs continue to adopt a paternalistic management style, offering even better welfare benefits to their employees than they once did as a result of the improved performance of the enterprise (Chan & Unger 2008).

Meanwhile, the opening up of the economy has attracted millions of rural migrant workers to seek employment in the urban areas. Indeed, they have played a pivotal role in China's contemporary economic development. The inflow of rural migrant workers to urban areas started in the late 1980s. In 1995, there were about 50 million rural migrant workers (Chen et al. 2001). This had increased to some 150 million by 2006, making up 58 per cent of the workers in the industry sector and 52 per cent in the service sector (State Council 2006). Initially working in manufacturing plants, on construction sites and as domestic helpers, they are now employed in a wide spread of industries and occupations, but primarily in private firms, foreign-investment sweatshop plants and the informal sector, where labour standards are low and employment regulations are often violated. The vast majority of them have no written employment contract, little training, few rest days, no social security and virtually no health and safety protection. They work excessively long hours, live in poor conditions and are largely unorganised and unrepresented (e.g. Chan 2001; Gallagher 2005; Lee 2007; Pun & Smith 2007). Delay of wage payment is common, especially in the construction industry (Cooke 2008a). The adversarial employment conditions endured by rural migrant workers is a legacy of the highly non-egalitarian socialist development strategy adopted by the government, in which urban development ironically has been achieved at the expense of the rural population (e.g. Solinger 1999; Meng 2000). Institutionalised discriminative practices continue when rural migrant workers enter urban employment. Although efforts have been made by the government to eliminate discriminative practices since the 1990s, mainly through regulatory and policy intervention, the lack of comprehensive legislative coverage and effective enforcement in the private and informal sectors means that these workers remain largely unprotected (Cooke 2008b).

In sharp contrast to the above two groups of workers are the younger generation of university graduates, who are employed in government and public sector organisations, well-performing private firms and prestigious multinational corporations. As a result of the expansion of higher education in the early 2000s, China now produces millions of university graduates each year, in addition to thousands who have been trained overseas. For example, in 2006, over four million students graduated from universities and colleges. This is in addition to 42 000 returnees from overseas with postgraduate qualifications (*China Statistical Yearbook 2007*). The well-documented talent shortage in China (e.g. Farrell & Grant 2005; Malila 2007) means that some of them hold a high level of bargaining power in determining their terms and conditions. This is in spite of the fact that an increasing number of university graduates are encountering problems finding employment, due to a lack of work experience. Firms are relying on financial rewards (e.g. pay rises, bonuses and stock options) and career development opportunities as the main mechanisms to attract and retain talented and experienced employees (Arkless 2007; Wang et al. 2007). This new generation of workers, particularly the post-1980s generation (i.e. those who were born after the implementation of the one-child policy in the 1980s), tends to have different values and work ethics from the older generation of workers, who were more influenced by the traditional Chinese cultural values and socialist work ethics such as loyalty, obedience and diligence. Young graduate employees have little knowledge of trade unions (Cooke 2008c) and are said to be more materialistic, have stronger career aspirations and be more eager to progress (Arkless 2007; Malila 2007).

The unions

Only one trade union—the All-China Federation of Trade Unions (ACFTU)—is recognised by the Chinese government. The union-Chinese Communist Party (CCP) tie dates back to the 1920s (the union was founded on 1 May 1925), when grassroots union organisations served as the Party member recruitment bases and provided vital support to the Communist Party by mobilising workers. Since the founding of Socialist China, the ACFTU has become one of the eight 'mass organisations' that have the function of organising and representing certain groups of people, such as women, youth and workers. A distinct feature of these political organisations is that they need to be recognised and led by the Communist Party. This institutionalises the master and subordinate relationships between the Party and the mass organisations, depoliticises the relationship and derecognises, upfront, any conflicts and power struggle that may exist between these organisations and the state. Although the relationship between the Communist Party and the ACFTU has not always been smooth, attempts by the ACFTU to gain greater power and autonomy have been suppressed by the Party (You 1998; Sheehan 1999). Similarly, attempts to form autonomous workers' unions have been clamped down on, as was the case during the Tiananmen Square incident in 1989.

The governance structure of ACFTU branches is in the form of both vertical and horizontal reporting lines. They are under the dual control of the local government at their level and their organisational branch at a higher level. ACFTU branches are responsible for liaising with union organisations at the enterprise level and are tasked to gain recognition by employers.

The roles and responsibilities of the unions are set out by a number of laws, namely the Trade Union Law (1950, 1992, amended 2001), the Labour Law (1995) and the recent Labour Contract Law (2008). According to the Trade Union Law (2001), 'the basic function and duty of the trade unions is to safeguard the legal rights and interests of the employees. While upholding the overall rights and interests of the whole nation, trade unions shall, at the same time, represent and safeguard the rights and interests of employees' (Article 6). Article 7 further stipulates that the 'trade union shall mobilise and organise the employees to participate in the economic development actively, and to complete the production and work assignments conscientiously, educate the employees to improve their ideological thoughts and ethics, technological and professional, scientific and cultural qualities, and build an employee team with ideals, ethics, education and discipline'.

According to Martin's (1989) typologies, the Chinese trade unions fall within 'the authoritarian' category as the 'state instruments', carrying out a 'decisively subordinate role' that is 'concerned with *both* production and protection' (1989: 78). The trade unions' primary responsibility is the state (Martin 1989), whose interests are not necessarily aligned with those of the workers. Under the Socialist system, in which the state employer and the workers are perceived to share the same interests, the trade unions' main function is to organise social events, take care of workers' welfare, help management implement operational decisions, organise skills training, raise employee morale and coordinate relations between management and workers (Verma & Yan 1995). They carry out this function effectively by acting as a 'conveyor belt' between the Communist Party and the workers (Hoffman 1981). The way the ACFTU is set up and operationalised has led to questioning by international trade union organisations, labour movement activists and scholars regarding the legitimacy of ACFTU as a trade union (e.g. Taylor & Li 2007).

Since the mid-1990s, when SOEs shed millions of their workers, skill training and assisting laid-off workers to regain employment have been two major functions of the unions. With the growth of new ownership forms outside of the state sector and the concomitant social welfare reforms that were carried out in the state sector, the welfare role of the state has been diminishing. The once relatively harmonious management–labour relationship has been replaced with one characterised by conflicting interests, rising numbers of disputes and increasing inequality in contractual arrangements between management and labour. However, the role of the unions—or, more specifically, the union officials' perception of their duties—has not changed in time to reflect the new reality. Union officials generally lack resources and power, skills and legal knowledge to fulfil their collective bargaining role and to defend their members' rights (Warner & Ng 1999; Cooke 2008c). They are often considered ineffective in representing workers' interests against management prerogatives and sometimes side with management (e.g. White 1996; O'Leary 1998; Lee 1999; Clarke 2005). It is not unusual to find that enterprise managers or Party secretaries assume the union chairman's role, despite the fact that it is against the regulations. Similarly, union officials at the branch level are rarely elected. Rather, they are appointed by the local government and often rotate their positions in government departments.

Nevertheless, the ACFTU is the largest national trade union body in the world, when measured by its official membership on paper (Warner & Zhu 2009). As shown by Table 12.2, the levels of union membership have been consistently high at over 90 per cent since 1990 in workplaces where grassroots union organisations are established. By the end of 2006, there were over 1.3 million grassroots union organisations and nearly 170 million union members. The number of full-time union officials in union branches has also been rising steadily, to over half a million by the end of 2006, after experiencing a brief period of decline between 2001 and 2004 when union organisations experienced a period of restructuring and downsizing as part of the state sector reform. By June 2008, there were 209 million union members and 1.7 million grassroots union organisations (*People's Daily Online* 2008). It must be noted here that the high level of membership in unionised workplaces has not brought any real power to workers. Once a union unit is established in a company, particularly in the urban sector, it is virtually mandatory for its employees to become members.

Table 12.2 Union membership level in organisations where unions were established

Year	Grassroots unions (000s)	Employees (000s)	Female employees (000s)	Membership (000s)	Female members (000s)	Union density (%)	Full-time union officials (000s)
1952	207	13 932	–	10 023	–	71.9	53
1962	165	26 671	–	19 220	–	72.1	86
1979	329	68 972	21 717	51 473	–	74.6	179
1980	376	74 482	25 186	61 165	–	82.1	243
1985	465	96 430	35 967	85 258	31 492	88.4	381
1990	606	111 569	42 910	101 356	38 977	90.8	556
1995	593	113 214	45 153	103 996	41 165	91.9	468
2000	859	114 721	45 345	103 615	39 173	90.3	482
2001	1 538	129 970	50 879	121 523	46 966	93.5	–
2002	1 713	144 615	51 576	133 978	46 652	92.6	472
2003	906	133 016	50 793	123 405	46 012	92.8	465
2004	1 020	144 367	55 026	136 949	51 353	94.9	456
2005	1 174	159 853	60 163	150 294	55 748	94.0	477
2006	1 324	181 436	67 193	169 942	61 778	93.7	543

Note: Since 2003, statistical coverage of the number of grassroots trade unions has been adjusted (original note)
Source: Adapted from the *China Statistical Yearbook 2007*, p. 883

The pattern of unionisation in China resembles that in developed and developing countries. In other words, the unionisation level in the state sector tends to be far higher than that in the private sector. It is estimated that only about 30 per cent of the private firms have established unions. Most grassroots-level union organisations do not have full-time officials (*Workers' Daily*, 2 November 2004). Nevertheless, official statistics suggest that union membership levels have been on the increase since 2003 (*China Labour Statistical Yearbook 2007*). This is a direct result of the ACFTU's recruitment drive. In August 2003, the ACFTU officially classified rural migrant workers in urban areas as 'members of the working class' and required union organisations to organise rural migrant workers (*Yangcheng Evening News*, 8 August 2003). By the end of 2004, 20 million rural migrant workers had been recruited as union members (*Workers' Daily*, 7 December 2004). This figure had increased to 66 million by June 2008 (*People's Daily Online* 2008). The ACFTU's strategy is to recruit as many rural migrant workers as possible into the union, disregarding where they are from, what types of jobs they do, how long they work or even whether or not they are in employment (*Workers' Daily*, 25 February 2005). This mode of organising outside the workplace by offering a range of services (e.g. labour market information, legal support and training) is similar to what Kelly and Heery (1989: 198–9) describe as a 'distant expansion' recruitment strategy. It is unlikely to help unions gain recognition and tackle rampant exploitation and mistreatment at workplaces.

The success in union member recruitment should not be over-estimated, and official statistics need to be interpreted with extreme caution. For example, the *China Labour Statistical Yearbook 2007* shows that there were more union members in the collectively owned enterprises (COEs) in 2006 (9.45 million members) than there were employees in total employment in COEs (7.64 million employees). It is highly questionable that the retired or laid-off employees from COEs can account for the missing 1.81 million union members. Similarly, the union density level in private enterprises and other non-state sectors reported in the *China Labour Statistical Yearbook 2007* also seems to be higher than those revealed in independent academic studies (e.g. Chan 2001; Cooke 2002, 2008c; Taylor et al. 2003; Gallagher 2005). The relatively low level of union density in the private and informal sector, where the majority of rural migrant workers are employed, is to a large extent an outcome of employers' formidable resistance to union recognition and the lack of demand from workers to establish a trade union. This is partly because workers are unfamiliar with the concept of workplace representation, but more because of the perceived inefficacy of the union in advancing workers' interests (Cooke 2008b).

THE PROCESS OF EMPLOYMENT RELATIONS

Collective consultation and collective contract

The notion of 'collective bargaining' was first introduced in employment relations in China in the early 1990s, after the Trade Union Law (1992) authorised unions at the enterprise level to conclude collective contracts with the employer. The term 'collective consultation' is preferred by the state to 'collective bargaining' when it comes to defining the official process of employment relations. It is believed that consultation is a more constructive approach than 'bargaining', as it conforms to the Chinese culture of non-confrontation and conflict avoidance. In 1994, the Provisions on Collective Contracts were issued by the Ministry of Labour, which provided detailed regulations to support the Collective Contract provision outlined in the Labour Law of China passed in 1994 (for more detailed discussion, see Taylor et al. 2003; Brown 2006). Trade unions have been given the official role of representing workers when it comes to consultation with employers. This position of the unions has been reinforced and expanded in the subsequent amended Trade Union Law (2001) and the improved Provisions on Collective Contract (2004), which superseded the 1994 version. According to Article 20 of the Trade Union Law (2001), a trade union shall represent employees in equal negotiation and signing a collective contract. Matters that can be concluded in a collective contract may include labour remuneration, working time, rest and vacations, occupational safety and health, professional training, and insurance and welfare. In addition, local labour authorities are responsible for facilitating and monitoring the consultation process.

The establishment of this tripartite consultation system is believed to be an important mechanism for the government, trade unions and enterprises to strengthen social dialogue and cooperation in coordinating labour relations. Achievements have been made after a decade's implementation of the system. According to the ACFTU, 754 000 collective contracts had been signed across the country by the end of September 2005, covering 137 800 enterprises and 103.84 million workers. Collective contracts signed are said to be increasingly being broadened to cover a range of aspects of labour standards, though wages remain the major issue (Zhang 2006). The ACFTU is also pushing for collective contracts that provide large coverage, such as region-based and industry-wide collective contracts. However, it has been argued that the collective consultation system does not provide a real independent framework for regulating employment relations

(Clarke et al. 2004) and that the majority of collective contracts were model agreements made between the employer and the union without the direct involvement of workers or any real negotiation process (Brown 2006). Equally, region- or nation-wide collective contracts may be too broad to be relevant to local needs and give enterprise managers excuses to ignore local union representatives. The recent Wal-Mart (China) example is a case in point (China Labor News Translations 2008). In addition, collective contracts appear to be more widely adopted in SOEs than in private firms (Warner & Ng 1999).

Resolution of labour disputes

A labour dispute reconciliation system was established in Socialist China in the early 1950s. After a period of disruption during the Cultural Revolution (1966–76), the system was resumed in 1987 with the promulgation of the Temporary Regulation for Labour Disputes Reconciliation in State-owned Enterprises. This temporary regulation was amended in 1993 and implemented as the Labour Disputes Reconciliation Regulation. The Regulation was later incorporated into the Labour Law of China (1995), which forms the legal basis for settling labour disputes. The Labour Law of China officially brought all labour disputes in all firms under the jurisdiction of the formal labour dispute resolution system (Cooke 2008a).

The labour dispute resolution system in China consists of three stages: mediation, arbitration and litigation (for a more detailed description, see Taylor et al. 2003). Mediation is the initial procedure that usually takes place in the enterprise where the labour dispute occurs through a mediation committee consisting of representatives of the employer, the employees and the trade union or a third party deemed acceptable to both parties in dispute. Resolution to the dispute through consultation and voluntary mediation is the approach encouraged by the state. Any agreements made at this stage and beyond are legally binding. If this approach fails, then one of the two parties in the dispute can apply to the labour dispute arbitration committee for resolution. An arbitration committee will then be formed to arbitrate the dispute. A dispute case can also be submitted directly to the arbitration committee without going through the initial stage of mediation at the enterprise level, if it is felt that mediation is unlikely to settle the dispute. A dispute case, however, will not be accepted for lawsuit until after it has been through the arbitration procedure. Cases resolved by the arbitration committees are classified as being by means of mediation, arbitration or other. If either party is not satisfied with the arbitration ruling, then the case can be appealed at the local People's Court. At each stage, emphasis is placed on resolving the conflict through negotiation, mutual understanding and voluntary agreement between the parties directly involved. Labour disputes in China are categorised as either individual or collective disputes; collective disputes should consist of at least three employees who share the same reason(s) for the dispute (Cooke 2008a).

A number of characteristics have emerged from the trends of labour disputes since the adoption of the Labour Law of China (1995). First, the number of labour disputes accepted by the arbitration committees at all levels has been rising each year, from 48 121 cases in 1996 to 317 162 cases in 2006 (*China Labour Statistical Yearbook 2007*). Second, pay, social insurance, alteration or termination of employment contract, and work injury/labour protection have been the major causes of disputes. In particular, disputes about pay and social insurance account for over half of the total dispute cases each year. Third, the nature of the labour disputes increasingly appears to be confrontational and antagonistic. There has been a continuous rise in the proportion of cases settled by arbitration and appeals, and a continuous decrease in resolutions by mediation. For example, in 1996 a total of 52 per cent of the dispute cases received by arbitration committees were settled by mediation and 27 per cent were settled by arbitration. In 2006, only 34 per cent of the cases were settled through mediation while over 45 per cent were settled through arbitration (*China Labour Statistical Yearbook 2007*). Fourth, the proportion of cases won by workers appeared to be significantly lower than the proportion of cases submitted by them. Fifth, businesses funded by FIEs and by Hong Kong, Macao and Taiwan have had the highest share of labour disputes, both in relation to their share of employment and in terms of the speed of increases in the 1990s (Cooke 2008a).

In addition to the official labour-resolution system, workers rely on other channels to voice their grievances and seek justice—for example, letters and petitions (Thireau & Hua 2003), as well as workplace industrial action and street protests, which are often spontaneous and illegal (Chan 2001; Chen 2003; Gallagher 2005; Lee 2007). There have also been numerous attempts by workers to set up autonomous organisations and launch political movements, but these have quickly been suppressed by the government (*China Labour Bulletin* 2005). It is worth noting that official statistics on labour disputes, legal or illegal, only reveal a partial picture. The precise number of labour disputes, industrial actions and street protests, and the total number of those who are involved, may never have been captured, and it is likely that they will never be published by the authorities.

CURRENT AND FUTURE ISSUES AND TRENDS

Labour market flexibility

If temporary employment, job-sharing, annualised hours, part-time and seasonal work are some of the key features in the labour deployment strategy adopted by firms in developed economies to combat labour/ skill shortages and the pressure of global competition, then Chinese labour market flexibility is achieved through the rapid expansion of the informal employment sector. Its primary motives are cost saving (from the employers' perspective) and creation of employment opportunities (from the government's). Thus China has been experiencing a sharp swing from a once rigid internal labour market dominated by the state sector to an increasingly informal and unprotected labour market since the mid-1990s. Laid-off SOE workers and rural migrant workers make up the majority of those in informal employment.

The use of informal employment in the form of temporary, seasonal, casual and hourly-paid work has long existed in China, albeit on a much smaller scale until recent years. The term 'informal employment', however, is a relatively new one in China, first introduced by the Shanghai labour authority in 1996 (Cooke 2008b). It is worth noting that the Chinese authorities tend to use the term 'flexible employment' to neutralise its negative image. The lack of consensus on the precise definition and classification of informal employment, and the absence of any official statistics on the total number of employed in this mode and what forms of employment they are engaged in, have been widely noted (e.g. Peng & Yao 2004; Shi & Wang 2007; Zhang 2004). Nevertheless, it is estimated that at least 150 million workers are engaged in informal employment in the urban area (State Council 2006).

The majority of workers in informal employment do not have an employment contract with their employers. Some employers take advantage of policy loopholes and hire and fire workers at will, leading to further job insecurity for the workers. Since the majority of these workers would have found their jobs through personal networks, workers are more likely to tolerate mistreatments by the employer due to personal ties (Zhang 2008). In some situations where the employment relationship is complicated—for example, agency workers and live-in nannies sent by employment agencies—it is unclear who the employer is; therefore the hiring parties tend to pass the parcel and evade their responsibilities (Cooke 2008b).

Employment agencies

Accompanying the growth of informal employment has been a significant growth in recent years has been a significant growth in the number of employment agencies tailored to the lower end of the labour market. In 2001, there were a total of 26 793 employment agencies, 70 per cent of them funded by the labour authorities at various levels as part of the multi-level employment service network. By 2005, the number of employment agencies had increased to 35 747, two-thirds of them funded by labour authorities. The number of employees working in these employment agencies increased from 84 440 in 2001 to 111 000 in 2005 (*China Labour Statistical Yearbook 2002* and *2006*). In principle, these employment agencies represent an institutional presence in the labour market by playing a number of roles. These include providing labour market information, training, screening, recruitment and placement of workers, influencing wage setting, regulating the contingent labour market, redistributing the risks associated with contingent employment and acting as employers. With regard the last of these, it is believed that this form of employment relationship benefits both the worker and the client in that the worker enjoys a higher level of job security and labour rights protection, whereas the client will have a continuous supply of labour (*Workers' Daily*, 22 February 2005). In practice, this triangle employment relationship proves to be complicated and is prone to abdication of responsibilities due to ambiguity of status, as mentioned above.

The Employment Agency Regulation promulgated by the state in 1995 stipulates that employment agencies established by the local labour authorities should be non-profit making, whereas those set up by private firms or organisations unrelated to the labour authorities can be either profit-making or non-profit-making. In reality, most employment agencies impose service charges, often beyond the price set by the local authority. Employment agencies have been criticised for a lack of professionalism, lack of up-to-date market information and lack of coordination between various organisations related to labour market services. Their training function is under-resourced and poorly equipped. Their training content is outdated and fails to reflect what is most needed by employers (Li 2000). The legitimacy of employment agencies as a labour market broker is also highly questionable amongst job seekers. Research findings suggest that only a small proportion of laid-off SOE workers and rural migrant workers have visited an employment agency, and few of them found their jobs through employment agencies (Li 2003; Mu 2003).

It was anticipated that the enactment of the Labour Contract Law (2008) would see a reduction in the number of those hired by employment agencies, promoting more direct and stable employment relationships between the worker and the employer. The reality so far has been a stark contrast. In anticipation of the negative impact of the new law on employment cost, many employers joined the rush in late 2007 to dismiss their workers who had been working for the firm for a number of years and rehire them under new temporary contracts. Others dismissed their workers and rehired them, or hired new ones as agency workers through employment agencies. As a result, employment agencies have prospered and the number of workers registered with employment agencies is growing.

Work–life balance

One direct consequence of the marketisation of the Chinese economy has been work intensification, particularly for those in the private and informal sectors. According to the annual sample survey conducted by the national labour authorities (see *China Labour Statistical Yearbook 2007*), the average working hours per week in the urban area have been rising steadily in recent years from over 45 hours in 2003 to over 47 hours in 2006. In particular, those who work in the manufacturing, construction, transport, logistics and postal service, wholesale and retail, hotel and catering, and community services sectors work the longest hours (all above 50 hours). In 2006, over 47 per cent of rural migrant workers in the survey worked more than 48 hours, compared with 31 per cent of workers with urban resident status who did so.

The actual number of hours worked by those in FIE sweatshop manufacturing plants and private firms may never be established officially, as employers have a vested interest in not disclosing the real figures in order to avoid overtime payments and legal sanctions. What is known from smaller scale academic studies is that workers in FIE manufacturing plants and private enterprises tend to work extensive hours—often beyond 60 hours—with few rest days (e.g. Chan 2001; Lee 2007; Pun & Smith 2007). In the low-paid jobs, workers often demand overtime opportunities and are willing to accept normal rates of pay instead of the overtime premiums stipulated by law. Employers are also happy to provide overtime work with reduced labour costs associated with additional headcounts. Work–life balance is undoubtedly an issue for these workers, but paradoxically, they prefer to work more hours than to participate in social activities organised by the employer or spend time with their families. Increasing their wage level is the most effective, albeit an unlikely, solution due to their lack of bargaining power and the cost pressure some employers are facing.

Work intensification associated with long hours and an intensive work pace is also becoming an issue for professional and managerial workers in fast-growing industries such as telecommunications, IT, consultancy, finance and real estate. This has led to health problems and retention issues. Some firms are now beginning to address these problems by organising an after-work social life for their employees, hiring professionals to provide counselling services and introducing some forms of employee assistance programs (EAPs). While organising social life for employees (and their families) has long been a workplace welfare provision in SOEs and to a lesser extent in private firms as part of the Chinese paternalistic culture, EAPs are relatively new and are mainly provided to professional and managerial employees. These examples suggest that work–life conflicts in China derive from a range of sources that may differ from those manifested in Western societies and require different HR initiatives and government policy interventions in the Chinese context.

CONCLUSIONS

Employment relations in China have undergone significant changes during its process of economic reform. It is clear that characteristics of employment relations are now diverging across different ownership forms, industrial sectors and groups of workers. This is a trend that reflects those in developed economies, despite fundamental differences that remain—notably union independence and strength. Due to the lack of representational strength of the unions and employers' associations, employment relations in China are shaped largely between the employer and the workers, with the majority of workers having little bargaining power. Where changes in employment practices are taking place, these are often a result of the enactment of employment-related laws and regulations. The role of the state therefore continues to be crucial in shaping employment relations in the foreseeable future. It must be noted here that, despite the government's desire to create a more humanistic employment environment for the workers through tightening legislative governance, the intended effect of laws and regulations are not always achieved. Employers continue to find ways to bypass legal constraints and workers may tolerate unlawful employment practices for fear of job losses.

Unions are active mainly in the state sector and private firms that have strong government ties, although new initiatives of organising, such as block unions for smaller enterprises, community unions for the unemployed and project unions for construction sites are promoted to organise those outside the state sector. Unions largely carry out a welfare role, which is inadequate for the representation needs of those in the private sector and those working in poorly managed SOEs. It is therefore not surprising that the level of union disaffection is high among SOE workers who have experienced radical changes with worsened employment outcomes. Equally, the level of union identification is low among rural migrant workers, due to their unmet representation needs. In comparison, public sector employees are more receptive to, and actually demand, the welfare role of the unions. In this sector, employment relations remain relatively stable and are less frequently challenged by the market economy. There is plenty of scope for the unions to improve their (welfare) functions (Cooke 2008c).

More broadly, the welfare role of the unions should not be dismissed, as it reflects both the government's ideology of building harmonious employment relations and the traditional Chinese culture. Benevolent paternalism, collectivism and harmony are some of the key characteristics of the Chinese culture, which feature prominently in workplace relationships. The workplace plays an important role in providing social bonding activities to develop and maintain a harmonious relationship amongst employees and between the firm and its workforce. The provision of employee welfare and employee entertainment is traditionally seen by Chinese firms as an important ingredient to improve morale and commitment in the workforce, and to enhance the productivity of the firm (Cooke 2008c). Trade unions are instrumental in organising social events and providing the welfare role that is needed to improve the working and family life of employees. This role is particularly important when the HR function in the majority of Chinese organisations remains under-developed.

To some extent, the ideal form of employment relations promoted by the Chinese government, and one that is influenced by the traditional Chinese culture, bears a resemblance to the neo-pluralistic approach to contemporary employment relations promoted by industrial relations scholars in Western economies. It is an approach that emphasises social cohesion and stresses the importance of social values over individual interests, cooperation over conflict and trust over power (Ackers 2002). What is clear in the Chinese context is that the diversification of union constituency consequential of the marketising economy presents different opportunities as well as challenges to the trade unions. This requires them to adopt different roles and organising strategies at the grassroots level to address multiple issues if they are to maximise the utility of the unions.

A CHRONOLOGY OF CHINESE EMPLOYMENT RELATIONS

1949	The founding of Socialist China, ruled by the Chinese Communist Party.
1950	Enactment of the Trade Union Law.
1966–76	The period of the notorious Chinese Cultural Revolution, during which production activities were slowed down or stopped, with the national economy on the brink of paralysis.
1978	The beginning of China's 'open door' economic policy, which has led to the growth of FIEs and private firms with different employment policies from SOEs.
1992	Enactment of the Trade Union Law.
1992	The famous Southern Tour by Deng Xiaoping, the architect of China's market economy, during which he gave an important speech that endorsed the important role of private economy and entrepreneurship, leading to a rapid growth of the sector which has become a major employer.
1993	Enactment of the Enterprise Minimum Wage Regulation, setting the monthly minimum wage for full-time workers for the first time.
1994	The Ministry of Labour issued the Provisions on Collective Contracts, which provided details to the collective contract system outlined in the Labour Law of China.
1995	Enactment of the Labour Law of China—the first major piece of employment law in China.
1997	The beginning of the radical restructuring of SOEs, which has led to millions of workers being laid off.
2000	The Ministry of Labour and Social Security (MoLSS) issues the Collective Wage Consultation Trial Implementation Measures, requiring employers and workers (represented by management and unions) to collectively consult on issues related to wage payments.
2001	Enactment of the Trade Union Law (amended).
2001	China joins the WTO, which intensifies competition and puts pressure on Chinese firms to change their business and employment practices.

2003	Premier Wen Jiabao and President Hu Jintao take office, marking the beginning of the pursuit of an economic development policy that emphasises social justice, social harmony and environmental protection instead of the efficiency-driven economic development policy of their predecessors.
2003	Premier Wen Jiabao initiates a government-led campaign in an attempt to solve the delayed wage payment problem endemic in industries employing primarily rural migrant workers, especially in the construction industry.
2003	The ACFTU launches a drive to recruit rural migrant union members; it also leads the campaign to put pressure on FIEs to recognise trade unions in China.
2004	The MoLSS issues the Provisions on Collective Contract, which regulate the acts of conducting collective negotiations and the signing of collective contracts.
2007	A large number of firms in China, including large and well-performing firms across all ownership forms, dismiss their long-serving workers and rehire them under different contracts to avoid legal responsibility in anticipation of the forthcoming Labour Contract Law.
2008	Enactment of the Labour Contract Law, the Promotion of Employment Law and the Labour Dispute Mediation and Arbitration Law.

CHAPTER 13

Employment relations in India

C.S. Venkata Ratnam and Anil Verma

India's system of industrial relations has evolved from its origins in British India, going back to the growth of industry in the nineteenth century. The legal foundation for unions, collective bargaining and worker rights in general has its roots in British common law, although Indian developments set their own pace during most of the twentieth century. India is a large multi-party democracy with a diverse population in terms of ethnicity, language, religion and caste. These characteristics also influence its industrial relations system. Most unions are concentrated in large enterprises and in government-related sectors. A majority of India's workforce is rural, and employed in the so-called 'informal' sector (Agarwala 2008). Unions are scarce in both these spheres, resulting in an overall unionisation rate that is less than 5 per cent of the workforce. Yet unions and collective bargaining are important ingredients in any strategy for sustained economic growth.

Since the mid-1990s,[1] India has pursued a successful economic growth strategy based in large part on liberalising its once heavily regulated economy. In the ten-year period 1996–2005, India's economy grew an average of 6 per cent per annum and in the four-year period 2002–05, economic growth was an even more impressive 8.5 per cent per annum. Up until the early 1990s, India's economy experienced a rate of growth that was slow relative to other major countries. Economists often referred to the 'Hindu rate of growth' as a derisive term to describe the sluggish pace of India's economy during the first four decades after independence from Britain in 1947.[2] The anemic growth rate can partly be attributed to the lack of flexibility in the

330

labour market. Indian labour laws were among the most favourable to workers anywhere in the world. Employers faced severe restrictions on their ability to discipline or lay off workers, or to close a plant (World Bank 2007).

This chapter provides a description of the framework of the industrial relations system followed by an overview of adaptation to economic reforms of the 1990s. We describe the historical evolution of the context for industrial relations in consideration of the forces that have shaped the industrial relations system. We examine the interplay between industrial relations and the high economic growth achieved in the years since the economic reforms of the 1990s. Finally, we consider the challenges that the industrial relations system faces in contributing to future growth while ensuring fairness and equity for workers.

THE ACTORS

Trade unions in India

The trade union movement emerged some time between the 1850s and 1870s, coinciding with the emergence of early manufacturing in textiles, jute and light engineering. The All India Trade Union Congress (AITUC), established in October 1920, was the first national federation of trade unions. It comprised of diverse ideological persuasions aligned in a struggle against colonial rule and capitalists, both foreign and local. With the change in political context on the eve of independence in 1947, the movement split into three major federations.

The Indian National Trade Union Congress (INTUC) was established on 3 May 1947, with the active support and encouragement of the Indian National Congress whose political ideology of peaceful and non-violent reform was at odds with the revolutionist focus of the communists who dominated the AITUC. A year later, in 1948, a group identifying themselves as socialists also broke away from the AITUC to form the Hind Mazdoor Sabha (HMS). In the late 1960s, there was a split in the Congress, followed by similar splits within the communist and other political parties. After the general election in 1967, the dominance of the Congress Party ended with communist parties being elected to power in Kerala and West Bengal. As more regional parties emerged and took power in several states, each of these parties set up its own trade union wing, leading to a significant proliferation in the number of unions. Among the largest of these is the Centre of Indian Trade Unions (CITU), established in 1970 and aligned with the

Communist Party of India—Marxist (CPI-M or simply, CPM). Its power is particularly strong in West Bengal where the CPM has held power for many decades. Another large federation, the Bharatiya Mazdoor Sangh (BMS), formed in 1955, is unaffiliated with any party officially but is close to the Bharatiya Janata Party (BJP) in ideological terms.

By the mid-2000s, there were over a dozen federations of trade unions in the country, with the largest five enjoying a membership of over five million. In 1982, largely in response to the proliferation of labour federations, the Indian Labour Conference developed the criteria of membership in at least four states and four industries/sectors for a union federation to be considered nationally representative. Though the official number of registered unions was around 50000, the actual number may well exceed 100000 unions. Accurate and reliable estimates of the number of unions, their membership and their finances remain problematic because no government or non-government agency systematically collects these data.

The prevalent form is the 'union shop', where union membership is acquired after employment in an establishment where a union is recognised by the employer. The 'closed shop' system—much less common—prevails informally in wholesale markets and on railway stations among manual workers.

The Indian Constitution and freedom of association

Article 19(c) of the Constitution of India guarantees the right of association—that is, the right to belong or not belong to a union. It is not compulsory for a worker to join a union. Equally, it is unconstitutional to prevent a person who wants to join a union from doing so. Trade union registration is not compulsory, nor is trade union recognition. In practice, all registered trade unions have de facto, not *de jure*, recognition. It is up to the employer to 'recognise' a trade union either willingly or by being compelled to do so by the workers.

Until 2001, as few as seven workers could band together to form a trade union. To discourage the proliferation of unions, the *Trade Union Act* 1926 was amended in 2001 to require a larger membership for registering a union. The requirement was increased to 10 per cent of the establishment or 100, whichever is the lesser figure. However, the requirement for forming an unregistered trade union remains at seven people. There are currently no legal restrictions on the administrative unit and/or place where the workers are employed for the purpose of registering a union. The law is silent on whether unions can be formed along craft, employment category or other lines. It can be inferred from

Section 15 of the Act that trade unions do not just pursue economic interests, but are also oriented towards political, social and welfare objectives. Unions can raise and maintain political funds.

The nexus between trade unions and politics

One of the defining characteristics of the trade union movement is its close affiliation with political parties. In India, as in other developing countries under colonial rule, trade unions played a major role in the struggle against colonial rule. Some of those who led the freedom struggle also led the trade union movement, such as Mahatma Gandhi and Subhash Chandra Bose. As a result, political leadership in early twentieth century—particularly during the inter-war years—pursued the policies of a welfare state.

This association also resulted in the Indian Constitution emphasising 'justice, liberty, and equality for all', together with an activist role for the state in guaranteeing the same. In the mixed (public/private) economy after independence, the state pursued socialist objectives, assigning public sector enterprises a dominant role in attaining high economic growth. The policy was a mix of nationalisation of critical industries such as insurance, banking and mining combined with new investments in large-scale public enterprises.

Adapting to a nascent democracy, politicians needed the votes of the working classes, for which the political parties formed alliances with trade unions. For their part, trade unions felt that if they aligned with political parties—particularly the ruling party—they would be better able to defend their members' interests *vis-à-vis* management.

Although the alliance between trade unions and political parties has served their mutual interest in many ways, there have nonetheless been some negative consequences. First, trade unions became fragmented whenever there was fragmentation in the political parties. Within a state, for instance, INTUC was divided whenever there was a division within the ranks of the Congress Party. The communist union movement also became divided due to divisions within the party.

Second, trade union unity suffered due to political polarisation. In India, the public sector suffers most if the ruling party in a state is different from the one ruling at the centre. The state government machinery has often been used to take on the central public sector in an attempt to settle scores with the central government. This has been possible because in most cases, barring banks, insurance, atomic energy, space, petroleum, oil field, railways, mines/quarries, and so on, the state government is the appropriate authority for the enforcement of labour laws and for the maintenance of industrial relations and law and order. Not infrequently, industrial relations issues also become law and order problems. By delaying action or using discretion rather indiscreetly, governments at both central and state levels have enormous power to influence the dynamics at the local/enterprise/establishment level.

Third, in the context of liberalisation and globalisation, having their own party in power is becoming a liability for trade unions because political parties of all ideological hues tend to follow policies of wooing investors and encouraging cost-based competition, and workers bear the brunt of those neo-liberal policies.

National trade union centres

According to the criterion set by the government of India after consultation with the unions in India, any union with a minimum of 500 000 members spread over at least four industries and four states will be recognised as a national trade union centre. The following five unions currently fulfil this criterion:

- the All India Trade Union Congress (AITUC), affiliated to the Communist Party of India and World Federation of Trade Unions (WFTU)
- Bharatiya Mazdoor Sangh (BMS), with close links to the Rashtriya Swayamsevak Sangh and Bharatiya Janata Party, but not affiliated to any political party as such
- Hind Mazdoor Sabha (HMS), with avowed commitment to socialist philosophy and no formal affiliation with any political party. It is affiliated to the International Trade Union Confederation.
- the Centre of Indian Trade Unions (CITU), affiliated to the Marxist Party of India
- the Indian National Trade Union Congress (INTUC), affiliated to the Congress Party and the International Trade Union Confederation.

Besides the above five, there are at least seven other national-level unions with which the government holds consultations.

Enterprise-level unions

Enterprise-level trade unions are of two kinds: those affiliated to national centres and those without any affiliation to political parties. Sometimes unions may be independent but their leaders may owe allegiance to a political party. Some large organisations may have over a hundred trade unions, the Kolkata Municipal Corporation being an example at one point. Up until the economic reforms of the 1990s took shape, the Steel Authority of India Limited, a public sector enterprise, had over 220 trade unions. In the private sector, Hindustan Lever, the Unilever affiliate in India, had 220 unions at one stage.

Trade unions based on craft, occupational or employment category, and even caste, are not uncommon in India. Indian Airlines and the Indian Railways both deal with classic examples of craft unions. Within an enterprise, there can be separate unions for workers (on the shopfloor), staff (attendants, drivers, clerks, typists, etc.), supervisory staff and executives/officers. In some public sector enterprises, the policy of reserving jobs for certain castes has resulted in caste-based unions.

Management and employers' organisations

The principal umbrella organisations for Indian employers are the All India Organisation of Indian Employers (AIOE) and the Council of Indian Employers (CIE). Chambers of commerce, industry associations and representative organisations of the public sector are all members of these organisations.

The earliest employer associations (e.g. chambers of commerce and industry associations) were formed primarily in industries such as jute, textiles and engineering in response to a plethora of labour laws that were enacted after independence from British rule. Rapid growth of the public sector, including public sector enterprises, followed as a direct result of government policy. A representative organisation for the public sector, called the Standing Conference on Public Enterprises (SCOPE), was formed in 1970. During the Emergency (1975–77), the then Labour Minister, the late K.V. Raghunath Reddy, insisted upon separate representation for public sector employers, at both national and international levels.

Amalgamation of employer organisations

Before independence, employer associations were divided by indigenous versus foreign, large versus small, and to some extent by region. After independence, more employer associations were formed in the small and medium sectors and in various sectors that wanted to advocate their unique needs. With the proliferation of employer associations, the need for consolidation arose. After several initiatives and meetings, in 1956 a super structure called the Council of India Employers (CIE) was formed to bring the AIOE and the EFI together under one umbrella.

Council of Indian Employers

The main objective in setting up the CIE was to ensure closer cooperation and coordination between the two bodies, which together represent the interests of large-scale industry. SCOPE joined the CIE in 1973, making the CIE the dominant employer organisation. On behalf of these three organisations, the CIE submits representations to the government of India on labour policies if a common approach is desired by all its constituents. The CIE represents Indian employers at the International Council of Employers and at the International Labour Organization.

REPRESENTATION

Employers' organisations in India play two types of role in representing the interests of their members. First, they nominate representatives of employers in voluntary or statutory bodies set up not only to determine wages and conditions of employment of workers in a particular industry/sector, but also for consultation and cooperation on social and labour matters in the national and global context. Second, they seek to redress the grievances of employers against legislative or other measures by making submissions to the authorities concerned. They also represent the interests of employers in various committees/institutions, and various bipartite and tripartite fora on various issues such as legislation, voluntary codes, social security and bonuses at national and international levels.

Lastly, employer organisations serve as fora for information sharing, policy formulation and consensus building on issues of strategic importance. Apart from obvious issues such as economic growth and wealth creation, the social obligations of employers as responsible corporate citizens have assumed greater importance in recent times. In the years since economic liberalisation, the role of employers' organisations has come into sharper focus in areas of corporate governance, business ethics and social responsibility.

Non-union firms

Whereas unions were synonymous with large-scale enterprise—private or public—in the pre-economic reform years, it has been increasingly common since the 1990s to find establishments operating without any union presence at all. Few software companies in India have unions. Several units of large firms such as Reliance, Nirma, Samtel, Toyota and Volvo operate without unions, as do large number of greenfield manufacturing units of otherwise unionised companies such as SRS and Hero Honda.

There are a number of strategies that employers follow to avoid unions. Typically, non-union firms are greenfield sites with high capital investment and technology and lower labour intensity. Wages are set a little higher but productivity is high enough to give them a relatively lower unit labour cost. In some high-tech firms, the employer would also set benefits at a level higher than in other comparable enterprises. The demographic background of the workforce of such companies can be diverse enough that the workers' interests do not easily or readily converge. For example, many of these new establishments would employ fewer blue-collar workers and more white-collar and professional workers. It is generally the case that knowledge workers and professionals have less interest in forming unions.

In some firms, prospective candidates are asked whether they would be inclined to join a union. In other firms, a senior manager would ask new recruits to join efforts to avoid a union. Such tactics are not legal, but in practice it is hard for workers or unions to stop such employer activity.

Collective bargaining

Only about 2 per cent of the total workforce, but over 30 per cent of the workers in the formal (organised) sector, participates in collective bargaining (Venkata Ratnam 2006). This figure would be much higher (70 per cent or more) within the public sector and the largest public and private sector enterprises (Frenkel & Kuruvilla 2002; Kuruvilla & Hiers 2000). The legal framework encourages adjudication in case of disputes, with the government acting as Big Brother.

The historical context for industrial relations

At the time of independence, the British gave India and other South Asian countries a legal framework aimed primarily at dispute resolution. After independence in 1947, the Indian government adopted the Soviet model of planned economic development and sought to achieve a socialist society. In the mid-1950s, the Nehru government embarked upon heavy industrialisation, with the public sector in control of the developing economy. Industrial harmony was considered a necessary prerequisite for achieving plan targets.

Prime Minister Indira Gandhi nationalised several industries—banks, coal and textiles—in the early 1970s, ensuring that the major inputs and infrastructure sectors of the economy were firmly under government control. She pursued a policy of import substitution in response to the oil price shocks of the 1970s, while many other countries in Asia opened up their markets with export-oriented industrialisation strategies. During the Emergency, from 1975 to 1977, some of the key labour law amendments resulted in increased restrictions on the ability of employers to sack workers and close operations that were no longer viable. Prime Minister Ghandi also amended the Constitution during this period to provide for certain fundamental duties of citizens, along with workers' participation in management, as a directive principle of state policy.

Even before economic reforms started in 1991, the need for a comprehensive overhaul of labour laws and the industrial relations framework was considered several times. In fact, the government of India established two national commissions on labour to recommend comprehensive reforms to labour laws. The first was in 1966 with a mandate to secure better welfare and improve the conditions of labour. The second was in 1999 with a mandate to align labour laws with the requirements of a globalising economy and the complementary task of recommending umbrella-type legislation for unorganised labour.

Freedom of Association

Article 19(c) of the Constitution of India guarantees freedom of association as a fundamental right. This was recognised in the *Trade Unions Act* 1926, *Industrial Disputes Act* 1947 and *Industrial Employment (Standing Orders) Act* 1946. The right of collective bargaining is not extended to industrial workers in government undertakings, such as the railways, posts, telecommunications, and the Central Public Works Department. Compensation and other monetary benefits for these workers are based on recommendations of pay commissions appointed periodically by the government. The labour laws at the national level do not mandate employers to either recognise unions or engage in collective bargaining. However, some states (for instance, Andhra Pradesh, Bihar, Gujarat, Karnataka, Madhya Pradesh, Maharashtra, Orissa and West Bengal) have provisions concerning recognition of trade unions.

Although India ratified ILO Convention No. 11 concerning the Right of Association for Agricultural Workers in 1923, it has not ratified ILO Conventions Nos 87 and 98 due to 'technical difficulties' involving trade union rights for civil servants. Nath (1997) speculates that the government's intention may be to restrict freedom of association rights to only manual workers, and to exclude supervisory and managerial workers.

Determination of a collective bargaining agent

Identification of a collective bargaining agent has remained a hotly debated issue since 1931 when the Royal Commission on Labour argued for the need to recognise even those unions that have only minority support among workers. The 1947 amendment to the *Trade Unions Act* 1926, and the Trade Union Bill 1950 provided for recognition of more than one union by an employer, though neither piece of legislation was passed by the Parliament. In 1956, the Second Five-Year Plan stressed the importance of one union in one industry. The First National Commission on Labour (Government of India 1969) left the matter of union recognition to be decided on the basis of local circumstances. The Second National Commission on Labour (Government of India 2002) made specific recommendations, but these have yet to be incorporated into formal policy.

There is no law at the national level for recognition of trade unions. However, some states—for example, Maharashtra and Madhya Pradesh—have specified recognition procedures in the law. There are a number of ways to determine a representative union for the purposes of collective bargaining. These methods include (1) the Code of Discipline, which is common across most public sector undertakings; (2) the secret ballot, which is mandatory in three states—Andhra Pradesh (since 1975), Orissa (since 1994) and West Bengal (since 1998); (3) a check-off system, which is favoured by some unions; and (4) membership verification.

Collective agreements and disputes

An agreement with one trade union is not biding on members of other unions unless arrived at during joint conciliation proceedings. Other unions, including a minority union, can therefore raise an industrial dispute even if one union has an agreement with the employer. Under section 36(1) of the *Industrial Disputes Act* 1947, which deals with workers' representation, a collective agreement is binding on the workers who have negotiated and individually signed the settlement, but not on other workers who have not signed the agreement.

However, a *settlement* (a written agreement between employer

339

and workers) arrived at in the course of conciliation proceedings is binding under section 18(3) of the Act, not only on the actual parties to the industrial dispute but also on the heirs, successors or assignees of the employer on the one hand and all the workers in the establishment—present or future—on the other.

Under section 2(p) of the *Industrial Disputes Act*, collective agreements to settle disputes can be reached with or without recourse to the conciliation machinery established by legislation. If the parties fail to reach an agreement through conciliation, then the matter is referred for arbitration or adjudication; the *award* of the arbitrator or adjudicator is then binding on the parties concerned.

An 'award' can be an interim or a final determination of an industrial dispute by a Labour Court, Industrial Tribunal, National Industrial Tribunal or an arbitrator under section 10A. Awards are enforceable under section 33(c) by the Labour Court or 17(B) of the *Industrial Disputes Act* after the expiry of 30 days from the date of publication in the official gazette. If an award is not honoured by either of the parties, the party that is guilty of not honouring can be prosecuted under the *Industrial Disputes Act*. The penalty for not honouring an award could be six months' imprisonment or a fine. The powers under section 29 of the *Industrial Disputes Act* are not vested in Labour Courts or tribunals. When an award is received by the Assistant Labour Commissioner/Regional Labour Commissioner, the commissioner tries to ascertain whether the award was implemented by the parties, or whether it been modified or rejected by the relevant government in its proceedings under section 17A. In case of non-implementation, the Assistant Labour Commissioner or Regional Labour Commissioner can issue a *show cause* notice to the party at fault.

Although various worker organisations exist in the informal sector, collective bargaining is rare.

Unfair labour practices

The *Industrial Disputes Act* 1947 does not contain any stipulation that only a recognised union can raise an industrial dispute. In this matter, the Code of Discipline (1958) is at variance with the *Industrial Disputes Act*. In 1982, the *Industrial Disputes Act* was amended to include the following as unfair labour practices: (1) refusal by the employer to bargain collectively in good faith with recognised trade unions; (2) refusal by a recognised union to bargain collectively in good faith with the employer; and (c) workers and trade unions of workers indulging in coercive activities against certification of a bargaining representative.

Section 2(p) of the *Industrial Disputes Act* defines 'settlement' and section 29 makes the breach of any term of the settlement punishable with imprisonment for a term of six months or with fine or both. Refusal to bargain collectively, in good faith, with recognised trade unions is an unfair labour practice under section 2(ra)/Schedule V of the Act and is punishable under Section 25(u) with imprisonment for a term that may extend to six months or with a fine that may extend to Rs1000 or both.

Management's use of financial promises, threats or coercion to discourage workers from joining unions, although illegal, not only appears to be widespread but also frequently remains unchallenged and unprosecuted. It is not uncommon to find some employers increasing wages in response to a union organising drive or after negotiations fail to achieve a settlement.

LEVELS OF BARGAINING AND AGREEMENTS

National-level agreements

Prior to the 1970s, wage boards appointed periodically by the government were setting wages and working conditions in some industries. The number of wage boards declined from nineteen in the late 1960s to one (for journalists) in the late 1990s. From the early 1970s, sectoral bargaining at the national level was prevalent mainly in industries in which the government was the dominant player—for instance, banking and coal (approximately 700 000 workers each), as well as steel and ports, and docks (approximately 200 000 workers each). About 60 private, public and multinational banks are currently members of the Indian Banks' Association. They negotiate long-term settlements with the all-India federations of bank employees. In the coal sector, over 200 coking and non-coking mines across the country were nationalised in the early 1970s. However, only once has a national agreement been negotiated for the entire coal industry. In steel, the National Joint Consultative Committee for the Steel Industry (NJCS), a permanent bipartite committee for integrated steel mills in the public and private sectors, has signed six long-term settlements since 1969 when the committee was first set up. In the port sector, thirteen major ports have formed the Indian Ports' Association, which negotiates with major national trade unions.

In pay determination, civil servants' pay provides the benchmark for the rest of the public sector. In turn, public sector pay becomes the benchmark for unionised workers in the private sector, where collective bargaining tends to be more adversarial and contentious as both parties respond to domestic and international competitive pressures.

Firm/plant-level agreements

While employers generally prefer decentralised bargaining at the plant level, unions press for bargaining at higher levels. They feel that plant-level bargaining reduces their bargaining power, particularly during periods of crisis. For instance, at Escorts Limited, a large private sector manufacturing conglomerate with many different products, collective bargaining was conducted at the firm level up until 1990. Post-liberalisation, management pressed for and achieved decentralised bargaining at the plant level after taking on a 39-day strike. For management, decentralised bargaining was instrumental in basing pay and other working conditions on prevailing economic conditions within specific product markets rather than on some kind of average across all products.

Duration of agreements

Until the 1970s, the duration of collective agreements was usually two to three years. During the 1970s and 1980s, the duration increased to between three and four years. In the 1990s, over 80 per cent of central public sector agreements were signed for five years each. Since 1997, when the sixth round of public sector pay revisions began, the duration of public sector wage agreements has risen from five to ten years. The duration of most private sector collective agreements, however, continues to be three, or in rare cases four, years.

Collective bargaining in practice

In practice, most unions are highly politicised and the government wields enormous discretionary power without the commensurate responsibility. This leads to poor enforcement of the law and collective agreement provisions. Frequently, trade unions are co-opted into the collective bargaining process either by the government or by management. This leads to a crisis of confidence, particularly when unions find the going tough and are unable to meet the expectations of their 'members'. As a result, workers' commitment to any solidarity-based ideology diminishes and they become increasingly utilitarian and short-term in their orientation. They will not hesitate to shift their allegiance to another leader or union that promises more in less time. The disturbing reality is that workers can choose a union to represent them without belonging to it; workers can enjoy the benefits of collective bargaining as 'free riders' without joining a union or paying union dues; unions can have collective bargaining rights without workers' support; and it is possible to make deals with minority unions, thus undermining the majority unions.

THE ECONOMIC CONTEXT FOR REFORMS

With the end of the Cold War and the fall of the Berlin Wall in 1989, Fabian socialism and communism gave way to neo-classical economic policies. Economic growth came to be seen as a prerequisite for social progress and well-being. Governments in emerging economies began to woo investors, which in turn led to a lower priority being placed on labour protection. If, in the past, labour laws were enacted to protect the interests of workers, labour reforms became more focused on the needs of enterprises, such as high-quality, efficient production and costs benchmarked to competition.

India was a major economic force in the seventeenth century, before becoming a British colony. Under British rule, India developed many industries such as textiles, steel and engineering. However, in 1973 India closed its doors and followed import substitution policies at a time when East and Southeast Asian economies were opening their doors and embarking upon export-oriented strategies for economic growth. The information revolution in the 1980s afforded new opportunities to India for economic development.

Nearly two decades after the commencement of the economic reform process, India has achieved significant integration with the global economy. Overall, India has done quite well, even though the majority of Indians remain poor. By early 2009, India had achieved a four-year unprecedented average growth of nearly 8 per cent in GDP. Among the large emerging economies, the World Economic Forum's *Global Competitiveness Report* ranks India in 50th position in 2008 (43rd in 2006 and 45th in 2005) against China (30th), Brazil (64th) and Russia (51st).[3] The European Cities Monitor (ECM) survey reports that Delhi and Mumbai rank 5th and 13th among preferred worldwide destinations for future investment from Europe. It also points out that 30 per cent of Europe's leading companies (against 36 per cent for China) look to India as the favored destination for relocation.[4]

India is expected to reap a significant demographic dividend because the bulk of India's population, as of 2001, was in the 20–59 years age group (486 million), while those in the 5–19 years age group numbered 354 million. By 2020, the potential working age population in the 20–59 years age group is estimated to be over 761 million.

However, it is disconcerting that the quality and skill set of the working-age population may nevertheless be lacking. Forecasts based on National Sample Survey Organization (NSSO) data for the 1990s point out that 'over 233 million Indians will still not have access to formal sources of education or crossed primary school levels in 2020, compared to 198 million in 2005. Another 157 million or so will have managed to complete their primary levels.' (TeamLease Services 2006) Fortunately the Government realised the gravity of the situation and established National Skills Mission under the direct charge of the Prime Minister and provided huge funds for rapid expansion of vocational skills through public-private partnerships and increased the budget for education.

EMPLOYMENT

While a small proportion of workers are winners under the market system, a large majority is worse off—hence the need for a more interventionist labour policy. In India, inequality is measured in terms of expenditures as opposed to income. Based on the 61st round Consumer Expenditure Survey of the National Sample Survey and the size-distribution of persons from the 61st Employment and Unemployment Survey, Sundaram (2007) observes:

> The period between 2000 and 2005 saw a sharp acceleration in workforce growth, and, on the observe side, a slowdown in the rate of growth of labour productivity across most sectors and in the economy as a whole, and a slowdown (a decline) in real wage growth. Consistent with the trends in labour productivity and real wages, relative to the 1994–2000 period, the pace of poverty reduction between 2000 and 2005 shows, at best a marginal acceleration (or a marginal deceleration, depending on the choice of poverty lines) in rural India and a clear slowdown in urban India. The period also saw a small rise in the number of working poor and a substantial rise in the number of self-employed and regular wage/salary workers in the 'above poverty line' households. (2007: 3)

If one looks at potential sources of employment opportunities within the Indian economy over the next decade and a half, one must first focus on agriculture, which is already overpopulated—60 per cent of the population is dependent on a sector that provides barely 20 per cent of India's GDP. Farming is becoming less rewarding and needs a boost in productivity, which cannot come without reducing the number of persons employed per hectare. Many households will no longer be able to rely on agriculture over the next decade or more. In manufacturing, which has started growing again after a long period of decline, job growth will remain low and the potential of the organised sector to offer regular employment will continue to be slow. The incidence of contract and casual employment in many large factories is already over half to three-quarters of the total workforce. The public sector, which used to be the engine of growth before economic reforms commenced, now barely employs 5 or 6 per cent of the total workforce. With the growing incidence of workforce reductions through voluntary separations,[5] pressure for privatisation and/or performance improvement future jobs will be more in the private sector, including self-employment.

The services sector is seen as India's great white-collar hope, although the Deutsche Bank has warned that India needs a blue-collar revolution to reinvigorate its manufacturing sector.[6] The success of the much-hyped IT[7] sector has some sceptics pointing to the low value added by Indian software engineers. The gross revenue generated by an IT employee in India at US$35 000 is supposed to be at least nine times less than for their counterparts in Israel, and over fourteen times less than for their counterparts in Ireland.

The search for flexibility in the post-reform period

One of the defining features of industrial relations since the economic reforms of the 1990s has been a rising chorus of demands for increasing flexibility in the labour market (Badigannavar 2006; Hill 2009). Employers and public policy experts from national and international organisations have voiced concerns about sustaining economic growth if the labour market is not flexible enough to facilitate new technologies and production methods. The issue of flexibility cannot be addressed through a single policy measure. In the following sections, we describe some of the responses to this need for increased flexibility from the courts, state governments and the national government. These responses are not always coordinated but they are all aimed at the same need to increase flexibility while maintaining the standards of worker protection that have been developed in the years since independence. Of course, this is a tough balancing act, and in many instances protections are diluted so that some measure of flexibility can facilitate new investments and jobs.

Some modifications of labour protection have come from the need to balance labour rights with consumer rights. The *Consumer Protection Act* 1986 and the redressal forum created in it have given consumers rights that threaten to subordinate the rights of workers and their unions. Both consumer courts and civil courts have indicated that labour rights cannot always take precedence over other rights. For instance, the right of disgruntled workers to agitate cannot impinge on the liberty and freedom of citizens. Thus political protests that paralyse cities (called *bandh)* cannot be allowed if they interrupt or impede the normal civic activities of citizens. The right to collective bargaining was taken away from insurance workers in the early 1980s when it was found that the agreement between management and workers in Life Insurance Corporation (LIC) was prejudicial to the interests of policy-holders. In separate cases, telecom unions in Orissa and loading labourers (*mathadi* workers) in Mumbai were ordered to pay damages for causing losses to consumers. Courts are holding individual employees as well as unions or union leaders/activists responsible. In rare cases, courts have allowed employers to recover damages even from Provident Fund (social security fund) accounts.

In *Common Cause v Union of India and Others* (National Consumer Disputes Redressal Commission, New Delhi, 9 May 1996), Common Cause, an NGO, filed a case under the *Consumer Protection Act* 1986 seeking action against both Air India and the erring group of its staff members for disrupting a large number of flights due to a sudden strike by members of the Indian Flight Engineers' Association. Even though there is no contract between consumers and the association, the *Consumer Protection Act* holds service providers (including employees and trade unions) responsible for the hardship and loss to passengers. Section 18 of the *Trade Union Act* is not a bar to complaints against a trade union under the *Consumer Protection Act*.

The National Consumer Disputes Redressal Commission held that employees in an organisation that renders service for consideration are equally accountable under the provisions of the Consumer Protection Act, 1986 along with the management of the said organisation even though there was no contract between the person hiring/availing the service (consumer) and the concerned employees.

While the Commission did not inflict any punishment on the air-line or the association, and no compensation was awarded to the petitioner in this case, two significant observations were made in the judgment. First, the Commission stated that if labour action were illegal it would deal with them in a 'very strict manner' and that the Commission would 'have no hesitation to award proper compensation to the consumers who are thereby affected and aggrieved'. On the other hand, if the disruption in productive activity takes place in conformity with the provisions of the law governing industrial relations, then 'no proceedings under the *Consumer Protection Act* can be instituted against the employees or their Associations/Unions'. Second, the Commission directed that the airlines must warn the travelling public through public advertisements if a strike were imminent. This decision uses consumer rights to impose certain limits on labour's ability to disrupt operations.

There is also the issue of whether an employer can recover damages from the concerned employees' Provident Fund (or other assets). In *Bharat Kumar K. Palicha and Another v State of Kerala and Others* (Kerala High Court, 1997), the petition sought a declaration that the calling for and holding of a *bandh* (a city-wide general strike, including suspension of all traffic) was unconstitutional and hence illegal. The petitioners said that a *bandh* prevented citizens from commuting or working, often with the use of force, harassment or threats. It caused disruption to civic life (through stoppages of transportation, forced closure of shops/establishments, and so on), could lead to violence and violated Article 21 of the Constitution of India in that it impinged on personal liberty and could even be a threat to life.

In an earlier case (*Railway Board v Niranjan Singh*, 1996), the Supreme Court held that:

> the fact that the citizens of this country have freedom of speech, freedom to assemble peaceably and freedom to form associations or unions does not mean that they can exercise those freedoms in whatever place they please. The exercise of those freedoms will come to an end as soon as the right of someone else to hold his property intervenes. Such a limitation is inherent in the exercise of those rights.

In this case, the court held that 'the calling for a *bandh* by any association, organisation or political party and the enforcing of that call by it is illegal and unconstitutional. We direct the state and its officials, including the law enforcement agencies, to do all that is necessary to give effect to this.'

In the *Kerala Case*, the Kerala High Court held that:

this Court has sufficient jurisdiction to declare that the calling of a *bandh* and the holding of it is unconstitutional especially since, it is undoubted, that the holding of 'bandhs' is not in the interests of the Nation by leading to national loss of production . . . The State cannot shirk its responsibility of taking steps to recoup and of recouping the loss from the sponsors and organizers of such *bandhs*. We think that these aspects justify our intervention under Article 226 of the Constitution.

Some political parties have continued to call for *bandhs* in complete disregard of these court decisions. In response, courts have begun to levy heavy fines on some political parties. These developments have begun to curb illegal labour action; however, the system is not perfect in that not every illegal action is prosecuted and many of them a long time to process through the courts.

Even as some court decisions have put limits on labour action, other decisions have expanded labour rights or their enforcement in the spirit of balancing the interests of workers and employers. The most significant such court ruling occurred in 2006 when the Supreme Court of India, in Writ Petition (Civil) Number 465/1986, directed the government to remove and rehabilitate children working in hazardous occupations. Dasgupta (2008) documents several cases where courts responded favourably to requests filed as public interest litigation (PIL) for better enforcement of labour rights.

AGENDA FOR LABOUR LAW REFORM

As described in this chapter, the industrial relations system in India has evolved in response to globalisation, reforms and subsequent restructuring of industry and workplaces. Yet most observers agree that further changes and reforms in labour policy are necessary if India is to sustain the high growth rate necessary to pull large segments of society out of poverty (Gurtoo 2008). We briefly note below some of the most significant areas for reform.

- *Fewer laws with better enforcement.* It would be more expedient and equitable to have one labour code instead of numerous pieces of legislation, as China and Vietnam realised in the mid-1990s. A large number of laws does not necessarily lead to better protection for workers.
- *Elimination of multiple definitions across different legislations.* Wages, for instance, are defined in a dozen ways in various laws. The same is true of the definition of which workers are covered.

A unified Labour Code can cover all classes of workers rather than have variations in coverage across different laws.

* *Clear rules for termination of employment.* Workforce adjustment is essential if an economy is to create new jobs. Notice, consultation and compensation provisions can and should be tightened. The requirement of prior permission of the government needs to be removed in matters of layoffs, retrenchment and closure; Section 9-A, concerning notice of change, should be amended. Notice is required, consultation is to be encouraged, but the employer should have the right to make changes necessary to maintain and improve competitiveness.
* *Remove managerial functions from the scope of bargaining.* There should be no bargaining in respect of recruitment, transfer, promotion, work assignment and workforce adjustment.
* *Independent industrial relations dispute-settlement machinery.* This has been recommended by the National Commission on Labour for quite some time.
* *Skills development funds outside of direct government control.* A dynamic economy needs to upgrade its skills constantly and to retrain workers when technological change makes certain skills obsolete.
* *A tripartite national wages council.* The wage-setting process is far too episodic and bureaucratic. It needs to engage all parties in a dialogue to ensure continuity, responsiveness and accountability.

CONCLUSIONS

By and large, labour policy in India has addressed itself mostly to the 7 per cent of the labour force employed in the organised sector. Therefore, the challenges of industrial relations in India are quite unique and different from most other countries, including other developing nations. India has too many laws offering too little protection to too few who are mainly engaged in the formal/organised sector that accounts for barely 7 per cent of the labour force.

Given the pluralism in the Indian labour market, the government is faced with a paradox: how to moderate the 'excessive' (at least on paper) protection to 7 per cent of the organised labour force and enhance social protection for the remaining 93 per cent of the labour force engaged in the unorganised/informal sector? While India will have, for decades to come, demographic dividends in terms of a young workforce, a vast proportion of them need basic education, vocational skills training, health services and social security. Unless these needs are met adequately, the so-called demographic dividend could turn into demographic liability. Perhaps the most glaring weakness of the industrial relations system in India is 'its failure to include all workers' (Hill 2009).

Labour administrators in India have vast discretionary powers without commensurate accountability, training or infrastructure to handle them. There is a need for building a cadre of professionals in labour administration and the labour judiciary. There is also a need for greater awareness and understanding of alternative dispute-resolution procedures. The tripartite partners need to work together to promote arbitration. Towards this end, training and certification of arbitrators should be encouraged and mechanisms put in place on a scale commensurate with the needs. Alongside this, there is also a need to develop *labour lok adalats* (people's labour courts) whereby the labour adjudication process is expedited closer to the place of work and living of the affected parties without recourse to the vexatious time- and money-consuming legal procedures.

The government has not revived the special national tripartite mechanism it initiated at the time of launching the economic reforms in 1991 to work for a consensus on 'flexicurity', a tradeoff between flexibility and security. Compensation for affected workers in the form of income protection can be traded in exchange for relaxing labour laws to accommodate employer need for flexibility. Workplace industrial relations systems need to facilitate change, promote flexibility and prepare the workforce to be able, adaptive and responsive to the challenges of the changes.

A CHRONOLOGY OF INDIAN EMPLOYMENT RELATIONS

1885	The Indian National Congress (INC) is formed to give Indians a political voice.
1919	India is one of the 44 founder members of the ILO.
1920	The All India Trade Union Congress (AITUC) is formed, aligned with the Communist Party of India and affiliated with the World Federation of Trade Unions (WFTU).
1926	The *Trade Union Act* comes into effect to give unions legal recognition, but specifies no procedure for employer recognition.
1946	*Industrial Employment Standing Orders Act.*
1947	India gains independence from British rule.
1947	*Industrial Disputes Act.*
1947	The Indian National Trade Union Congress (INTUC) is formed, aligned with the Indian National Congress, affiliated with the ICFTU (now the International Trade Union Confederation, ITUC).
1948	Hind Mazdoor Sabha (HMS) is formed, aligned with the socialists and affiliated with the ICFTU (now ITUC).
1948	*Factories Act.*
1948	*Minimum Wages Act.*
1955	Bharatiya Mazdoor Sangh (BMS) is formed, unaffiliated with any international federation.
1956	Council of India Employers (CIE) formed by amalgamating the All India Organisation of Indian Employers (AIOE) and the Council of Indian Employers (CIE).
1965	*Payment of Bonus Act.*
1966	First National Commission on Labour is appointed (1966–69).
1970	Centre of Indian Trade Unions (CITU) formed, aligned with the Communist Party of India—Marxist (CPI-M).
1970	Standing Conference on Public Enterprises (SCOPE) formed to represent employers in public sector enterprises.
1976	*Bonded Labour Abolition Act.*

1986	The *Child Labour (Prohibition and Regulation) Act* prohibits employment of children under the age of 14 in hazardous work.
1991	Economic reforms introduced to begin deregulating the economy and to make it more open to international markets.
1996	Supreme Court of India, in Writ Petition (Civil) Number 465/1986, directs the government to remove and rehabilitate children working in hazardous occupations.
1999	The second National Commission on Labour is appointed (1999–2002).
2006	Government of India order to ban employment of children under the age of 14 in domestic work, restaurants, roadside tea stalls and the hotel industry.

Notes

Chapter 3   Employment relations in the United States

[1]   The authors thank Hoyt Wheeler for permission in this historical section to draw from material in the US chapter co-authored by him, which appeared in the prior edition of this volume.

Chapter 6   Employment relations in Italy

[1]   The above unionisation rates are solely based on union members affiliated to CGIL and CISL, and not also to UIL (due to a lack of data).
[2]   See the OECD database on Union Members and Employees in OECD.Stat (web access restricted).
[3]   The data are courtesy of IRES-CGIL.
[4]   Data available at <www.aranagenzia.it> (accessed 15 January 2009).
[5]   The official data on union density in the public sector presented in the previous sub-section are a result of this legal requirement.
[6]   Own calculations on data available at <www.aranagenzia.it> (accessed 15 January 2009).
[7]   This happened, for example, with the metalworking contract of 2001 and with the proposed 'Pact for Milan' in early 2000, which was signed only by CISL and UIL. This was a local-level concertation agreement aimed at allowing municipal authorities a more flexible use of fixed-term contracts in exchange for employment creation.
[8]   The concept of reducing inflation by predetermining wage increases was an old (and brilliant) idea of an Italian economist, Ezio Tarantelli (see Tarantelli 1986), who unfortunately paid with his life for this innovative idea as he was murdered by the Red Brigades in 1985.

Chapter 9   Employment relations in Denmark

[1]   The unemployment insurance funds and the unions have always been treated in the legislation as formally separate, but have never been perceived as such in practice, until recent years. To utilise the sociological paradigm of definition, one might say that when a situation is defined as real, it becomes real in its consequences (Ritzer 1977).

[2]   We should add that regulation via legislation has also been practised in such important areas as the working environment. This is partly because the first factory laws were enacted before the new labour market organisations were fully developed. But the labour market parties have also played a considerable role in the system via their participation in national councils and a special system of cooperation at enterprise level. The parties have also been involved in formulating the regular amendments to the legislation. The trend in recent years has been for the labour market parties to be accorded greater responsibility.

[3]   The expression 'yellow' trade unions is of French origin. Some of the first such alternative organisations were established in France in 1887, where they acted as strike-breakers. In the violent conflict that then arose, striking workers smashed windows in a building housing the strike-breakers, which were subsequently patched with yellow paper (Friis & Hegna 1974: 550–1).

Chapter 10   Employment relations in Japan

[1]   Because of the nature of the job, it sometimes has been difficult to distinguish one type of non-regular worker from another. In addition, different statistics have used different definitions of non-regular workers.

[2]   In Japan, the poverty rate is 15.3 per cent.

[3]   Performance in this context does not mean firm performance; rather, it means individual performance, which is assessed by managers.

Chapter 11   Employment relations in South Korea

[1]   The FKTU was formed in 1946 as the anti-communist union organisation, which was patronised by the right-wing political leaders to fight against the All-Korean Labour Union (AKLU), led by socialists at that time. The FKTU was a sub-partner to support the labour policy by the authoritarian regime until 1987.

[2]   The share of male members in total union membership has increased from 63.8 per cent in 1980 to 77.9 per cent in 2006.

[3]   Australian Prime Minister Hawke, who visited Korea in 1989, gave

President Tae-woo Roh advice about the social dialogue model and its achievements for forging labour–management cooperation and overcoming economic difficulties in Australia. President Roh was impressed with the tripartite approach, and sent government officials and research fellows to study the social dialogue model in Australia in early 1990.

4   The government expanded the coverage of the *Minimum Wage Act* to include all businesses from November 2000.

5   There has been a intense debate on the size of non-standard workforce, drawing upon the Economic Active Population-Supplementary Survey conducted by the National Statistics Office yearly since 2000. The labour circle has insisted that the number of people in the non-standard workforce has to include the workers under recurrent renewal of temporary employment contracts, who are excluded by the government's statistics. According to the labour circle's estimation, the workforce share of the non-standard workforce has consistently been around 55 per cent of the total working population.

6   Multiple unions were allowed for the national and industrial levels by the revision of the TULAA in 1997.

Chapter 12   Employment relations in China

1   For details of Chinese laws and regulations (including labour-related laws and regulations), see the China Law Database of Beijing University: <www.lawinfochina.com> (accessed 20 May 2010).

Chapter 13   Employment relations in India

1   Although reforms were first introduced in 1991, their effect on economic growth did not achieve a clearly identifiable new profile until a few years later. This lag can be attributed to the fact that reforms were introduced gradually over a number of years.

2   The Hindu rate of growth was described as roughly 3.5 per cent per annum by the late Raj Krishna of the Delhi School of Economics.

3   *Global Competitiveness Report 2008–09*, published by the World Economic Forum. These findings are in contrast to the dismal picture painted in the report, *Doing Business in India*, published annually by the International Finance Corporation (IFC), an arm of the World Bank. It ranked India 120th (2008) and 122nd (2009) out of 175 countries in terms of doing business (rankings available from <www.doingbusiness.org>. While the IFC study examines the government regulatory framework and infrastructure, it gives high marks to India for innovation, and for sophistication of firm

operations and adoption of technologies from abroad. The *Global Competitiveness Report* survey expresses concern about fiscal deficit and infrastructure, and notes that the benefits of economic growth need to be more broadly distributed.

4   The *Economic Times*, 2 October 2006.

5   For example, the Steel Authority of India reduced its workforce from 220 000 in 1986 to 130 000 in 2005; several private sector companies reduced their labour force to one-quarter, doubled wages and increased output by four times over the past two decades.

6   See *India Rising: A Medium-term Perspective India Special*, report by Deutsche Bank, available at <www.bankresearch.org>.

7   IT enabled services, business process outsourcing and knowledge process outsourcing included.

References

Abegglen, J.C. (1958) *The Japanese Factory: Aspects of its Social Organisation*. Glencoe, IL: The Free Press.

Abegglen, J.C. & Stalk, G. Jr (1985) *Kaisha: The Japanese Corporation*. New York: Basic Books.

ACAS (annually) *Annual Report*. London: Advisory, Conciliation and Arbitration Service, Her Majesty's Stationery Office.

—— (2008) *Annual Report and Accounts 2007/08*. <www.acas.org.uk> (Accessed 1 October 2008).

Australian Council of Trade Unions (ACTU) (2008) *Submission to the House Standing Committee on Employment and Workplace Relations: Inquiry into Pay Equity and Associated Issues Related to Increasing Female Participation in the Workforce* (27 October).

Accornero, A. (1976) 'Problemi del movimento sindacale in Italia: 1943–73', in *Annali Della Fondazione Giangiacomo Feltrinelli*. Milan: Feltrinelli, pp. 685–1013.

Ackers, P. (2002) 'Reframing employment relations: The case for neo-pluralism'. *Industrial Relations Journal*, 33(1): 2–19.

Ackers, P. & Payne, J. (1998) 'British trade unions and social partnership: Rhetoric, reality and strategy'. *International Journal of Human Resource Management*, 9: 529–50.

Adams, G. (1995) *Canadian Labour Law*, 2nd ed. Aurora, ON: Canada Law Book.

Adams, R.J. (1980) *Industrial Relations Systems in Europe and North America*. Hamilton, ON: McMaster University.

Adell, B., Grant, M. & Ponak, A. (2002) *Strikes in Essential Services*. Kingston, ON: Queen's University IRC Press.

Agarwala, R. (2008) 'Reshaping the social contract: Emerging relations between the state and informal labor in India'. *Theory and Society*, 37(4): 375–408.

Allen, M. (2004) 'The varieties of capitalism paradigm: Not enough variety?', *Socio-Economic Review*, 2: 87–108.

Almond, P. & Ferner, A. (eds) (2006) *American Multinationals in Europe: Managing Employment Relations Across National Borders*. Oxford: Oxford University Press.

Almond, P. & Tempel, A. (2006) 'Multinationals and national business systems: A "Power and Institutions Perspective"', in P. Almond & A. Ferner (eds), *American Multinationals in Europe: Managing Employment Relations Across National Borders*. Oxford: Oxford University Press, pp. 10–35.

Amable, B. (2003) *The Diversity of Modern Capitalism*. New York: Oxford University Press.

Ambruster-Sandoval, R. (2005) 'Workers of the world unite? The contemporary anti-sweatshop movement and the struggle for social justice in the Americas'. *Work and Occupations*, 32(4): 464–85.

Anderman, S. 1986. 'Unfair dismissal and redundancy', in R. Lewis (ed.), *Labour Law in Britain*. Oxford: Blackwell, pp. 415–47.

Andersen, S.K. (2001) *Mellem politik og marked. Interesseorganisering og lønregulering på de kommunale/regionale arbejdsmarkeder i EU*. Copenhagen: DJØF Publishing.

—— (2003) 'Danmark: Vejen mod en erga omnes model', in S.K. Andersen (ed.), *EU og det nordiske spil om lov og aftale. De nordiske lande og de europæiske aftaler/direktiver om deltid og tidsbegrænset ansættelse*, Stockholm: Institute for Working Life, pp. 41–72.

Andersen, S.K. & Mailand, M. (2005) 'Flexicurity of det danske arbejdsmarked—et review med fokus på overenskomstsystemet', in *Flexicurity—udfordringer for den danske model*. Copenhagen: Ministry of Employment.

Andolfatto, D. (ed.) (2007) *Les syndicats en France*. Paris: La Documentation Française.

Andolfatto, D. & Labbé, D. (2006) *Histoire des syndicats (1906–2006)*. Paris: Seuil.

Annual Reports of the Certification Office, London (1980–2000).

Aoki, M. (1988) *Information, Incentives and Bargaining in the Japanese Economy*. Cambridge: Cambridge University Press.

Appelbaum, E. (2008) 'Fairness at work pays off'. Paper presented at the University of Manchester Fairness at Work Research Group Launch, 22 October.

Appelbaum, E., Bailey, T., Berg, P. & Kalleberg, A. (2000) *Manufacturing Competitive Advantage: The Effects of High Performance Work Systems on Plant Performance and Company Outcomes*. New York: Cornell University Press.

Applebaum, E. & Batt, R. (1994) *The New American Workplace*. Ithaca, NY: ILR Press.

Arkless, D. (2007) 'The China talent paradox'. *China-Britain Business Review*, June: 14–15.

Armstrong, M. (2002). *Employee Reward*, 3rd ed. London: CIPD.

Arrowsmith, J. & Marginson, P. (2006) 'The European cross-border dimension to collective bargaining in multinational companies'. *European Journal of Industrial Relations* 12(3): 245–66.

Artus, I. (2001) *Krise des deutschen Tarifsystems: Die Erosion des Flächentarifvertrags in Ost und West*. Wiesbaden: Westdeutscher Verlag.

Asian Development Bank (ADB) (2005) *Asian Labour Market Indicators*. Manila: ADB.

Attali, J. (2008) *Rapport pour la libération de la croissance française*. Paris: La Documentation française.

Auer, P. (2008) 'Labour market institutions and the European social model in a globalizing world', in R. Rogowski (ed.), *The European Social Model and Transitional Labour Markets: Law and Policy*. Aldershot: Ashgate, pp. 323–50.

Auroux, J. (1981) *Report on the Right of Workers*. Paris: Ministère du Travail.

Australian Bureau of Statistics (ABSa) *Australian System of National Accounts* cat. no. 5204.0, Canberra: ABS (quarterly).

—— b *Labour Force Australia* cat. no. 6202.0, Canberra: ABS (quarterly).

——c *Employee Earnings, Benefits and Trade Union Membership Australia* cat. no. 6310.0 Canberra: ABS (quarterly).

—— d *Consumer Price Index* cat. no. 6401.0 Canberra: ABS (quarterly).

Badigannavar, V. (2006) 'Industrial Relations in India', in M. J. Morley, P. Gunnigle and D. G. Collings (eds), *Global Industrial Relations*, London: Routledge, 198–217.

Baccaro, L. (2001) 'Union Democracy Revisited: Decision-Making Procedures in the Italian Labour Movement', *Economic and Industrial Democracy*, 22, 183–210.

Baccaro, L. (2007) 'Political economy della concertazione sociale'. *Stato e Mercato*, 1: 47–77.

Baccaro, L., Carrieri, M. & Damiano, C. (2003) 'The resurgence of the Italian confederal unions: Will it last?' *European Journal of Industrial Relations*, 9: 43–59.

Baccaro, L. & Simoni, M. (2004) 'Il referendum sull'articolo 18 E gli interventi per la flessibilità del mercato del lavoro', in V. Della Sala & M. Fabbrini (eds), *Politica in Italia*. Bologna: Il MuliNo.

—— (2007) 'Centralized wage bargaining and the "Celtic Tiger" phenomenon'. *Industrial Relations*, 46: 426–55.

Bach, S., Bordogna, L., Della Rocca, G. & Winchester, D. (eds) (1999) *Public Service Employment Relations in Europe: Transformation, Modernization or Inertia*. London: Sage.

Bain, G.S. & Price, R.J. (1983) 'Union growth in Britain: Retrospect and prospect'. *British Journal of Industrial Relations* 11(1): 46–68.

Baird, M. & Charlesworth, S. (2007) 'After the baby: A qualitative study of working time arrangements following maternity leave'. *Labour and Industry*, 17(3): 97–118.

Bamber, G.J., Gittell, J.H., Kochan, T.A. & von Nordenflytch, A. (2009) *Up in the Air: How Airlines Can Improve Performance by Engaging their Employees*, Ithaca: Cornell University Press.

Bamber, G., Lansbury, R. & Wailes, N. (2004) 'Introduction', in G. Bamber, R. Lansbury & N. Wailes (eds.) *International and Comparative Employment Relations: Globalisation and the Developed Market Economies*, 4th ed. Sydney: Allen & Unwin, pp. 1–35.

Bamber, G., Ryan, S. & Wailes, N. (2004) 'Globalisation, employment relations and human resources indicators in ten developed market economies: International data sets'. *The International Journal of Human Resource Management*, 15(8): 1481–1516.

Bamber, G., Sheldon, P. & B. Gan (2010) 'Collective bargaining: Facing growing challenges', in R. Blanpain (ed), *Comparative Labour Law and Industrial Relations in Industrialized Market Economies*, 10th ed. The Netherlands: Kluwer Law International, (in press)

Barbash, J. (1967) *American Unions: Structure, Government and Politics*. New York: Random House.

Barbash, J. & Barbash, K. (eds) (1989) *Theories and Concepts in Comparative Industrial Relations*. Columbia, SC: University of South Carolina Press.

Barca, F. & Magnani, M. (1989) *L'industria tra capitale e lavoro: Piccole e grandi imprese dall'autunno caldo alla ristrutturazione*. Bologna: Il MuliNo.

Barrell, P. & Pain, N. (1997) 'The EU, an attractive investment', *New Economy* 4(1): pp. 50–54

Bean, R. (1994) *Comparative Industrial Relations: An Introduction to Cross-National Perspectives*, rev. ed. London: Routledge.

Beardsmore, R. (2006) 'Labour disputes in 2005'. *Labour Market Trends*, June: 174–90.

Beaumont, P.B. (1987) The *Decline of the Trade Union Organisation*. London: Croom Helm.

Beggs, J.J. & Chapman, B.J. (1987) 'Australian strike activity in an international context: 1964–1985'. *Journal of Industrial Relations*, 29(2): 137–49.

Bell, D. (1962) *The End of Ideology: On the Exhaustion of Political Ideas in the Fifties*. New York: The Free Press.

Bellmann, L., Kohaut, S. & Schnabel, C. (1999) 'Flächentarifverträge im Zeichen von Abwanderung und Widerspruch: Geltungsbereich, Einflußfaktoren und Öffnungstendenzen', in L. Bellman & V. Steiner (eds), *Panelanalysen zu Lohnstruktur, Qualifikation und Beschäftigungsdynamik*. Nürnberg: IAB, pp. 11–40.

Bennett, L. (1995) 'Bargaining away the rights of the weak: Non- union agreements in the federal jurisdiction', in P. Ronfeldt & R. McCallum (eds), *Enterprise Bargaining, Trade Unions and the Law*. Sydney: Federation Press.

Berger, S. (1996) 'Introduction', in S. Berger & R. Dore (eds), *National Diversity and Global Capitalism*. Ithaca, NY: Cornell University Press, pp. 1–27.

Bernstein, I. (1970) *The Turbulent Years*. Boston: Houghton Mifflin.

Berridge, J., Cooper, C.L. & Highley-Marchington, C. (1997) *Employee Assistance Programmes and Employee Counselling*. Chichester: John Wiley and Sons.

Bertelsmann-Stiftung & Hans-Böckler-Stiftung (1998) *Mitbestimmung und neue Unternehmenskulturen—Bilanzen und Perspektiven: Bericht der Kommission Mitbestimmung*. Gütersloh: Verlag Bertelsmann-Stiftung.

Betcherman, G., McMullen, K., Leckie, N. & Caren, C. (1994) *The Canadian Workplace in Transition*. Kingston, ON: IRC Press, Queen's University.

Bevort, A. (2008) 'De la position commune sur la représentativité au projet de loi: renouveau et continuité du modèle social français'. *Droit Social*, 7–8: 823–33.

Bevort, A. & Jobert, A. (2008) *Sociologie du travail: les relations professionnelles*. Paris: Armand Colin College University.

Biagi, M., Sacconi, M., Dell'Aringa, C., Forlani, N., Reboani, P. & Sestito, P. (2002) *White paper on the labour market in Italy, the quality of European industrial relations and changing industrial relations*. The Netherlands: Kluwer Law International.

Bishop, V., Korczynski, M. & Cohen, L. (2005) 'The invisibility of violence: Constructing violence out of the Job Centre workplace'. *Work, Employment and Society*, 19(3): 583–602.

Bispinck, R. & WSI-Tarifarchiv (2008) *Tarifhandbuch 2008*. Frankfurt: Bund-Verlag.

Blake, D. (2000) 'Two decades of pension reform in the UK'. *Employee Relations* 22(3): 223–45.

Blanchflower, D., Bryson, A. & Forth, J. (2007) 'Workplace industrial relations in Britain 1980–2004'. *Industrial Relations Journal*, 38(4): 285–302.

Blanden, J., Machin, S. & Van Reenen, J. (2006) 'Have unions turned the corner? New evidence on recent trends in union recognition in UK firms'. *British Journal of Industrial Relations*, 44(2): 169–90.

Blanpain, R. (2010) 'Comparativism in labour law and industrial relations', in R.Blanpain (ed), *Comparative Labour Law and Industrial Relations in Industrialized Market Economies*, 10th ed. The Netherlands: Kluwer Law International, pp.3–24.

Blau, F.D. & Kahn, Lawrence L.M.K. (1996) 'International differences in male wage inequality: Institutions versus market forces'. *Journal of Political Economy*, 106: 791–837.

Block, R.N., Friedman, S., Kaminski, M & Levin, A. (2006) 'An introduction to the current state of workers' rights' in R. N. Block, S. Friedman, M. Kaminski & A. Levin (eds), *Justice on the Job: Perspectives on the erosion of collective bargaining in the United States* W.E. Kalamazoo, Michigan: Upjohn Institute for Employment Research, pp. 1–17.

Bordogna, L. (1994) *Pluralismo Senza Mercato: Rappresentanza E Conflitto Nel Settore Pubblico*. Milan: Angeli.

—— (1997) 'Un decennio di contrattazione aziendale nell'industria'. In L. Bellardi & L. Bordogna (eds), *Relazioni Industriali E Contrattazione Aziendale. Continuita' E Riforma Nell'esperienza Italiana Recente*. Milano: Angeli.

—— (1999) 'Il fattore dimensionale nelle relazioni industriali e nella contrattazione collettiva in azienda', in F. Trau (ed.), *La 'Questione Dimensionale' Nell'industria Italiana*. Bologna: Il MuliNo, pp. 561–592.

Bordogna, L. & Provasi, G.C. (1989) 'La conflittualita', in G.P. Cella & T. Treu (eds), *Relazioni Industriali. Manuale Per L'analisi Dell'esperienza Italiana*. Bologna: Il MuliNom, pp. 275–306.

Bosch, G. & Weinkopf, C. (eds) (2008) *Low-wage work in Germany*. New York: Russell Sage Foundation.

Bray, M. & Walsh P. (1998). 'Different paths to neo-liberalism? Comparing Australia and New Zealand'. *Industrial Relations*, 37(3): 358–87.

Brewer, M., Goodman, A., Muriel, A. & Sibieta, L. (2007) *Poverty and Inequality in the UK: 2007*. London: Institute for Fiscal Studies.

Briggs, C. (2005) 'Lockout law in comparative perspective: Corporatism, pluralism and neo-liberalism'. *International Journal of Comparative Labour Law and Industrial Relations*, 21(3): 481–502.

Briggs, C. & Cooper, R. (2006) 'Between individualism and collect-ivism? Why employers choose non-union collective agreements', *Labour and Industry*, 17(2): 1–23.

Bronfenbrenner, K. (1997) 'The role of union strategies in NLRB certification elections'. *Industrial and Labor Relations Review*, 50: 195–212.

Brown, D. & Harrison, M.J. (1978). *A sociology of industrialisation: An introduction*. London: Macmillan.

Brown, D.J.M. & Beatty, D.M. (2005) *Canadian Labour Arbitration*. 5th ed (looseleaf). Agincourt, ON: Canada Law Book.

Brown, R. (2006) 'China's collective contract provisions: Can collective negotiations embody collective bargaining?' *Duke Journal of Comparative and International Law*, 16: 35–77.

Brox, H., Rüthers, B. & Henssler, M. (2007) *Arbeitsrecht*, 17th rev. ed. Stuttgart: Kohlhammer.

Bryson, A. (2004) 'Managerial responsiveness to union and non-union worker voice in Britain'. *Industrial Relations*, 1: 213–41.

Bryson, A. & Gomez, R. (2005) 'Why have workers stopped joining unions? The rise in never-membership in Britain'. *British Journal of Industrial Relations*, 43(1): 67–116.

Buchanan, J. & Briggs, C. (2002) 'Works councils and inequality at work in contemporary Australia', in P.J. Gollan & G. Patmore (eds), *Partnership at Work: The Challenge of Employee Democracy*. Sydney: Pluto Press, pp. 48–73.

Bureau of Economic Analysis (2008) 'Gross domestic product 2008: Second quarter 2008 (final)'. Media release, 26 September, <www.bea.gov/newsreleases/national/gdp/gdpnewsrelease.htm> (accessed 18 January 2010).

Bureau of Labor Statistics (2008a) 'Union members in 2007'. Media release, 25 January, www.bls.gov/news.release/union.nr0.htm (accessed 9 March 2010).

———(2008b) 'Labor force statistics from the current population survey: Civilian labor force for September 2008', <http://data.bls.gov/cgi-bin/surveymost?ln> (accessed 25 October 2008).

Bureau of National Affairs (2000) 'Kaiser, AFL-CIO detail contract hailed as model for health care sector'. *Daily Labor Report*, Washington, DC, 27 September, 188: A–6.

——— (2005) 'SEIU, IBT disaffiliate from AFL-CIO, announce plan to set up new federation', *Daily Labor Report*, Washington, DC, 26 July, 142: AA–1.

—— (2007) 'Groundbreaking UAW-GM contract receives 66 percent union membership approval vote', *Daily Labor Report*, Washington, DC, 11 October, 196: A–14.

—— (2008) 'High priority in Democrats' 2008 platform is "Good jobs with good pay and benefits"', *Daily Labor Report*, Washington, DC, 29 August, 168: A–7.

Burgess, J. & Campbell, I. (1998) 'Casual employment in Australia: Growth, characteristics, a bridge or a trap?'. *Economic and Labour Relations Review* 9 (1): 31–54.

Burns, P. (2001) 'A telling intervention'. *People Management*, 7(14): 30–3.

Calmfors, L. & Driffill, J. (1988) 'Bargaining structure, corporatism and macroeconomic performance'. *Economic Policy*, 6: 13–61.

Cammack, P. (1997) *Capitalism and Democracy in the Third World: The Doctrine for Political Development*. London: Leicester University Press.

Cappelli, P. (1985) 'Competitive pressures and labor relations in the airline industry'. *Industrial Relations*, 24: 316–38.

——(1999) *The New Deal at Work*. Boston: Harvard Business School Press.

Carlin, W. & Soskice, D. (2009) 'German economic performance: Disentangling the role of supply-side reforms, macroeconomic policy and coordinated economy institutions'. *Socio-Economic Review*, 7: 67–99.

Carrieri, M. (1985) 'Accordi non conclusi, accordi non efficaci, accordi non voluti', in Carrieri, M. and Perulli, P. (eds), *Il Teorema Sindacale*. Bologna: Il MuliNo.

—— (1995) *L'incerta Rappresentanza*. Bologna: Il MuliNo.

—— (1996) 'Le rsu nel sistema Italiano di relazioni Industriali'. *Lavoro e Diritto*, 1: 153–185.

—— (1997) *Seconda Repubblica: Senza Sindacati?* Rome: Ediesse.

—— (2008) *L'altalena Della Concertazione*. Rome: Donzelli.

Cella, G.P. (1976) 'Stabilita'e crisi del centralismo nell'organizzazione sindacale', in A. Accornero (ed.), *Problemi Del Movimento Sindacale in Italia 1943–76*. Milan: Feltrinelli, pp. 639–72.

Cella, G.P. & Treu, T. (1989) 'La contrattazione Collettiva', in G.P. Cella & T. Treu (eds), *Relazioni Industriali. Manuale Per L'analisi Dell'esperienza Italiana*. Bologna: Il MuliNo.

—— (2009) *Relazioni Industriali E Contrattazione Collettiva*. Milano: Il MuliNo.

Certification Officer (2008) *Annual Report of the Certification Officer 2007–2008*. London: Certification Office for Trade Unions and Employers' Associations.

—— (1980–2000) *Annual Reports*. London: Certification Office for Trade Unions and Employers' Associations.

Chan, A. (2001) *China's Workers Under Assault: The Exploitation of Labour in a Globalising Economy*. New York: M.E. Sharpe.

Chan, A. & Unger, J. (2008) 'Is China's core industry closer to the Japanese-German or the Anglo-American model? Management–employee relations at a Chinese state enterprise'. Paper presented at the international conference, Breaking Down Chinese Walls: The Changing Faces of Labor and Employment in China, Cornell University, Ithaca, NY, 26–28 September.

Charlesworth, S. & Campbell, I. (2008) 'Right to request legislation: Two new Australian models'. *Australian Journal of Labour Law*, 21(2): 116–36.

Chaykowski, R. & Verma, A. (1992) *Industrial Relations in Canadian Industry*. Toronto: Holt, Rhinehart and Winston.

Chen, F. (2003) 'Between the state and labour: The conflict of Chinese trade unions' double identity in market reform'. *China Quarterly* 176: 1006–28.

Chen, J.G., Lu, Z. & Wang, Y.Z. (2001) *China Social Security System Development Report*. Beijing: Social Science Document Publishing House.

China Labor News Translations (2008) 'Promising Wal-Mart trade union chair resigns over collective contract negotiations', <http://news.ifeng.com/opeinion/200807/0729> (Accessed 24 September 2008).

China Labour Bulletin (2005) 'ACFTU unit stunned as Siemens China sacks sales force', <www.china-labour.org.hk/public/contents/articles> (Accessed 13 November 2005).

China Labour Statistical Yearbook 2002, 2006 & 2007. Beijing: China Statistics Press.

China Statistical Yearbook 2003 & 2007. Beijing: China Statistics Press.

Clark, I. & Almond, P. (2006) 'Overview of the US Business System', in P. Almond & A. Ferner (eds), *American Multinationals in Europe—Managing Employment Relations Across National Borders*. London: Oxford University Press, pp. 37–56.

Clark, T., Gospel, H. & Montgomery, J. (1999) 'Running on the spot? A review of twenty years of research on the management of human resources in comparative and international perspective'. *International Journal of Human Resource Management*, 10(3): 520–44.

Clarke, S. (2005) 'Post-socialist trade unions: China and Russia'. *Industrial Relations Journal* 36(1): 2–18.

Clarke, S., Lee, C. & Li, Q. (2004) 'Collective consultation and industrial relations in China'. *British Journal of Industrial Relations* 42(2): 235–54.

Claydon, T. (1989) 'Union derecognition in Britain in the 1980s'. *British Journal of Industrial Relations* 27(2): 214–24.

—— (1998) 'Problematising partnership', in P. Sparrow & M. Marchington (eds), *Human Resource Management: The New Agenda*. London: Financial Times/Pitman, pp. 180–92.

CNEL (2007) *Lineamenti Della Contrattazione Aziendale Nel Periodo 1998–2006*. Rome: CNEL.

Cochrane, J.L. (1976) 'Industrialism and industrial man in retrospect: A preliminary analysis', in J.L. Stern & B.D. Dennis (eds), *Proceedings of the Twenty-ninth Annual Winter Meetings, Industrial Relations Research Association Series*. Madison, WI: IRRA, pp. 274–87.

Cole, R.E. (1971) *Japanese Blue Collar:The Changing Tradition*. Berkeley, CA: University of California Press.

Colling, T. (1997) 'Managing human resources in the public sector', in I. Beardwell & L. Holden (eds), *Human Resource Management*, 2nd ed., London: Pitman, pp. 654–80.

—— (2000) 'Personnel management in the extended organisation', in S. Bach & K. Sisson (eds), *Personnel Management: A Comprehensive Guide to Theory and Practice*. Oxford: Blackwell, pp. 70–90.

Colvin, A.J.S. (2006) 'Flexibility and fairness in liberal market economies: The comparative impact of the legal environment and high performance work systems'. *British Journal of Industrial Relations*, 44: 73–97.

—— (2007) 'Empirical research on employment arbitration: Clarity amidst the sound and fury?' *Employee Rights and Employment Policy Journal*, 11: 405–47.

Combet, G. (2003) 'Employee consultation in the Australian context', in P. Gollan & G. Patmore (eds), *Partnership at Work: The Challenge of Employee Democracy*. Sydney: Pluto Press, pp. 134–9.

Commons, J.R. (1909) 'American shoemakers'. *Quarterly Journal of Economics*, 24: 39–81.

Cooke, F.L. (2002) 'Ownership change and the reshaping of employment relations in China: A study of two manufacturing companies', *Journal of Industrial Relations* 44(1): 19–39.

—— (2005) *HRM, Work and Employment in China*. London: Routledge.

—— (2008a) 'The dynamics of employment relations in China: An evaluation of the rising level of labour disputes'. *Journal of Industrial Relations* 50(1): 111–38.

—— (2008b) 'Labour market regulations and informal employment in China: To what extent are workers protected?' Paper presented in Annual China Task Force Meeting, 25–27 June, University of Manchester, UK.

—— (2008c) 'Are Chinese women workers protected? A study of female workers' representational needs and forms and effects of (un)organizing'. Paper presented at international conference, Breaking Down Chinese Walls: The Changing Faces of Labor and Employment in China, Cornell University, Ithaca, NY, 26–28 September.

Cooney, S. (2007) 'China's labour law, compliance and flaws in implementing institutions'. *Journal of Industrial Relations* 49(5): 673–86.

Cooper, R. (2000) 'Organise, organise, organise! The 2000 ACTU Congress'. *Journal of Industrial Relations* 42(4): 582–94.

—— (2002) 'Trade unionism in 2001'. *Journal of Industrial Relations*, 44(2): 247–62.

Cooper, R. & Ellem, B. (2008) 'The neoliberal state, trade unions and collective bargaining in Australia'. *British Journal of Industrial Relations*, 46(3): 532–54.

Coupar, W. & Stevens, B. (1998) 'Towards a new model of industrial partnership: Beyond the "HRM versus industrial relations" argument', in P. Sparrow & M. Marchington (eds), *Human Resource Management: The New Agenda*. London: Financial Times/Pitman, pp. 145–59.

Cox, A., Zagelmeyer, S. & Marchington, M. (2006) 'Embedding employee involvement and participation at work'. *Human Resource Management Journal*, 16(3): 250–67.

Coyle-Shapiro, J., Morrow, P. & Kessler, I. (2006) 'Serving two organizations: Exploring the employment relationship of contracted employees'. *Human Resource Management*, 45(4): 561–83.

Crouch, C. (1993) *Industrial Relations and European State Traditions*. Oxford: Clarendon Press.

—— (2005) *Capitalist Diversity and Change: Recombinant governance and institutional entrepreneurs*. Oxford: Oxford University Press.

Crouch, C. & Pizzorno, A. (eds) (1978) *The Resurgence of Class Conflict in Western Europe Since 1968*. New York: Holmes & Meier.

Cully, M., Woodland, S., O'Reilly, A. & Dix, G. (1999) *Britain at Work: As Depicted by the 1998 Workplace Employee Relations Survey*. London: Routledge.

DA (1998) *Arbejdsmarkedsrapport 1998*. Copenhagen: Dansk Arbejdsgiverforening.

—— (2007). *Arbejdsmarkedsrapport 2007*. Copenhagen: Dansk Arbejdsgiverforening.

—— (2008) *Arbejdsmarkedsrapport 2008*. Copenhagen: Dansk Arbejdsgiverforening.

DARES Research Institute of the French Ministry of Labor (2006) *'Premières synthèses'*. L'individualisation des hausses de salaire de base, Ministère de l'emploi, de la cohésion sociale et du logement, mars, n° 09.1.

—— (2007) *'Premières synthèses'*, Des conflits du travail plus nombreux et plus diversifiés, Ministère de l'emploi, de la cohésion sociale et du logement, février, n° 08.1.

—— (2008) *'Premières synthèses'*, Les élections aux comités d'entreprise en 2005–2006 Ministère de l'emploi, de la cohésion sociale et du logement, octobre, n° 40.3.

Dasgupta, M. (2008) 'Public interest litigation for labour: How the Indian Supreme Court protects the rights of India's most disadvantaged workers'. *Contemporary South Asia*, 16(2): 159.

Davies, P. & Kilpatrick, C. (2004) 'UK worker representation after single channel'. *Industrial Law Journal*, 33(2): 121–51.

Deakin, S. & Morris, G.S. (2005) *Labour Law*, 4th ed., Oxford: Hart.

Debroy, B. (1997) 'Labour market reform'. Policy Paper No. 22 prepared for *Project LARGE (Legal Adjustments and Reforms for Globalizing the Economy)*. New Delhi: Allied Publishers.

Deeg, R. & Jackson, G. (2007) 'Towards a more dynamic theory of capitalist diversity'. *Socio-Economic Review*, 5(1): 149–79.

Dell'Aringa, C., Della Rocca, G. & Keller, B. (eds) (2001) *Strategic Choices in Reforming Public Service Employment*. London: Macmillan.

Denis, J.-M. (ed.) (2005) *Le conflit en greve: Tendances et perspectives de la conflictualité contemporaine*. Paris: La Dispute.

Department of Trade and Industry (DTI) (1998) *Fairness at Work*, Cmnd 3968. London: HMSO.

—— (2007) *Success at Work: Consultation on Measures to Protect Vulnerable Agency Workers*. London: HMSO.

Dickens, L. (2000) 'Doing more with less: ACAS and individual conciliation', in B. Towers & W. Brown (eds), *Employment Relations in Britain: 25 Years of the Advisory, Conciliation and Arbitration Service*. Oxford: Blackwell, pp. 67–92.

Dickens, L. & Hall, M. (2006) 'Fairness—up to a point: Assessing the impact of New Labour's employment legislation'. *Human Resource Management Journal*, 16(4): 338–56.

Dilger, A. (2002) *Ökonomik betrieblicher Mitbestimmung. Die wirtschaftlichen Folgen von Betriebsräten*. München: Hampp.

Dix, G. (2000) 'Operating with style: The work of the ACAS conciliator in individual employment rights cases', in B. Towers & W. Brown (eds), *Employment Relations in Britain: 25 years of the Advisory, Conciliation and Arbitration Service*. Oxford: Blackwell, pp. 93–122.

Doellgast, V. (2008) 'National industrial relations and local bargaining power in the US and German telecommunications industries'. *European Journal of Industrial Relations*, 14(3): 265–87

Doeringer, P.B. (1981) 'Industrial relations research in international perspective', in P.B. Doeringer, P. Gourevitch, P. Lange & A. Martin (eds), *Industrial Relations in International Perspective: Essays on Research and Policy*. London: Macmillan, pp.1–21.

Doeringer, P. & Piore, M. (1971) *Internal Labor Markets and Manpower Analysis*. Lexington, MA: D.C. Heath.

Dølvik, J.-E. & Waddington, J. (2005) 'Can trade unions meet the challenge? Unionisation in the marketised services', in G. Bosch & S. Lehndorff (eds), *Working in the Service Sector*. London: Routledge, pp. 316–41.

Donovan, T.N. (1968) *Royal Commission on Trade Unions and Employers' Associations: Report*, Cmnd 3623. London: Her Majesty's Stationery Office.

Dore, R. (1973) *British Factory, Japanese Factory: The Origins of National Diversity in Industrial Relations*. London: Allen & Unwin.

—— (1987) *Taking Japan Seriously*. Stanford, CA: Stanford University Press.

Drache, D. & Glasbeeck, H. (1992) *The Changing Workplace: Reshaping Canada's Industrial Relations System*. Toronto: James Lorimer.

Dreyfus, M. (1995) *Histoire de la CGT*. Bruxelles: Editions complexes.

Dreyfus, M., Gautron, G. & Pigenet, M. (eds) (2003) *La naissance de FO: Autour de Robert Bothereau*. Rennes: Presses Universitaires de Rennes.

Duclos, L. & Mériaux, O. (2001) 'Autonomie contractuelle et démocratie sociale: Les implicites de la refondation'. In *Regards sur l'actualité*. Paris: La Documentation française, janvier, pp. 19–33.

Due, J. & Madsen, J.S. (2003) *Fra magtkamp til konsensus. Arbejdsmarkedspensionerne og den danske model*. Copenhagen: DJØF Publishing.

—— (2005) 'Denmark: The survival of small trade unions in the context of centralised bargaining', in J. Waddington (ed.), *Restructuring Representation: The Merger Process and Trade Union Structural Development in Ten Countries*. Bruxelles: PIE/Peter Lang, pp. 87–112.

—— (2006). *Fra storkonflikt til barselsfond. Den danske model under afvikling eller fornyelse*. Copenhagen: DJØF Publishing.

—— (2008a) 'The Danish model of industrial relations: Erosion or renewal'. *Journal of Industrial Relations*, 50: 513–29.

—— (2008b). *OK 2007 og OK 2008—Perspektiver og konsekvenser.* FAOS' Forskningsnotat 100. København: FAOS, Sociologisk Institut, Københavns Universitet.

Due, J., Madsen, J.S. & Strøby Jensen, C. (1993). *Den danske Model. En historisk sociologisk analyse af det kollektive aftalesystem.* Copenhagen: DJØF Publishing.

Due, J., Madsen, J.S., Strøby Jensen, C. & Petersen, L.K. (1994) *The Survival of the Danish Model: A Historical Sociological Analysis of the Danish System of Collective Bargaining.* Copenhagen: DJØF Publishing.

Dunlop, J.T. (1958) *Industrial Relations Systems.* New York: Henry Holt and Company.

Dunlop, J.T. et al. (1994) *The Dunlop Commission on the Future of Worker-Management Relations: Final Report.* Washington DC: US Department of Labor: <www.ilr.cornell.edu/library/e_archive/> (accessed 20 May 2010).

Dustmann, C. & Weiss, Y. (2007) 'Return migration: Theory and empirical evidence from the UK'. *British Journal of Industrial Relations*, 45(2): 236–56.

Earnshaw, J. & Cooper, C.L. (1996) *Stress and Employer Liability.* London: Institute of Personnel and Development.

Eaton, J. (2000) *Comparative Employment Relations: An Introduction.* Oxford: Polity Press.

Ebbinghaus, B. (2003a) 'Die Mitgliederentwicklung deutscher Gewerkschaften im historischen und internationalen Vergleich', in W. Schroeder & B. Wessels (eds), *Die Gewerkschaften in Politik und Gesellschaft der Bundesrepublik Deutschland. Ein Handbuch.* Wiesbaden: Westdeutscher Verlag, pp. 174–203.

Ebbinghaus, B. (2003b) 'Ever larger unions: Organisational restructuring and its impact on union confederations' industrial relations'. *Industrial Relations Journal*, 34: 446–60.

Ebbinghaus, B. & Visser, J. (2000) *Trade Unions in Western Europe Since 1945.* London: Macmillan.

Economic Report of the President (2001) Washington DC: US Government Printing Office.

Edwards, P. (1995) 'Strikes and industrial conflict', in P. Edwards (ed.), *Industrial Relations: Theory and Practice in Britain.* Oxford: Blackwell.

Edwards, P. & Ram, M. (2006) 'Surviving on the margins of the economy: Working relationships in small, low-wage firms'. *Journal of Management Studies*, 43(4): 895–916.

Edwards, T., Almond, P., Clark, I., Colling, T. & Ferner, A. (2005) 'Reverse diffusion in US multinationals: Barriers from the American business system'. *Journal of Management Studies*, 42(6): 1261–86.

Edwards, T., Colling, T. & Ferner, A. (2007) 'Conceptual approaches to the transfer of employment practices in multinational companies: An integrated approach'. *Human Resource Management Journal* 17(3): 201–17.

Egels-Zandén, N. (2008) 'TNC motives for signing international framework agreements: A continuous bargaining model of stakeholder pressure'. *Journal of Business Ethics*, 84: 529–47.

Egels-Zandén, N. & Hyllman, P. (2007) 'Evaluating strategies for negotiating workers' rights in transnational corporations: The effects of codes of conduct and global agreements on workplace democracy'. *Journal of Business Ethics*, 76: 207–23.

Ehrenstein, I. (2007) 'Mitbestimmte Unternehmen 2006'. *Die Mitbestimmung*, 53: 70.

Elgar, J. & Simpson, B. (1993) 'The impact of the law on industrial disputes in the 1980s', in D. Metcalf & S. Milner (eds), *New Perspectives in Industrial Relations*. London: Routledge, pp. 70–114.

Ellem, B. (2001) 'Trade unionism in 2000'. *Journal of Industrial Relations*, 43(2): 196–218.

Ellguth, P. & Kohaut, S. (2007) 'Tarifbindung und betriebliche Interessenvertretung: Aktuelle Ergebnisse aus dem IAB-Betriebspanel 2006'. *WSI-Mitteilungen*, 60: 511–14.

Elvander, N. (2002) 'The new Swedish regime for collective bargaining and conflict resolution: A comparative perspective'. *European Journal of Industrial Relations*, 8(2): 197–216.

Engerman, S. (2003) 'The history and political economy of international labour standards', in K. Basu, H. Horn, L. Roman & J. Shapiro (eds), *International Labour Standards: History Theory, Policy Options*. London: Blackwell, pp. 9–45.

Equal Opportunities Commission (2001) *Just Pay: Report of the Equal Pay Task Force*. Manchester: EOC.

Equal Opportunity for Women in the Workplace Agency EOWA (2008) *EOWA Survey on Workplace Flexibility*, Sydney.

Erickson, C.L. (1992) 'Wage rule formation in the aerospace industry'. *Industrial and Labor Relations Review*, 45: 507–22.

—— (1996) 'A re-interpretation of pattern bargaining'. *Industrial and Labor Relations Review*, 49: 615–34.

Esping-Andersen, G. & Regini, M. (2000) 'The dilemmas of labor market regulation', in G. Esping-Andersen & M. Regini (eds), *Why Deregulate Labor Markets?* Oxford: Oxford University Press, pp. 11–29.

Estevez-Abe, M. (2006) 'Gendering the varieties of capitalism: A study of occupational segregation by sex in advanced industrial societies'. *World Politics*, 59(1): 142–75.

European Industrial Relations Observatory (EIRO) (2008) *Developments in industrial action 2003–2007*. Dublin: European Foundation for the Improvement of Living and Working Conditions.

Evans, P. (1997) 'The eclipse of the state? Reflections on stateness in an era of globalisation'. *World Politics* 50(1): 62–87.

Ewing, K., Moore, S. & Wood, S. (2003) *Unfair Labour Practices: Trade Union Recognition and Employer Resistance*. London: Institute of Employment Rights.

Faini, R. & Sapir, A. (2005) 'Un modello obsoleto? Crescita e specializzazione dell'economia Italiana', in T. Boeri, R. Faini, A. Ichino, G. Pisauro & C. Scarpa (eds), *Oltre Il Declino*. Bologna: Il Mulino, pp. 19–65.

Fairbrother, P. (2002) 'Unions in Britain: Towards a new unionism?' in P. Fairbrother, & G. Griffin (eds.), *Changing Prospects for Trade Unionism: Comparisons Between Six Countries*. London: Continuum.

Fajertag, G. & Pochet, P. (eds) (1997) *Social Pacts in Europe*. Brussels: ETUI.

—— (2000) *Social Pacts in Europe—New Dynamics*. Brussels: ETUC.

Farber, H.S. (1998) 'Has the rate of job loss increased in the nineties?' unpublished working paper, Industrial Relations Section, Princeton University.

Farrell, D. & Grant, A. (2005) 'China's looming talent shortage'. *The McKinsey Quarterly*, 4, <www.mckinseyquarterly.com/article_page.aspx?ar=1685> (Accessed 3 March 2007).

Ferner, A. (1997) 'Country of origin effects and HRM in multinational companies'. *Human Resource Management Journal*, 7(1): 19–37.

Ferner, A. & Hyman, R. (1998) 'Introduction: Towards European industrial relations?' in A. Ferner & R. Hyman (eds), *Changing Industrial Relations in Europe*, 2nd ed. Oxford: Blackwell, pp. xi–xxvi.

Ferner, A. & Quintanilla, J. (1998) 'Multinationals, national business systems and HRM: The enduring influence of national identity or a process of "Anglo-Saxonisation"?' *International Journal of Human Resource Management*, 9(7): 10–31.

Ferner, A., Quintanilla, J. & Varul, M. (2001) 'Country of origin effects, host country effects and the management of HR in multinationals: German companies in Britain and Spain'. *Journal of World Business*, 36(2): 107–27.

Feuille, P. & Wheeler, H.N. (1981) 'Will the real industrial conflict please stand up?' in J. Stieber, R.B. McKersie & D.Q. Mills (eds), *US Industrial Relations 1950–1080: A Critical Assessment*, Madison WI: IRRA, pp. 255–95.

Finkelman, J. & Goldenberg, S. (1983) *Collective Bargaining in the Public Service: The Federal Experience in Canada*, 2 vols. Montreal: Institute for Research on Public Policy.

Fleisher, B. & Yang, D. (2003) 'Labour laws and regulations in China'. *China Economic Review*, 14: 426–33.

Foner, P.S. (1947) *History of the Labor Movement in the United States Vol. 1*. New York: International Publishers.

Förster, M. & d'Ercole, M.M. (2005) *Income Distribution and Poverty in OECD Countries in the Second Half of the 1990s*. Paris: OECD.

Fox, A. (1985) *History and Heritage: The Social Origins of the British Industrial Relations System* London: Allen & Unwin.

Francis, H. & Keegan, A. (2006) 'The changing face of HRM: In search of balance'. *Human Resource Management Journal*, 16(3): 231–49.

Franzese, R. & Hall, P. (2000) 'Institutional dimensions of coordinating wage bargaining and monetary policy', in T. Iversen, J. Pontusson & D. Soskice (eds), *Unions, Employers and Central Banks: Macro-Economic Coordination and Institutional Change in Social Market Economies*. New York: Cambridge University Press, pp. 173–204.

Freeman, R.B. (1989) *On the Divergence in Unionism Among Developed Countries*. Discussion Paper No. 2817. Cambridge MA. National Bureau of Economic Research.

—— (2008) 'Labour market institutions around the world', in P. Blyton, N. Bacon, J. Foirito & E. Heery (eds), *Sage Handbook of Industrial Relations*. London: Sage, pp. 640–58.

Frege, C. & Kelly, J. (eds) (2004) *Varieties of Unionism: Strategies for Union Revitalisation in a Globalising Economy*, Oxford: Oxford University Press.

Frenkel, S. & Kuruvilla, S. (2002) 'Logics of action, globalization, and the changing employment relations in China, India, Malaysia and the Philippines'. *Industrial & Labor Relations Review* 55(3): 387–512.

Freyssinet, J. (ed.) (2006) *Travail et emploi en France, état des lieux et perspectives*. Paris: La Documentation française.

Frick, B. (ed.) (2003) 'Symposium "The economics of mandated code-termination"'. *Schmollers Jahrbuch*, 123: 337–454.

Frick, B., Kluge, N. & Streeck, W. (eds) (1999) *Die wirtschaftlichen Folgen der Mitbestimmung. Expertenberichte für die Kommission Mitbestimmung*. Frankfurt: Campus.

Friis, J. & Hegna, T. (eds) (1974) *Arbeidernes Leksikon*. Oslo: Pax.

Fukao.T. (2002) "Chokusetsu Tohshi to Koyo no Kudoka" (Foreign Direct Investment and Hollowing of Employment) The Japanese Journal of Labor Studies 44, (4), April. pp.34–37.

Galenson, W. (1952) *The Danish System of Labor Relations: A Study of Industrial Peace*. Cambridge, MA: Harvard University Press.

Gall, G. (2003) 'Employer opposition to union recognition', in G. Gall (ed.), *Union Organizing: Campaigning for Trade Union Recognition*. London: Routledge, pp. 79–96.

—— (2004) 'Trade union recognition in Britain, 1995–2002: Turning a corner?' *Industrial Relations Journal*, 35(3): 249–70.

Gall, G. & McKay, S. (1994) 'Trade union derecognition in Britain, 1988–1994'. *British Journal of Industrial Relations* 32(3): 433–48.

Gallagher M. (2005) *Contagious Capitalism: Globalisation and the Politics of Labor in China*. Princeton, NJ: Princeton University Press.

Garavini, S. (1976) 'La centralizzazione contrattuale e le strategie del sindacato', in A. Accornero (ed.), *Problemi Del Movimento Sindacale in Italia: 1943–76*. Milan: Feltrinelli, pp. 673–84.

Garnaut, R. & Huang, Y.P. (2001) *Growth Without Miracles: Readings on the Chinese Economy in the Era of Reform*. Oxford: Oxford University Press.

Garrett, G. (1998) 'Global markets and national policies: Collision course of virtuous circle?' *International Organization* 52(4): 787–824.

Georgi, F. (1995) *L'invention de la CFDT 1957–1970* Paris: L'Atelier-CNRS Editions.

Gerum, E. (2007) *Das deutsche Corporate-Governance-System. Eine empirische Untersuchung*. Stuttgart: Schäffer-Poeschel.

Getman, J.G. (1998) *The Betrayal of Local 14*. Ithaca, NY: Cornell University Press.

Giacinto, E. (2007) 'Sindacalizzazione in Bilico', in A. Bianco & E. Giacinto (eds), *Sindacato Oh Sindacato! Quarto Rapporto Della Biblioteca Centrale Cisl*. Rome: CISL, pp. 118–28.

Giles, A. (2000) 'Globalisation and industrial relations theory'. *Journal of Industrial Relations* 42 (2): 173–194.

Gill, C. & Krieger, H. (1999) 'Direct and representative participation in Europe: Recent evidence'. *The International Journal of Human Resource Management* 10(4): 572–91.

Gleason, S.E. (ed.) (2006) *The Shadow Workforce: Perspectives on Contingent Work in the United States, Japan, and Europe*. Kalamazoo, MI: W.E. Upjohn Institute for Employment Research.

Godard, J. (2000) *Industrial Relations: The Economy and Society*, 2nd ed., North York, ON: Captus Press.

—— (2005) 'The new institutionalism, capitalist diversity and industrial relations', in B.E. Kaufman (ed.), *Theoretical Perspectives on Work and the Employment Relationship*. Champaign, IL: Industrial Relations Research Association, pp. 229–264.

Goetschy, J. (1983) 'A new future for industrial democracy in France'. *Economic and Industrial Democracy* 1: 85–103.

—— (1995) 'Major developments and changes in French industrial relations since the 1980s', in M. Mesh (ed.), *Sozialpartnerschaft und Arbeitsbeziehungen in Europa*. Wien: Manz Verlag.

—— (1998) 'France: The limits of reform', in A. Ferner & R. Hyman (eds), *Changing Industrial Relations in Europe*. Oxford: Blackwell, pp. 357–95.

Golden, M. (1988) *Labor Divided: Austerity and Working-Class Politics in Contemporary Italy*. Ithaca, NY: Cornell University Press.

Goldthorpe, J.H. (1984) 'The end of convergence: Corporatist and dualist tendencies in modern Western societies', in J.H. Goldthorpe (ed.), *Order and Conflict in Contemporary Capitalism: Studies in the Political Economy of Western European Nations*. Oxford: Clarendon, pp. 315–343.

Gollan, P.J., Markey, R. & Ross, I. (eds) (2002) *Works Councils in Australia*. Sydney: Federation Press.

Gollan, P.J. & Patmore, G. (eds) (2003) *Partnership at Work: The Challenge of Employee Democracy*. Sydney: Pluto Press.

Gomez-Mejia, L.R., Balkin, D.B. & Cardy, R.L. (1995) *Managing Human Resources*. Englewood Cliffs, NJ: Prentice-Hall.

Goodman, J.F.B. & Earnshaw, J. (1995) 'New industrial rights and wrongs: The changed framework of British employment law'. *New Zealand Journal of Industrial Relations* 19(3): 305–21.

Goodman, J.F.B. (1994) 'The United Kingdom', in *Towards Social Dialogue: Tripartite Co-operation in National Economic and Social Policy-Making*. Geneva: ILO, pp. 273–96.

—— (2000) 'Building bridges and settling differences: Collective conciliation and arbitration under ACAS', in B. Towers & W. Brown (eds), *Employment Relations in Britain: 25 Years of the Advisory, Conciliation and Arbitration Service*. Oxford, Blackwell, pp. 31–65.

Goodman, J.F.B. & Earnshaw, J. (1995) 'New industrial rights and wrongs: The changed framework of British employment law'. *New Zealand Journal of Industrial Relations* 19(3): 305–21.

Goodman, J.F.B. & Whittingham, T.G. (1969) *Shop Stewards in British Industry*. London: McGraw-Hill.

Gordon, A. (1985) *The Evolution of Labor Relations in Japan*. Cambridge: Council on East Asian Studies, Harvard University.

Gospel, H.F. & Littler, C.R. (1983) *Managerial Strategies and Industrial Relations: An Historical and Comparative Study*. London: Heinemann.

Gospel, H. & Pendleton, A. (2005) 'Corporate governance and labour management: An international comparison', in H. Gospel & A. Pendleton (eds), *Corporate Governance and Labour Management: An International Comparison*. Oxford: Oxford University Press, pp. 1–32.

Gottlieb, B., Kelloway, E. & Barham, E. (1998) *Flexible Work Arrangement: Managing the Work/Family Boundary*. Chichester: John Wiley & Sons.

Government of India (1931) *Royal Commission on Labour: Report*. New Delhi: Government of India Press.

—— (1969) *Report of the National Commission on Labour*. New Delhi: Government of India Press.

—— (2002) *Annual Report of the Ministry of Labour*. New Delhi: Ministry of Labour.

Grant, D. (1997) 'Japanisation and new industrial relations', in I. Beardwell (ed.), *Contemporary Industrial Relations: A Critical Analysis*. Oxford: Oxford University Press, pp. 201–33.

Gratton, L., Hope Hailey, V., Stiles, P. & Truss, C. (1999) *Strategic Human Resource Management*. Oxford: Oxford University Press.

Green, F. (1992) 'Recent trends in trade union density'. *British Journal of Industrial Relations* 30(3): 445–58.

Grimshaw, D. (2009) 'The UK: A progressive statutory minimum wage in a liberal market economy context', in D. Vaughan-Whitehead (ed.), *Minimum Wage Systems in an Extended Europe*. Geneva: ILO, pp. 465–500.

Grimshaw, D., Earnshaw, J. & Hebson, G. (2003) 'Private sector provision of supply teachers: A case of legal swings and professional roundabouts'. *Journal of Education Policy*, 18(3): 267–88.

Grimshaw, D., Willmott, H. & Vincent, S. (2002) 'Going privately: Practices of partnership in the outsourcing of services in the public sector'. *Public Administration*, 80(3): 475–502.

Grote, J.R., Lang, A. & Traxler, F. (2007) 'Germany', in F. Traxler & G. Huemer (eds), *Handbook of Business Interest Associations, Firm Size and Governance. A Comparative Analytical Approach*. London: Routledge, pp. 141–76.

Groux, G. & Pernot, J.M. (2008) *La greve*. Paris: Sciences Po, les Presses.

Guest, D. & Conway, N. (2000) *The Psychological Contract in the Public Sector*. London: Chartered Institute of Personnel and Development.

Guest, D. & Hoque, K. (1994) 'The good, the bad and the ugly: Employment relations in new non-union workplaces'. *Human Resource Management Journal* 5(1): 1–14.

Guest, D. & Peccei, R. (1998) *The Partnership Company: Benchmarks for the Future. The Report of the IPA Survey Principles, Practice and Performance*. London: Involvement and Participation Association.

—— (2001) 'Partnership at work: Mutuality and the balance of advantage'. *British Journal of Industrial Relations*, 39(2): 207–36.

Gumbrell-McCormick, R. (2008) 'International actors and international regulation', in P. Blyton, N. Bacon, J. Foirito & E. Heery (eds), *Sage Handbook of Industrial Relations*. London: Sage, pp. 325–45.

Gunderson, M. & Taras, D.G. (2008) *Union–Management Relations in Canada*. 5th ed. Toronto: Pearson.

Gurtoo, A. (2008) 'A framework for labour policy reforms in India: Balancing economic growth and social development'. *The International Journal of Sociology and Social Police*, 28(11/12): 472–84.

Hall, L. & Torrington, D. (1998) *The Human Resource Function: The Dynamics of Change and Development*. London: Pitman.

Hall, M. (2006) 'A cool response to the ICE regulations? Employer and trade union approaches to the new legal framework for information and consultation'. *Industrial Relations Journal*, 37(5): 456–72.

Hall, P. & Gingerich, D. (2004) *Varieties of Capitalism and Institutional Complementarities in the Macro-Economy*, Discussion Paper 04/5. Cologne: Max Plank Institute for the Study of Societies.

Hall, P.A. & Soskice, D. (eds) (2001) *Varieties of Capitalism: The Institutional Foundations of Comparative Advantage*. New York: Oxford University Press.

Hall, R. (2008) 'The politics of industrial relations in Australia in 2007'. *Journal of Industrial Relations*, 50(3): 371–82.

Hall, R. & Wailes, N. (2009) 'International and comparative human resource management', in A. Wilkinson, N. Bacon, T. Redman & S. Snell (eds), *Sage Handbook of Human Resource Management*. London: Sage, pp. 115–32.

Hamann, K. & Kelly, J. (2008) 'Varieties of capitalism and industrial relations', in P. Blyton, N. Bacon, J. Fiortio & E. Heery (eds), *Sage Handbook of Industrial Relations*, London: Sage, pp. 129–48.

Han, J. & Jang, J. (2000), 'Job history and career in the transition between regular and non-regular jobs'. *Korean Journal of Labor Economics*, 23(2): 33–53. (in Korean)

Hanami, T. (1979) *Labour Relations in Japan Today*. Tokyo: Kodansha-International.

Hancke, B., Rhodes, M. & Thatcher, M. (2006) 'Introduction: Beyond varieties of capitalism', in B. Hancke, M. Rhodes & M. Thatcher (eds), *Beyond Varieties of Capitalism: Conflict, Contradictions and Complementarities in the European Economy*. Oxford: Oxford University Press, pp.3–38.

Hancock, K. (1984) 'The first half century of wage policy', in B. Chapman, J. Isaac & J. Niland (eds), *Australian Labour Relations Readings*. Melbourne: Macmillan, pp. 44–99.

Hansen, J. & Andersen, S.K. (2008) *Østeuropæiske arbejdere i bygge- og anlægsbranchen*. FAOS Forskningsnotat. University of Copenhagen, Department of Sociology.

Harcourt, M. & Wood, G. (2007) 'The importance of employment protection for skill development in coordinated market economies'. *European Journal of Industrial Relations*, 13(2): 141–59.

Hashimoto, M. (1990) *The Japanese Labor Market in a Comparative Perspective with the United States*. Kalamazoo, MI: W.E. Upjohn Institute for Employment Research.

Hassel, A. (2006) 'What does business want? Labour market reform in CMEs and its problems', in B. Hancke, M. Rhodes & M. Thatcher (eds), *Beyond Varieties of Capitalism: Conflict, Contradictions and Complementarities in the European Economy*. Oxford: Oxford University Press, pp.253–277.

—— (2008) 'The evolution of a global labour governance regime'. *Governance: An International Journal of Policy, Administration and Institution*, 21(2): 231–51.

Haworth, N. (2005) '"You've got to admit it's getting better..." Organised labour and internationalisation', in B. Harley, J. Hyman & P. Thompson (eds), *Participation and Democracy at Work*, London: Palgrave, pp. 186–203.

Haworth, N. & Hughes, S. (2003) 'International political economy and industrial relations'. *British Journal of Industrial Relations*, 41(4): 665–82.

Haynes, P. & Allen, M. (2001) 'Partnership as union strategy: A preliminary evaluation'. *Employee Relations* 23(2): 164–87.

Hearn Mackinnon, B. (2008) 'Employer matters in 2007'. *Journal of Industrial Relations*, 50(3): 463–74.

Hebdon, R. & Brown, T. (2007) *Industrial Relations in Canada: An HR Perspective*. Toronto: Nelson Education.

Hébert, G., Jain, H.M. & Meltz, N.M. (eds) (1989) *The State of the Art in Industrial Relations*. Kingston: Industrial Relations Centre, Queen's University and Centre for Industrial Relations, University of Toronto.

Heery, E. (1998) 'The relaunch of the Trades Union Congress'. *British Journal of Industrial Relations*, 36(3): 339–60.

—— (2002) 'Partnership versus organising: Alternative futures for British trade unionism'. *Industrial Relations Journal*, 33(1): 20–35.

Heery, E., Bacon, N., Blyton, P. & Fiorito, J. (2008) 'Introduction: The field of industrial relations', in P. Blyton, N. Bacon, J. Fiortio & E. Heery (eds), *Sage Handbook of Industrial Relations*. London: Sage, pp. 1–32.

Heery, E., Delbridge, R. & Simms, M. (2003) *The Organising Academy*. London: Trades Union Congress.

Heery, E., Simms, M., Delbridge, R., Salmon, J. & Simpson, D. (2000) 'Union organizing in Britain: A survey of policy and practice'. *International Journal of Human Resource Management*, 11(5): 986–1007.

Hession, C.H. & Sardy, H. (1969) *Ascent to Affluence: A History of American Economic Development*. Boston: Allyn & Bacon.

Hill, E. (2009) 'The Indian industrial relations system: Struggling to address the dynamics of a globalizing economy'. *Journal of Industrial Relations*, 51: 395–410.

Himmelweit, S. (2007) 'The right to request flexible working: A "very British" approach to gender (in)equality?' *Australian Bulletin of Labour*, 33(2): 246–63.

Hirschmeier, J. & Yui, T. (1975) *The Development of Japanese Business, 1600–1973*. Cambridge, MA: Harvard University Press.

Hirst, P. & Thompson, G. (1996) *Globalisation in Question: The International Economy and the Possibilities of Governance*. Cambridge: Polity Press.

Hodson, R. (2001) *Dignity at Work*. Cambridge: Cambridge University Press.

Hoel, H. & Beale, D. (2006) 'Workplace bullying, psychological perspectives and industrial relations: Towards a contextualized and interdisciplinary approach'. *British Journal of Industrial Relations*, 44(2): 239–62.

Hoffman, C. (1981) 'People's Republic of China', in A. Albert (ed.), *International Handbook of Industrial Relations*, Westport, CT: Greenwood Press.

Holgate, J., Hebson, G. & McBride, A. (2006) 'Why gender and "difference" matter: A critical appraisal of industrial relations research'. *Industrial Relations Journal*, 37(4): 310–28.

Höpner, M. (2005) 'What connects industrial relations and corporate governance? Explaining institutional complementarity' *Socio-Economic Review*, 3: 331–58.

Houseman, S. & Osawa, M. (eds) (2003) *Nonstandard Work in Developed Economies: Causes and Consequences*. Kalamazoo, MI: W.E. Upjohn Institute for Employment Research.

Howell, C. (1992) *Regulating Labor: The State and Industrial Relations Reform in Postwar France*. Princeton, NJ: Princeton University Press.

—— (2003) 'Varieties of capitalism: and then there was one?' *Comparative Politics* 36(1): 103–22.

—— (2005) *Trade Unions and the State: The Construction of Industrial Relations Institutions in Britain, 1890–2000*. Princeton, NJ: Princeton University Press.

Hu, X.J. (2004) 'On the legal system of China's labour market'. *Journal of Anhui University of Technology* (Social Sciences Edition) 21(5): 19–20.

Hughes, S. (2005) 'The International Labour Organisation'. *New Political Economy*, 10(3): 413–25.

Hughes, S. & Wilkinson, R. (1998) 'International labour standards and world trade: No role for the World Trade Organisation'. *New Political Economy*, 3(3): 375–89.

Human Resources and Social Development Canada (n.d.) Website: <www.hrsdc.gc.ca/en/labour/labour_relations/info_analysis/index/shtml> (accessed 21 November 2008).

Hyman, R. (1997) 'The future of employee representation'. *British Journal of Industrial Relations* 35(3): 309–36.

—— (1999) 'Imagined solidarities: Can trade unions resist globalization', in P. Leisink, (ed.), *Globalization and Labour Relations*. Cheltenham: Edward Elgar, pp. 94–115.

—— (2005) 'Trade unions and the politics of the European social model'. *Economic and Industrial Democracy*, 26(1): 9–40.

Ilsøe, A. (2008) *Tillidsrepræsentanter i industrien. Udbredelsen af tillidsrepræsentanter på overenskomstdækkede danske produktionsvirksomheder*. FAOS Research notes No. 93. Copenhagen: FAOS, University of Copenhagen.

Ilsøe, A., Due, J. & Madsen, J.S. (2007) 'Impacts of decentralisation—erosion or renewal? The decisive link between workplace representation and company size in German and Danish industrial relations'. *Industrielle Beziehungen*, 14(3): 201–22.

Industrial Relations Services (1999) 'Trends in employee involvement'. *IRS Employment Trends*, 683: 6–16.

Institute for Employment Research (2001) *Projections of Occupations and Qualifications 2000/2001*. London: Department for Education and Employment.

International Labour Organisation (ILO) (2009) *Rules of the Game: A*

Brief Introduction to International Labour Standards, rev. ed. Geneva: International Labour Organisation.

ISTAT (2002) *La Flessibilità Del Mercato Del Lavoro Nel Periodo 1995–96*, Rome: ISTAT.

Iversen, T. (1999) *Contested Economic Institutions: The Politics of Macroeconomics and Wage Bargaining in Advanced Democracies.* Cambridge: Cambridge University Press.

Jackson, G. (2001) 'The origins of non-liberal corporate governance in Germany and Japan', in W. Streek & K. Yamamura (eds), *The Origins of Nonliberal Capitalism: Germany and Japan in Comparison.* Ithaca, NY: Cornell University Press, pp. 121–70.

Jacobi, O., Keller, B. & Müller-Jentsch, W. (1998) 'Germany: Facing new challenges', in A. Ferner & R. Hyman (eds), *Changing Industrial Relations in Europe*, 2nd ed., Oxford: Blackwell, pp. 190–238.

Jacoby, S. (1985) *Employing Bureaucracies.* New York: Columbia University Press.

—— (1999) 'Are career jobs headed for extinction?' *California Management Review* 42: 123–45.

—— (2005) *The Embedded Corporation: Corporate Governance and Employment Relations in Japan and the United States.* Princeton, NJ: Princeton University Press.

Japan Institute of Labour (1996) 'Industrial relations and labour law in changing Asian economies'. *Proceedings of the 1996 Asian Regional Conference on Industrial Relations.* Tokyo: Japan Institute of Labour.

Japan Institute of Labour Policy and Training (2003) *Kigyo no zinzi senryaku to rodosya no syugyo ishiki ni kansuru chosa (Survey on Firms' Human Resource Management Strategy and Sentiment of Workers).* Tokyo: Japan Institute of Labour Policy and Training.

—— (2006) *Gendai nihon kigyo no zinzai manezimento (Human Resource Management of the Modern Japanese Firm).* Tokyo: Japan Institute for Labour Policy and Training.

—— (2006) *Human Resource Management of Today's Japanese Firms: Interim Report of the Research Project 'Comprehensive Analysis of Firms' Management Strategies, Personnel Treatment Systems, Etc.'.* Tokyo: JILPT Research Report No. 61.

Jobert, A. (2000) *Les espaces de la négociation collective, Europe et territories.* Toulouse: Octarès.

Jung, E. (2006) *Political Economics of Modern Labor Markets.* Seoul: Humanitas.

Juravich, T. & Bronfenbrenner, K. (1999) *Ravenswood: The Steelworkers'*

Victory and the Revival of the American Labor Movement. Ithaca, NY: Cornell University Press.

Kassalow, E.M. (1974) 'The development of Western labor movements: Some comparative considerations', in L.G. Reynolds, S.A. Masters & C. Moser (eds), *Readings in Labor Economics and Labor Relations.* Englewood Cliffs, NJ: Prentice-Hall.

Katz, H.C. (1985) *Shifting Gears.* Cambridge, MA: MIT Press.

—— (1993) 'The decentralization of collective bargaining: A literature review and comparative analysis'. *Industrial and Labor Relations Review* 47(1): 1–22.

—— (1997) 'Introduction and comparative overview', in H.C. Katz (ed.), *Telecommunications: Restructuring Work and Employment Relations Worldwide.* Ithaca, NY: Cornell University Press, pp. 1–28.

—— (2005) 'Industrial relations and work', in S. Ackroyd, R. Bart, P. Thompson & P. Tolbert (eds), *The Oxford Handbook of Work and Organisations.* Oxford: Oxford University Press, pp. 263–82.

Katz, H.C., Batt, R. & Keefe, J.H. (2000) 'The revitalization of the CWA: Integrating political action, organizing, and collective bargaining', unpublished manuscript. NYSSILR-Cornell University.

Katz, H.C. & Darbishire, O. (2000) *Converging Divergences: Worldwide Changes in Employment Systems.* Ithaca, NY: Cornell University Press.

Katz, H.C., Kochan, T.A & Colvin, A.J.S. (2007) *An Introduction to Collective Bargaining and Industrial Relations*, 4th ed. New York: Irwin-McGraw Hill.

Katzenstein, P. (ed.) (1978) *Between Power and Plenty: Foreign Economic Policies of_Advanced Industrial States.* Madison, WI: University of Wisconsin Press.

—— (1985) *Small States in World Markets: Industrial Policy in Europe.* Ithaca, NY: Cornell University Press.

Kaufman, B.E. & Taras, D.G. (2000) *Non-union Employee Representation.* Armonk, NY: M.E. Sharpe.

Keller, B. (1993) *Arbeitspolitik des öffentlichen Sektors.* Baden-Baden: Nomos.

—— (1999) 'Germany: Negotiated change, modernization and the challenge of unification', in S. Bach, L. Bordogna, G. Della Rocca & D. Winchester (eds), *Public Service Employment Relations in Europe: Transformation, Modernization or Inertia?* London: Routledge, pp. 56–93.

—— (2007) 'Wandel der Arbeitsbeziehungen im öffentlichen Dienst: Entwicklungen und Perspektiven'. *Die Verwaltung. Zeitschrift für Verwaltungsrecht und Verwaltungswissenschaften*, 40: 173–202.

Keller, B. & Henneberger, F. (1999) 'Privatwirtschaft und öffentlicher Dienst: Parallelen und Differenzen in den Arbeitspolitiken', in W. Müller-Jentsch (ed.), *Konfliktpartnerschaft*. 3rd ed., München: Hampp, pp. 233–56.

Keller, B. & Seifert, H. (eds) (2007) *Atypische Beschäftigung—Flexibilisierung und soziale Risiken*. Berlin: edition sigma.

Kelly, J. (1982) *Scientific Management, Job Redesign and Work Performance*. London: Academic Press.

—— (1998) *Rethinking Industrial Relations: Mobilization, Collectivism and Long Waves*. London: Routledge.

—— (1990). 'British trade unionism 1979–1989: Change, continuity and contradictions', *Work, Employment and Society*, 4 (special issue): 29–65.

—— (1996) 'Union militancy and social partnership', in P. Ackers, C. Smith & P. Smith (eds), *The New Workplace and Trade Unionism*. Routledge: London, pp. 77–109.

Kelly, J. & Heery, E. (1989) 'Full-time officers and trade union recruitment'. *British Journal of Industrial Relations* 27(2): 196–213.

Kerala High Court (1997) *Bharat Kumar K. Palicha and Another v. State of Kerala and Others* <http://kerala.indlaw.com/search/caselaw> (accessed 24 May 2010).

Kerr, C. (1983) *The Future of Industrial Societies: Convergence or Continuing Diversity?* Cambridge, MA: Harvard University Press.

Kerr, C., Dunlop, J.T., Harbison, F.H. & Myers, C.A. (1960) *Industrialism and Industrial Man: The Problems of Labour and Management in Economic Growth*. London: Penguin.

Kersley, B., Alpin, C., Forth, J., Bewley, H. & Oxenbridge S. (2006) *Inside the Workplace: Findings from the 2004 Workplace Employment Relations Survey*. London: Routledge.

Kessler, I. & Purcell, J. (1994) 'Joint problem solving and the role of third parties: An evaluation of ACAS advisory work'. *Human Resource Management Journal*, 4(2): 1–21.

Kessler, S. & Bayliss, F. (1998) *Contemporary British Industrial Relations*, 3rd ed. Basingstoke: Macmillan.

Kim, S. & Sung, J. (2005) *Employment Policy in Korea*. Seoul: KLI. (in Korean)

Kim, Y. (2005) *Wage Policy for Korean Workers*. Seoul: Humanitas. (in Korean)

King, W.L.M. (1973 [1918]) *Industry and Humanity*. Toronto: University of Toronto Press.

Kitay, J. & Lansbury, R.D. (eds) (1997) *Changing Employment Relations in Australia*. Melbourne: Oxford University Press.

Knell, J. (1999) *Partnership at Work*. Employment Relations Research Series Number 7. London: Department of Trade and Industry.

Kochan, T. (1998) 'What is distinctive about industrial relations research?' in K. Whitfield and G. Strauss (eds), *Researching the World of Work: Strategies and Methods in Studying Industrial Relations*. Ithaca: Cornell University Press, pp. 31–49.

Kochan, T., Katz, H. & McKersie, R.B.(1994) *The Transformation of American Industrial Relations*. 2nd ed. Ithaca, NY: Cornell University Press.

Kochan, T.A., Lansbury, R.D. & MacDuffie, J.P. (eds) (1997) *After Lean Production: Evolving Employment Practices in the World Auto Industry*. Ithaca, NY: Cornell University Press.

Kohaut, S. (2007) 'Tarifbindung und tarifliche Öffnungsklauseln: Ergebnisse aus dem IAB-Betriebspanel'. *WSI-Mitteilungen* 60: 94–97.

Kohaut, S. & Schnabel, C. (2007) 'Tarifliche Öffnungsklauseln— Verbreitung, Inanspruchnahme und Bedeutung'. *Sozialer Fortschritt* 56: 33–40.

Koike, K. (1977) *Shokuba no Rodo Kumiai to Sanka* (Worker Participation and Labour Unions at Workplace level) Tokyo: Toyo Keizai Shinpo Sha.

—— (1988) *Understanding Industrial Relations in Modern Japan*. Macmillan, London.

Korean Labor Institute (2008) *2008 KLI Labor Statistics*. Seoul: KLI (in Korean).

Koshiro, K. (1983) *Nihon no roshi Kankei* (Industrial Relations in Japan). Tokyo: Yuhikaku.

Kramer, R.J. (1998) 'Equal employment opportunities', in M. Poole & M. Warner (eds), *The IEBM Handbook of Human Resource Management*. London: Thomson Learning, pp. 736–44.

Kronauer, M. & Linne, G. (eds) (2007) *Flexicurity: Die Suche nach Sicherheit in der Flexibilität*, 2nd ed., Berlin: edition sigma.

Kubo, K. (2008) 'Japan: The resilience of employment relationship and the changing condition of work', in S. Lee & F. Eyraud (eds), *Globalization, Flexibilization and Working Conditions in Asia and the Pacific*. London: Chandos.

Kumar, P. (1993) *From Uniformity to Divergence: Industrial Relations in Canada and the United States*. Kingston, ON: IRC Press, Queen's University.

Kuruvilla, S. & Hiers, W. (2000) *Globalization and industrial relations in India*. Report for the International Labour Organization, Regional Office for Asia and the Pacific, Bangkok.

Kuruvilla, S. & Ranganathan, A. (2008) 'Economic development strategies and macro-and micro-level human resource policies: The case of India's "outsourcing" industry'. *Industrial & Labor Relations Review*, 62(1): 39.

Kuruvilla, S. & Venkata Ratnam, C.S. (1996) 'Economic development and industrial relations: The case of South Asia and Southeast Asia'. *Industrial Relations Journal* 27(1): 9–23.

Kuwahara, Y. (1989) *Industrial Relations Systems in Japan: A New Interpretation*. Tokyo: Japan Institute of Labor.

Labour Canada *Chronological Perspectives on Work Stoppages in Canada*. Toronto: Human Resources Development Canada (HRDC) http://srv131.services.gc.ca/dimt-wid/pcat-cpws/recherche-search. aspx?lang=eng> (accessed 9 March 2010)

Labour Canada (various issues, unpublished data, 1966–2000) *Strikes and Lockouts in Canada*. Toronto: Human Resources Development Canada (HRDC).

Labour Market Trends (various issues, monthly) Central Statistical Office. London: Her Majesty's Stationery Office.

Lallement, M. (2008) *Sociologie des relations professionnelles*. Paris: La Découverte, coll. Repères.

Lama, L. (1976) *Intervista Sul Sindacato*. Bari: Laterza.

Lange, P. & Vannicelli, M. (1982) 'Strategy under stress: The Italian union movement and the Italian crisis in developmental perspective', in P. Lange, G. Ross & M. Vannicelli (eds), *Unions, Change, and Crisis*. Boston, George Allen & Unwin, pp. 95–206.

Lansbury, R.D. (1985) 'The Accord: A new experiment in Australian industrial relations'. *Labour and Society*, 10(2): 223–35.

—— (2009) 'Workplace democracy and the global financial crisis: Implications for Australia'. *Journal of Industrial Relations*, 51(5): 599–616.

Lansbury, R.D. & Wailes, N. (2003) 'The meaning of industrial democracy in an era of neo-liberalism', in P.J. Gollan & G. Patmore (eds), *Partnership at Work: The Challenge of Employee Democracy*. Sydney: Pluto Press, pp. 37–46.

—— (2008) 'Employee involvement and direct participation', in P. Blyton, N. Bacon, J. Fiortio & E. Heery (eds), *Sage Handbook of Industrial Relations*. London: Sage, pp. 434–46.

Lebergott, S. (1984) *The Americans: An Economic Record*. New York: W.W. Norton.

Ledvinka, J. & Scarpello, V.G. (1991) *Federal Regulation of Personnel and Human Resource Management*, 2nd ed. Belmont, CA: Kent.

Lee, B. (2003), 'Industrial relations system', in J. Kim (ed.), *Employment and Industrial Relations in Korea*. Seoul: KOILAF, pp. 171–213.

—— (2005), 'Solidarity crisis of Korean labor movement'. *Korea Focus*, 13(1): 86–106.

—— (2006), 'Policy recommendation for collective bargaining of the public sector', Report presented to Tripartite Commission.

—— (2008), *Labor 20 Year in Statistics*. Seoul: KLI. (in Korean)

Lee, B. & Kwon, H. (2008) *Strategies for Union Organizing in the Era of Globalization*. Seoul: KLI. (in Korean)

Lee, C.K. (1999) 'From organized dependence to disorganized despotism: Changing labour regimes in Chinese factories'. *The China Quarterly*, 157: 44–71.

—— (2007) *Against the Law: Labor Protests in China's Rustbelt and Sunbelt*. Berkeley, CA: University of California Press.

Lee, J. (2002), 'Industrial unionization and change of bargaining structure'. Paper presented to the International Conference of International Labor Standards and Korean Industrial Relations, held by KLI and ILO in Seoul, South Korea.

Lee, W. & Lee, B. (2003), 'Industrial relations and labor standards in Korea', in O. Kwon (ed.), *Korea's New Economy Strategy in Globalization Era*. Cheltenham: Edward Elgar, pp. 173–91.

Legge, K. (2007) 'Networked organizations and the negation of HRM?' in J. Storey (ed.), *Human Resource Management: A Critical Text*, 3rd ed., London: Thomson.

Leibfried, S. & Wagschal, U. (eds) (2000) *Der deutsche Sozialstaat: Bilanzen—Reformen—Perspektiven*. Frankfurt: Campus.

Levine, S.B. (1984) 'Employers' associations in Japan' in J.P. Windmuller & A. Gladstone (eds) *Employers' Associations and industrial Relations: A Comparative Study*. Oxford: Clarendon, pp. 318–56.

Levy, F. & Murname, R.J. (1992) 'U.S. earnings levels and earnings inequality: A review of recent trends and proposed explanations'. *Journal of Economic Literature*, 30: 1333–81.

Lewin, D. (2008) 'Employee voice and mutual gains'. In *Proceedings of the 60th Annual Meeting*. Champaign, Illinois: Labor and Employment Relations Association.

Li, H. (2000) 'An analysis of the situation of China's labour market'. *Journal of Beijing College of Management of Planning and Labour*, 3: 14, 57.

Li, Y.B. (2003) 'The progress and forecast of the Chinese labour market'. *Contemporary Finance and Economics*, 3: 15–19.

Linden, M. (1998) 'Doing comparative labour history: Some essential preliminaries', in J. Hagan & A. Wells (eds), *Australian Labour and Regional Change: Essays in Honour of R.A. Gollan*. Sydney: University of Wollongong in association with Halstead Press.

Lobel, S. (1996) *Work/Life and Diversity: Perspectives of Workplace Reponses*. Boston, MA: Center on Work and Family, Boston University.

Locke, R.M. (1992) 'The decline of the national union in Italy: Lessons for comparative industrial relations'. *Industrial and Labor Relations Review*, 45: 229–49.

—— (1995) *Remaking the Italian Economy*. Ithaca, NY: Cornell University Press.

Locke, R.M., Kochan, T.A. & Piore, M. (1995) *Employment Relations in a Changing World Economy*. Cambridge, MA: MIT Press.

Locke, R.M., Piore, M. & Kochan, T.A. (1995) 'Reconceptualising comparative industrial relations: Lessons from international research'. *International Labour Review* 134(2): 139–61.

Locke, R. & Thelen, K. (1995) 'Apples and oranges compared: Contextualized comparisons and the study of comparative politics'. *Politics and Society* 23(3): 337–67.

Low Pay Commission (2000) 'The national minimum wage: The story so far'. Second Report of the LPC, Cmnd 4571.

Macintyre, S. (1989) 'Neither labour nor capital: the policies of the establishment of arbitration' in S. Macintyre & R. Mitchell (eds), *Foundations of Arbitration: The origins and effects of state compulsory arbitration*, 1890–1914. Melbourne: Oxford University Press, pp. 176–201.

Macintyre, S. & Mitchell, R. (eds) (1989) *Foundations of Arbitration: The Origins and Effects of State Compulsory Arbitration, 1890–1914*. Melbourne: Oxford University Press.

Mailand, M. (2008) *Regulering af arbejde og velfærd—Mod nye arbejdsdelinger mellem staten og arbejdsmarkedets parter*. Copenhagen: DJØF Publishing.

Malila, J. (2007) 'The great look forward: China's HR evolution'. *China Business Review* 34(4): 16–19.

Manow, P. & Seils, E. (2000) 'Adjusting badly: The German welfare state, structural change, and the open economy', in F.W. Scharpf & V.A. Schmidt (eds), *Welfare and Work in the Open Economy, Vol. II: Diverse Responses to Common Challenges*. Oxford: Oxford University Press, pp. 264–307.

Marchington, M. (1995) 'Employee relations', in S. Tyson (ed.), *Strategic Prospects for Human Resource Management*. London: Institute of Personnel and Development, pp. 81–111.

Marchington, M. & Cox, A. (2007) 'Employee involvement and participation: Structures, processes and outcomes', in J. Storey (ed.), *Human Resource Management: A Critical Text*, 3rd ed. London: Thomson.

Marchington, M., Grimshaw, D., Rubery, J. & Willmott, H. (eds) (2005) *Fragmenting Work: Blurring Organizational Boundaries and Disordering Hierarchies*. Oxford: Oxford University Press.

Marchington, M. & Parker, P. (1990) *Changing Patterns of Employee Relations*. Hemel Hempstead: Harvester Wheatsheaf.

Marchington, M. & Wilkinson A. (1998) 'Partnership in context', in P. Sparrow & M. Marchington (eds), *Human Resource Management: The New Agenda*. London: Financial Times/Pitman, pp. 208–25.

—— (2001) 'Employee involvement at work', in J. Storey (ed.), *Human Resource Management: A Critical Text*, 2nd ed. London: Thomson, pp. 232–52.

—— (2002) *People Management and Development*. London: Chartered Institute of Personnel and Development.

—— (2008). *Human Resource Management at Work*, 4th ed. London: CIPD.

Marchington, M., Wilkinson, A., Ackers, P. & Dundon, T. (2001) *Management Choice and Employee Voice*. London: Chartered Institute of Personnel and Development.

Marginson, P., Gilman, M., Jacobi, O. & Krieger, H. (1998) *Negotiating European Works Councils: An Analysis of Agreements Under Article 13*. Dublin: European Foundation for the Improvement of Living and Working Conditions.

Martin, R. (1989) *Trade Unionism: Purposes and Forms*. Oxford: Clarendon Press.

Martin, R. & Bamber, G.J. (2004) 'International comparative employment relations theory: Developing the political economy perspective' in *Theoretical Perspectives on Work and the Employment Relationship*, Annual Research Volume, ed. B.E. Kaufman. University of Illinois: The Industrial Relations Research Association, pp. 293–320.

Martinez Lucio, M. & Perret, R. (2009) 'The diversity and politics of trade union responses to minority ethnic and migrant workers: The context of the UK'. *Economic and Industrial Democracy* 30(3): 234–47.

Martinez Lucio, M. & Stuart, M. (2005) *Partnership and Modernisation in Employment Relations*. London: Routledge.

Mascini, M. (2000) *Profitti E Salari*. Bologna: Il MuliNo.

Mason, B. & Bain, P. (1993) 'The determinants of trade union membership in Britain: A survey of the literature'. *Industrial and Labor Relations Review*, 46(2): 332–51.

Matthews, K. & Minford, P. (1987) 'Mrs Thatcher's economic policies, 1979–1987'. *Economic Policy*, 2(2): 57–101.

McCallum, R. (1997) 'Australian workplace agreements: An analysis'. *Australian Journal of Labour Law*, 10(1): 50–61.

McCallum, R. & Patmore, G. (2002) 'Works councils and labour law', in P.J. Gollan, P.J., Markey & I. Ross (eds) (2002) *Works Councils in Australia*. Sydney: Federation Press, pp. 74–101.

McClendon, J.A., Kriesky, J. & Eaton, A. (1995) 'Member support for union mergers: An analysis of an affiliation referendum'. *Journal of Labor Research* 16(1): 9–23.

McDonald, T. & Rimmer, M. (1989) 'Award restructuring and wages policy'. *Growth* 37: 111–34.

McGovern, P. (2007) 'Immigration, labour markets and employment relations: Problems and prospects'. *British Journal of Industrial Relations*, 45(2): 17–35.

McKay, S. (2001) 'Between flexibility and regulation: Rights, equality and protection at work'. *British Journal of Industrial Relations*, 39(2): 285–303.

Mercer, S. & Notley, R. (2008) *Trade Union Membership 2007*. London: Department for Business, Enterprise and Regulationary Reform (National Statistics), <http://stats.berr.gov.uk/UKSA/tu/tum2008. pdf> (Accessed 18 January 2010).

McLaughlin, C. (2009) 'The productivity-enhancing impacts of the minimum wage: Lessons from Denmark and New Zealand'. *British Journal of Industrial Relations*, 47(2): 327–48.

McLoughlin, I. & Gourlay, S. (1994) *Enterprise Without Unions: Industrial Relations in the Non-Union Firm*. Buckingham: Open University Press.

Mehrotra, R. (1998) 'Notice of change: A must for voluntary retirement scheme? Impact of Bombay High Court decision in *KEC International Case*'. *Current Law Reporter*, July: 3–10.

Meng, X. (2000) *Labour Market Reform in China*. Cambridge: Cambridge University Press.

Mesh, M. (ed.) (1995) *Sozialpartnerschaft und Arbeitsbeziehungen in Europa*. Wien: Manz Verlag.

Metcalf, D. (1991) 'British unions: Dissolution or resurgence?' *Oxford Review of Economic Policy*, 7: 18–32.

—— (1999) 'The British national minimum wage'. *British Journal of Industrial Relations* 37(2): 171–201.

—— (2005) 'Trade unions: Resurgence or perdition? An economic analysis', in S. Fernie & D. Metcalf (eds), *Trade Unions: Resurgence or Demise?* London: Routledge, pp. 83–117.

Milkman, R. & Kye, B. (2008) 'The state of the unions in 2008: A profile of union membership in Los Angeles, California, and the nation'. Los Angeles, CA: UCLA Institute for Research on Labor and Employment, <www.irle.ucla.edu/research/pdfs/unionmembership08-color.pdf> (Accessed 18 January 2010).

Millward, N., Bryson, A. & Forth, J. (2000) *All Change at Work? British Employment Relations 1980–1998, as Portrayed by the Workplace Industrial Relations Survey Series.* London: Routledge.

Millward, N., Stevens, M., Smart, D. & Hawes, W. (1992) *Workplace Industrial Relations in Transition.* Aldershot: Dartmouth

Ministry of Health, Labour and Welfare (2010) *Basic Survey on Wages* 1985 to 2004 [statistics]. Available from *Rodo Tokei Deta Kensaku Sisutemu (Labor Statistics Search System)* <http://stat.jil.go.jp/> (Accessed 16 February 2010).

Ministry of Internal Affairs and Communications (2010) *Labour Force Survey* 1987 to 2006 [statistics]. Available from *Rodo Ryoku Chosa Choki Zikeiretsu Deta (Labor Force Survey, Long-term Data)*, <http://www.stat.go.jp/data/roudou/longtime/03roudou.htm> (Accessed 16 February 2010).

Ministry of Labour (*Rodosho*). (1975) *Rodo Hakusho* (White Paper on Labour). Japan: Ministry of Finance Printing Office.

Molina, O. & Rhodes, M. (2002) 'Corporatism: The past, present, and future of a concept'. *Annual Review of Political Science*, 5: 305–31.

Morehead, A., Steele, M., Alexander, M., Stephen, K. & Duffin, L. (1997) *Changes at Work: The 1995 Australian Industrial Relations Survey.* Melbourne: Longman.

Morishima, M. (1992) 'Use of joint consultation committees by large Japanese firms'. *British Journal of Industrial Relations* 14(1): 5–16.

Moss, B.H. (1980) *The Origins of the French Labour Movement 1830– 1914: The Socialism of Skilled Workers.* Berkeley, CA: University of California Press.

Mouriaux, R. (1994) *Le syndicalisme en France depuis 1945.* Paris: La Découverte, coll. Repères.

Mu, J. (2003) 'Building a unified urban–rural labour market is an inevitable trend'. *Journal of Kunming University*, 2: 11–14.

Muir, K. (2008) *Worth Fighting For: Inside the Your Rights at Work Campaign.* Sydney: University of New South Wales Press.

Mukherjee, D. & Majumder, R. (2008) 'Tertiarisation of the Indian labour market: A new growth engine or sending distress signals?' *Journal of the Asia Pacific Economy*, 13(4): 387–413.

Müller-Jentsch, W. & Ittermann, P. (2000) *Industrielle Beziehungen: Daten, Zeitreihen, Trends 1950–1999.* Frankfurt: Campus.

Nam, J. & Kim, T. (2000), 'Are non-standard jobs a bridge or a trap?' *Korean Journal of Labor Economics*, 23(2): 85–105. (in Korean)

Nankervis, A., Compton, R. & Baird, M. (2008) *Human Resource Management: Strategies and Processes*, 6th ed. Sydney: Thompson.

Nath, S. (1997) Labour Policy and Economic Reforms in India, 1991–1996: A Study in the Context of Restructuring. MPhil dissertation. New Delhi: Indian Institute of Public Administration.

Nienhüser, W. & Hossfeld, H. (2004) *Bewertung von Betriebsvereinbarungen durch Personalmanager. Eine empirische Studie.* Frankfurt: Bund-Verlag.

Niland, J.R. (1976) *Collective Bargaining in the Context of Compulsory Arbitration.* Sydney: University of New South Wales Press.

Nitta, M. (1988) *Nihon no Roudousha Sanka* (Worker Participation in Japan). Tokyo: University of Tokyo Press.

Nolan, P. (2001) *China and the Global Economy.* London: Palgrave.

O'Leary, G. (ed.) (1998) *Adjusting to Capitalism: Chinese Workers and the State.* New York: M.E. Sharpe.

OECD (1984) *Economic Surveys: Italy*. Paris: OECD.

—— (1986) *Flexibility in the Labour Market. The Current Debate.* Paris: OECD.

—— (1997a) *Employment Outlook*. Paris: OECD.

—— (1997b) *Implementing the OECD Job Strategy: Lessons from Member Countries' Experience.* Paris: OECD.

—— (2006) *Employment Outlook 2006*. Paris: OECD.

—— (2008) *Employment Outlook 2008*. Paris: OECD.

Ohmae, K. (1990) *The Borderless World: Power and Strategy in the Interlinked Economy*. New York: Harper Business.

—— (1995) *The End of the Nation State*. New York: The Free Press.

Ohtake, F. (2005) *Nihon no fubyodo—kakusa shakai no genso to mirai* (Inequality in Japan). Tokyo: Nihon Keizai Shimbun. (in Japanese)

Orth, J.V. (1991) *Combination and Conspiracy: A Legal History of Trade Unionism, 1721–1906*. New York: Oxford University Press.

Osterman, P. (1994) 'How common is workplace transformation and how can we explain who does it?' *Industrial and Labor Relations Review*, 47: 175–88.

—— (1999) *Securing Prosperity*. New York: Oxford University Press.

—— (2000) 'Work reorganization in an era of restructuring: Trends in diffusion and effects on employee welfare'. *Industrial and Labor Relations Review*, 53: 179–96.

Page, R. (2006) *Co-determination in Germany: A beginners' guide*. Düsseldorf: Hans-Böckler-Stiftung.

Palmer, B.D. (1983) *Working class experience: The rise and reconstitution of Canadian labour, 1800–1980*. Toronto: Butterworths.

Panitch, L. & Swartz, D. (1993) *The Assault on Trade Union Freedoms: From Wage Controls to Social Contract*. Toronto: Garamond Press.

Papadakis, K. (2008) 'Research on transnational social dialogue and International Framework Agreements (IFAs)'. *International Labour Review*, 147(1): 100–104.

Park, J. (1992), *A Study on the Industrial Relations at Korean Large Firm*. Seoul: Baeksanseodang. (in Korean)

Park, W. & Roh, Y. (2001) *Changes in Human Resource Management and Industrial Relations in the Period of Post-Crisis*. Seoul: KLI.

Patmore, G. (2003) 'Industrial conciliation and arbitration in New South Wales before 1998', in G. Patmore (ed.), *Laying the Foundations of Industrial Justice: The Presidents of the NSW Industrial Relations Commission 1902–1998*. Sydney: Federation Press.

Pedersen, O.K. (2006) 'Corporatism and beyond: The negotiated economy', in J.L. Campbell, J.A. Hall & O.K. Pedersen (eds), *National identity and the Varieties of Capitalism: The Danish Experience*. Toronto: McGill-Queens University Press, pp. 245–70.

Peetz, D. (1990) 'Declining union density'. *Journal of Industrial Relations*, 32(2): 197–223.

—— (1998) *Unions in a Contrary World: The Future of the Australian Trade Union Movement*. Melbourne: Cambridge University Press.

Peirce, J. (2003) *Canadian Industrial Relations*, 2nd ed. Scarborough, ON: Prentice Hall Canada.

Peng, X.Z. & Yao, Y. (2004) 'Clarifying the concept of informal employment and promote the development of informal employment'. *Social Science*, 7: 63–72.

People's Daily Online (2008) 'Wang Zhaoguo: 209 million membership, the ACFTU becomes the largest trade union in the world'. <http://acftu.people.com.cn/GB/8188849.html> (Accessed 19 December 2008).

Perraton, J., Goldblatt, D., Held, D. & McGrew, A. (1997) 'The globalisation of economic activity'. *New Political Economy*, 2(2): 257–77.

Pernot, J.M. (2005) *Syndicats: lendemains de crise*. Paris: Gallimard.

Piore, M.J. (1981) *Convergence in Industrial Relations? The Case of France and the United States*. Working Paper No. 286. Cambridge, MA: Massachusetts Institute of Technology, Department of Economics.

Pittard, M. (1997) 'Collective employment relationships: Reform of arbitrated awards and certified agreements'. *Australian Journal of Labour Law*, 10(1): 62–88.

Pizzorno, A., Regalia, I., Regini, M. & Reyneri, E. (1978) *Lotte Operaie E Sindacato in Italia: 1968–1972*. Bologna: Il MuliNo.

Plowman, D. (1989) 'Forced march: The employers and arbitration', in S. Macintyre & R. Mitchell (eds), *Foundations of Arbitration: The Origins and Effects of State Compulsory Arbitration, 1980–1914.* Melbourne: Oxford University Press, pp. 135–55.

Pocock, B., Elton, J., Preston, A., Charlesworth, S. et al. (2008) 'The impact of Work Choices on women in low paid employment in Australia'. *Journal of Industrial Relations,* 50(3): 475–88.

Pontusson, J. (1995) 'From comparative public policy to political economy: Putting political institutions in their place and taking interests seriously'. *Comparative Political Studies* 28(1): 117–48.

Potter, P. (1999) 'The Chinese legal system: Continuing commitment to the primacy of state power'. *China Quarterly* 159: 673–83.

Preston, A. & Jefferson, T. (2007) 'Trends in Australia's gender–wage ratio'. *Labour & Industry,* 18(2): 69–84.

Przeworski, A. & Teune H. (1970). *The Logic of Comparative Social Inquiry.* New York: Wiley.

Pugno, E. & Garavini, S. (1974) *Gli Anni Duri Alla Fiat: La Resistenza Sindacale E La Ripresa.* Turin: Einaudi.

Pulignano, V. (2006) 'The diffusion of employment practices of US-based multinationals in Europe: A case study comparison of British- and Italian-based subsidiaries between two sectors'. *British Journal of Industrial Relations,* 44: 497–518.

—— (2007) 'Going national or European? Local trade union politics within transnational business contexts in Europe'. In K. Bronfenbrenner (ed.), *Global Unions: Challenging Global Capita through Cross-Border Campaigns.* Ithaca, NY: Cornell University Press, pp. 137–54.

Pun, N. & Smith, C. (2007) 'Putting transnational labour process in its place: The dormitory labour regime in post-socialist China'. *Work, Employment and Society* 21(1): 47–65.

Purcell, J. & Hutchinson, S. (2007) *Bringing Policies to Life: The Vital Role of Front Line Managers in People Management.* London: CIPD.

Purcell, J., Purcell, K. & Tailby, S. (2004) 'Temporary work agencies: Here today, gone tomorrow?' *British Journal of Industrial Relations,* 42(4): 705–25.

Purcell, J. & Sisson, K. (1983) 'Strategies and practice in the management of industrial relations', in G. Bain (ed.), *Industrial Relations in Britain.* Oxford: Blackwell, pp. 95–120.

Ramsay, H. (1977) 'Cycles of control: Worker participation in sociological and historical perspective'. *Sociology,* 11: 481–506.

Ray, P.K. (2006) 'Labour policy and employment generation: A comparative note on India and China'. *Indian Journal of Labour Economics,* 49(2): 353–68.

Regalia, I. & Regini, M. (1998) 'Italy: The dual character of industrial relations'. In A. Ferner & R. Hyman (eds), *Changing Industrial Relations in Europe*, 2nd ed. Malden, MA, Blackwell, pp. 459–503.

Regini, M. (1985) 'Relazioni industriali e sistema politico: L'evoluzione eecente e le prospettive degli anni '80', in M. Carrieri & P. Perulli (eds), *Il Teorema Sindacale*. Bologna: Il MuliNo.

Regini, M., Kitay, J. & Baethge, J. (eds) (2000) *From Tellers to Sellers: Changing Employment Relations in Banks*. Cambridge, MA: MIT Press.

Reich, R. (1995) *Address to the Delegates of the 10th World Congress of International Industrial Relations Association*. Washington, DC: IRRA, 31 May–4 June.

Reilly, P., Tamkin, P. & Broughton, A. 2007. *The Changing HR Function: Transforming HR?* London: CIPD.

Reynaud, J.-D. (1975) *Les syndicats en France*. Paris: Seuil.

Rhodes, M. (1996) *Globalisation, Labour Markets and Welfare States: A Future of' 'Competitive Corporatism'?* Florence: European University Institute.

—— (2001) 'The political economy of social pacts: 'Competitive corporatism' and European welfare reform'. In P. Pierson (ed.), *The New Politics of the Welfare State*. Oxford: Oxford University Press, pp. 165–94.

Rideout, R.W. (1971) 'The *Industrial Relations Act* 1971'. *The Modern Law Review*, 34(6): 655–75.

Riisgaard, L. (2005) 'International Framework Agreements: A new model for securing workers' rights?' *Industrial Relations* 44(4): 707–37.

Rimmer, M. (1987) 'Australia: New wine in old bottles', in B. Bilson (ed.), *Wage Restraint and the Control of Inflation: An International Survey*. London: Croom Helm.

Ritzer, G. (1975) *Sociology: A Multiple Paradigm Science*. Boston: Allyn and Bacon.

Rollinson, D. & Dundon, T. (2007) *Understanding Employment Relations*. London: Addison-Wesley.

Romagnoli, U. & Treu, T. (1981) *I Sindacati in Italia Dal '45 Ad Oggi: Storia Di Una Strategia*. Bologna: Il MuliNo.

Rosanvallon, P. (1988) *La question syndicale*. Paris: Seuil.

Rose, J. & Chaison, G. (2001) 'Unionism in Canada and the United States in the 21st Century'. *Relations Industrielles/Industrial Relations* 56(1): 34–65.

Rosenblum, J. (1995) *Copper Crucible*. Ithaca, NY: Cornell University Press.

Rossi, F. & Sestito, P. (2000) 'Contrattazione aziendale, struttura nego- ziale e determinazione del salario'. *Rivista di Politica Economica*, 90: 129–83.

Rostow, W.W. (1960) *The Stages of Economic Growth: A Non-Communist Manifesto*. Cambridge: Cambridge University Press.

Rubery, J., Carroll, M., Cooke, F.L., Grugulis, I. & Earnshaw, J. (2004) 'Human resource management and the permeable organisation: The case of the multi-client call centre'. *Journal of Management Studies*, 41(7): 1199–1222.

Rubery, J., Earnshaw, J., Marchington, M., Cooke, F. & Vincent, S. (2002) 'Changing organisational forms and the employment relationship'. *Journal of Management Studies*, 39: 645–72.

Rubinstein, S.A. & Kochan, T.A. (2001) *Learning from Saturn*. Ithaca, NY: Cornell University Press.

Ryan, S., Wailes, N. & Bamber, G.J. (2004) 'Globalisation, employment and labour: Comparative statistics', in G. Bamber, R. Lansbury and N. Wailes (eds), *International and Comparative Employment Relations*, 4th ed. Sydney: Allen & Unwin, pp. 357–402.

Sabel, C. (1982) *Work and Politics*. New York: Cambridge University Press.

Saich, T. (2001) *Governance and Politics of China*. Basingstoke: Palgrave.

Salamon, M. (2000) *Industrial Relations: Theory and Practice*, 4th ed. Harlow: Financial Times/Prentice Hall.

Salisbury, D. (2001) 'The state of private pensions', in S. Friedman & D.C. Jacobs (eds), *The Future of the Safety Net: Social Insurance and Employee Benefits*. Champaign, IL: Industrial Relations Research Association.

Salvati, M. (1984) *Economia E Politica in Italia Dal Dopoguerra Ad Oggi*. Milan: Garzanti.

Santi, E. (1983) 'L'evoluzione delle strutture di categoria: Il caso cisl'. *Prospettiva Sindacale*, 48:102-122.

Schettkat, R. (2006) *Lohnspreizung: Mythen und Fakten. Eine Literaturübersicht zu Ausmaß und ökonomischen Wirkungen von Lohngleichheit*. Düsseldorf: Hans-Böckler-Stiftung.

Scheuer, S. (2008). 'Den danske model er under pressure'. *Ugebrevet A4*, 32: pp. 21–22.

Schmid, G., Reissart, B. & Bruche, G. (1992) *Unemployment Insurance and Active Labor Market Policy*. Detroit MI: Wayne State University Press.

Schmidt, V. (2002) *The Futures of European Capitalism*. Oxford: Oxford University Press.

Schnabel, C. (1998) 'The reform of collective bargaining in Germany: Corporatist stability vs firm flexibility', in R. Hoffmann, O. Jacobi, B. Keller & M. Weiss (eds), *The German Model of Industrial Relations Between Adaptation and Erosion.* Düsseldorf: Hans-Böckler-Stiftung, pp. 83–95.

—— (2000) *Tarifautonomie und Tarifpolitik.* Köln: Deutscher Industrie-Verlag.

Schroeder, W. & Wessels, B. (eds) (2003) *Die Gewerkschaften in Politik und Gesellschaft der Bundesrepublik Deutschland. Ein Handbuch.* Wiesbaden: Westdeutscher Verlag.

—— (eds) (2010) *Arbeitgeber-und-Wirtschaftsverbände in Deutschland. Ein Handbuch,* Wiesbaden, Verlag für Sozialwissenschaften.

Schuler, R., Budhwar, P. & Florkowski, G. (2002) 'International human resource management: Review and critique'. *International Journal of Management Reviews,* 4(1): 41–70.

Schulten, T., Bispinck, R. & Schäfer, C. (eds) (2006) *Mindestlöhne in Europa.* Hamburg: VSA-Verlag.

Sefton, T. & Sutherland, H. (2005) 'Inequality and poverty under New Labour', in J. Hills & K. Stewart (eds), *A More Equal Society? New Labour, Poverty, Inequality and Exclusion.* Bristol: Policy Press.

Seifert, H. (ed.) (2005) *Flexible Zeiten in der Arbeitswelt.* Frankfurt: Campus.

—— (2006) *Konfliktfeld Arbeitszeitpolitik. Entwicklungslinien, Gestaltungsanforderungen und Perspektiven der Arbeitszeit.* Bonn: Friedrich-Ebert-Stiftung.

—— (2008) 'Regulated flexibility: Flexible working time patterns in Germany and the role of works councils'. *The International Journal of Comparative Labour Law and Industrial Relations,* 24: 227–40.

Sethi, A. (ed.) (1989) *Collective Bargaining in Canada.* Scarborough, ON: Nelson.

Sexton, P.C. (1991) *The War Against Labor and the Left.* Boulder, CO: Westview.

Shalev, M. (1980) 'Industrial relations theory and the comparative study of industrial relations and industrial conflict'. *British Journal of Industrial Relations* 18(1): 26–43.

Sheehan, J. (1999) *Chinese Workers: A New History.* London: Routledge.

Sheldon, P. & Thornthwaite, L. (1999) 'Employer matters in 1998'. *Journal of Industrial Relations,* 41(1): 152–69.

Shephard, R.J. (1996) 'Financial aspects of employee fitness programmes', in J. Kerr, A. Griffiths & T. Cox (eds), *Workplace Health.* London: Taylor & Francis, pp. 29–54.

Shi, M.X. & Wang, B.Q. (2007) 'Modelling of labour relations in informal employment'. *China Labour*, 11: 22–4.

Shirai, T. (ed.) (1983) *Contemporary Industrial Relations in Japan.* Madison, WI: University of Wisconsin.

Shorter, E. & Tilly, C. (1974) *Strikes in France: 1830–1968.* Cambridge: Cambridge University Press.

Siaroff, A. (1999) 'Corporatism in 24 industrial democracies: Meaning and measurement'. *European Journal of Political Research*, 36: 175–205.

Simpson, B. (2000) 'Trade union recognition and the law: A new approach'. *Industrial Law Journal*, 29(3): 193–222.

Sims, A.C.L., Blouin, R. & Knopf, P. (1995) *Seeking a Balance: Canada Labour Code Review Part 1.* Ottawa: Minister of Public Works and Government Services.

Sisson, K. (ed.) (1994) *Personnel Management.* Oxford: Blackwell.

Skopcol, T. & Somers, M. (1980). 'The uses of comparative history in macrosocial inquiry'. *Comparative Studies in History and Society* 228(2): 174–92.

Smith, M. & Lyons, M. (2006) 'Women, wages and industrial relations in Australia: The past, the present and the future'. *International Journal of Employment Studies*, 14(2): 1–18.

Smith, P. & Morton, G. (2001) 'New Labour's reform of Britain's employment law'. *British Journal of Industrial Relations* 39(1): 119–38.

Solinger, D. (1999) *Contesting Citizenship in Urban China: Peasant Migrants, the State, and the Logic of the Market.* Berkeley, CA: University of California Press.

Somerville, W. (2007) *Immigration Under New Labour.* Bristol: Policy Press.

Soskice, D. (1990) 'Wage determination: The changing role of institutions in advanced industrialised countries'. *Oxford Review of Economic Policy*, 6: 36–57.

Standing, G. (2008) 'The ILO: An agency for globalisation?' *Development and Change*, 39(3): 355–84.

State Council (2006) *Report on Rural Migrant Workers in China.* Beijing: State Council of China.

Statistics Canada (2007). *Perspectives on Labour and Income.* Catalogue 75–001 XIE, August, Volume 8, No. 8. Toronto: Statistics Canada.

—— (2008), Anonymous, 'Unionization', in *Perspectives on Labour and Income*, Vol 20, No. 3, pp. 70–78.

—— (2009). 'Unionization'. *Perspectives on Labour and Income.* Vol. 20, No. 8. Toronto: Statistics Canada.

Statistics Canada *Literacy skills among Canada's immigrant population* <www.statcan.gc.ca/pub/81-004-x/2005005/9112-eng.htm> (accessed 25 February 2010).

Statistics Denmark (2006) *External Trade of Denmark 2006.* Copenhagen: Statistics Denmark.

Stewart, J. & Walsh, K. (1992) 'Change in the management of public services'. *Public Administration*, 70(4): 499–518.

Stone, K. (1996) 'Mandatory arbitration of individual employment rights: The yellow dog contract of the 1990s'. *Denver Law Review* 73: 1017–34.

Strauss, G. (1998) 'Comparative international industrial relations', in K. Whitfield & G. Strauss (eds), *Researching the World of Work: Strategies and Methods in Studying Industrial Relations.* Ithaca: Cornell University Press, pp. 175–92.

Streeck, W. (1987) 'The uncertainty of management in the management of uncertainty: Employers, labour relations and industrial adjustments in the 1980s'. *Work, Employment and Society* 1(3): 281–308.

—— (1997) 'Beneficial constraints: On the economic limits of rational voluntarism', in J.R. Hollingsworth & R. Boyer (eds), *Contemporary Capitalism: The Embeddedness of Institutions.* Cambridge: Cambridge University Press, pp. 197–219.

—— (2000) 'Competitive solidarity: Rethinking the "European social model"', in K. Hinrichs, H. Kitschelt & H. Wiesenthal (eds), *Kontingenz Und Krise: Institutionenpolitik in Kapitalistischen Und Postsozialistischen Gesellschaften.* Frankfurt: Campus Verlag, pp. 245–62.

Streeck, W. & Thelen, K. (2005) 'Introduction: Institutional change in advanced political economies', in W. Streeck & K. Thelen (eds), *Beyond Continuity: Institutional Change in Advanced Political Economies.* Oxford: Oxford University Press, pp. 1–39.

Streeck, W. & Yamamura, K. (eds) (2001) *The Origins of Nonliberal Capitalism: Germany and Japan in Comparison.* Ithaca, NY: Cornell University Press.

—— (2003) *The End of Diversity? Prospects for German and Japanese Capitalism.* Ithaca, NY: Cornell University Press.

Sturmthal, A. (1973) 'Industrial Relations Strategies', in A. Sturmthal & J. Scoville (eds), *The International Labor Movement in Transition.* Urbana, IL: University of Illinois Press.

Sugeno, K. (2002) *Shin Koyo Shakai no Ho to Keizai.* Tokyo: Yuuhikaku.

Sundaram, K. (2007) 'Employment and poverty in India, 2000–2005'. *Economic and Political Weekly*, 28 July: 3121–31.

Suzuki, H. (1998) *Senshinkoku ni okeru Hitenkeikoyo no Kakudai* (Growth of Atypical Employment in Industrialised Countries). Tokyo: Japan Institute of Labor.

Swenson, P. (1991) 'Bringing capital back in, or social democracy reconsidered: Employer power, cross-class alliances, and centralization of industrial relations in Denmark and Sweden'. *World Politics* 43(4): 513–45.

Swimmer, G. (2001) *Public Sector Labour Relations in an Era of Restraint and Restructuring.* Don Mills, ON: Oxford University Press.

Swimmer, G. & Thompson, M. (eds) (1995) *Public Sector Collective Bargaining in Canada: The End of the Beginning or the Beginning of the End?* Kingston, ON: IRC Press, Queen's University.

Tachibanaki, T. (2005). *Confronting Income Inequality in Japan: A Comparative Analysis of Causes, Consequences, and Reform.* Cambridge, MA: MIT Press.

Taft, P. (1964) *Organized Labor in American History.* New York: Harper & Row.

Tarantelli, E. (1986) *Economia Politica Del Lavoro.* Turin: UTET.

Taylor, B., Chang, K. & Li, Q. (2003) *Industrial Relations in China.* Cheltenham: Edward Elgar.

Taylor, B. & Li, Q. (2007) 'Is the ACFTU a union and does it matter?' *Journal of Industrial Relations*, 49(5): 701–15.

TeamLease Services (2006) *India Labour Report, 2006: A Ranking of Indian States by their Labour Ecosystem—Labour Demand, Supply and Labour Laws.* Bangalore: TeamLease Services.

Tempel, A. Wachter, H. & Walgenbach, P. (2006) 'The comparative institutional approach to human resource management in multinational companies', in M. Geppert and M. Mayer (eds), *Global, National and Local Practices in Multinational Companies.* London: Palgrave Macmillan.

Terry, M. & Dickens, L. (eds) (1991) *European Employment and Industrial Relations Glossary: United Kingdom.* London: Sweet and Maxwell/Luxembourg: Office for Official Publications of the European Communities.

Thelen, K.A. (1991) *Labor Politics in Postwar Germany.* Ithaca: Cornell University Press.

—— (1993) 'Western European labour in transition: Sweden and German compared'. *World Politics* 46(1): 15–27.

—— (2000) 'Why German employers cannot bring themselves to dismantle the German model', in T. Iversen, J. Pontusson & D. Soskice (eds), *Unions, Employers and Central Banks: Macro-*

Economic Coordination and Institutional Change in Social Market Economies. New York: Cambridge University Press, pp. 138–70.

—— (2001) 'Varieties of labor politics in the developed democracies'. In P.A. Hall & D. Soskice (eds), *Varieties of Capitalism: The Institutional Foundations of Comparative Advantage*. New York: Oxford University Press.

Thireau, I. & Hua, L. S. (2003) 'The moral universe of aggrieved Chinese workers: Workers' appeals to arbitration committees and letters and visits offices'. *The China Journal*, 50: 83–103.

Thomas, C. & Wallis, B. (1998) 'Dwr Cymru/Welsh Water: A case study in partnership', in P. Sparrow & M. Marchington (eds), *Human Resource Management: The New Agenda*. London: Financial Times/Pitman, pp. 160–70.

Thompson, M., Rose, J. & Smith, A. (eds) (2003) *Beyond the Regional Divide: Regional Dimensions of Industrial Relations*. Kingston: Queen's Centre for Policy Studies and Mc-Gill-Queen's University Press.

Towers, B. (1997) *The Representation Gap: Change and Reform in the British and American Workplace*. Oxford: Oxford University Press.

Trades Union Congress (1999) *Partners in Progress: New Unionism in the Workplace*. London: TUC.

Traxler, F. (1995) 'Farewell to labor market associations? Organized versus disorganized decentralization as a map for industrial relations', in C. Crouch & F. Traxler (eds), *Organized Industrial Relations in Europe: What Future?* Aldershot: Avebury, pp. 3–19.

——(2003) 'Bargaining (de)centralization, macroeconomic performance and control over the employment relationship'. *British Journal of Industrial Relations*, 41: 1–27.

—— (2004) 'The metamorphosis of corporatism: From classical to lean patterns'. *European Journal of Political Research*, 43: 571–98.

Traxler, F., Blaschke, S. & Kittel, B. (2001) *National Labour Relations in Internationalized Markets: A Comparative Study of Institutions, Change and Performance*. Oxford: Oxford University Press.

Turner, H.A. (1962) *Trade Union Growth, Structure and Policy: A Comparative Study of the Cotton Unions*. London: Allen & Unwin.

Turner, L. (1991) *Democracy at Work: Changing World Markets and the Future of Labour Unions*. Ithaca, NY: Cornell University Press.

Turner, L., Katz, H.C. & Hurd, R.W. (2001) *Rekindling the Movement*. Ithaca, NY: Cornell University Press.

Turone, S. (1992) *Storia Del Sindacato in Italia*. Bari: Laterza.

Ulrich, D. & Brockbank, W. (2005) *The HR Value Proposition*. Boston, Harvard Business School Press.

Undy, R. (1999) 'New Labour's industrial relations settlement—The Third Way'. *British Journal of Industrial Relations* 37(2): 315–36.

Undy, R., Ellis, V., McCarthy, W. & Halmos, A. (1981), *Change in Trade Unions*. London: Hutchinson.

Unger, J. & Chan, A. (1995) 'China, corporatism, and the East Asian model'. *The Australian Journal of Chinese Affairs*, 33: 29–53.

US Census Bureau (2008) 'US trade in goods and services—balance of payments (BOP) basis'. Media release, 10 June, <www.census.gov/foreign-trade/statistics/historical/index.html> (Accessed 18 January 2010).

Vaciago, G. (1993) 'Exchange rate stability and market expectations: The crisis of the EMS'. *Review of Economic Conditions in Italy*, 1: 11–29.

Vartia, M. & Hyyti, J. (2002) 'Gender differences in workplace bullying among prison officers'. *European Journal of Work and Organizational Psychology*, 11(1): 113–26.

Vatta, A. (2007) 'Italy', in F. Traxler & G. Huemer (eds), *Handbook of Business Interest Associations: Firm Size and Governance*. London: Routledge, pp. 204–39.

Venkata Ratnam, C.S. (1997a) *Competitive Labour Policies in Indian States*. Working Paper prepared for Project LARGE. New Delhi: Allied Publishers.

Venkata Ratnam, C.S. (1997b) 'The role of the state in industrial relations in the era of globalization'. Paper presented at the sub-regional tripartite meeting on Globalization and Transformation of Industrial Relations in South Asia at New Delhi. New Delhi: ILO-South Asia Multidisciplinary Advisory Team (Mimeo).

—— (2006) *Industrial Relations*. New Delhi: Oxford University Press.

—— (2007) *Labour Reforms in Northern India*. New Delhi: Confederation of Indian Industry and International Management Institute (Mimeo).

Verma, A. & Chaykowski, R.P. (eds) (1999) *Contract & Commitment: Employment Relations in the New Economy*. Kingston, ON: Queen's University IRC Press.

Verma, A. & Yan, Z.M. (1995) 'The changing face of human resource management in China: Opportunities, problems and strategies', in A. Verma, T. Kochan & R. Lansbury (eds), *Employment Relations in the Growing Asian Economies*. London: Routledge, pp. 315–35.

Visser, J. (1990) 'In search of inclusive unionism'. *Bulletin of Comparative Labour Relations*, 18: 245–78.

—— (1996) 'Interest organizations and industrial relations in a changing Europe', in J. Van Ruysseveldt & J. Visser (eds), *Industrial Relations in Europe: Traditions and Transitions*. London: Sage, pp.1–41.

—— (2006) 'Union membership statistics in 24 countries'. *Monthly Labor Review*, 129: 38–49.

Visser, J. & Van Ruysseveldt, J. (1996) 'Robust corporatism, still? Industrial relations in Germany', in J. Van Ruysseveldt & J. Visser (eds), *Industrial Relations in Europe: Traditions and Transitions.* London: Sage, pp. 124–74.

Voelkl, M. (2002) *Der Mittelstand und die Tarifautonomie. Arbeitgeberverbände zwischen Sozialpartnerschaft und Dienstleistung.* München: Hampp.

Voos, P. (1984) 'Trends in union organizing expenditures: 1953–1977'. *Industrial and Labor Relations Review*, 38(1): 52–63.

Waddington, J. (1992) 'Trade union membership in Britain, 1980–1987: Unemployment and restructuring'. *British Journal of Industrial Relations*, 30(2): 287–324.

—— (2000) 'United Kingdom: Recovering from the neo-liberal assault', in J. Waddington & R. Hoffman (eds), *Trade Unions in Europe: Facing Challenges and Searching for Solutions.* Brussels: European Trade Union Institute, pp. 575–626.

—— (2003) 'Heightening tension in relations between trade unions and the Labour government'. *British Journal of Industrial Relations*, 41(2): 335–58.

—— (ed.) (2005) *Restructuring Representation. The Merger Process and Trade Union Structural Development in Ten Countries.* Brussels: Peter Lang.

Waddington, J. & Hoffmann, J. (2000) 'The German union movement in structural transition: Defensive adjustment or setting a new agenda?' in R. Hoffmann, O. Jacobi, B. Keller & M. Weiss (eds), *Transnational Industrial Relations in Europe.* Düsseldorf: Hans-Böckler-Stiftung, pp. 113–37.

Waddington, J. & Whitson, C. (1997) 'Why do people join unions in a period of membership decline?' *British Journal of Industrial Relations*, 35(4): 515–46.

Wade R. (1996) 'Globalisation and its limits: Reports of the death of the national economy are greatly exaggerated', in S. Berger & R. Dore (eds), *National Diversity and Global Capitalism.* Ithaca, NY: Cornell University Press, pp. 60–88.

Wagner Act (1935) *National Labor Relations Act.* Washington DC: National Labor Relations Board.

Wailes, N. (2007) 'Globalization, varieties of capitalism and employment relations in retail banking'. *Bulletin of Comparative Labour Relations*, 64: 1–14.

—— (2008) 'Are national industrial relations regimes becoming institutionally incomplete?' in M. Ronnmar (ed.), *EU Industrial Relations v National Industrial Relations: Comparative and Interdisciplinary Perspectives*. Alphen aan den Rijn, Netherlands: Wolters Kluwer, pp. 3–14.

Wailes, N., Lansbury, R. & Kirsch, A. (2009) 'Globalisation and varieties of employment relations: An international study of the automotive assembly industry'. *Labour and Industry*, 20/1: 89–106.

Wailes, N., Ramia, G. & Lansbury, R. (2003) 'Interests, institutions and industrial relations'. *British Journal of Industrial Relations*, 41(4): 617–37.

Walton, R.E., Cutcher-Gerschenfeld. J.E. & McKersie, R.B. (1994) *Strategic Negotiations: A Theory of Change in Labor–Management Relations*. Boston, MA: Harvard Business School Press.

Walton, R.E. & McKersie, R.B. (1965) *A Behavioral Theory of Labor Negotiations: An Analysis of a Social Interaction System*. New York: McGraw-Hill.

Wang, X., Bruning, N. & Peng, S.Q. (2007) 'Western high performance HR practices in China: A comparison among public-owned, private and foreign-invested enterprises'. *International Journal of Human Resource Management*, 18(4): 684–701.

Warner, M. & Ng, S.H. (1999) 'Collective contracts in Chinese enterprises: A new brand of collective bargaining under "Market Socialism"?' *British Journal of Industrial Relations* 37(2): 295–314.

Warner, M. & Zhu, Y. (2009) 'Labour–management relations in the People's Republic of China: Whither the "harmonious society"?' *Asia Pacific Business Review*, forthcoming.

Warrian, P. (1996) *Hard Bargain: Transform Labour–Management Relations*. Toronto: McGilligan Books.

Weber, H. (1986) *Le parti des patrons, le CNPF 1946–1986*. Paris: Seuil.

Wedderburn, K. (1986) *The Worker and the Law*, 3rd ed. Harmondsworth: Penguin.

Weiler, P. (1980) *Reconcilable Differences*. Toronto: Carswell.

Weiss, L. (1998) *The Myth of the Powerless State: Governing the Economy in a Global Era*. Cambridge: Polity Press.

Weiss, M. & Schmidt, M. (2000) *Labour Law and Industrial Relations in the Federal Republic of Germany* 3rd rev. ed. Deventer: Kluwer.

Wever, K.S. (1995) *Negotiating Competitiveness: Employment Relations and Organizational Innovation in Germany and the United States*. Boston: Harvard Business School Press.

Wheeler, H.N. (1985) *Industrial Conflict: An Integrative Theory*. Columbia, SC: University of South Carolina Press.

White, G. (1996) 'Chinese trade unions in the transition from socialism: Towards corporatism or civil society?' *British Journal of Industrial Relations*, 34(3): 433–57.

Whitehouse, G., Baird, M., Diamond, C. & Hosking, A. (2006) *The Parental Leave in Australia Survey: November 2006 Report,* St Lucia: University of Queensland.

Whitfield, K. & Strauss, G. (1998) 'Research methods in industrial relations', in K. Whitfield and G. Strauss (eds), *Researching the World of Work: Strategies and Methods in Studying Industrial Relations.* Ithaca, NY: Cornell University Press, pp. 5–31.

Whittaker, D.H. (1997) *Small firms in the Japanese Economy.* Cambridge: Cambridge University Press.

Wilkinson, R. (2002a) 'The World Trade Organisation'. *New Political Economy* 7(1): 129–41.

—— (2002b) 'Peripheralising Labour: the ILO, the WTO and the completion of the Bretton Woods Project', in J. Harrod & R. O'Brien (eds), *Global Unions? Theory and Strategy of Organised Labour in the Global Political Economy* London: Routledge, pp. 204–20.

—— (2002c) 'Locked out, shut down: Worker rights and the World Trade Organisation'. Paper presented to *British Journal of Industrial Relations* Conference on Politics and Industrial Relations, Windsor September.

Wills, J. (1998) 'Taking on the Cosmo-Corps? Experiments in transnational labour organization'. *Economic Geography* 74(2): 111–31.

—— (1999) 'European works councils in British firms'. *Human Resource Management Journal*, 9(4): 19–38.

Winchester, D. & Bach, S. (1995) 'The state: The public sector', in P. Edwards (ed.), *Industrial Relations: Theory and Practice in Britain.* Oxford: Blackwell.

Womack, J., Jones, D. & Roos, D. (1990) *The Machine that Changed the World.* New York: Rawson-Macmillan.

Woods, H.D., Carruthers, A.W.R., Crispo, J.H.G. & Dion, G. (1969) *Canadian Industrial Relations.* Ottawa: Information Canada.

Workers' Daily, 2 November 2004; 7 December 2004; 22 and 25 February 2005.

Workplace Information Directorate (various issues) *Workplace Gazette* (collective agreement data).

World Bank (2004) *Doing Business in 2004: Understanding Regulation.* Washington, DC: World Bank.

—— (2007) *Doing Business in India.* Washington, DC: World Bank.

WSI Tarifarchiv (2007) *Tarifbindung 1998–2006,* <www.boeckler.de>.

WSI-Projektgruppe (1998) 'Ausgewählte Ergebnisse der WSI-Befragung von Betriebs und Personalräten 1997/98'. *WSI-Mitteilungen*, 51: 653–67.

Yangcheng Evening News, 8 August 2003.

You, J. (1998) *China's Enterprise Reform: Changing State/Society Relations after Mao.* London: Routledge.

Zhang J.G. (2006) 'Chinese trade unions actively promoting development of tripartite consultation and collective contract mechanism'. <www.acftu.org.cn/template/10002/file.jsp?cid=70&aid=125> (Accessed 25 October 2008).

Zhang, L.B. (2004) 'On the definition and policy of "informal employment"'. *Economic Research Reference*, 81: 38–43.

Zhang, Y.H. (2008) 'On labour rights protection for workers in informal sector'. *Journal of China Institute of Industrial Relations*, 1: 43–6.

Index